ECDL
Made Simple

Business Communications Development Ltd

MADE SIMPLE
BOOKS

OXFORD AUCKLAND BOSTON JOHANNESBURG MELBOURNE NEW DELHI

Made Simple
An imprint of Butterworth-Heinemann
Linacre House, Jordan Hill, Oxford OX2 8DP
225 Wildwood Avenue, Woburn MA 01801-2041
A division of Reed Educational and Professional Publishing Ltd

℞ A member of the Reed Elsevier plc group

First published 2000
© BCD Ltd 2000

TRADEMARKS/REGISTERED TRADEMARKS
Computer hardware and software brand names mentioned in this book
are protected by their respective trademarks and are acknowledged.

British Library Cataloguing in Publication Data
A catalogue record for this book is available from the British Library.

ISBN 0 7506 4835 X

Typeset by P.K.McBride, Southampton
Icons designed by Sarah Ward © 1994
Printed and bound in Great Britain

PLANT A TREE
British Trust for
Conservation Volunteers

FOR EVERY TITLE THAT WE PUBLISH, BUTTERWORTH-HEINEMANN
WILL PAY FOR BTCV TO PLANT AND CARE FOR A TREE.

Contents

Preface

This book was designed to cover two aspects of instruction and training: To enable the user to follow the instruction, either as part of a tutor-led course or as a self-study guide. It is specially aimed at those users who have little or no experience of computers and the applications described within it. The aim is introduce the computer and its application and then to bring added value and skill-building instruction to the user.

This book covers the ECDL syllabus version 1.5, and is based upon the Microsoft Office 97 suite of applications.

Further information on the course in general, and availability of courses can be obtained from:

Business Communications Development Ltd
14 Cavendish Road
Southsea, Hampshire, PO5 2DG
Telephone: 01705.750137
Fax: 01705.751304
e-mail: info@hitweb.co.uk
Website: bcdtraining.co.uk

Screenshot permissions

Microsoft: Screenshots reprinted with permission from Microsoft Corporation.

Microsoft Windows, Windows NT, Microsoft Word, Microsoft Excel, Microsoft PowerPoint and Microsoft Outlook are either registered trademarks or trademarks of Microsoft Corporation.

Apple, the Apple logo, Macintosh are registered trademarks of Apple Computers, Inc.

Business Communications Development Ltd, has attempted to include trademark information for products, services and companies referred to in this guide. Although Business Communications Development Ltd has made reasonable efforts in gathering this information, it cannot guarantee its accuracy. All brand names and product names used in this book are trade names, service marks, or registered trademarks of their respective owners. Business Communications Development Ltd are not associated with any product or vendor mentioned in the document, other than its associated company, Hitweb Ltd.

Limit of liability/disclaimer of warranty

Business Communications Development Ltd and the authors have used their best efforts in preparing this book. Business Communications Development Ltd and its authors make no representations or warranties with respect to the accuracy or completeness of the contents of this book and specifically disclaim any implied warranties of merchantability or fitness for a particular purpose. There are no warranties which extend beyond the descriptions contained in this paragraph. No warranty may be created or extended by sales representatives or written sales materials. The accuracy and completeness of the information provided herein and the opinions stated herein are not guaranteed or warranted to produce any particular results, and the advice and strategies contained herein may not be suitable for every individual. Neither Business Communications Development Ltd, nor its authors shall be liable for any loss of profit or any other commercial damages, including but not limited to special, incidental, consequential, or other damages.

1 Basic concepts of IT

The components of a computer

Types of computer systems

Personal Computer (PC) IBM Compatible

A PC is a computer designed for a single user. The term 'PC' is generally used to identify an IBM compatible system – IBM set the standard and other companies followed. A single PC is often referred to as a stand-alone system, indicating that it is not connected to a network.

The popularity of PCs has grown at a phenomenal rate in recent years. They are to be found in homes, business, industry, schools and the Armed Forces. The majority of PCs run the Microsoft Windows operating system.

The Apple Macintosh computer

The Apple Mac is also to be found in many homes, and is the favoured system with organisations that specialise in the production of graphics, publishing and multimedia products.

The Apple Mac was the first computer system to use a Graphical User Interface (GUI), more on that later.

Mainframe systems

The mainframe was at one time the only system generally available. IBM made its name and money selling its mainframe systems. Mainframe systems, are large compared to a PC, and process and store large amounts of data and support many users simultaneously.

A mainframe computer terminal usually only consists of a monitor and a keyboard. There is no local processor or storage device, as the mainframe handles these functions.

A mainframe computer normally supports a network system and may be found in many locations such as: multinational companies, military defence systems, telephone companies and universities.

The component parts

We are only going to deal with the PC, IBM compatible system. Computer systems are generally referred to as either:

a desktop system

a tower system – this one has separate speakers

The case

Whether the system has a desktop or tower case, it is what is inside the case that is of interest now. Here you will find most of the major components on a computer system.

Externally only two or three components are readily identifiable – all storage devices:

- The CD-ROM, or DVD drives.
- The floppy drive.
- Possibly a tape backup device.
- A Zip/Jaz or LS-120 (high-capacity removable disks) drive.

We will return to these items in due course.

Plextor's 40X internal and external CD-ROMs

Jaz drive

HP CD Writer Plus 8100i

Front panel controls

The controls on the front panel of the case are fairly universal, irrespective of type or manufacturer, and you may expect to find:

- The main power On/Off switch.
- A Reset switch.
- Several LEDs (Light Emitting Diodes).

Computer interface

Most external devices are connected to the system at the rear of the case, at the 'interface'.

The monitor

The monitor is used to display the computer output. There are two main types of monitors.

The **CRT (Cathode Ray Tube) monitor** comes in a variety of screen sizes, starting at 14-inch and progressing up to 21-inch.

Screen size is measured diagonally from the top left to the lower right corner.

Mitsubishi CRT type monitor

Monitors are generally classified by their screen size, but other factors to be considered are:

- **Dot size**. The maximum dot size should not exceed 0.28. The lower the number the better but at a greater cost.
- **Refresh rate**. This is the number of times per second that the screen is updated. A rate of 72 Hz, or higher, is recommended.
- **Resolution** is the number of horizontal and vertical pixels (screen dots). Lower resolutions, 640 x 480, give larger images, so you can see details more clearly. Higher resolutions, 1024 x 768 or more, give smaller images, but show more information at once.

The second type of monitor, is the **Liquid Crystal Display (LCD)**. This employs newer technology, and offers distinct advantages. It:

- Takes up less space on the desk.
- Is lighter in weight
- Uses less power.

Mitsubishi LCD type monitor

3

Environmental Protection Agency (EPA)

The EPA developed an energy saving system, known as Energy Star, which is now incorporated in most monitors. Energy Star technology reduces waste, and hence pollution, by switching the monitor, after a set period of inactivity, into a 'sleep mode', which uses less power.

If yours is an EPA Monitor, the use of a screen saver actually defeats the EPA purpose.

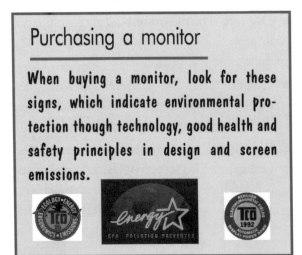

Purchasing a monitor

When buying a monitor, look for these signs, which indicate environmental protection though technology, good health and safety principles in design and screen emissions.

The keyboard

The keyboards is an *input* device – typing on it sends instructions to the computer. Keyboards come in several different shapes and styles.

Digital Free Wire, cordless keyboard

Traditional QWERTY keyboard

The mouse

A mouse is a hand-held device used to select or move items on screen. They also come in several different shapes and styles.

Microsoft Intellimouse Trackball

Microsoft Intellimouse PRO

The modem

The modem is a device that the computer uses to communicate to other computers, fax machines and suchlike, over the standard telephone lines.

Modems have increased greatly in speed and reliability in recent years. The current standard is known as V90 56K x2, and has a reasonable good data transfer rate.

If you wish to access the Internet, then a modem is a must. For more information on this subject, go to Chapter 7 page 203.

3COM (US Robotics) V90 56K Message Modem

ISDN modems

There are specialist modems used for ISDN (digital telephone) connections. For more on this subject, go to Chapter 7 page 203.

Zoom Telephonics ISDN Fax/Modem

Other peripherals

The scanner

A scanner is an input device that captures a picture or photograph from a paper copy and displays the images on the screen.

Suitable software, such as Optical Character Recognition (OCR) can be used to scan in text documents and then converts the text for use in a word procesing package.

Most scanners usually come with a cut-down version of specialist graphic editing software as part of the package.

Agfa 310 flat bed scanner

The printer

A printer is an output device, which converts copies of electronic documents to paper format, which are known as hard copies.

There are an abundance of printers on the market, ranging from:

Dot matrix printers

These use a set of pins which impact on an inked ribbon. The print is of fairly low quality as it is made-up from a series of dots.

Inkjet printers
- An extremely popular type of printer.
- Produces high quality print.
- The ink is usually a water-based product which degrades over a period of time.
- Do not allow print to come in contact with water, because it will run.

HP DeskJet 670C printer

HP DeskJet 1600C

Laser printers
- High quality print output.
- Does not use ink but a toner, hence no problem with dampness, etc.
- Laser printers are generally more expensive to purchase and to run.

HP LaserJet 6P/6MP printer

One of HP's advanced workgroup LaserJet 8000 series of printers

Inside the computer

The case contains a number of other important sub-units, that make up the computer system.

The motherboard

This is the main circuit board of the computer – all other items or units connect or plug into it. There are various types of boards available.

AT motherboards are old and have been largely replaced by the ATA motherboard.

ATX Slot 1 motherboards support both the Pentium II and III processors.

There are also other types of motherboards, designed for certain processors. They are re-ferred to by the type of processor housing, e.g.:

AT Super Socket 7

ATX Super Socket 7

CPU Super Socket 7

TMC A15VG+ Super Socket 7 motherboard

Take note

Some motherboards will support more than one processor, usually the Pentium II series.

The TMC T16NBD Slot 1 ATX motherboard (66-100MHz)

- Pentium II slot 1
- RAM slots
- AGP slot
- PCI slots
- Expansion facilities
- ISA slots

On-board systems

Motherboard technology has advanced leaps and bounds in recent years. It is not unusual to find some or all of the following built-in to the motherboard:

- Two channels for the floppy drives.
- Four channel EIDE support for hard disk, CD and LS-120 super floppy drives.
- VGA support for the monitor.
- Various types of SCSI support.
- Sound facilities.

The Central Processing Unit (CPU)

The CPU is the main chip in the computer. It processes instructions, carries out calculations and controls the flow of information through the computer. The CPU is the computer 'brain'.

CPU manufacturers

Intel is by far the greater producer of CPUs. Their processors are known by names.

- The current Intel processor is the Pentium III, with speeds from 533 to 750 MHz, and has generally replaced the Pentium II CPU.

- The Pentium II, with speeds from 233 to 500 MHz. With the introduction of the Pentium III processor it is unlikely that you will be able to purchase a Pentium II CPU.

Intel Pentium II CPU
Shown here without its fan
and heat sink assembly. CPUs run at
high temperatures so need these to keep cool.

- The Celeron, socket 370, is a fast inexpensive CPU. Based on the Pentium II, but with less built-in memory, this was designed to meet the needs of home and budget users.

Other manufacturers of CPUs

AMD offer a range of CPUs, such as the AMD-K6-2 and AMD-K6-3 series, and the recently introduced Athlon, Slot A CPU.

Cyrix with their range of 6x86 and Media GX CPUs.

Some AMD CPUs

AMD-K6-2 CPU

AMD-K6-3 CPU

AMD Athlon, Slot A CPU

Computer technology advances in leaps and bounds. With the operating system upgrades, applications upgrades, CPUs are not being left behind. New CPUs are in the pipeline, as are faster speeds for the current range of CPUs. Intel is currently working on a new CPU, aimed specifically at larger network systems.

> ## Take note
>
> Processor speed is measured in megahertz and the higher the number, e.g. 450 MHz, the faster the computer. However, if you have a fast processor but only a limited amount of RAM, you will not be able to get the best out of your system. CPUs and RAM, together, produce the speed.

Random Access Memory (RAM)

RAM, found on the motherboard, is a temporary storage device. RAM is only active when the computer is switched on and powered up. Any data still in RAM when the system is shut down, or subjected to a power failure, is lost never to be regained.

There are a number of different types of RAM with differing speeds and compatibility requirements.

72 pin SIMM RAM chip

Expansion slots

There are usually a number of spare slots on the motherboard, for expansion or upgrading. Generally there are only two types of slots used on current systems. The slots are known as ISA, the older slot and PCI, the newer slot.

There are usually several of each type of slot on each motherboard, thus allowing the user a degree of flexibility. You preference, wherever possible, should be for the PCI slot cards.

Creative Labs PCI
128 sound card

The hard disk drive (HDD)

The hard disk drive, also known as the fixed disk, is mounted within the computer case. Currently the minimum HDD storage capacity is 13Gb which is rather large.

The HDD is connected to the motherboard via a special ribbon cable to the EIDE (Enhanced Integrated Drive Electronics) socket.

The internal view of a 3.5 inch hard disk drive

The floppy disk drive (FDD)

The floppy disk drive is also connected to the motherboard, by a similar type of cable as used by the HDD, though this has a different type of connector. The FDDs capacity is typically limited to 1.4Mb, thus limiting its usefulness.

The CD-ROM drive

The CD-ROM (Compact Disk-Read Only Memory) drive is connected to an EIDE socket on the motherboard, by the same type of cable as that used by the HDD.

CD-ROMS use a disk similar to audio CDs, with a capacity of 650Mb. You can only read files – you cannot store your own on a CD-ROM.

CD-ROMs are gauged by the speed that they run at and this is often referred to as 36X or 40X. The higher the number the faster the CD-ROM will function.

Digital Versatile Disk Drive

The DVD is gaining in popularity and is now quite often fitted in new computer systems as standard, instead of the CD-ROM. The DVD has a capacity of 5Gb.

Panasonic LF-D101U, a rewritable DVD RAM drive.

The Power Supply Unit (PSU)

The PSU connects to an external mains supply, converting it from 250 volts Alternating Current (AC) to Direct Current (DC), with voltages between 3.3 to 12 volts. Power consumption is between 200 to 250 watts. Compare that to the average household bulb of 60 watts.

A fan within the PSU draws air out from the case to assist in keeping the components cool.

Operating systems

An operating system (OS) is the link between the hardware and the software. It ensures that all the components, that make-up the computer system, function together and efficiently.

When you start your computer, the operating system is started first. Applications software, such as MS Word can only be started after the OS is loaded. Without the operating system the applications cannot and will not function.

MS-DOS

Microsoft Disk Operating System, MS-DOS, was the earlier and a command line OS. The user performed tasks by typing in short text-based commands, which the PC then executed.

Windows

Windows is the follow-on OS after MS-DOS and likewise is a Microsoft product.

Windows is a Graphical User Interface, GUI, operating system. Instead of typing in commands, the user performs tasks by selecting icons, small images, or selecting commands from menus. GUIs makes it easier to use the OS, speeds up operations, and are more user friendly.

First generation Windows OS still required the presence of MS-DOS, because the two systems functioned together. MS-DOS had to be installed first, followed by Windows, which basically sat on top of MS-DOS, with the GUI. Windows still used various MS-DOS facilities, as and when required.

Other Operating Systems

Unix

Unix is a powerful OS that has been around for sometime now and is enjoying a revival in some areas.

Unix is used on many computer systems that support the Internet.

The Apple Macintosh OS

The Apple company produced the first GUI for computers. Unfortunately, due to Apple Mac's marketing policy and strategy, they really lost out to Microsoft over time.

Unix and Apple Mac OS are mentioned simply to indicate that there are other operating systems available, other than Microsoft products.

A short history

MS-DOS was basically the first OS for PCs and over a period of time, numerous versions of the OS were released.

GUIs arrived with Windows and most users first encountered Windows at version 3. Windows was upgraded to version 3.11, which in many ways was the forerunner of the next OS – Windows 95.

Windows version 3, by the introduction of the GUI, was a major step forward in operating systems for PCs.

Windows 95 was the next major step forward, still using a GUI. This time however, the GUI had undertaken a major revamp. It was even easier to use, and allowed the user to carry out tasks and actions much quicker.

Various patches and upgrades appeared for Windows 95, until the arrival of Windows 98.

Windows 98 still uses the 95 GUI, with increased functionality and facilities.

New Technology (NT)

During the transition and development of the variously mentioned operating systems, Microsoft was developing another system, called New Technology, NT for short.

The earlier versions of Windows NT used the same style GUI as that used in Windows 3x operating systems, up to NT version 3.51. With the introduction of Windows NT version 4, the switch was made to the Windows 95/98 style GUI.

Windows NT was developed specifically as a more powerful and secure operating system for business and industry.

Windows NT OS appears in two forms, the Workstation user system and the Network version, known as NT Server.

Platform

The term 'platform' refers to the type of operating system used by a computer. MS-DOS, Windows 3xx, Windows 95/98, Windows NT and Unix are all platforms.

You cannot run any Windows applications on MS-DOS, though you can run most MS-DOS applications on a Windows platform. This is due to the fact that Windows has 'backward compatibility'. Within Windows, there is a section of the software that is specifically written to cater for MS-DOS applications.

Functions of the OS

Other than ensuring that all the components of the computer work together, the OS has many other areas of responsibility and functionality.

File management

It is the OS that is responsible for all file management aspects on the computer. To this end, Windows has a particular program for file management, called Windows Explorer.

File Naming

Under MS-DOS and Windows 3, file names consisted of a maximum of eight letters followed by a full stop, a period, and then a three-letter extension for example, '.doc'

With the introduction of Windows 95 there came a far more sensible file naming system using long file names. This permitted the user to use up to 255 characters, in place of the original eight. The name is still followed by the full stop and a three-letter extension. This system allows the use of more descriptive names, making file recognition and management that much easier.

For more information on file management, see Chapter 2.

Utilities

The OS also provides a number of utilities, smaller programs, as integral elements of the OS to assist in the efficient performance of the computer. For example:

Disk formatting

Before a disk can be used on a computer, it must be formatted, in a manner that the OS will recognise. It is the OS that provides the program to format the disk.

See Chapter 2 for further information.

Computer performance

If the computer finds a fault or error on any disk, there is a program within the OS to deal with this problem. This is called Scandisk. It conducts a series of checks on the disk and will attempt to fix any faults found. Scandisk will advise the user on the current status of the disk on completion of the scan.

Defragmentation

Because of the way data is stored on disks, there will come a time when you will notice a slowing down of the system when attempting to open files. This is due to the fact that often the file is broken down in to smaller sections. These sections are then stored in different locations on the disk, fragmentation.

The procedure used to overcome fragmentation is known as Defrag. This locates the various sections of the files and moves them, if possible, next to each other, in contiguous locations. This will assist in opening the files quicker and free up wasted space on the disk.

Networking

Windows 95/98 supports networking, with all the necessary software included as an integrated part of the OS.

The only additional requirement to establish your own network, assuming that you have two or more computers, is to install the Network Interface Cards (NIC), and the appropriate cabling and connectors.

Plug and Play

Windows 95/98 supports Plug and Play technology. What this means is that the OS will detect any new hardware that you install and load the necessary *drivers*. These are short programs that support the hardware items connected to the computer, and allow them to function.

File storage

FAT16

MS-DOS, Windows 3.x and Windows 95 use a file storage system known as FAT16. The FAT (File Allocation Table) remembers where the various parts of a file are stored on the disk.

FAT16 is quite wasteful in the way it stores data on the disk. To overcome the problem of wasted space, Windows 98 introduced a new system known as FAT32.

FAT32

FAT32 is more economical in the manner that stores data on the disk. Less space is lost and the system is more efficient.

There is a problem however, only Windows 98 recognises FAT32. Be careful if you elect to use FAT32, you do have a choice. If you pass files to colleagues and friends who are running MS-DOS, Windows 95 or Windows NT, then those disks must use FAT16.

NTFS

New Technology Filing System (NTFS) is used by Windows NT operating systems. Only NT OSs can read this filing system, and it is through the use of NTFS that Windows NT gains some of its increased security features.

With the introduction of Windows 2000, yet another filing system will emerge. This new system is based on NTFS but it is believed that there will be no backward compatibility with the original NTFS system, thus making it reliant upon Windows 2000 operating systems.

Customisation

All Windows programs permit the user to customise the computer set-up and the user interface. Windows 98 provides increased functionality in this area, for instance:

Twin monitors

Windows 98 allows for up to two monitors to be connected to the same computer. This is particularly useful if you give presentations (see Chapter 6). You may have your own monitor adjacent to the computer or you may set it up, along with the second monitor for audience use.

To run two monitors, you must install a second video card in the computer, and of course you will require longer cables.

Other features

There are more features within the OS, and they are not all listed here. Read the appropriate user handbook. Failure to even scan the handbook briefly will almost certainly result in you not being fully aware of the capabilities and functionality of the OS.

Internet browser

Microsoft includes its browser software, Internet Explorer, with the operating systems. The browser is necessary if you intend to access the Internet.

See Chapter 7 for more details.

Programs and applications

Application software

The term application software, such as that contained within the Microsoft Office suite, refers to a number of different programs specifically written to accomplish specialist tasks and functions.

These applications are used to write letters, manage finances, to create databases, to draw pictures and to play games.

Application software is platform-related. That is to say, you must have the appropriate operating system loaded to run the application.

When application software is released, it has a name and a version number. Inevitably, even after considerable testing, the software will have faults in it, known as bugs. The software manufacturer will periodically issue an update or 'patch', designed to correct the various problems. When applied to the applications, the patch will also update the version number of that product.

It is important to be aware of what version your software is, particularly if access and security are concerns to you.

MS Word – word processing

This application is used to produce letters and a variety of other types of documents, which would, until the introduction of computers, have been produced on a typewriter.

MS Excel – spreadsheets

This application was specifically written to manage and analyse finances and information as well as create charts and graphs.

Excel can also be used to create simple databases.

MS Access – databases

This application was specifically written to create databases, to enable information and data to be assembled and collated.

Access is a powerful application that lends itself to simple databases, such as a list of names and addresses of your friends, to more complex ones such as stock control and ordering in warehouses and supermarkets.

MS PowerPoint – presentations

PowerPoint produces a series of slides, including audio and video inserts, to be assembled for presentation to audiences.

MS Outlook

Outlook is much more than a Personal Information Management (PIM) system.

Outlook lists your contacts, assists you in organising your time and such like, but much more:

- Outlook produces and manages your electronic mail, e-mail.

  E-mail is covered in Chapter 7.

- If your computer is connected to a network, Outlook provides a group working facility to enable, a team for instance, to collate their activities, meetings and so on.

Outlook is well worth investigating more deeply, in time. There are many features not readily apparent on the surface, such as tracking and logging the time you spend working on a particular document, spreadsheet or database. This feature is particularly useful if you are self-employed and charge for your time by the hour.

Application integration

All applications within the MS Office suite are written by Microsoft and therefore support cross-application functionality. What this means is that instead of each application carrying out similar functions independently, the same functions are centrally located and each application accesses these functions.

Through the use of integrated functions, the applications do not waste precious space on the hard disk. Further more, as a consequence of integration, many of the menus and toolbars, within the applications, are very much the same, in respect of look, content and feel.

Naturally there are specialist menus and toolbars specifically related to the particular application.

Because of the similarity and layout of the application GUI, user training and experience is much easier and quickly transferred.

Summary

Applications are platform-specific and will not function without the appropriate operating system.

Integrated applications are frequently cheaper to purchase rather than buying each application singularly.

Furthermore, by purchasing a suite of applications, cross-application and functionality is greatly enhanced.

Storage and memory

Storage devices

Permanent storage

All storage devices such as hard disk drives and floppy disk drives are known as permanent storage devices. What this means is that any data that is written to the drives can be retrieved and reused at a later date.

The action of shutting down the computer and turning off the power will not result in the loss of this data.

These types of drives use a magnetic medium on which the data is stored. That is why it is particularly important never to use any other magnetic material in the vicinity of computer disks. The magnetic influence will corrupt and destroy the data stored on the disk.

Identifying disk drives

The operating system employs letters to identify the various drives installed in a computer system.

If only one hard drive is fitted, it is allocated the letter C and this is known as the Root drive.

If other hard drives are fitted, then they will be allocated the next available letters.

Most computers now have a CD drive installed and it too is allocated a drive letter, usually the letter D.

So, we have the letters C and D but what happened to A and B? The letters A and B are reserved solely for the use of floppy drives.

It is uncommon to see more than one floppy disk drive installed these days and it is always allocated the letter A. Even though there is not a second floppy drive installed, the letter B is not available for use elsewhere.

If a second drive unit is installed at a later date, the user must set up the drive through the computer BIOS, and only then will the operating system see the drive.

Consult the documentation that came with your computer for more information, such as what type of BIOS installed on your computer.

Types of storage devices

There are numerous types of storage devices available. Some, such as the hard and floppy disk drives will permit the user to read and write to the disk any number of times. Other storage devices will only permit read actions.

CD drives

The average CD disk has a storage capacity of 650 MB. Compare that to the everyday floppy disk, which has a capacity of 1.44 MB.

There are three types of CD drive:

- **CD-ROMs** can only be used to read data, you cannot write, save files, to a CD-ROM.
- **CD-R** drives permit the user to read from the CD any number of times; however, the write capability can only take place once. You cannot go back at a later date and perform another write action to the same CD.

15

- **CD-RW** drives permit multiple read write operations to be carried out on the same CD, until such time that it is, of course, full.

CD-ROMs do not require any specialist software, other than the appropriate drivers. Whereas the CD-R and CD-RW drives do require specialist software to function and cost a great deal more.

DVD Drives

Digital Versatile Disks, come in two types:

- **DVD ROM** looks just like a CD-ROM, in shape and size but stores over 26 times the amount of data. A standard DVD disk can hold over two hours of high quality video with improved CD quality audio.

  The DVD-ROM will also read standard CD disks. Storage capacities vary from 4.7 GB to 17 GB, making them ideal for distribution of large multimedia applications.

  DVD players are now also available for use in the home for viewing full-length feature films.

- **DVD RAM** also looks very like a CD-ROM drive and has the same features as a DVD ROM drive. The difference is that the DVD-RAM allows the user to record data. The DVD-RAM is a read-write system

  The recently introduced Panasonic LF-D101U is a DVD-RAM system. This drive has a capacity of 5.2 GB, and will also read the Panasonic optical disk. About the only thing it cannot do is write to the standard CD disk.

Other permanent storage devices

The optical disk

This requires a special drive unit to write to the disk. The first series of optical disk had a storage capacity of 250 MB. The current series of disks now have a capacity of 650 MB.

The super floppy

This recently introduced drive, is rumoured to eventually replace the older floppy disks. The super floppy is known as the LS-120. The figure 120 indicates the capacity of the floppy disk. It is 120 MB, compare that to the older floppy disk with a capacity of 1.44 MB.

The external appearance of the LS-120 drive is almost identically to that of the old 3½ inch floppy drive unit.

The LS-120 will also read and write to a 1.44 MB floppy disk.

Memory

When the computer is running and you decide to use one of the applications, the essential elements of the program and data are loaded into the Random Access Memory, RAM.

There are a number of different types of memory and their locations vary, as follows:

CPUs have a limited amount of memory, built into them. This memory is known as **internal cache** or primary cache or L1.

Working in conjunction with the CPU cache is another memory cache, known as **external cache**. This resides on the motherboard and consists of Static RAM (SRAM) chips.

In the Pentium II and Pentium III CPUs the external RAM is built into the CPU, this makes accessing the cache much quicker.

Random Access Memory (RAM) is the main memory of the computer.

Memory is not a permanent storage medium – RAM is volatile. This means that any data stored in the RAM will be lost when the computer is switched off.

Accessing data

As already stated, a certain amount of data is loaded into the internal cache of the CPU. If the processor cannot find the data it needs in the internal cache, it looks in the external cache for the data. If it cannot find the data it needs in the internal or external cache, the processor then looks in the slower main memory, the RAM.

Data movement

Each time the computer requests data from RAM, the computer places a copy of the data in the memory cache. This process constantly updates the memory cache so that it always contains the most recently used data.

As a consequence of the movement of data to the internal and external cache, these memory areas will quickly become full. So not only is data going into the cache, it is also being moved out. The older data, that has not been used recently, is moved out down the chain.

Another memory area that the computer uses is sometime called a Swap file or dynamic memory. This is an area on the disk drive that the operating system reserves for its own use. If the computer system has limited amounts of RAM installed, this area on the hard disk is used more often. This process slows down the access time considerably.

Operating systems

Different operating systems use memory in different ways. In the older Windows 3xx, the OS generally set swap files. The user could change the size, providing the hard disk size was adequate and space was available.

Windows 95/98 uses a dynamic system. What this means is that the OS automatically adjusts the size of the file as and when necessary.

Take note

Do not confuse 'storage' and 'memory'. Both are memory mediums but handle data in two completely different ways. For instance, the HDD stores data, through the use of a magnetic medium. If the computer is switched off the data is retained.

RAM stores data but only while the computer is switched on. RAM requires a constant supply of electricity to function.

The basic units of stored data

The aim is to introduce the various terms used, their relationship and how it all comes together in the computing process.

Bit

A bit (*bi*nary dig*it*) is the smallest unit of information that a computer can process, and is usually represented as either 0 or 1.

Byte

A combination of 8 bits is referred to as a byte. Each byte can represent a single character or letter. For example: the letter A = 01000001.

Kilobyte

One kilobyte, abbreviated as KB, is 1,024 bytes. In terms of space in a document, it is approximately equal to one page of double-spaced text.

Megabyte

One megabyte (MB) is 1,024 KB or 1,048,576 bytes, roughly equal to a 300 page paperback.

Gigabyte

Gigabyte (GB) is 1,024 MB or 1,073,743,824 bytes.

Terabyte

One terabyte (TB) is 1,024 GB or 1,099,551,627,776 bytes.

Records

A record is a small amount of data that is stored, processed, and retrieved as a single convenient unit. It is a group of related facts describing one item contained in a number of separate locations called fields.

Databases are made up of fields and records. Any number of fields can be used to create a record. For instance, if you are creating a database of your contacts, it may have a field for the details: first name, last name, address line1, address line2, address line3 and so on.

The rows of data within a table of a database, are its records. Each row of information is considered a separate entity that can be accessed or sequenced as required.

Files

A file is a set of data with an identifying label held in a computer storage device. Files are the end result of writing a letter, of creating a spreadsheet or the database.

Applications may well call their particular end product by a different name. For instance, a letter created in MS Word, would usually be called a document. Remember the three letter extension after the filename and the period, *doc*. This is an abbreviation for 'document'.

It is irrelevant which application, or how that application refers to files created by it. For instance, Excel produces a spreadsheet, but when stored on a storage device, it is a *file*. Likewise an Access database is a file.

For further details on files and file management, please refer to Chapter 2, *Using the Computer*.

Using a graphical user interface

Windows and Macintosh operating systems use a Graphical User Interface system, GUI (pronounced 'gooey').

A GUI is a visual means of interacting with the computer and provides an easy means of issuing instructions and commands without the user having an extensive knowledge of commands and programming by using windows, icons, mouse and pull-down menus.

The GUI system uses small pictures, known as *icons* to represent actions and commands. The interface is also made up of a series of *menus*.

The menus, once activated, open a drop down list containing further commands. Even more menus may be concealed within the initial drop list and this system of menus is known as cascading.

Icon method

Icons are a visual means of issuing instructions, for instance 'print the document', by the use of one mouse click on the appropriate icon.

To issue the same instruction to the computer, using the menus, would require three separate mouse actions, which is still quicker than the older method of command line instructions.

Menu method

Though the use of icons is normally a quicker method of issuing instructions, menus often offer greater flexibility. For instance:

Refer back to the icon method of printing a document; one click on the icon was all that was needed however, to print the document using the menus required three separate actions to do the same thing. Now suppose that you only wanted to print the one page. The icon method could not be used as it prints the entire document.

Using the menu method opens a print dialog box, which offers a number of options for printing the document. For instance:

- Print one page.
- Print a range of pages.
- Change the printer properties.
- Change choice of printer for the current print job.

The application window

Each application window consists of a number of different areas:

For instance, the MS Word application window, starting at the top:

- The strip along the top is the Title bar. When it is coloured blue it indicates that it is the active window.
- The Title bar will also list the document name, and subject to customisation, the file path as well.
- Below the title bar is the Menu bar usually with nine drop-down menu lists.
- Below the Menu bar is the first of the toolbars, usually the Standard toolbar.
- Below the Standard toolbar, usually, is the Formatting toolbar.

19

Each of the three items listed above can be customised by you, with additions and subtractions being made to the content of the menus and likewise to the toolbars.

The overall appearance, such as which colour scheme you prefer, whether the ruler is displayed, and any additional toolbars that you may wish displayed permanently, can all be customised.

Standardisation

With the majority of application suites, standardisation and integration has greatly improved. For instance, the majority of the icons that appear on the Word Formatting toolbar will also appear on the Excel Formatting toolbar.

This increases your productivity, in as much as that, having already used one application, you can immediately apply that knowledge to the second application.

The same applies to the drop-down menu contents, even to such a degree that different software companies are conforming to a common standard layout.

Customisation

As touched upon previously, customisation allows you to set up the screen display, and suchlike, to best suit your preferences.

Within the operating system, there exists a means of changing the screen resolution.

This is particularly useful for anyone who is visually impaired. By changing the resolution to a lower setting, the images will appear larger on the screen, thus improving the visibility for the user.

Productivity

Productivity is increased. This is due to the fact that you can often, on the click of a mouse button, issue instructions extremely quickly, and then proceed to another task without having to wait for the last instruction to by carried out and speeds up the work process tremendously.

To gain the maximum use of any application, it is necessary to experiment and try out the various options available.

Use the online Help system, via the Help menu on the Menu bar.

Further detail

For further detail on the layout and content of the various applications covered by the ECDL course, please refer to Chapters 4 to 7.

Multimedia

Multimedia, literally 'many media', for example, using sound, pictures and text to make a more effective, understandable presentation.

Multimedia CD-ROM disks

A CD-ROM disk can store multimedia presentations. The CD disk is currently the main medium used by the multimedia industry, though the introduction of the DVD disk will impact on its future greatly in time.

You will recall from previous sections on this module, that the CD disk has a capacity of 650 MB, which when compared to the floppy disk, is considerable. However, when compared to the DVD disk, which has a capacity in the region of 5.2 GB, the CD disk has its limitations.

DVD multimedia

DVD multimedia, in the computer and home entertainment environment offers far greater opportunities for advancement.

Already on sale, on the High Street, are DVD players and full length feature films. The systems connect up to the TV in a similar manner to that of the video recorder.

Current DVD home entertainment systems do not offer a record facility, as do the video recorders, though this will change shortly.

Computer DVD

The initial DVD systems for computers were read only, though available now, at some cost, are read-rewrite units. The system offers several features that make it a very attractive item. For instance the unit is not only able to read and write to DVD disks; it can read CD disks and optical disks as well.

Cost is of course a major consideration with any recently-introduced new technology.

Some examples

There are numerous multimedia products on the market, such as encyclopaedias and teaching aids – particularly on computer subjects.

If you are a classical music buff, the extended audio disk will be of interest. With all the necessary hardware installed, you can of course play the audio disk through the computer.

So what's new? Well before playing the music, it installs a small program that is also on the disk, and then whilst playing the music you can research, from the audio disk, the history of the music as it is played.

Multimedia and the Internet

More and more areas on the Internet and for that matter, company intranets, are using multimedia.

Intranets are much the same as the Internet except that they are run on private networks within organisations and are not normally accessible to the general public.

OnLine shopping

Imagine that you have decided to do some shopping on the Internet. You are going to place you weekly grocery order with your local online supermarket.

Imagine how boring it would be once you are logged on, to simply have a screen display listing products and a series of tick boxes. Not a very good sales pitch.

Now imagine, you log on, a voice greets you by your first name, which is picked-up from your log-on process. You are then advised of the store's special offers accompanied by the appropriate images of the products.

By clicking on a series of buttons, which identify the various sections of the store, you are taken to that section and you select the items you require. Quite often there is an image of a shopping basket and to select an item, you simply left-click on it and drag it to the shopping basket and drop it in.

While you are placing your order, the supermarket computer is checking the availability of products and suchlike and if there is a lack of stock, you will be advised of such immediately and possibly offered an alternative item if one is available. If you decline the alternative, you are will be advised of the anticipated delivery time.

Quite a difference to simply a screen with lines of text and tick boxes!

Drawbacks

There are of course certain drawbacks to such a system.

How often do you go to the fresh produce section? You almost always pickup an item and feel it for freshness and suchlike!

When the supermarket is assembling your order for you, are they so discerning? Of course they would have us all believe so, but this is an area that requires further investigation on the part of the user once again.

Tip

Multimedia lends itself ideally to the application covered in Chapter 6, *Presentations*.

Developing a computer-based system

Business use

When an organisation, or for that matter an individual, decides that they require a computer system, either from new or upgrading current systems, there are a series of steps and procedures that should be followed.

The following is essential to the process:

Systems analysis

Identify the requirements – the input processes, the output and control mechanisms operating in the current system.

Systems design

Specify the inputs, processes, outputs and control for a new system, designed so as to overcome the shortcomings of the old system.

Program design

Using a high level programming language to write the programs necessary to perform the processing operations required by the system specification.

Feasibility study

Is the proposal economically, technically and socially practicable?

Program testing

With real time and test data to iron out any bugs and test the system to extremes.

Implementation

Either parallel, direct, phased in, or a pilot system.

Training

Is re-training required, if so prioritise the training requirement. Key personnel head the list.

Conversion of files

Will the new system read old formats or will manual conversion be required.

Maintenance and monitoring

To deal with any problems that come to light after implementation and to maintain and upgrade the system as and when required, either in programming or through the introduction of new hardware.

Home use

An individual's assessment

As an individual, the procedure is much less complicated and the overall deciding factor will almost always be that of finance.

The following are a number of questions that you should take into consideration when thinking of buying a computer for personal use:

Finance

The first consideration is how much can I afford? If money is no object then the assessment is somewhat easier, though it should still be carefully thought out.

Requirement

What do you want or expect the system to do? For example, is the use solely for adults or will children have access to the system?

Security

Is security going to be of importance? If so, then the type of operating system required should be carefully considered. For general home use and low-level office requirements Windows 98 would be satisfactory.

If security is likely to be a problem then maybe Windows NT will meet your security requirements. The increase in security has a corresponding increase in price as well.

Applications

What applications will you require? Will the built-in Windows 98 word-processor meet your requirements, or will you require compatibility with applications in use at the office.

Multimedia

Almost all systems come pre-packaged with CD drives and sound cards and speakers. It is worth checking just to be sure.

Brand names

Do you go for a brand name, for example an IBM or Compaq computer, or buy a clone by mail order. There is a great deal to be said for purchasing clone systems. There are many good deals to be had at slightly lower prices.

Monitors

Careful consideration should be given to the monitor size. It is suggested that the minimum size that should be considered is 15-inch.

What does 15-inch mean, what is the actual viewable size? In many cases the actual viewing area on the screen is less than that stated, because some of the screen is behind the moulded plastic case. Be aware, always check.

Games

Do you intend to play games, if so then a good quality joystick is required. You are limited when using a mouse to control games.

Disc size

This is less than a problem today than it used to be, however, still check the size.

RAM (Memory)

A system with a fast CPU will be degraded by a lack of RAM. The more RAM the better and more efficient the system.

Always remember that the OS has a minimum RAM requirement as do the applications. Minimum requirements for a modern system is suggested as 128 MB.

Warranties

Ensure you understand the warranty offered, and do you purchase an extended warranty?

Pay particular attention to monitors in respect of warranties. Many mail order houses offer what is known as swoop-out warranties. If the monitor becomes faulty, a simple telephone call will generally have a fully re-conditioned monitor at your door the next working day.

No need to return the faulty item to the High Street store, it is taken back by the delivery service and most warranties are for three years.

Applications and use of computers

The importance and growing use of computers

Throughout history there have been numerous technological introductions and advances that have resulted in major impacts upon the way of life and approach to manufacturing.

The arrival of the computer, though initially slow to affect us, has in recent years made tremendous changes to almost all ways of life and work. The computer, whether it be a mainframe, mini-computer or the PC, has impacted to some degree or another on almost everyone's life. This may take the form of a person actually using a PC at home, in the office or in the way they work, for instance in a car plant where a considerable volume of work is now automated.

Computers are ideal systems to carry out unattended repetitive actions, with a very high degree of accuracy. This is seen particularly in manufacturing industry.

Computers have lessened the risk to people by their use in dangerous areas and processes, for instance in the nuclear industry and by the police and armed forces in bomb disposal.

The above fields were mentioned to highlight the use of multimedia. In both of these fields, visual, and often audio, requirements exist. The use of a computer coupled with video and audio equals one form of multimedia.

Development continues at a pace within the computer industry, in the form of new CPUs arriving on the market, new systems of data storage such as the DVD RAM, and the continual upgrading of operating systems and applications.

Surrounding the introduction of the new or upgraded applications there is also the introduction of new or expanded use of computer systems and applications.

Computer systems in business

There exist numerous systems and platforms in use in business today, for instance:

Banking
- Automatic Transaction Machines, better known as cash machines.
- Automatic cheque readers. These not only read the cash details, etc., by the use of magnetic or other medium, but also monitor the number of cheques issued by the individual or company, to determine if a new cheque book is required. Once it detects that the user is down to their last four or five cheques, the system initiates a process that will order and dispatch a new chequebook.
- Cash transfer, whether national or international.

Stock Exchange
- Trading on numerous Stock Exchanges is now conducted by the use of computers. There were some problems in the earlier days. The systems were designed, and programmed, to monitor the sale of stocks and

shares, and should there appear to be a run on them, the system automatically initiated sales. This in turn was picked up by other Exchanges and the computer systems actually started a panic selling spree.

Advertising

- Advertising is taking advantage of computers, particularly in the mail shot, 'junk mail' to many of us. The mail merge feature of the word-processing and Desktop Publishing, DTP, programs, has introduced the automation of bulk mail addressing.

Accountancy

- The use of spreadsheets has introduced an automation capability to accountancy.
- The spreadsheet can also be used as a modelling tool for simple forecasting, and the use of the 'what if' feature can assist in the development of strategy and business planning.

Management

- Specialist software exists to assist management in the decision-making process.

Project management

- Project management software is available to assist in the management of different types of projects.
- This software will program in events, sequences, etc., and will warn of over-runs or conflicts between events.

Group working

- Many tasks involve group working. The information must be available to more than one person, hence the development of group working through the use of networking.

- The network allows the sharing of information and resources, thus speeding up processing time and production of documentation in relation to the projects.

Office automation

- Numerous areas within an office now have automated features, such as:
  - Customer administration.
  - Company calendars.
  - Production of in-house publications.
  - Company contacts and address book.
- E-mail is a fast and cost-effective method of communications. With suitable hardware and applications installed, text and graphics can be transmitted quickly and easily.

Computer systems in industry

The car industry has seen over the last ten years, completely new systems of work introduced. The manufacture of a motor vehicle is extensively an automated process, where large areas of the car plant are manned by but a few personnel, mainly technicians in attendance of the robots that actually assemble the car body and shell.

Advantages

There are many advantages to be gained by the use of computer control robotic systems:

- **Reliability**: The system carries out, repeatedly, the same actions without fatigue.
- **Accuracy**: The same actions, no matter how often done, are consistently accurate.
- **Re-programming**: All systems can be re-programmed quickly and easily from one focal point.

- **Staff training**: With manual handling and assembly by staff, staff must be retrained when changes are introduced. A consequence of robotic assembly and of re-programming is that the need for staff training is minimal and therefore reduces the likelihood of error in the assembly of the product.

Disadvantages

- Loss of employment opportunities
- The introduction of robotic assembly lines saw a major reduction in numerous car plant work forces.

Take note

The banking industry has also seen the impact of the computers affect their manpower situation enormously. With the introduction of automated systems, less and less personnel are required.

Computers in education

When computers were first introduced into schools, the BBC commissioned a computer system that was known as the Acorn.

The Acorn, in its early days was quite farsighted, however, it required its own hardware and specially written software. Cross-platform compatibility did not exist. The Acorn can still be found in many schools but is now in decline, with the introduction of Windows-based systems. The Acorn was available to the public but due to the limited quantities sold, costs of the system, including software, were high.

In 1997, the government decided that all schools would have up-to-date systems as soon as possible. In addition, and as part and parcel of the government initiative, the 'schoolnet' was introduced. The idea was to link schools via, and to give access, to the Internet.

Educational software

With the introduction of the PC into schools, the availability of educational software has increased and its cost has been correspondingly reduced.

The software available ranges from that of basic applications for use in primary schools, to more advanced applications for high schools.

There is one particular application that employs multimedia. This is a Desktop Publishing package, incorporating sound, video and hyperlinks.

Advantages

- Because most educational software is either CD or network based, information can quickly and easily be recalled.
- The student can quickly and easily return to a passage, carry out the same task, or re-read the same passage for clarification.
- A student can pace his or her own study rate.
- Some applications will monitor the student's progress and test and advise if there is a problem.

Disadvantages

- The student cannot question the tutor for clarification or request assistance.
- The computer is impersonal, and offers only limited feedback to the student.

Computers for home use

The majority of home-based computer systems are multimedia systems, incorporating CD-ROM drives and sound systems.

Office software

If the home system is to be used for business then the applications should be the same as in the office, to ensure compatibility.

Home accounts

If the system is to be used to run household accounts and your bank details, including online banking, then specialist software exists to meet your requirements. Microsoft Money 2000 provides online banking, assists in tax returns to managing your shares portfolio. There are of course other applications that will also carry out the same functions.

Hobbies

This area is too large to list everything that one could do using a computer: Some uses are discussed briefly below.

If you are keen to assemble your **family history** there are packages that will assist you in this area.

By the use of the numerous CDs that are available, you can conduct **research** into a vast array of subjects and topics. Do not forget the availability of the Internet for research as well.

There exists an ever-increasing volume of CDs for home study and revision. Whether it is for GCSEs or the Open University, the computer is an excellent tool to assist with revision, and of course, the presentation of the course work.

Computers in everyday life

Computers are encountered in our everyday life to such an extent that we are sometimes not aware of their presence. Some examples are:

Supermarkets

Barcode reader

At the checkout, the barcode reader is connected to the store's computer. When the product is passed in front of the reader, the details are read and passed to the computer, which identifies the item, advises the checkout of its price and then the details are printed out on to the customer's receipt.

Stock holdings

As well as recognising the item and pricing it, the computer will also advise its stock holding section that the item has been sold.

Re-ordering

The stock holding section will have built-in, as a feature of the software, a re-order code. Once a certain level of stock is reached, the system will automatically scan to see if stock is already on-route, when it is due to arrive and what the quantity is. In the event that there is a rush for certain products, and the on-route stock quantity maybe inadequate, then a further request for stock is placed on the company warehouse for future delivery.

Stocktaking

This is also carried out much more quickly. The staff will download, to a hand-held device, the details, such as the name and code, of the stock on hand. The staff then count the items on the shelves, and enter the quantity on the device. The two figures are tallied back on the main computer, taking in to account damaged goods and write-offs.

Another method use a hand-held device, this time with a barcode reader. Each item has a stock code displayed on the front of the shelf, the reader is wiped across the code, and the quantity on the shelf is also entered. The detail is in turn downloaded at the main computer.

Pricing

As all pricing is handled at one point, the computer, changes can be implemented quickly.

Libraries

Computerisation of library holdings has now replaced most of the old methods. Computers lend themselves to this area particularly well.

The master list

The library will have a master list of all publications on its inventory. This list is in turn arranged into categories such as: crime, historical and so on.

Each item will also be listed by title, author, and date of publication, with some specialist publications having a keyword list, on which the staff may conduct searches.

The borrower

For a person to borrow a publication, that person must first be registered at the library.

The registration will include some form of identification, usually a number, which identifies the borrower, along with that person's details such as home address, etc.

Library smart card

Some libraries issue the borrower with a swipe card, which records the above details. The borrower presents the book to the library staff, who in turn passes the card through a card reader. The detail is transferred to the computer and the book details are also entered. The date for return of the book is recorded on the computer. At this stage, the system returns to that of the old system, the library staff then stamps the return date on the sheet inside the book.

Accountancy procedures

Different libraries have different procedures however; at some stage the system will run a check on all loaned publications and produce a list of those publications overdue. This list will contain the details of whom the book was loaned to, the person's address, etc., for further action.

Doctors' surgeries

More and more doctors' surgeries are using computers to store patients' details and records as well as treatment received.

These systems are bespoke systems, especially written for the task and not available from the average computer/software retailer.

This is an area where security implications are enormous. The system must protect the patients' rights of confidentiality and the information must be access protected.

Driving licences

The recently introduced driving licence is a smart card, and has given some organisations a growing concern in respect of the 'Big Brother Watching' syndrome.

The card will record the driver's details on the face of the card, as well as storing that detail, and possibly more, on a chip in the card.

Systems and applications software

Systems software

- Systems software, the operating system, is the software required to run the computer.
- Without the systems software, the applications software cannot be loaded and will not function.

- Any number of applications may run on top of the systems software, provided that it was written for that platform.

Applications software

- Applications software is platform-specific and will use various functions within the systems software to carry out instructions on its behalf.
- It is the application software that has been especially written to perform specific tasks, such as spreadsheets for financial aspects and so on.

Smart cards

Smart cards come in many shapes and forms and include bank debit cards, credit cards, supermarket loyalty cards, fuel cards and so on. The use and potential use of smart cards is endless and is only currently limited by the need for greater security measures.

The range of uses is as diverse as:

Hotel use
In hotels to replace doors keys. The card is programmed, on issue, to open the room allocated to the customer.

Bank use
For use with Bank cash machines. The card is issued to a bank customer, as is a personal identification number (PIN).

The customer inserts the card into a slot and the card is read by the system. The user is then asked to type in the PIN, which is transmitted back to a central location and checked as correct. Once confirmed correct, the user is offered a number of options, which will include the option to withdraw cash.

The bank cash machines are another form of computer network. All the banks that own machines are eventually connected to the main system, where all the customers and their details are stored.

In addition to their own machines, a majority of banks allow other bank customers to withdraw cash from their machines, via the network of interconnected systems. Be aware though, some banks offer this service for free, while others impose a surcharge.

IT and society – the Information Age

This is the age of information. Never before has information been so freely and easily accessible by so many people, to such an extent that there is almost too much available, hence the term 'information overload'.

The abundance of information has lead to the development of specialist applications, designed to sort, filter and present it in various formats.

Impact on society

The way in which information is handled has resulted in a massive loss of jobs in administration, for example in payroll staff.

The computer is more accurate and is extremely fast when compared to a human carrying out the same or similar tasks.

Everything is required and expected to be instant resulting in an increase of stress related problems.

Medical

Medical technologies have benefited with faster and more accurate testing, scanning devices and monitoring equipment.

Weather forecasting

Computers, along with satellite communications and radar have greatly improved the accuracy of weather forecasting.

The information society

The availability of information has created an information profession. These are the people who spend a large portion of their working day processing information. The information may be as a result of filling a tax return, the census form, the driving licence application, the electoral roll and an application for a bank loan, to name but a few sources of information.

The computer vs. man

There are undoubtedly situations where a computer system, either as a computer on a desktop or controlling a robotic device, can carry out functions better than a person does.

Occasions when this may be appropriate are:

- The same repeated tasks.
- Actions that require accuracy and speed.
- Rapid processing of large quantities of information.
- Hazardous operations involving nuclear materials, deep-water operations and such-like.

There are also occasions when man is the better choice for a certain task, such as:

- When the task is a one-off. The time spent programming a computer would prove non-cost-effective.
- When the information relating to the task is free-flowing and the computer would either have to be re-programmed or to have as part of its programming a learning function. Again most likely non-cost-effective.
- Situations when interpretation on the ground is vital. The computer cannot see or hear, at this point in time, to assimilate the data.

- A situation develops where no programming has foreseen the circumstances or likelihood of such an event.

Care of the computer system

Cleanliness is next to godliness, and that is equally true in relation to the use of computers.

- Keep all liquids away from the systems components. Tea, coffee or whatever spilt over the keyboard will spoil your day as well as ruining the keyboard.

- Because the system creates static electricity, dust will gather and penetrate in to the tiniest of locations. For example; erratic mouse control usually indicates a build-up of dirt inside the case. Follow the manufacturer's instructions and clean it regularly.

- Do not expose or subject the system to excessive heat or likewise excessive cold.

- Store all disks in containers and ensure that there are no magnetic devices in the vicinity of the disks or the computer system.

- When you have finished with the computer do not simply switch it off. There is a shutdown procedure that should be adhered to. If the system fails for whatever reason, the only way to resolve the problem may be to switch off the computer without following the shutdown procedure. Refer to the operating system handbook for more details.

Elementary fault finding

Warning, if you do not feel confident in any way to tackle the following, stop and seek assistance. Do not struggle, you may place yourself in danger or compound the situation and make it worse.

- Check the obvious first, are all the on/off switches in the on position?

- Before moving and adjusting any power cables, ensure that the mains supply is switched off.

- If the system fails to respond when first switched on, ensure that that the power cable to the computer, and the monitor cables, are fully located in their sockets at the back of the computer.

- Now switch the power back on at the source and attempt to restart the computer.

- If the above fails, switch off the supply and plug in another electrical item, at the wall socket, that you know is functioning. This will help to eliminate doubts regarding the power socket on the wall.

- If the problem cannot be resolved after carrying out the above actions, seek professional assistance.

Repeated problems

In the event that a problem recurs over a period of time, make a note of the error message that may appear. Note the circumstances and what you did that caused the error or problem to happen. This will assist the support staff and will, hopefully, save time in solving the problem.

Tip

Always have an up-to-date Emergency Repair Disk (ERD) to hand. This will assist if the system fails to start-up correctly.

Computer crashes

If your computer crashes, all may not be lost.

1 Press the [Ctrl] + [Alt] + [Del] keys simultaneously.

2 The Close program dialog box will open. If you are lucky, it will indicate what the problem is, highlighting the name of the offending program and adding a comment like: 'is not responding'.

3 Press the End Task button.

4 Sometimes another dialog box appears,and this may tell you that the program is busy. Press the End Task button again. This may solve the problem.

Be careful of continually pressing the **[Ctrl]** + **[Alt]** + **[Del]** keys, as this will most likely cause the computer to restart completely.

Health and safety

A problem with computer systems is the abundance of cables that connect their various items.

Ensure that cables are kept tidy and are not likely to cause accidents, for example people tripping over them and perhaps pulling the item off the desk, compounding the problem.

In the work place, it is the employer's responsibility to provide a safe working environment. Likewise it is the home user's responsibility to ensure that the home environment is also safe.

In the office environment, the employer should ensure that the correct office furniture is purchased and installed. For instance:

● Desks with cable management systems should be purchased for all workstations.

● Printer stands should allow stacking and also permit the correct paper feed.

● Some dot matrix printers, particularly the larger machines, can be very noisy. If necessary the printer should be placed inside a noise-reducing cabinet.

● During printing, laser printers will, over time, extrude fine particles of toner. The printer should not be placed where particles can be blown over people working nearby.

Mains power points

Never overload the mains power point. Never use the adapter units that allow more than one plug to be inserted into a socket outlet. There are appropriate means on the market, to permit the running of a number of computer items from one socket.

As most computer items have low power consumption, it is acceptable to use an extension lead. Keep this as short as possible and cut it to length. Do not coil it up if it is too long.

Always ensure that the appropriate fuse is in the plug. Most when purchased, will have a 13-amp fuse installed. That is too high a fuse for the average computer item.

If in doubt, seek professional advice.

Security, copyright and the law

Software copyright

Programs are usually covered by copyright. You are personally liable if you contravene the copyright of the software.

You break the law if you:

- Copy the software and distribute the copies.
- Lend the software to friends to install the software on their computers.

You may make a copy of the software solely as a safeguard, in the event that the original disk becomes damaged.

Licences held

You may only load the software on the number of computers that you hold licences for.

Security

You must afford the original disks and any legally held copies the same level of security.

You must retain all copies of licences for all software used, and maintain a list of where and on what computers the software is loaded.

Freeware

This is software that is freely available, such as demonstration disks, or some educational programs. Read the licences, to ensure that you are not inadvertently contravening any agreements.

Shareware

Software that is made freely available for a limited time, to enable you to decide whether or not you wish to buy it. If you decide that you wish to continue using the software after the trial period, you will be required to register the product and pay a fee.

You must delete the software at the end of the trial period if you are not interested in it, otherwise you will be liable to pay the producers for the product.

Software on the Internet

Pirated copies of software are sometimes available on the Internet. Be sure to check before downloading such software.

End User Licence Agreement

The End User Licence Agreement (EULA) is included as part of the installation program on all software.

As the installation of the software progresses, the user is prompted to agree to the terms and conditions of the EULA, or to discontinue the installation. A section of the EULA states that if you do not agree with the EULA, the user should not to continue with the installation and return the software to the supplier from whom it was purchased.

The supplier however, generally, has in his small print a clause that states that should the cellophane wrapping be removed, the product will not be accepted for any other reason than faulty disks.

Be aware. Ensure you know what you require before you buy.

Data Protection Act 1984

This was introduced to meet concerns arising from the threat which misuse of the power of computers might pose to individuals. These derive from the ability of computing systems to store vast amounts of data, to manipulate data at high speed and, with associated communications, to give access to data from locations far from the site where the data is stored.

All public and private organisations that hold data about individuals or companies on computer systems must register this fact with the Data Registrar, giving the purpose for which the data is held. Data held can only be used for the purpose specified.

Data users must register:

● what data they hold

● how they use it

● how it is obtained

Individuals can obtain a copy of the data held about themselves, and data users must disclose it if requested.

An extract from the Data Protection Act 1984

Schedule 1

The Data Protection Principles Part 1

1. The information to be contained in personal data shall be obtained, and personal data shall be processed, fairly and lawfully.

2. Personal data shall be held only for one or more specified and lawful purposes.

3. Personal data held for any purpose or purposes shall not be used or disclosed in any manner incompatible with that purpose or those purposes.

4. Personal data held for any purpose or purposes shall be adequate, relevant and not excessive in relation to that purpose or those purposes.

5. Personal data shall be adequate and, where necessary, kept up to date.

6. Personal data held for any purpose or purposes shall not be kept for longer than is necessary for that purpose or those purposes.

7. An individual shall be entitled –

(a) at reasonable intervals and without undue delay or expense -

(i) to be informed by any data user whether he holds personal data of which that individual is the subject; and

(ii) to access any such data held by a data user; and

(b) where appropriate, to have such data corrected or erased.

Appropriate security measures shall be taken against unauthorised access to, or alteration, disclosure or destruction of, personal data and against accidental loss or destruction of personal data.

Rights of Data Subjects – Part III

Subject to the provisions of this section, an individual shall be entitled –

(a) to be informed by any data user whether the data held by him includes personal data of which that individual is the data subject; and

(b) to be supplied by any data user with a copy of the information constituting any such personal data held by him;

and where any of the information referred to in paragraph (b) above is expressed in terms which are not intelligible without explanation the information shall be accompanied by an explanation of those terms.

The UK Data Protection Act 1984 is a complex document and the extracts quoted, on the preceding page, were taken from the Website listed below, and was current at the time of writing this publication.

Web site: http://www.hmso.gov.uk/acts/acts1984/1984035.htm#aofs.

A full version of the Data Act can be obtained from The Stationary Office Limited, ISBN 0 10 543584, £6.60.

Security

Computer security not only covers the aspects of theft of the computer, and its associated equipment, but the security of the data stored on the computer itself.

Data

Only legitimately held data can be stored on a computer, as covered by the Data Protection Act.

Passwords

Computer passwords must be guarded carefully, in particular that of the person afforded administrator rights on the computer system.

Copies of the passwords should be maintained and sealed in an envelope and then locked in a secure container, i.e. the company safe.

- Instructions as to who may open the envelopes should be clearly written on the outside of the envelopes.
- Any person permitted to open the envelopes should sign a document stating why, by what authority, etc. that the person is accessing the password lists.

Backup policy

As data may become damaged, lost or otherwise destroyed, there should exist a policy for creating back-up copies of all-important data.

Subject to the degree of importance attached to the data, backups may be required daily or more frequently.

The backup policy may only require the backing-up of new or recently amended data, termed **incremental backup.** A **full backup** occurs less frequently.

Backup storage

During the course of backing up data it is important to use a different set of tapes for each backup period. This is due to possible damage to the tape, such as tape stretch or breakage.

One copy of the backup tapes should be held on site for easy access. At least one copy of the backup tapes should be held off site as a precaution against fire of theft.

Backup procedures must be documented and clearly understood and practised by the staff responsible for creating the backups.

Equally important is that the **Backup Restore** procedures must be tried and tested. It's all well and good having a good looking document telling the staff what to do, then only to find that the system does not function.

Anti-virus protection

Viruses are becoming more and more of a problem to computer users. Viruses are, generally, small computer programs that are written to disrupt the normal operation of a computer.

Viruses cause a variety of problems, such as:

● Annoying little messages that pop-up on the screen periodically.

● The destruction of the data on the computer.

A virus hit the computer world just before Easter 1999 and caused considerable chaos within companies running e-mail.

The virus arrived via the Internet and once on a computer, would search the system for that person's e-mail address book. It would create 50 e-mail messages based on the address book, then attach itself to those e-mails and sent them through the system. On arrival at each of the 50 addressees, it started all over again.

Clearly for some systems, this created an overload and the systems crashed.

Virus intrusion

Viruses gain access to computers in many different ways, for instance:

● A floppy disk may have a virus on it. The virus transfers itself to the computer hard disk and in turn spreads to other disks.

● Documents can transfer viruses by way of macros contained within them. The viruses will transfer to the computer and spread.

● The Internet is an obvious source of viruses coming in a number of different ways such as downloading files and data.

Virus protection

All systems should employ some form of anti-virus protection, not just anti-virus software, but also company policy as to who may load programs, to what disk may be used and how they should be transported.

Power failure

Security also comes in the form of protection against power failures or power surges.

Uninterrupted Power Supplies

There exists on the market today numerous types of Uninterrupted Power Supplies (UPS) systems. These contain powerful batteries that are on constant standby and will switch in if there is a power failure.

The batteries are not usually powerful enough to allow long continuing use of the computer system, but have sufficient power to give the system adequate time to perform an orderly shut-down without losing any data.

UPS systems have specialist software working in conjunction with the power supply designed to sense a power problem.

Anti-surge protection

Power supply systems are often not running at the correct voltage, etc., due to the strain on the systems or to adverse weather conditions.

These conditions create power surges, increases and fall in the output, which if powerful enough could cause data corruption. Sufficiently powerful surges may actually cause some systems to re-boot, particular in times of storms.

UPS systems can provide considerable protection, by the way of built-in circuitry, and reduce the likelihood of data loss.

Home users can also benefit from such protection by purchasing smaller protective devices, rather than a full-blown UPS system, which can be quite costly.

Hardware, software and ergonomics

Hardware and software

Hardware is the term used to describe a component part or sub-assembly of a computer system. For example:

- the monitor
- the computer case.
- the keyboard.

Software is the term used to describe a program that is run on a computer, for example:

- Windows 98 Operating system.
- Microsoft Office Suite 97.
- Adobe PhotoShop 5.

Types of memory

Random Access Memory (RAM)

RAM is a non-permanent memory system. For RAM to function the computer system must be up and running and functioning correctly.

The operating system and application are loaded in to RAM, as is the information that is currently being processed.

RAM can be written to, that is when information is placed into the memory, and can be read from, that is when information can be retrieved from the memory.

When the computer is shutdown, any data that was in RAM is lost. Once the system is switched off, that data cannot be recovered.

RAM is known by a number of different names, e.g. memory, internal storage.

Read Only Memory (ROM)

As the name suggests ROM can only be used to retrieve information. ROM comes in many forms and can be found burnt into a chip that resides inside the computer.

The chip that comes immediately to mind is the one that contains the start-up instructions for the computer. This is also referred to as the BIOS or CMOS.

- The BIOS or CMOS contains the basic instructions required by the computer on start-up, including information such as what hard drives and other devices are installed, and the instructions to enable it to carry out the POST test before handing the system over to the operating system.

A CD-ROM is also a ROM device.

A floppy disk can be set to a read only state by moving the slide button to expose an aperture. This will prevent the disk being written to until such time that the slide switch is adjusted again to close the aperture.

The purpose of backup

The purpose of backing up information is to ensure that in the event of either:

- an equipment failure, resulting in the loss or damage to data
- the physical destruction of the data by fire
- the actual theft of the data

that the organisation can continue to function by having a second copy of the data available.

A point of fact

Following the bombing of the World Trade Center in New York, some years ago, it was some considerable time before access to the buildings was permitted.

A number of companies, working out of the centre, had backup plans and procedures in place. However, only a small percentage of these stored their backup data off-site and therefore could immediately access that data. The remaining companies did not have access to their data for weeks and in some cases months.

It was estimated, 12 months after the event that some 40% of those companies had gone out of business as a direct consequence of poor backup policy and procedures.

Procedures

There are numerous procedures for backing up data, however, no matter how good the procedures may look on paper, they must function in practice.

Run the backup procedures and the restore element to ensure the data is actually restored.

Input and output devices

Input devices, as the name suggest, input data, instructions and so on into the computer. Examples of input devices are:

- The keyboard
- A scanner

Output devices display the result of the computation. Examples of output devices are:

- The monitor
- A printer

Printers

There are a wide range of printers available for use with computers. The printers are varied in the type and purpose that they are intended for.

Printers are listed under three main headings:

- Laser printers.
- Inkjet printers
- Dot matrix printers.

There are other types, but these tend to be for more specialist use and are not covered here.

All three types of printer are available in either black and white or colour.

Laser printers

Laser printers are generally more expensive and use toner, not ink, to produce the image.

Colour laser printer prices are falling, but compared to the inkjet colour printers, are still extremely expensive.

There are other considerations to be taken in to account other than just the purchase price:

- Toner is expensive.
- Replacement drums are expensive.

39

- The printing time is longer and slower.
- Most current Laser colour printers have a maximum resolution of 600 x 600, and this is often too low to produce very high quality graphics.

The final printed product, unlike that of the inkjet, is stable and will not run if it comes in contact with moisture.

Inkjet printers

Inkjet printers are quite cheap when compared to laser printers. They use an inkjet to produce the printed document. There are limitations with the ink. Should it be exposed to moisture, the ink will run and if exposed to prolonged sunshine, will fade.

The high majority of inkjet printers are usually a dual inkjet system; that is to say, colour is almost always built-in as standard.

Apart from price, other considerations are:

- What is the end product and what it is intended to convey? Will it include high-end quality graphics and photography?
- Inkjet printers are available with many different resolutions. Some of which are quite low, while others are higher.
- High-resolution printers are a must if it is intended to print photographic images.
- Will special paper be required to produce the imagery on, and how will this look with the everyday paper used in the document.
- Some ink cartridges contain multiple colour inks, which can means that you are throwing away unused ink in these. Others have individual ink cartridges for each colour ink.

Dot matrix printers

The dot matrix printer was once a very common printer however, with the fall in prices of both the inkjet and laser printers, it has declined in use and popularity. They are not often seen in the average office of today.

Dot matrix printers are available in colour as well as black and white.

The print is made up of a series on small dots, from a set of pins, which first must punch onto a ribbon and then impact on to the paper.

There are two sizes for the print head, 9-pin and 24-pin. 9-pin print quality is often poor.

Health and Safety considerations

The European Union issued a series of publications, which became known as the 'six pack'. One of the publications specifically dealt with computer workstation ergonomics and the following areas were addressed:

- Display screens
- Keyboards.
- Work desk/surface.
- Work chair.
- Space requirements.
- Lighting.
- Reflections and glare.
- Noise.
- Heat.
- Humidity.
- Computer/user interface.

All the above items will, in some way or another, have an impact on the working environment of the user. For instance:

- Glare from the monitor screen or from a glossy desktop.
- A strong light behind the monitor, i.e. windows.
- A chair that is not adjustable or does not meet the safety standards laid down in the regulations.
- Cramped and restraining working space.
- Poor lighting conditions that reflect on to the monitor screen.
- The monitor set either too high or, most commonly, too low.

Breaks

The user must take short breaks if involved with prolonged work involving the display screen. The break does not necessarily mean leaving the location of work, but a change of activity away from the display screen.

Eye Tests

Regulation 5 of the Health and Safety (Display Screens Equipment) Regulations 1992 gives the user or those about to become users the opportunity to have an appropriate eye and eyesight test as soon as practicable after request and at regular intervals.

- Special corrective appliances are to be provided by the employer for users where normal ones cannot be used.
- The costs of the tests and special corrective appliances are to be met by the employer of the user.
- The term 'special appliance' will be those prescribed to meet vision defects at the viewing distance – anti-glare screens are not special corrective appliances.

Further regulations

There are a number of further regulations that the employer and casual user should be aware of. The regulations are not simply for guidance but are to be implemented as a matter of law.

Common sense

Most problems can be quickly overcome by the application of a common sense approach however; common sense must not override the application and enforcement of the rules and regulations that apply to the working environment, etc.

Advice

If in doubt, contact your local Health and Safety Executive (HSE) office for advice.

Information network services

A network is a group of connected computers, which can share files, printers and in some cases, applications. All information on a network is potentially shareable. The sharing of information helps to increase the productivity of personnel and of workgroups.

There is also a capital saving to be made by the sharing of printers and other devices. All in all, networks better utilise computer resources and the availability of information.

Network connections

There are a different number of systems used to connect computers, to create the network.

Networks vary in size and complexity. The number of computers on a network will vary, subject to factors such as traffic volume, workgroup design, function, style and much more.

Workgroups

'Workgroup' is another term for a network and is usually used to describe a small group of people, within a small establishment or office and often employs peer-to-peer networking.

Peer-to-peer

In peer-to-peer networking, all the people on the network usually store their files on their own computers, and give access to some, or all, of the files to other users.

This method of networking is cheap and easy to install and is often sufficient for a small office.

Printer sharing

In peer-to-peer networking it is normal to share printers. A shared printer is connected to one computer and the others on the network use that computer's resources to access the printer, thereby saving on costs.

A Local Area Network

A Local Area Network (LAN) may describe a number of computers connected together, in one room, on one floor, in one building or generally in an immediate locality.

A peer-to-peer network, in strict terms, is a LAN. However LAN systems usually employ what is known as a client/server network.

The *client* is the computer at which the user sits – the workstation. All computers are connected to the *server*, via their workstations. The server is a central computer that stores all the files used in common by the company or organisation.

Also running off the server may well be a number of other shared facilities, such as printers and modems.

Wide Area Networks

Wide Area Networks (WAN) interconnect smaller networks. These networks can be close or at a great distance to each other.

The Internet is a series of smaller networks interconnected.

Standard network topologies

All network designs stem from three basic topologies, connection structures.

Bus

The bus topology is the simplest to install and maintain. It consists of a single cable, known as a truck, backbone or segment, that connects all the computers together in a single line.

One disadvantage of the system is that if a cable fails, the complete network will crash.

Star

The star topology connects all the computers, by individual cable runs, to a centralised component called a hub. Unlike the bus topology, if one cable fails, the network as a whole will not crash. However, one hub failing may cause a network crash.

Token ring

The token ring topology connects the computers to a single circle of cable. The signal travels around the cable in one direction and passes through each computer in turn. Each computer acts as a repeater to boost the signal.

The failure of one computer may impact on the entire network and cause a crash.

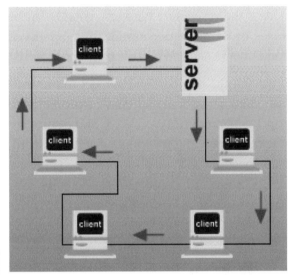

Telephone systems in computing

Telephone systems play a major part in computer networking.

Modems

A modem (*mo*dulator–*dem*odulator) is an device that coverts binary data to analogue tones and voltages that are suitable for transmission over standard dial-up or leased telephone lines.

Many modems also have a fax capability, and in addition, many now offer voice mail facilities, via the software bundled with the modem.

Most home computers now include a modem, which will allow you to connect to the Internet. If you work from home, you can, with the appropriate authorisation, connect to your company's own network. The method used is called dial-up networking.

Dial-up networking

To use dial-up networking, you must have a modem and access to a phone line or a suitable mobile telephone and its associated hardware. You must also have the necessary authority to access the respective network, usually in the form of a telephone number, an approved logon name and the correct password.

You dial the number, and subject to the software and network set-up, may be prompted to logon and provide a password. Some software packages store the logon name and password, thus speeding up the dial-up process. There are of course security implications of such a system.

The handshake

The modem, before it can start transmitting data, carries out what is known as a handshake with the distant modem. This establishes how the modems will exchange information. After the handshake, the modems are ready to pass or receive data as required.

Data compression

The transmitting modem will compress the data, then send it to the distant modem, which will decompress the data. The modems will use what is known as error control, to ensure that the data reliably reaches its destination.

Speeds

Modems have the option of using different speeds to transfer data. When communicating, modems must use the same speed. A fast modem can talk to a slow modem, but both will communicate at the slower speed.

Current Standard

The current standard for most common modems, for everyday use, is V90 56K x2. The explanation of this standard is somewhat involved and is beyond the scope of this book.

Terminology

Online

You are online when the modem has connected to another modem, and is ready to exchange information.

Offline

When the modem is not connected to another, you are offline.

Integrated Services Digital Network (ISDN)

Instead of using standard telephone lines and a standard modem, some companies use an ISDN line. ISDN transfers information four times faster than the standard modem. ISDN requires the use of a specialist modem, called a terminal adapter.

The Internet

The Internet is extremely useful in many ways, shapes and forms and is covered in more detail in Chapter 7.

E-mail

Electronic mail, e-mail, is a very popular feature of the Internet. E-mail can be exchanged with anyone around the world, provided of course that both parties have access to the Internet and have an e-mail address.

To send e-mail, you must have in addition to the above, a computer with suitable software, a modem, telephone line and an Internet Service Provider (ISP).

You can access your e-mail from anywhere in the world, simply by dialling the appropriate telephone number for their ISP, and their e-mail can be accessed using their logon name and password.

Internet browser

To access the Internet, you must have a suitable browser, which translates the Internet data in to a usable visual display on the screen.

Costs

E-mail is fast, easy, inexpensive and cuts out the use of paper, thus creating a saving of resources in one respect.

Voice over the Internet

In the not-too-distant future, greater use of the Internet will be made in the field of voice communications.

Information access

The Internet gives the user access to an abundance of information, often free, through locations far and wide, via newspapers, magazines, academic papers, government documents, television transcripts, speeches, job listings and much, much more.

Entertainment

Hundreds of games are available on the Internet, again often free of charge. Music is now also downloadable. Using the Internet, you can review current movies, theme songs and have interactive conversions around the world, sometimes with celebrities.

Discussion groups

You can join discussion groups around the world, with people who have similar interests. The discussion usually takes place mainly by text. You can ask questions and respond to questions posed by other members of the discussion group.

Online shopping

Online shopping is becoming more and more popular, as more organisations and companies become online shopping providers.

You can buy books, flowers, music CDs, pizza, stocks and shares and order your weekly grocery requirements and have them delivered to your door.

Sample paper1: Basic concepts of IT

	Section 1	
1	Name three 'peripheral' items that can be attached to a PC.	1. 2. 3.
2	Name three components typically found WITHIN a PC (i.e. within the case)	1. 2. 3.
3	Which operating system (OS) came first, MS-DOS or MS Windows?	
4	What does 'GUI' (pronounced 'gooey') stand for?	
5	Name three functions of the PC's Operating System (OS)	1. 2. 3.
6	Name three types of application software typically found on a PC.	1. 2. 3.
7	What is the difference between memory and data storage media on a computer?	
8	Which is bigger, a terabyte or megabyte?	Terabyte/ Megabyte
	Section 2	
9	Name one advantage and one disadvantage of the use of computer systems in industry.	
10	Cash dispenser points or 'hole in the wall' machines are more accurately known as 'ATM's'. What does ATM stand for?	
11	When computers were first introduced into schools a specially designed computer system commissioned by the BBC was used. What was the name of this system?	
12	Name two current uses of the 'Smart Card' in everyday life.	

Section 3		
13	Name two occasions where it is considered that a computer is more appropriate to a given task than a human; and two where the human is a more appropriate choice than a computer.	
14	Give two fundamental rules when considering the care of your computer.	
15	When your computer crashes there are three keys which when pressed simultaneously may assist you in discovering the nature of the fault and allow you to shut down your computer in a controlled manner. Which keys are they?	
16	Name a possible Health and Safety issue associated with dot-matrix printers, and how this issue can be overcome.	
Section 4		
17	Under what circumstances are users allowed to make copies of copyrighted software?	
18	What is the difference between 'freeware' and 'shareware'?	
19	Under the Data Protection Act of 1984 data users must register three pieces of information pertaining to their data. What are these three pieces of information?	
20	Name three aspects of security that must be addressed to ensure the safety of the data on your computer system.	1. 2. 3.
Section 5		
21	Which of the following can be classified as hardware and which as software?	
	Computer Monitor	Software/Hardware
	MS Windows operating system	Software/Hardware
	Microsoft Office	Software/Hardware
	Mouse	Software/Hardware
	Floppy Disk	Software/Hardware

22	Which of the following statements are true:	
	Random Access Memory (RAM) will store data after the PC has been switched off	True/False
	RAM may be referred to as memory or internal storage	True/False
	ROM stands for Read Once Memory	True/False
	The ROM chip that holds a computer's start-up instructions is called the BIOS or CMOS	True/False
24	Name three common types of printers	1. 2. 3.
25	Which ONE of the following is a likely consequence of increasing the RAM on a PC?	
	You can store more files and folders on the PC	True/False
	The graphics on your monitor will be clearer	True/False
	Your PC will process and run quicker	True/False
	You will be protected against certain viruses	True/False
26	Name FIVE factors associated with working on a PC that have Health and Safety considerations associated with them.	1. 2. 3. 4. 5.
Section 6		
27	Give two reasons why you would want to network a number of PCs in an office.	1. 2.
28	Is the Internet an example of a LAN or a WAN?	LAN/WAN
29	Which ONE of these is NOT a network topology:	
	Shuttle	True/False
	Token Ring	True/False
	Bus	True/False
	Star	True/False
30	Which transfers data the quickest, modems over a telephone line, or a terminal adapter over an ISDN line?	
31	What does the 'E' in 'E-mail' stand for?	
32	Name two uses for the Internet.	

2 Using the computer

Using the computer

System start up

Chapter 1 gave you a basic introduction to the computer hardware. We now move on and take a look at how we get the system up and running, what it is doing during this phase and what the display should look like. Finally, there is a section on the mouse and common fuctionality aspects across applications.

Before you switch on the system always check that there is not a floppy disk in the drive unit. We will return later to why there should not, in most cases, be a disk in the drive when the system starts. Now cast your mind back to the previous lesson and you will recall that the system on/off switch is normally located on the front panel of the main unit. Switch it on.

A power unit built into the computer supplies all the components with power, and you will most likely hear the fan whirr and maybe hear the hard disk drive start to spin as well.

The POST test routine

At this stage the computer carries out a self-test, to determine that everything that should be there is present and functioning. This is known as the POST routine (Power On Self Test) and is stored in a permanent memory area in the system.

During this phase the computer checks that various systems are functioning and will also detect any errors. If the POST discovers a problem, for instance with the floppy drive, it will return an error message, e.g. 'Floppy Disk Drive Failure'.

Numerous errors can be detected by the POST routine, but successful completion of the test does not guarantee that your system is actually free of all errors and problems. On completion of the POST routine, we will assume that the system is fully functional.

The system then loads the routines that are essential to the operation of the computer into the memory. The operating system (OS), Windows 95/98, Windows NT or any other OS is loaded as required. The special files adapt the OS to the hardware requirements.

Finally the Windows interface is loaded and the Desktop appears.

The Desktop display

Think of the computer Desktop as being similar to an office desk and how you arrange the various items that you often find on a desk, such as the documents that you are reading or writing, your telephone, file trays, pens and pencils and so on.

As desktops are configurable to your requirements and preferences, there is no such thing as a standard display. There are, however, certain items that most people retain on their Desktop.

The Desktop display is made up of a number of areas and items.

● **The Background** may be a plain colour, or may be made up of patterns and/or images. These patterns and images are referred to as the wallpaper and a number are pre-packaged in Windows 95/98 operating system.

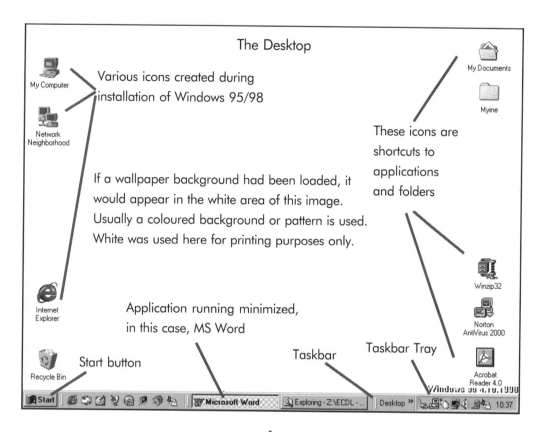

The Desktop

My Computer

Network Neighborhood

Internet Explorer

Recycle Bin

Various icons created during installation of Windows 95/98

If a wallpaper background had been loaded, it would appear in the white area of this image. Usually a coloured background or pattern is used. White was used here for printing purposes only.

Application running minimized, in this case, MS Word

Start button

My Documents

Myine

These icons are shortcuts to applications and folders

Winzip32

Norton AntiVirus 2000

Acrobat Reader 4.0

Windows 98 4.10.1998

Taskbar

Taskbar Tray

Start | Microsoft Word | Exploring - Z:\ECDL - ... | Desktop » | 10:37

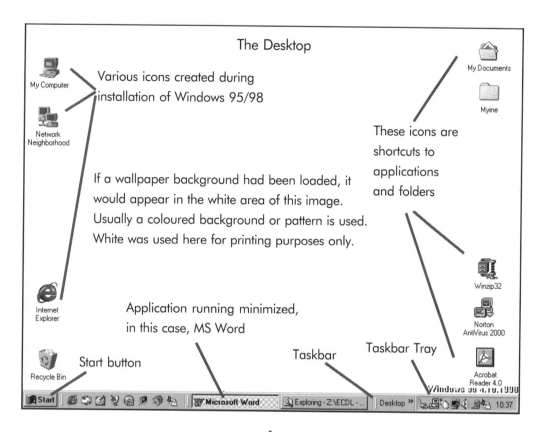

You can, once you master the system, create your own backgrounds if you so desire.

- It is from the **Taskbar** that you will generally select and start the applications you wish to use. The Taskbar is usually located along the bottom area of the screen, and has a number of regions that are independent of each other.

- At the extreme left edge of the Taskbar is the **Start button**. This has the word Start on it, and the Microsoft Flying Window logo.

Move the cursor over the Start button and pause. A Tool Tip will pop up.

Click here to begin.

Start

The Start menu

Click once on the Start button and a pop-up menu will appear.

This is divided into three regions.

The lower region will, in most cases, have only one option available and this is the **Shut Down** command, used to shut down the system.

The middle region has seven options. The top four of these have right-facing arrows, to the right of the items. These indicate that there are secondary menus, and by moving the cursor over the item, a further menu will open. This type of system is known as a cascading menu.

Move your cursor over the option **Programs**.

The secondary menu will open and you may find that there are more right arrows by some of its items.

Do not start any of the applications at this stage. Move the cursor back over the main Start menu and the Programs menu will close.

51

Point to Programs to open its menu

The upper region of the main menu is customisable – you can insert or remove items.

Ensure that the Taskbar is still visible and look to the extreme right-hand side. What you will see is subject to how the computer has been set up, however, there is usually at least one item in this region, and it is the clock.

Move the cursor over the clock, pause and the date will be displayed in the area above the clock.

Other items may well be displayed on the Taskbar and this again will depend on the operating system version and computer setup.

Once an application is open, its name will appear on the Taskbar. If you have two running simultaneously, both names will appear on the Taskbar. It is from here that you can switch between applications. Click once on the application name to bring it up on the screen.

Click to switch to the application

Elsewhere on the Desktop are a number of icons. This again is subject to how the computer has been set up and personalised. Where the icons appear is irrelevant to its operation. In general, one would expect to see the following:

A small image of a computer with the label 'My Computer'.

An image of two computers connected together and the words 'Network Neighborhood'.

An image of a waste bin. This is the Recycle Bin and its name appears below the image.

Other icons may well be on the Desktop but we will end our brief tour at this point.

Starting applications

It's now time to run an application. Move the cursor over the **Start** button and click once. Move up to **Programs,** pause and a cascade menu will open. Move to the right and select .

Microsoft Word will open and the user is ready to either edit an existing document or start a new document altogether.

System shut down

You should never simply switch off the computer using the on/off switch. There is a set procedure for closing down, and the computer itself will tell you when it is safe to switch off.

Restarting the computer

You may sometimes need to shut down the computer and restart it. For instance, if you install new software, for the operating system to recognise the presence of the application, it is often necessary to restart the system.

The **Shut Down Windows** dialog box has an option to restart the computer. Simply select the **Restart** option and click on the **Yes** button, and the computer will shut down and then automatically restart.

Basic steps

1 Ensure all programs have been closed down, in this case, Word.

2 Click the Start button.

3 Select Shut Down from the pop-up menu. A dialog box will open.

4 Select Shut down the computer or Restart the computer as required.

5 Click Yes to confirm the action.

6 The system carries out a series of checks and saves any changes that you may have made to the Desktop, etc.

7 On shut-down, you will then see the message '*It is now safe to switch off your computer*'. Switch off the computer and any peripherals that are connected to it.

4 Shut down or Restart?

5 Confirm the shut-down

Using the mouse

The mouse is essentially a pointing device and is extremely important because many Windows applications rely heavily on the mouse to initiate actions or functions. This short section will introduce you to a number of mouse actions and the terminology used in association with the mouse throughout this course.

Types of mouse

There are different types of computer pointing devices available, but basically all devices have the following:

- **Roller Ball**. Built into the body of the mouse is a heavy roller ball, which responds to your movements of the mouse by moving the mouse pointer in the vertical and horizontal plains on the screen.

- **Buttons**. There are always at least two buttons, located on top and to the front of the mouse body.

The left button is generally the most used. This is used to select, highlight or in Drag and Drop operations. Generally, when directed to select or highlight an item, it is the left button that is used and is expressed as 'left-click' or simply 'click'.

The right button has recently been given more functionality and acquired an increased importance within Windows applications. The most common result of using of the right mouse button is to bring up a context or pop-up menu. When directed to use the right mouse button, the term generally used is 'right-click'.

Shortcut keys

There are certain actions that when carried out using the mouse can actually slow you down. For instance if you are typing text with both hands on the keyboard, and decide to save your work. To do this requires you to remove a hand from the keyboard and place it on the mouse, then move the mouse pointer up to the Standard toolbar, and then click the Save icon.

This all takes time. Consider the same situation, but this time you keep both hands on the keyboard and you use the keyboard shortcut Ctrl+S. Simultaneously press the Control (Ctrl) and the letter 'S' keys and the item that you are working on is saved. Much quicker, with both hands still at the keyboard.

Common shortcut keys

The really good thing about shortcut keys is that a majority of them are available to you irrespective of the application you are using. The shortcut, Ctrl+S, will save any work in Word, Excel, Access and many more applications.

The 'Save' shortcut combinations uses the Control key. You should be aware that there are other shortcuts, that use combinations of Shift, Control and Alt(ernative) keys. To learn more of these keys, use the online Help.

- **Abbreviations**. Control is abbreviated to Ctrl, Delete is Del and Escape is Esc.

- **Applying the shortcut**. In this book, the shortcut combination is written as Ctrl+S for Save. The plus (+) sign is only shown to indicate that you must press the indicated combination simultaneously. You do not have to press the plus key as well.

Listed below are some of the most common shortcut key combinations and we suggest that you memorise and use them when appropriate. You will be occasionally reminded to use the appropriate shortcut key method.

The list is not exhaustive and you should be aware that applications will have their own unique shortcut keys, which apply only to them. Do remember that common functions, such as Copy and Paste, are common to all Windows based applications.

For further information and lists of shortcut keys, use the online Help for each application.

Shortcut	Action	Shortcut	Action
Ctrl+S	Save current work	**Ctrl+X**	Cut selection to Clipboard
Ctrl+Z	Undo last action	**Ctrl+C**	Copy selected text/image
Ctrl+V	Paste Clipboard contents	**Ctrl+A**	Select entire document
Ctrl+Right Arrow	Move one word to the right	**Ctrl+Left Arrow**	Move one word to the left
End	Move to end of line	**Home**	Move to start of line
Ctrl+End	Move to end of document	**Ctrl+Home**	Move to start of document

Cut, Copy and Paste

Throughout this book you will often encounter the terms cut, copy, paste and Clipboard. So what are we talking about and how does it work? Listed below are a series of short explanations on each item and how the computer deals with each action.

With a sound understanding of these, you will develop a greater understanding of how the computer carries out relatively simple commands, which will increase your productivity, afford you considerable flexibility and reduce the sometimes repetitive tasks.

Clipboard

The Clipboard is a reserved area of computer memory, which cannot be used for any other purpose, that stores data, which originates from the Cut and Copy commands.

The Clipboard can normally only store one section of data/image at any time. For instance, if you cut a section of text and move it, then later cut a different section of text, the previously Cut text is over-written and lost. The situation changes somewhat with Office 2000, which extends the Clipboard so that it can hold up to a dozen separate items of data.

The Clipboard contents can be reused repeatedly, if required, it is not lost until such time that it is either over-written or the computer is switched off.

The commands

In any Windows application, the Cut, Copy and Paste commands can be found as items on the Edit menu and as buttons in the Standard toolbar.

Cut

The Cut action is used to remove a section of selected text, data or image from one location in a document, retains it in memory, ready to be placed in a different location of the same document, or in a different document or application.

Copy

Copy functions in a similar manner as the Cut command, except it does not remove the selected text, it only copies it. Whatever was copied, is retained in memory, and can be placed in another location within the same document, or in a different document or application.

Paste

The Paste command instructs the computer to look in the Clipboard and then to copy, whatever is found, to the cursor location within the current document.

File management

File management is just what the name implies, a means of filing or storing, in a logical and orderly manner all the documents, spreadsheets, databases and images that one creates on the computer. There is no requirement to differentiate between a Word document or an Excel spreadsheet, or any other such item, because in file management terms they are all the same and known as *files*.

Imagine having no system or management of all the files already on the computer; that is even before you start saving anything. Clearly we would spend more time looking for files than actually using them.

Included within the Windows operating system is a program especially designed to assist in file management. It is called Windows Explorer and it is this that we shall investigate.

Most computers only have one hard disk drive and this is referred to as the 'C:' drive, or root directory. Don't concern yourself too much at this stage about remembering all the names and alternatives. We will return to it in more detail later.

Think of the C: drive as a large filing cabinet that has a number of drawers. Within these drawers are a number of folders. 'Folders' is the same term used by Explorer and these folders serve the same purpose as those in the filing cabinet with one exception; the folders in Explorer are electronic folders.

You can do most things with the computer folder that you can with those in a real cabinet.

You can move the folder from one drawer to another. You can insert documents (files) into the folders and likewise you can remove items. If you so decide, you could throw the folder away for good, by deleting it.

You can copy a file, so that you have two identical files, but be careful though this could lead to confusion, and Windows will not allow you to do this in some instances.

Exploring Windows Explorer

Okay, it's now time to take a look at Windows Explorer. Move the cursor over the Taskbar and then click on the Start button once.

The Start menu will pop up. Move the cursor up to **Programs** and another menu will open the right. Remember that a right-facing arrow on a menu means that there is a further menu.

Windows Explorer is usually situated in the lower area of the Programs menu. Click once on Windows Explorer and after a short while Explorer will open. The screen should look similar to the one shown here. The main areas that are of interest to us at the moment have been labelled.

Look first at the All Folders pane that fills the left-hand side of the window. At the very top of this is an icon that represents the Desktop. Imagine that you are sitting at a conventional desk and all your various items and equipment are placed on the desktop. The principle is the same here, the Desktop is the visual focal point of the computer.

Windows Explorer

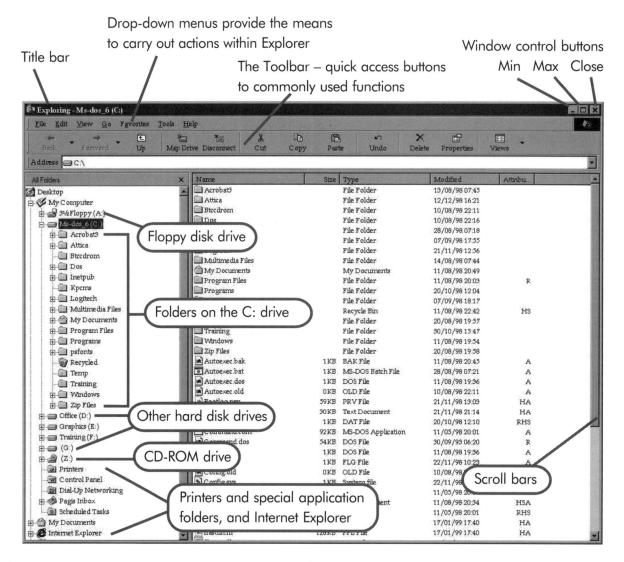

Title bar

Drop-down menus provide the means to carry out actions within Explorer

The Toolbar – quick access buttons to commonly used functions

Window control buttons
Min Max Close

Floppy disk drive

Folders on the C: drive

Other hard disk drives

CD-ROM drive

Printers and special application folders, and Internet Explorer

Scroll bars

You will see that the system is laid out in a hierarchy.

- The highest level is the Desktop.

- The second level down after the Desktop is My Computer, with other items below.

- You will also see that a number of the items shown have a + adjacent to them, to the left. Clicking once on the + sign will open a branch below that item.

Return to the top of the window and you will see a number of drive units.

- The first drive listed is the 3½" floppy (A:). The letter A identifies it as the A: drive.

- Below the floppy drive is the first hard drive, C. In the example the drive also has a name, MS-dos_6 which is followed by (C:).

All storage units are assigned letters to identify each one.

58

- The letters A and B are reserved for the floppy drives, even though only one floppy is usually fitted in most computers today.

- Below the floppy drive is the C drive, the only hard disk drive in most computers.

- The CD-ROM drive and any other types of unit are also assigned drive letters. If your computer is connected to a network, letters will be assigned to identify the various network connections and drives.

- As the alphabet has 26 letters, so you can assign up to 26 letters to drives.

Folders

Folder names

Windows 95 introduced long file names to the Windows based PC. Prior to the arrival of Windows 95, MS-DOS rules applied and one could use no more than 8 letters in a file name.

With the long file name rules and conventions, you can use up to 256 characters, including hyphens and spaces when naming folders.

There are a number of characters, such as the colon and full stop, that are reserved for the operating system, which means we cannot use them. Windows will usually prompt you if you do attempt to use them and will give you the opportunity to change the name.

Folder structures

Folders' names should be unambiguous and relate to their content. For instance, if you deal with invoices, a first level folder could be named *INVOICES IN* and another folder called *INVOICES OUT*.

Within each folder there could be a subfolder for each financial quarter, perhaps called *IN-VOICES 1-98*, *INVOICES 2-98*.

The optimum name should contain a maximum of 15 characters. Long names only cause confusion and consume time and space.

Naming files

The rules and conventions for file naming are much the same as for naming folders. You can use upper and lower case letters as well as hyphens and spaces and up to 256 characters.

The notable exception when naming files is the use of the extension. This consists of a full stop followed by a group of three letters and comes at the end of the file name. The letters indicate what type of file it is.

In this example you will see that there are two files, each with a different extension. The first, *6Test.doc*, is a Word document, indicated by the extension *.doc*.

The second, *7Test.xls*, is an Excel spreadsheet indicated by the extension *.xls*.

Opening folders

Sometimes you will have to open several subfolders to locate a file. In this example I am looking for the file *Basic.dll*. To reach the file I first have to open three folders.

We now are looking at the folder called *Logitech*. This is on the C drive and has a + sign to its left. I click once on the + sign.

Note the + sign next to some of the folders. This indicates that there are subfolders within them.

In this example note that the + sign has changed to a – sign. We now see that there is a folder within *Logitech*, called *Mouse*, and it too has a + sign next to it. A click on the + sign will open the folder.

In this example the *Mouse* folder has been opened to reveal a further three folders.

Note the absence of any + or - signs adjacent to any of the three folders.

In this example the folder called *System* has been opened. In the window on the right you can see the files that are stored in the *System* folder.

Take note

Folders can appear in the left and right panes of Explorer. Files only appear in the right pane of Explorer – never in the left.

Creating folders

You can create folders as required. Folders can be created within folders, and are referred to as subfolders.

For this exercise we will create a number of folders, using the names listed in the sequences outlined below.

Basic steps

1   Run Windows Explorer and click once on the C: drive.

2   Open the File menu, point to New and select Folder.

2   Use File > New > Folder

3   Type in the name *0Student*, the 0 is actually a zero not a letter O.

4   When you finish typing, press [Enter]. This tells the computer that it should now carry out the instruction, in this case, apply the new file name.

5   Now press the F5 key, at the top of the keyboard to refresh the screen display. The folder will now appear at the top of the C: drive listings.

❑   That's it. You have just created your first folder. However, we are not going to stop at just one folder. We require a number of folders to complete this exercise, so carry on as outlined below, and remember to read each instruction carefully.

Tip

If you make a mistake while typing in the file name and have not yet pressed [Enter], you can erase the error with [Backspace].

If you have pressed [Enter] and then realise that the name is incorrect, click on the file name, then press [F2] which will highlight the name so that you can overtype it.

Creating additional folders

Create another folder, following the sequence already described. Select the C: drive in the left pane first, so that the new folder is created at that level, and call this new folder *1Student*, use the figure '1' not the letter 'I'.

We still require another folder. This one is to be placed within the folder you have just created, *1Student*. This will be a subfolder.

Basic steps

1   Click on the folder *1Student*.

2   Select File > New > Folder.

3   The new folder will appear in the right pane. Name this folder *Exercise*.

4   When you pressed [Enter], a '+' sign appeared adjacent to the folder *1Student*. Click once on the '+' sign and *Exercise* will appear below *1Student*.

4   Open the folder

5   The '+' sign will change to a '-' sign. Click on the '-' sign and *Exercise* will no longer be visible.

Creating files

At this stage we have created three folders, which are empty. We will now create a number of files and place them in the new folders. In this exercise we will create the files without actually opening any applications.

Basic steps

1   Select the folder *0Student*.

2   Move up to the menu bar and select File.

3   Point to New, then select Microsoft Word Document.

61

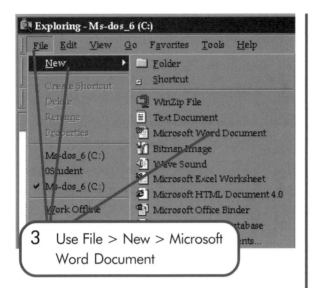

3 Use File > New > Microsoft Word Document

4 Look in the right pane and you will see a new file, called *New Microsoft Word Document*. It may have an extension .doc.

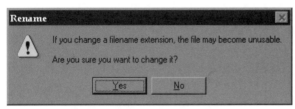

5 Note that the file name is highlighted ready for you to type in the name for the file. As soon as you start typing, you will overwrite the name in the box.

6 Enter the name *2Test.doc* – do not include any spaces. If you do not type in the .doc at the end of the name the following dialog box will appear:

Rename

> ⚠ If you change a filename extension, the file may become unusable.
> Are you sure you want to change it?
>
> [Yes] [No]

7 Should this occur, click No, and you will be returned to Explorer. Retype the name, with the .doc, and press [Enter].

To continue with this exercise we require a number of additional files. Carry on, follow the instructions and create the files, with the names given, in the stated folders.

In the folder *0Student*, create another Microsoft Word Document, and call it *3Test.doc*.

We are now going to create two spreadsheet files. Follow the procedure as above, but in this instance select Microsoft Excel Worksheet. Before you type in the name, note that the extension, now reads *.xls*. This will identify the file as an Excel worksheet.

In the folder *1Student*, create the files *4Test.xls* and *5Test.xls* – **remember** not to insert any spaces in the names.

Finally, create one Word and one Excel file (named *6Test.doc* and *7Test.xls*) in the folder *Exercise*. Remember that this is a subfolder within *1Student*.

That's it. We have all the folders and files needed to enable us to move onto the next phase of the exercise, which is, to copy and move files between folders.

Copying and moving files

The Copy command allows you to copy a file and place the copy in a different location. As is often the case with Windows, there are a number of ways to do this. For this exercise, we will use the pop-up menu. Pop-up menus are available within most applications, and apply to specific areas within each application.

Basic steps

1 In the left pane of Explorer, click on the '+' sign adjacent to the folder *1Student* to expand it and reveal its subfolder *Exercise*. We will need access to this folder shortly.

2 Select the folder *0Student* and move the cursor over the file *2Test.doc.*

Take note

You cannot copy a file to a folder that already contains a file with the same name. If you attempt to, you will be prompted and asked if you wish to overwrite the existing file. If in doubt click **No** on the prompt, investigate the File and then decide what course of action to carry out.

3 DO NOT select the file, but right-click once over it – a menu will pop up.

4 Take a moment to investigate the options, but note that your menu may differ from this, depending on your PC's configuration.

Use Cut to move items. The Cut command will remove the file, or folder, from its current location and store it in temporary memory. It can then be Pasted into its new location.

Copy stores a copy of the file or folder in memory, ready for use in a different location.

Paste completes the Copy or Cut command and inserts the file in its new location. Paste does not appear in the menu that pops up from a file.

5 Point to the file *2Test.doc,* in the folder *0Student.* Right-click and select Copy.

6 Move across to the left pane and point to the folder *1Student.* Right-click on it and select Paste from the pop-up menu.

❑ At this point in time you will not see the result of the Copy command because Explorer is still looking at the *0Student* folder.

7 Click on the folder *1Student* to select it. Look in the right pane of Explorer and you will see that there is now an additional file, *2Test.doc* present, in the folder.

8 Open the folder *0Student* and you will see that it is now empty.

Tip

The Cut, Copy and Paste commands were introduced on page 56.

Alternative method

We are now going to use another method of moving files and folders. This is known as 'Drag and Drop'.

Basic steps

1 Move the cursor over the folder *Exercise*. Click once on the left button but *DO NOT* release the button. Keep holding it down.

2 Move the mouse, keeping the left button pressed, up to the folder *0Student*. This will become highlighted as the cursor moves over it.

3 Once the folder is highlighted release the mouse button.

4 The folder *Exercise* will now appear in the right pane and a '+' sign will appear next to *0Student* and disappear from *1Student*.

The Edit menu

The actions carried out above introduced you to the pop-up menu, the Toolbar and the Drag and Drop methods. There remains another method and it is available via the Edit menu.

Left-click once on Edit and you will find the Cut, Copy and Paste commands are available from this point also.

Deleting files

You have already deleted one file earlier in the exercise. However it is necessary to explain how Windows 95/98 actually deletes items, because it is not quite as straightforward as first appears.

Windows reserves a portion of hard disk, usually about 10%, for use by the **Recycle Bin**. When you select an item and then press the Delete key, the file is actually moved to the Recycle Bin. It is not deleted immediately.

● If an item was accidentally deleted, it could be recovered from the Recycle Bin, provided the Bin has not been 'emptied'.

● To restore a file, open the Recycle Bin, highlight the file, and select **File > Restore**. The file will be restored back to its original location.

● To empty the Recycle Bin, open the Bin, select **File > Empty Recycle Bin**, and click **Yes** when prompted. After this stage, there is no recovery – the item is gone forever.

Multiple file selection

It is possible to copy, move or delete a group of files rather than handling files individually.

If the files are listed one after the other, simply select the file at the top of the list, press and hold down **[Shift]**, then select the last file in the list. All the files in the group will be highlighted. Double-check that you have selected only those files that you wish to delete.

If the files are not in a contiuous block, select the first file, press and hold down **[Control]**, then individually select each file. Should you inadvertently make an incorrect selection, keep **[Control]** down and click once more on the incorrectly selected file to deselect it.

The highlighted files can then be cut, copied or deleted as a group, using the same methods as for individual files.

Renaming files

There may come a time when you will want to change a file name. There are several ways to do this – we will use Explorer.

Basic steps

1 In Explorer, open the folder *1Student*. In the right pane you will see four files.

2 Right-click once over the name area of the file *4Test.xls* to get the pop-up menu.

3 Select Rename. The file name will become highlighted.

4 Type in the new name *Exel.xls*. You must remember to type in the extension (.xls) or you will be prompted for a response from the operating system.

An alternative method

You could rename a file by using the command **File > Rename**, or by pressing **[F2]**. In both cases, you must select the file first.

Saving files

When saving files you will have the option of where, or more accurately, on which storage device you store the file. In most cases, it will be either the hard disk, usually the C: drive or the floppy disk A: drive.

Of course other storage devices are available and are being used more and more. However, for the sake of simplicity, we will assume, at this stage, that only the A: and C: drives are available to you.

You will recall that earlier in the book the subject of creating folders and managing files was discussed, along with a number of recommendations and suggestions as to how you can structure your filing system.

● Initially when saving a file, either the **Save** option is selected from the **File** menu, or by clicking on the **Save** icon on the Standard Toolbar.

● When a file is saved for the first time, the Save As dialog box will open. This is because the system recognises the fact that the file does not currently have a file name.

● Once a file has a name, subsequent changes are saved to the same file name.

If at any time you should decide that you need to save the file using a different name, then the **Save As** option should be selected. You then simply allocate the file a different name, and straightaway what you have is actually a copy of the orginal file.

This option of saving the same file under a different name is extremely useful and permits you to modify either file to suit your requirements, while retaining a copy of the original.

The Save As dialog box

Shown below is the **Save As** dialog box and it is within this that you select where the file will be stored and allocate it a name.

The selected storage device, in this instance the 3½" floppy disk

The File name box

Path

The term 'path' is used to identify the route to, or to express it in another way, the location of a file. Let's assume that we have just saved a file, using the name *Sales*, in a folder called *August* and that folder is on the *A:* drive. Using the Path method of description it would appear as *A:\August\Sales*. This is a quicker and simpler method of describing the file's location.

Disk drives

Floppy disks and hard disks consist of platters, coated with a magnetic surface. It is this magnetic material that is the storage medium and the data is stored by rearranging the magnetic pattern on the disk.

Damage and misuse of disks can result in data loss. Floppy disks in particular are susceptible to damage simply by being left too close to items that have a magnetic field. Do not bend or touch the disk inside the plastic casing.

Disks must be formatted before they can be used.

Formatting disks

What is formatting? To enable the computer to store information on a disk, in an orderly and logical manner, some form of structure is required. Formatting creates this structure on the disk. Without going too deep into it at this stage, formatting creates sectors on the disk and each sector becomes addressable.

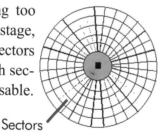

Sectors

The size of the sectors depends upon the disk size, and is not easily changed once set. Basically the larger the disk, the larger the sector.

When you save a file to disk, the file may well be smaller, or for that matter greater, than the sector size on the disk. Let us assume that the file to be saved is greater than the sector size. The file is saved to disk and fills up one sector, the remaining part of the file is placed in another sector. If this portion of the file does

Take note

If you format a disk with data on it, that data is lost and cannot be recovered. Always check the disk content before formatting.

not fill the sector, the remaining area of this sector cannot be used for saving any other files. It effectively becomes wasted space.

To keep track of where all the individual pieces of file are stored, a particular area on the disk is reserved, and it is known as the File Allocation Table, FAT for short.

File fragmentation

Now imagine that you had originally saved a file to disk, then deleted that file. The FAT takes this in to account and when you next save a file, this space is available and may be used. Because this space is almost certainly spaced out around the disk, file fragmentation occurs. What this means is that the file is not saved as one long continuous file but rather sections of the file fill up any space available, irrespective of where on the disk the space is.

Over a period of time, fragmentation can become a problem and slow down the time it takes to find and open programs and files. To assist in overcoming this problem, Windows includes a number of tools, and we will return to the subject of tools later.

Basic steps

1 Place the floppy disk into the disk drive – the metal shutter end goes in first, and the label should be uppermost.

2 Minimise any open windows so that you can see the Desktop. Double-click on the My Computer icon.

My Computer

3 Once open, right-click over the 3½" Floppy (A:) and select Format from the pop-up menu.

Open
Explore
Find...

Copy Disk...

Sharing...
Add to Zip

Format...

Create Shortcut

Properties

4 The Format dialog box will open and it is here that you can set your format options.

5 The Capacity will indicate the disk type, in the instance 1.44 Mb(3.5").

6 In the Format type area select *Full*.

7 You can, if you wish, type in a Label.

8 Ensure that the Display summary when finished checkbox is ticked.

9 Click Start. You can see the progress made by checking the Formatting progress bar at the bottom of the dialog box.

10 The Format Results dialog box gives you a full status report on the disk when the formatting is complete. Click Close.

11 Back at My Computer, double-click on the 3½" Floppy (A) and its window will open. This is empty because you have just formatted the disk. Any data that was on the disk has now been lost.

Backups of data

The expression 'Backup' means that you make copies of your important data in case a disaster occurs and the original data is corrupted, or is destroyed in some way or another.

There are a number of different, and some complex, methods of backing up data. The hardware involved could be as simple as a floppy disk however, for large quantities of data other methods are used.

On networks, the hard disk drives can be connected in a manner known as mirroring. What this means is that when data is saved, the information is saved simultaneously to two or more hard disks. In the event of a drive failure, the other drives will continue to function and data is not lost. A drive failure occurs when either the drive develops a fault, or a poor cable connection occurs.

Another method, used in conjunction with the above, is daily backups to a tape drive. A different tape is used each day and copies are stored off-site for additional security, for instance in the event of a fire.

Companies who have vast quantities of data will sometimes take their backup systems to the extent of actually having empty offices with duplicated computer systems running in parallel to the operational in-use system.

Creating backup files

We are not going to go to the extent of duplicating computer systems however, we are going to make backup copies of a number of files.

These files, because they are not large, will be stored on a floppy disk. Remember the standard floppy disk can only hold a maximum of 1.44 MB of data.

Basic steps

1 Open Windows Explorer.
2 Insert a floppy disk in to the disk drive.
3 Right-click on the folder *1Student*.
4 The pop-up menu will open. Point to the Send To command, and from its submenu select $3^1/_2$ Floppy (A).

5 A dialog box will open and you will see a visual display of the files being copied to the floppy drive.

6   Now double-click on the 3½ Floppy (A:) and you will see the folder, *1Student*, has been copied to the floppy disk.

Identifying file details

Once you have made copies of your important data, you must remember to change the backup copies each time you amend or change the master files.

How do you do this? When you save a file, not only is your data saved but this additional information is also saved:

- The file name and extension.
- The file size.
- The file type.
- The date and time the file was modified.

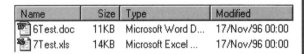

Not only does the above information assist in keeping track of backups, but it will also assist you when you are searching for a file. If you have forgotten where you stored a file, or you just remember that you last amended it on a certain date, these details will speed up your search. More on this later.

Backup software

Windows has, as part of the operating system, a backup software package, which is fairly elementary but quite adequate, in most cases for home and small office use.

To access the backup software, open Windows Explorer and right-click over the drive on which the files are stored that you wish to backup. Select **Properties** from the pop-up menu and when the Properties dialog box opens, select **Tools**.

The backup application is located in the central area of the dialog box.

It is recommended that you read the online Help section on backups before attempting to backup any data, so that you have a better understanding of the application, which may initially appear somewhat confusing.

Third party products

If you have a requirement to backup large volumes of data, the backup application in the Windows operating systems may not be adequate. You like most business users will probably require a third party specialist product.

The term 'third party product' means an application or utility produced by a company or organization other then the operating system vendor. The product is not supplied as a part of the operating system, but must be purchased separately and then loaded on to the computer in the same manner as any other application.

Most of these products will employ a compression method. What this does is to 'squeeze' the data, which makes the file smaller and it then takes up less space on the storage medium used. However, there are drawbacks to this method, mostly in that it takes quite a long time to backup large quantities of data, and it is not always easy to recover a single file rather than whole blocks of data.

Winzip

A well known and often quoted product, that is extremely handy for the home user, is Winzip. This product is given away for free on most computer magazines. There are one or two limitations of the free version of the product, however, it is still a very useful utility to have for home and small office use. Winzip is not designed for large-quantity data backup.

Caring for floppy disks

Never leave disks exposed to direct sunlight

Never expose disks to magnetic or electrical fields

Do not bend the disk

Do not open the shutter and touch the disk directly

Store disks at room temperature

Selecting printers

The computer is a tool to produce letters, spreadsheets, databases and much more. The end products of most of these are frequently required to be printed out for distribution and so on. To this end a printer is installed and connected to the computer.

More than one printer can be installed on a computer, though there is only one connection port, known as LPT1, for the printer. Additional ports can be installed if required.

Methods of connecting printers

There are a number of ways that one could connect additional printers to the computer using switch boxes, or what is becoming the norm, using the USB ports available with Windows 98. Refer to your computer manual for further details.

Another method of connecting to a different printer is through a network. The printer is connected directly to a network and can be set up in such a manner that anyone can use it, or a password list can authorise access to the printer.

Yet another connection could be used where another computer is on the network, and its printer is 'shared'. What this means is that the printer is set up by the operating system to be available to anyone on the network.

Networked printer

Shared printer

When more than one printer is installed on a computer, one is designated the default printer. What this means is that printing will always be carried out by this printer unless the setup is specifically changed (see below). If you look in the *Printers* folder, the default printer is indicated by a tick next to its icon.

A document can be sent to the printer using two different methods.

The first is by clicking once on the printer icon on the Toolbar. This will send the whole file to the default printer, using the current settings.

The printing of single pages in covered later in the book.

The Print dialog box

The other method of printing is to open the **File** menu and select **Print**. This will open up a dialog box, shown overleaf, where you may change the printer selection, or the number of copies to be printed and other factors.

To select a different printer, click on the down arrow at the end of the printer name slot. A drop down-list will appear, click once on the printer that you require and the list will close; that particular printer is now selected.

When the drop-down list closes, you are ready to print. Left-click on the OK button and the document is sent to the printer.

The dialog box will close and you are returned to whichever application you were using.

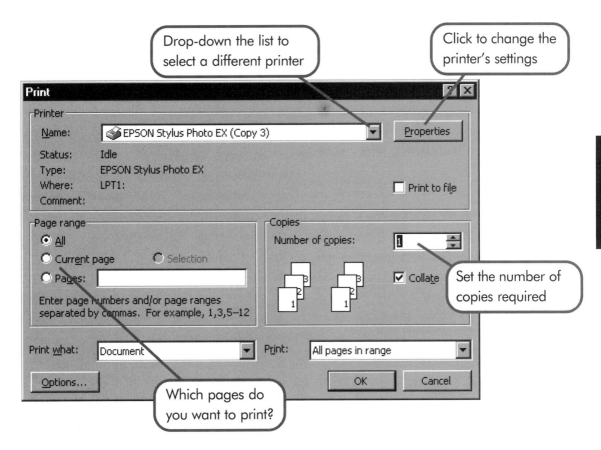

Drop-down the list to select a different printer

Click to change the printer's settings

Set the number of copies required

Which pages do you want to print?

Printing selected pages

There will be times when you have a multi-page document, but do not want to print it all.

To print just one page, place the cursor on that page before you use **File > Print** and when the dialog box opens, select *Current page* from the Page range section.

If you decide that you do not require the complete document to be printed, say for example, you have amended a number of pages, you can specify which pages are to be printed. For example, to print pages 2, 4, 5, 6 and 8, type 2,4-6,8 into the *Pages* slot. Click **OK** to print the selected range.

Printing multiple copies

To print more than one copy of your document select **File > Print** to open the dialogue box. Move the cursor over to the **Copies** section and click the up arrow next to *Number of copies* to set the number required.

Changing printer properties

Most modern printers will display a **Properties** button on the Print dialog box. Clicking this will open a further dialog box from which you may make adjustments to the quality of the printing, select specialist paper, if you are using a colour printer, and change the printer resolution. We are not going to make any adjustments at this time, but you should be aware of this facility.

Online Help

The Help functions can be accessed in two ways.

- Either click the **Start** button on the Taskbar and select **Help**,
- or from within Windows Explorer open the **Help** menu and select **Help topics**.

Either method will take you to the same window, where you can find help in several ways. Here's how to use the Index.

Basic steps

1 Select the Index tab.

2 Type into the slot a 'keyword' a word which describes the feature for which you want Help.

3 As you start typing, the pane below will scroll through the index to match the letters that you are typing.

4 Select a topic from the list.

5 Click Display.

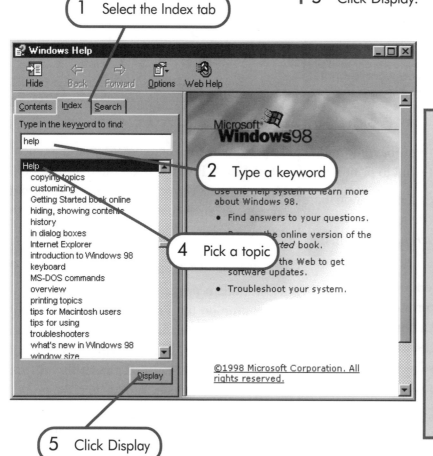

Tip

If you can't find what you want in the Index, try typing one or more keywords into the Search tab. The routine here will search through the text — not just the titles — of all the pages in the Help system to find matching words.

❏ If there is only one Help page available on the topic, it will be displayed in the right-hand pane. If there are several pages the Topics Found dialog box will open.

6 Select a subject and click Display.

7 The dialog box will close and the selected Help topic will be displayed.

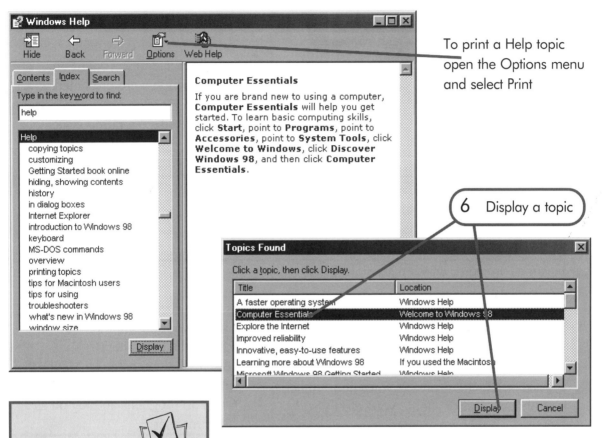

To print a Help topic open the Options menu and select Print

6 Display a topic

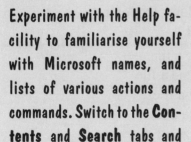

Tip

Experiment with the Help facility to familiarise yourself with Microsoft names, and lists of various actions and commands. Switch to the Contents and Search tabs and explore their possibilities.

Take note

Windows' online Help is not dissimilar to that of applications such as Word or Access, though these have more flexibility, or in the case of Access more interactivity with the application. Experiment and you will learn considerably from the Help system.

Sample paper 2: Using the computer

1	When switched on, the computer runs a self-test routine sometimes called a 'POST' routine. What does 'POST' stand for?	
2	When referring to a Personal Computer, what is usually meant by 'The Desktop'?	1. A piece of furniture you place your computer and/or keyboard on. 2. The screen you are presented with on your monitor upon successful loading of the operating system. 3. The background wallpaper you may have on your computer monitor.
3	When clicking on the **Start** button on the Taskbar, you are presented with a pop-up menu. Name two options or commands typically found within that pop-up menu.	1. 2.
4	Name two icons, which may typically be found on your Desktop.	1. 2.
5	When switching off your computer there is a set procedure you should follow. First you should click the 'Start' button on your Taskbar, which will present you with a number of options. Which should you select next?	1. Shutdown the computer? 2. Restart the computer? 3. Restart the computer in MS-DOS mode? 4. Close all programs and log on as a different user.
6	What is the name of the program specifically designed to assist you with File Management on your Personal Computer.	1. File Manager. 2. Internet Explorer. 3. Windows Explorer. 4. Excel.
7	Which of these can you NOT do using the Windows file management system?	1. Move a file. 2. Rename a file. 3. Copy a file. 4. Delete a file. 5. Re-size a file.
8	The buttons, at the top right of a window, control the window itself. What does the 'X' button enable you to do?	

9	Which letter is normally used to represent the floppy drive on a PC?	
10	What does the '+' sign next to a folder indicate.	1. The folder is 'open'. 2. The folder is 'closed'. 3. The folder has subfolders within it. 4. There are no subfolders within it.
11	When deleting a file within Windows 95/98 the system temporarily stores the file on a reserved portion of the hard disk. What is this area known as?	
12	When examining a file using Windows Explorer you can see certain information about the file. File name and type are two things, name a further two.	1. 2.
13	Why do floppy and hard disk drives have to be formatted?	
14	The FAT keeps track of where information on a disk is stored. What does FAT stand for?	
15	What happens to data stored on a disk if that disk is then formatted?	
16	Name three factors, which may damage a disk.	1. 2. 3.
17	Making copies of data to use in case the original data is lost is known as what?	
18	What is the most common connection port for a printer called?	
19	What symbol next to a printer indicates that it is the default printer?	
20	When you choose to print a document via the **File** menu you are presented with a **Print** dialog box which allows you to set options. Selecting the printer to use, and which pages to print are two, name another option.	

3 Word processing

Introducing Microsoft Word

Word is the word processing application included in the Microsoft Office suite. You will recall from Chapter 2 that any document, produced by a computer is in electronic form. As such, we can move, copy or delete various sections of the document easily. Images can be inserted, as can tables and columns.

Starting Word

You can start Word a number of different ways. If Word is installed as part of the Office suite, a shortcut bar is also installed, and you can start the applications from it. We, however, will use the Start button method.

Locate the Taskbar and click [Start] the Start button. Move the cursor up to the Programs area of the menu. A second menu will open out to the right, locate [Microsoft Word] and click on it.

Below is an example of Word's main window, showing the key areas and features. There are a number of items and controls not shown and these will be identified and discussed later.

Title bar Menu bar Standard toolbar Formatting toolbar

Rulers Application Control buttons

Document Control buttons

Text insertion point

Scroll bar

Active document window

View buttons Status bar

Menus and toolbars

Microsoft applications can be customised by their users, so you may find that some of the examples in this book do not match exactly what you see on your screen. Do not concern yourself because we will only use the standard menus and toolbar commands when telling you how to carry out a particular procedure.

The Menu bar

This is the uppermost bar located immediately below the Title bar. It is from the Menu bar that most commands and functions are located. In the example shown below the Format drop-down menu is shown open, listing all the standard default formatting options available.

There are several different ways to access commands and functions in Word, as in all Windows applications.

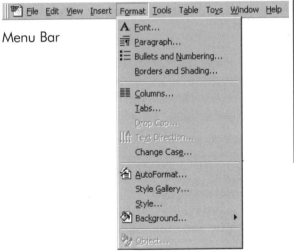

Menu Bar

Standard Toolbar

The Standard toolbar

The Standard toolbar gives you one click access to the commands and functions that are most commonly used in Word. As you move the cursor over the icons, a Tool Tip will appear to identify the purpose of the respective icon. The icons are grouped together on the toolbar in accordance to their functions.

Starting at the left of the toolbar, the first group on icons relates to opening a new blank document, opening an existing document and saving a document.

You will often find yourself using the third group of icons. The icon with the scissors image is the Cut icon, followed by the Copy and Paste icons. For more on Cut, Copy and Paste, please refer back to page 56.

The Formatting toolbar

It is from the Formatting toolbar that most text based formatting can be carried out.

As already mentioned, there are a number of ways that you can access various commands, and if you look at the drop-down menu in the Menu Bar example, you will see that the Formatting toolbar duplicates a number of the Format menu options.

Formatting Toolbar

Viewing a document

When Word starts up, a new blank document is displayed, and if you check the Title Bar you will see that Word has given the document a default name. If it is the first document opened, default name will be Document1. The number at the end of the word 'Document' will increase as you open subsequent new documents, until you actually save the document.

There are four ways that you can view the document: Normal, Online Layout, Page Layout and Outline.

To understand the how the different views display text, I suggest that you open a document that has text in it. When the document is open, select **View** on the menu bar and select each of the above options, in turn, to seen the manner in which the page and text is displayed.

You will, in time, find the best View to suit your methods and way of working, however for the duration of this course please use the Page Layout view.

The examples shown in the exercises that are used in this course are all in Page Layout view.

Opening documents

We will use the toolbar icons to open and save documents, though you can carry out the same functions by selecting New, Open, or Save from the File menu. The icons are:

- Open a blank new document
- Open an existing document
- Save a document.

Entering text

Open a blank new document and type in the text shown below. Save the document to the 3½ Floppy (A:) disk, and call it 'Colliery'.

The Colliery

The news had just leaked out that the Pit was to close. Pop had never known any other work, except of course when he was sent to France during the First World War. Pop, as man and boy, from the age of fourteen had worked this pit, and now it was all to end.

The closure program was to be formally announced later that afternoon, even so, the news swept around the colliery in no time at all. Even the men at the coal-face knew the news before they even came up from underground. They questioned the man at the gate guard as they stepped out of the cage, "is it true, are they really closing us down?" they asked. Just the look on his face was sufficient to confirm their worst fears.

Some four hundred men worked the colliery, and a high percentage of them were in their late forties and early fifties. Even though some of the men would move to other collieries, the future looked bleak for the majority of the men.

Remember

- Press **[Enter]** twice to insert a new line after each title and paragraph.
- Do **not** press **[Enter]** when you reach the end of a line. Word will automatically wrap the text to the next line.
- Insert two spaces after each full stop, one space between each word and after a comma.

Formatting text

- We are going to format the heading, so must first select it. Place the cursor in the margin to the left of the line, and it will change to an arrowhead. Click and the heading will be highlighted. This is a good way to select an entire line.

- Move to the Formatting toolbar, and click the down arrow to the right of the text size box. Select 14 and Word will change the high-lighted text to that size.

- With the text still highlighted, press **[Shift]** and **[F3]** keys together. This shortcut will change the text to all capitals.

- Highlight '*fourteen*' in the first paragraph, by double-clicking in the middle of the word. Select the Italic icon, on the For-matting toolbar, to change the word to italic.

- Save the changes to the document. Use the **Save** icon on the Standard toolbar.

Time for more text. Enter the new paragraphs (on the right) as given, including the mistakes, the spell check it.!

Spell checking

Dependent on how Word is configured, you may see a red wavy line below some words. This indicates that Word has not recognised them.

adressing

To spell check the document, select the icon on the Standard toolbar. The **Spelling and Grammar** dialog box will open.

After the shift change, and when the men had washed and showered, the shift assembled in the canteen. One of the Deputies caled for order and the Manager walked in. The canteen fell silent and the men waited forlornly for the formal announcement of the closure.

The Manager, Jack Harkins, not used to adressing such a large audience, cleared his throat and started to speak. "I'm sure that you have all heard, at least something to the effect, that the colliery is to close. Gentlemen, I am afraid that the rumour is true, and the colliery will close in four months time".

The men, even though they were expecting the whorst, groaned loudly. They turned to their pals and the noise in the canteen rose from a deady silence to such a level that the Manager could not be heard, and he had to bang on the table to regain the men's attention.

The suspect word is indicated in green

The buttons are self-explanatory

Word offers its suggestions

Formatting the layout

Change the margins of the document as follows:

- Use **File > Page Setup** to open this dialog box. Click the **Margins** tab.
- Change the Top and Bottom margins to 3 cm and the Left and Right margins to 2.5 cm.
- Ensure the **Apply To** option is set to *Whole document*. If not, use the drop-down arrow and select it from the list.
- Click the **OK** button, and the changes will take place.

Further text formatting

- Highlight the heading of the text and move the cursor to the Formatting toolbar.
- Click ☰ the **Centre** icon, the heading text will now move to the centre of the page.
- Click **U** the **Underline** icon on the Formatting toolbar and the text will be underlined.

Save the changes by clicking 💾 the Save icon.

Enter the additional text, given on the right, exactly as shown, then spell and grammar check the document again.

Justified text

At the moment the document is formatted *Left Justified*. What this means is that the text on the left of the page is lined up on the left margin, while the right margin is ragged.

We will now change the document formatting to *Full Justified*. What this means is that the application will adjust the text. The text closest

The talk in the pubs and clubs that evening was only of the forthcoming closure. Wives had joined their husbands, all hoping that someone else knew a little more than they did, only to find that there was no further news.

A number of the young men thought that they would be better off leaving the indudtry altogether, the question was, where else was there to go? The general consensus of opinion was that the closure would be the death of the valley.

The Manager waited until there was silence, he then told the men that the majority of the equipment underground, that could bt used elsewhere, would be removed. This meant that there would be a requirement, after the mine had formally closed, for a limited work force to remain ot remove the equipment. The response from the men was utter silence. The shock of the closure, and its speed of implmentation, was still working its way home for most.

to the right margin will now line up and the ragged edge will disappear.

- Highlight all the text, except for the heading.
- Click ▤ the **Full Justification** button on the Formatting toolbar.
- The text will adjust and you will see the difference, mainly in the right margin area, which will be lined up vertically.
- Save the changes to the document.

Moving text

Some of the text is clearly in the wrong place within the general story and has to be moved.

- Place the cursor at the beginning of the last paragraph starting '*The Manager waited until there...*'. Drag the cursor to the right and down to include the full stop after the word '*...most*'. All of the paragraph should now be highlighted.
- Click ✄ the **Cut** icon on the Standard toolbar. The selected text will disappear.
- Move the cursor and click to place the insertion point directly below the fifth paragraph, then press **[Enter]** once to insert an additional line.
- Click 📋 the **Paste** icon on the Standard toolbar, and the text will appear at the insertion point.

Tip

To select a whole paragraph quickly, click three times anywhere within it.

- Make any adjustments necessary, ensure the space above and below the inserted paragraph is consistent.
- Save the document changes.

Indenting text

- Place the cursor to the left of the first word of the first paragraph, starting '*The news had just...*'
- Press **[Tab]** and the first line of text will move to the right. This is 'first line indentation'.
- Now select the whole paragraph starting '*The Manager waited until...*'
- Move the cursor up to the Formatting toolbar and click ⬝≣ the **Increase Indent** icon. The paragraph will adjust and move to the right.
- Spell and Grammar check the document.
- Save the changes to the document and then close it.

Hyphenation

The following is an extract from the online Help, which gives considerable information about Word's hyphenation feature.

To give your documents a polished and professional look, use the hyphenation feature. For example, hyphenate text to eliminate gaps or 'rivers of white' in justified text or to maintain even line lengths in narrow columns.

You can hyphenate text automatically or manually. If you hyphenate manually, Word searches the document for words to hyphenate and then asks you whether to include a hyphen and where to position it.

For even more control over hyphenation, you can use optional hyphens and nonbreaking hyphens. Use an optional hyphen to control where a word or phrase (such as 'AutoFormat') breaks if it falls at the end of a line (for example, 'Auto-Format'). Use a nonbreaking hyphen to prevent a hyphenated word or phrase (such as 'MS-DOS') from breaking if it falls at the end of a line.

Hyphenate text automatically

On the **Tools** menu, point to **Language**, and then click **Hyphenation**. Select the **Automatically hyphenate document** check box.

In the **Hyphenation zone** box, enter the amount of space to leave between the end of the last word in a line and the right margin.

To reduce the number of hyphens, make the hyphenation zone wider. To reduce the raggedness of the right margin, make the hyphenation zone narrower.

In the **Limit consecutive hyphens to** box, enter the number of consecutive lines that can be hyphenated.

If the **Hyphenation** command does not appear on the **Language** submenu, you need to install the hyphenation tool.

Further assistance

Refer to the online Help for more information, particularly if you wish to manually control hyphenation, though most users will generally accept the default settings for hyphenation.

Create a new document

Open a new blank document save this document as Word2, on the 3½ Floppy (A) drive.

Type in the following text, exactly as shown below and remember to save the document, calling it *Word2*, as you progress.

Six months after the colliery had closed, and all the equipment that was worth removing had gone, the demolition started. Reinforced retaining walls were built at the shatf bottom. The wals were there to stop the in-fill spilling out into the galleries. Ton upon ton of rock and gravel was poured down the shaft until it was full, and finally a plug was set in at the top of the shaft.

Mid-way through March a short service was held at the pit head, to remember men and boys lost in accidents over the long years that the mine had been worked. Pop Jones, Alun Davis and Jim Walker stood together, each thinking back to when the number four gallery had flooded. The speed and rush of water was such that they, even though they were some considerable distance from the source, were swept off their feet. In all the cofusion and chaos they lost sight of their pal Peter Dillion. It was not for some time after the evnet that Peter was found dead, trapped between two drams that had overturned.

Eventually the winding gear and superstructure was dismantled. The filling of the shaft seemed to most to be the end of the colliery, but in actual fact it was the removal of the winding gears and towers that really brought home the fact that the pit was no more.

Carry out a Spell and Grammar check and then save the document.

Copying and moving text

Examine the new document and you will see that it does not flow or follow in a logical order.

- Place the cursor to the left of '*Eventually*', at the start of the last paragraph. Hold the left button down and drag it right and down to highlight the complete paragraph.
- Click ✂ the **Cut** icon.
- Now place the cursor after the last word, '*shaft*', of the first paragraph and press **[Enter]** twice to insert two additional blank lines. Leave the cursor at this position.
- Click 📋 the **Paste** icon and the text will be inserted between the two existing paragraphs.
- Carry out any formatting required, such as deleting the double line spacing between the paragraphs.
- Do not close the document.

Copying between documents

We require a number of blank new lines in the document. Place the cursor after '*overturned*', the last word of the last paragraph and press **[Enter]** to insert ten blank lines.

Enter the following text:

Any resemblance to actual events, or to persons living or dead, is purely coincidental.

We are now going to copy text from this document, *Word2*, to the *Colliery* document.

- Highlight the text, from '*Any resemblance…*' to '*…purely coincidental.*' and then click the Copy icon.

- Re-save the document, but do not close it.
- Open the document *Colliery* and place the cursor at the end of the last paragraph. Press **[Enter]** five times to insert five new lines.
- Click the Paste icon and the text from *Word2* will be copied over to this document. Save the changes to this document.
- Close *Word2* but keep *Colliery* open, because we require it for the next exercise.

Inserting a file

We are now going to combine two separate documents and produce one new document. This procedure is extremely useful if two people have been working on a project and each has produced a separate document.

The end product will result in the two individual files remaining intact, with an entirely new document being produced.

- Place the cursor at the end of the paragraph ending '*death of the valley.*' and press **[Enter]** twice to insert two new blank lines.
- Open the **Insert** menu and select **File…** At the **Insert File** dialog box select *3½ Floppy (A:)* in the **Look In** slot.
- Select *Word2.doc* from the list, then press the **OK** button.
- The file *Word2.doc* is inserted into the current document, as an integral part of it.
- We are going to save the document with a different name. Select **File > Save As** and a dialog box will open. Save the document as *Word3.doc* on the floppy disk.

You will now have three documents: the original document; the source of the additional text; the document produced after text insertion.

Deleting text

There is now a duplicate paragraph in the *Colliery* document. Locate the first instance of the paragraph:

"Any resemblance to actual events, or to persons living or dead, is purely coincidental."

- Highlight the paragraph and press **[Delete]**. (If you delete the wrong one, by mistake, use **Edit > Undo** to restore it.)
- Save the changes.

Re-formatting the heading text

With the Word3 document still open, select the heading '*The Colliery*'. We are going to change the format of the heading as follows:

- Click on the Bold icon on the Formatting toolbar.
- Click on the drop-down arrow to the right of the Font box and select the font name *Arial*.
- Save the changes to the document.

Fonts

Word offers you an assortment of fonts to use in your documents. Each font has a specific **typeface**, which determines the appearance of the characters. These are identified by names such as Arial, Courier and Times New Roman.

Each font also has a **size**, which is specified in points. One point is equal to 1/72 of an inch, so a 72 point font would measure 1 inch from the bottom of its lowest hanging character (g, y) to the top of its largest letter (T, I).

Fonts are classified as *proportional* or *non-proportional*. A proportional font such as Times New Roman, will use more space on the paper for the letter "w", than it does for the letter "I". A non-proportional font such as Courier uses the same amount of space on the paper for every character.

Here are some examples of fonts and sizes:

This line is in Times New Roman, size 12.

This line is in Times New Roman, size 16.

```
This line is in Courier, size 12.
```
This line is in Helvetica, size 12.

THIS LINE IS IN ALGERIAN, SIZE 12.

This line is in Lucida Handwriting, size 12.

Printing documents

The time has come to print the documents. We require one copy of each of these files. Open each in turn and print all their pages. (Refer to page 73, if necessary.)

Compare each document, starting with *Colliery.doc*. Find the section where you inserted the file and compare it with the document *Word3.doc*. Confirm that the file inserted is the same as the document *Word2.doc*.

Take note

Printed copies of documents are known as "Hard Copies". Keep all copies of the print outs for future reference.

Headers and Footers

The Headers and Footers function is a particularly useful feature of Word, and is a means of producing the same text, or image, on each page without repeated retyping or insertions. If you require each page to be numbered, it is through the use of Footers that this is achieved.

Inserting file names

Frequently people produce documents and do not use them for some time. You may well have a paper copy of the document, but may not recall what the saved document was called. Headers and Footers provide a means of indicating the file name. You can save the name, along with the name of the person who created the file and the date it was last modified.

To enter text or imagery in the Headers and Footers follow the example below:

- Open the document that you want headers and footers in, in this instance *Colliery.doc*.
- Open the **View** menu and select **Header and Footer**.

The active document will adjust its position on the screen, moving up to the top of the document and you will see a broken line box.

It is within here that the header or footer items will appear. In addition, another toolbar will appear, either roughly at the centre of your screen or underneath another toolbar.

Move the cursor over each of the icons on the toolbar and a Tool Tip will appear indicating what that icon's function is.

You can select text and change its font style and size, in the usual manner, in the Header or Footer. If necessary change the font size to 10.

- Type your name in the Header area.
- Click ▣ the **Switch Between Header and Footer** icon to change to the Footer area.
- Change the font size to 8 and then type in *Colliery.doc* and press the spacebar once.
- Click ▦ the **Insert Page Number Icon**.
- Click the **Close** button.

If you cannot see the Header and Footer, open the **View** menu and select **Page Layout**. Move to the top of the document and you will see the Header text, dimmed; move to the bottom and you will see the Footer, also dimmed.

Header area

Header

Header and Footer toolbar

Switch between Header and Footer

Header and Footer

Insert AutoText ▾   Close

Insert Page Number

Insert Number of Pages

Format Page Number

Insert Date

Insert Time

Find and Replace

The Find and Replace feature of Word is extremely powerful and can speed up changes or amendments to documents immensely.

- Open the **Edit** menu and select **Replace**. The **Find and Replace** box will open. In the **Find what** slot type in what you wish to find and change. Press **[Tab]** to go to the **Replace with** slot and type in the new word. In the example, we are about to replace '*box*' with '*window*'.

- Click the **Find Next** button. Word will search the document and will highlight the first occurrence of '*box*' and moves the document to enable you to see the word.

- If this occurrence of the word is one that you wish to change, click the **Replace** button. Word will replace '*box*' with '*window*' and move on to look for the next occurrence. This will continue until Word cannot find another occurrence of the word, or you end the search by clicking on the **Cancel** button.

- Alternatively, if you are satisfied that you can safely change all occurrences of the word '*box*', click the **Replace All** button.

Paragraph numbers

If it is not already in use, open the document 'Colliery.doc'.

- Select the first two paragraphs at the start of the document.

- On the Formatting toolbar, select the **Paragraph Numbering** icon.

Word will automatically insert paragraph numbers adjacent to the two selected paragraphs. Close the document but **DO NOT** save the changes. We do not require the paragraph numbering.

If you know, before you actually start typing a document, that paragraph numbering is a requirement, you can start paragraph numbering immediately by just clicking on the icon, and then start typing. Word will insert paragraph numbers as you progress. There are limitations with this feature, experiment to find out how best you can use it.

Creating tables

Tables are an extremely useful feature of Word, and with the latest version of Word, the options available in the design and use of tables have increased tremendously. When it is particularly important to maintain good control over the alignment and positioning of one area of text with another section of text, use a table. Also consider using a table without any borders or inside lines.

You can design the table yourself, with different border styles, the use of colour and suchlike. Word also has some predefined table layouts. These can be found in the **Autoformat** option in the **Insert Table** dialog box.

- To create a table, open a New blank document and save as 'Temp.doc'.

- Open the **Table** menu and select **Insert Table** to open the **Insert Table** dialog box.

It is here that you can set the number of columns and rows for the table, and if desired, select one of the predefined table layouts.

- Change the number of columns to three and the rows to four, using the up/down arrows. **Do not** select any **Autoformat** options at this time – just click the **OK** button.

The table will appear on screen with three columns and four rows, all the same size. This cann be adjusted as required. Here's how to merge two cells into one. Any block of cells can be merged in this way.

- Place the cursor in the second column of the first row, click and drag the cursor to the right through into the third column, highlighting the two cells.

- Release the mouse button. Open the **Table** menu and select **Merge Cells**. Word will join the two cells together into one large cell. Click anywhere in the table to remove the highlight from this new cell. This is how your table should look:

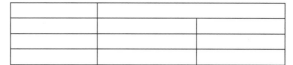

- Select the merged cell and click the Bold and Centre text icons.

Entering text in tables

- Place the cursor in the first cell, of the first row and type 'REGION' in capitals. Select the word and click the Bold icon.

- Press **[Tab]** to move the cursor into the next cell. Type 'TEMPERATURES', again all in capital letters. Note that the text is in the centre of the cell and is emboldened.

- Using **[Tab]**, move to the second column of the second row and type in 'Mid-Summer'. Press **[Tab]** once more to move to the third column. Type in 'Mid-Winter'.

- Still using **[Tab]**, move along to the next row and type in '*North*'.

- Move to the next column, which now appears under the heading of *Mid-Summer*. Type in '*85*'.

Follow the example below and enter the remaining text as shown:

REGION	TEMPERATURES	
	Mid-Summer	Mid-Winter
North	85	56
West	92	61

Changing the cell width in tables

Ensure that the cursor is placed in the table. The first column is a little wider than necessary, move the cursor over the outside left line of the table. The cursor will change to a double headed arrow with small vertical lines. Once the cursor has changed, keep the left button pressed; drag the line in the required direction, in this case to the right. When the table looks satisfactory, release the mouse.

Inserting columns and rows

To insert additional columns and rows, place the cursor where the additional column or row is required. Open the **Table** menu and select the appropriate **Insert** command. (Experiment inserting rows and columns at a later date.)

Deleting columns and rows

Highlight the column or row that you wish to delete then select **Delete Row** or **Delete Column**, as appropriate, from the **Table** menu.

Lines and borders

Lines and borders can be changed by placing the cursor anywhere in the table, then opening the **Format** menu and selecting **Borders and Shading**.

Create a second table

We need another table, for use later in the Mail Merge section. Proceed as follows:

- Open a new blank document.

- Change the page layout to Landscape. Open the **File** menu and select **Page Setup**. At the **Page Setup** dialog box open the **Paper Size** tab and choose *Landscape* in **Orientation**, to give a page that is wide rather than deep.

- Now click on the **OK** button.

Title	LastName	Company	Address1	Address2	City	PostalCode
Mr	Jones	Jones Heating Contractors	5 Marylebone Road	Bolton	Lancs	B19 8YH
Mr	Bryon	Lington Heating Controls Limited	12 High Street	Logton	Lincs	LM8 3HJ
Mr	Collins	Collins and Son Heating Contractors	56 Bridge Street	Middletown	Notts	NH32 4AG
Mrs	Kaye	Kaye's Engineering and Heating	98 Benton Road	Longparish	York	YM6 6JK

- Create a table, which has seven columns and five rows. **Do not** apply any Auto-Formatting to the table.

- You will find however that when the table was inserted into the document that all the columns were of equal size. We will adjust the column widths later, simply type in the sample data given above.

Now adjust the column widths until you can fit all the text in the columns as shown on page 92. Ensure the cursor is placed in the table, so that you can view the column widths. Place the cursor over the vertical lines of the columns and when it changes to a double arrow, drag the line in the appropriate direction to match the text formatting as seen in the table above.

Once all formatting has been completed, save the document as: *Data Source Information*.

Print a copy of the document and keep it safe as you will require it later when working through the Mail Merge section.

Take note

[Tab] is used to move from cell to cell within the table. If you wish to indent text — the normal function of [Tab] — you must use the key combination of [Control] and [Tab] together.

Page breaks

You will have noticed that Word senses when it has reached the end of the page, and inserts an additional page as required.

There will be occasions when you will require text to appear on a new, or the next, page. To achieve this, there are a number of different ways. The simplest and easiest way is the Quick Key method. Open *Word3.doc*.

- Place the cursor at the end of the text where you want the new page to start from, press **[Control]** and **[Enter]** at the same time and Word will insert a *Forced Page Break*.

- To try out this feature, place the cursor in the blank line above the paragraph starting 'Six months after the colliery had closed….'

- Press **[Control]** and **[Enter]** simultaneously and release immediately. Word will force the text on to the next page. When you are in Normal View note the broken line indicating where the Page Break is.

································Page Break································

If you find that you have placed the Page Break in the wrong place, or simply wish to remove it, place the cursor to the left of the Page Break symbol and press **[Delete]**.

There are other types of Breaks that are available within Word however, we will not cover them here. Experiment on your own later by investigating the options available from Insert command on the Menu Bar.

Save the changes to the document and close it.

Using tabulation

Tabulation is a method of lining up text and numbers in vertical columns or evenly spaced text on horizontal lines. By default, Word tabs are set at ½ inch intervals, but you can adjust the setting as required. Open a new document.

Enter the text as shown below, insert one Tab before the words 'Chapter' and after the chapter number and again before the page numbers.

Section 1		
Chapter 1	The first chapter of eight	4
Chapter 2	The second, a short chapter	8
Chapter 3	The third chapter	25
Chapter 4	The fourth chapter	35
Section 2		
Chapter 5	The fifth chapter	56
Chapter 6	The sixth chapter	68
Chapter 7	The seventh chapter	88
Chapter 8	The eighth and last chapter	118

Save this document as *Tabulation.doc*.

Word has a number of tab types, which you can apply to suit your own requirements:

⌊L⌋	The default tab is left justified
⌊⊥⌋	Centre justified
⌊⌐⌋	Right justified
⌊⌐⌋	Decimal aligned tab

Tabulation options

To change the tab settings, ensure that the Ruler is visible. If it is not, open the **View** menu and select **Ruler**. Located in the top left-hand corner of the Ruler is a small square with a symbol indicating the type of tab currently selected. The example below indicates a left justified tab is selected.

To change the tab, click the symbol and it will change to centre tab, and each subsequent click will change the setting to right justified, decimal aligned, then back to left justified.

Changing tabulation settings

If it is not already open, open the document *Tabulation.doc*, and make the Ruler visible.

- Open the **Edit** menu and select **Select All** so that the whole text is highlighted.

- Select the left justified symbol on the Ruler. Click on the Ruler at the 2.5cm position. A faint symbol will appear, indicating a left justified tab has been set. The text will now adjust the first tab position to 2.5cm.

- Ensure that all the text is still selected, and that the tab is still set to left justified. Click on the Ruler at 6cm. The tab is set and the text will move along to align at 6cm.

- Click twice on the tab symbol to select a right justified tab. Click on the Ruler at the 12.5cm to insert a right justified tab there. The text is moved along to align under the 12.5 location. Note that the numbers have aligned in number order alignment. Had you not selected the right justified tab but left it as a left justified tab, the numbers would not have aligned correctly, as shown in the example opposite.

Save the changes to the document.

Your document *Tabulation* should now match the example shown opposite.

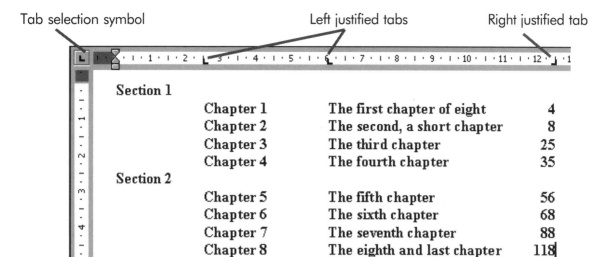

Tab selection symbol   Left justified tabs   Right justified tab

Section 1

Decimal aligned tabulations

Decimal tabs are used to align columns of figures that include decimal places. Open a new blank document.

● Create a list as shown below. Insert one tab after each item before the price:

Chocolate mix	£1.45
Flour	£1.65
Sugar	£0.99
Eggs	£1.25
Milk	£0.65
Baking tin	£12.45

● Save the document as *Decimal.doc*.
● Now select all the text and numbers.
● Change to the decimal tab 🔲 on the Ruler.
● Click on the Ruler at the 4.5 position. The figures will now align on the decimal point.

Chocolate mix	£1.45
Flour	£1.65
Sugar	£0.99
Eggs	£1.25
Milk	£0.65
Baking tin	£12.45

● Save the document changes and close it.

Changing line spacing

When producing draft copies of fairly long and complex documents it is common practice to use double spacing. This leaves room for hand written amendments to be inserted.

Open a new blank document and type in:

Goals
The individual shall have a sound knowledge of how a word processing application can be used. He or she shall be able to understand and accomplish normal everyday operations; editing or creating new documents.

Save the document as *Double.doc*, then:

● Select all the text, including the heading.
● Open the **Format** menu and select **Paragraph** and the **Paragraph Formatting** dialog box will open.
● In the **Spacing** section, select *Double* for **Line spacing**, then click **OK**.
● Save the changes and close.

If you know beforehand that you want a document in double-spacing, you can set this selection before typing any text.

Inserting graphics

A graphic, whether it's a photograph or a clip art image, will add impact to a document and enhance its appearance. Use imagery to draw attention to the subject matter, but use it with care as too much may distract the reader.

In the following exercise, we are going to create a simple 'no smoking' sign.

- Open a new blank document and save it as *Sign.doc*.

- Open the **File** menu and select **Page Setup**. At the **Page Setup** dialog box, select the **Paper Size** tab, then choose *Landscape* in **Orientation**.

  The page orientation will change to Landscape, so that the longest edge of the paper is now at the top, not the side. This orientation is ideal for making most signs.

- Change the Font style to Arial and the size to 72. Right-click anywhere on the document and select Font to open the Font dialog box. Click the down-arrow by the **Color** slot and select *Red*. Click on the **OK** button to close the dialog box and make the changes.

- The text will look better if it is centred on the page. Click ≡ the Centre icon on the Formatting toolbar, then press **[Enter]** once.

- Type in the words 'No Smoking' and press **[Enter]**. The text is large and coloured red. Of course you will have to print out the document on a colour printer to have the colour effect.

- Open the **Insert** menu, point to **Picture** and select **Clip Art**. The Clip Gallery window will open. Ensure that the Clip Art tab at the top has been selected.

- Select *Signs* from the **Categories** list. Find and highlight the smoking cigarette image or an appropriate alternative, then click the **Insert** button.

- The image will appear on the page, probably not quite where you want it and its size may also require some adjustment.

- Right-click over the image and from the pop-up menu select **Format Object**. When the Format Object dialog box opens, ensure that the **Size** tab is selected.

- Locate the **Scale** section of the Size box and ensure that the **Lock aspect ratio** and **Relative to original picture size** tick boxes are ticked as shown below. You should be aware that these figures will not necessarily match what you have on your screen.

- When you change the size figures you will only have to make one change to either the **Height** or **Width** boxes, not both. This is because Word, with the two boxes ticked, will automatically maintain the proportions relevant to its original size.

- This next adjustment is a judgement call on your part. Increase or decrease, if necessary, the size of the image until it occupies the lower central area of the page.

Finally we should now check the overall layout of the poster, the positioning of each element in relation to each other and general presentation.

To do this, we must first change the page view so that you can see the full-page size, and we can do that using the Zoom control.

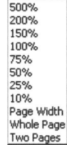

- Left-click over the drop-down arrow located to the right of the **Zoom** control on the Standard toolbar.

- Select *Whole Page* from the Zoom drop-down list.

- Move the cursor over the image once more and when cursor changes to a four-headed arrow, left-click and hold the button down.

- Drag the image to the centre of the page below the text 'No Smoking'. When the image is in place, release the mouse button. Your sign should resemble the example shown below.

- Save the document changes and close.

Inserting images is as simple as that. Obviously Word offers more options and features when working with imagery and you should experiment later.

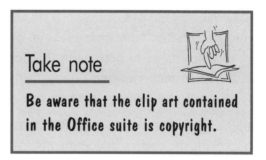

Take note

Be aware that the clip art contained in the Office suite is copyright.

No Smoking

Mail merge

One of the many features of Microsoft Word is Mail Merge. Mail Merge is designed to assist the user who has to produce numerous similar letters to send to many clients. Each letter will contain very much the same content, with minor changes, though each letter is personalised in its salutation and address details.

Imagine having a database of several hundred clients, and you wish to inform just one hundred of those clients of a change in a specification to an item they have an interest in. In the days of typewriters, to personalise the letters would have meant someone typing them all out separately. No longer – read on.

Mail Merge will produce bulk letters, using two previously prepared documents. Word uses particular names in the merge process, so it is important to remember these names and exactly what they are.

The Form Letter

This is the skeleton of the letter that contains the common information each client will receive. One advantage of a Form Letter is that should you later have to amend it, you only have one document to change. You can build-up a set of Form Letters for different uses.

It is not strictly necessary to create the Form Letter first; you will decide in time your preferred method of working.

The Data Source

This is the document that contains the personal details of the clients, including their names, how you will address each and of course, the addresses. Data Sources, like the Form Letter, are reusable. You can produce a Data Source in Word or use another application as the source.

To use names and addresses of contacts in your Outlook Contact List, as a data source, with the Mail Merge in Word, first add your Outlook Address Book to your user profile.

- Open Word and click **Mail Merge** on the **Tools** menu.
- Click **Get Data**, and then click **Use Address Book**. Select *Outlook Address Book*.

For powerful sorting and searching capabilities, use Access or Excel to edit longer lists of data.

When you consider that you are most likely already using other lists or applications for data, it is worth spending a little time investigating if these sources can be utilised. After all, that's one reason for using a computer; to store and reuse information without duplication.

The Main Document

It is from the Form Letter and the Data Source, that the Main Document is produced. This is the document that you will send to the clients after the Mail Merge has been completed.

Creating the components

We will use Word to create the various components necessary for the following exercise, and will start by creating the Form Letter.

Creating the Form Letter

- First open a new blank document, and save it as '*Form Let1.doc*'.
- We will use the standard business layout for the Form Letter. To save time and space, we have omitted our company details, logo, etc. which would usually appear above the Ref. and client address.

Follow the example shown below:

- Once you have completed the Form Letter, save the document.
- With the document still open, drop-down the **Tools** menu and select **Mail Merge**. The **Mail Merge Helper** dialog box will appear.

Ref: JAW/ct

Date (Read the *Take note* below)

Dear

<u>PRICE REDUCTIONS ON ALL HIGH EFFICIENCY PUMPS</u>

This is to advise you that we have once again reduced the cost price of our low energy, high efficiency water pumps.

As a valued client, we thought that you should be amongst the first to be advised of the price reduction. Furthermore, with your customer discounts applied, this will add up to a substantial saving to you.

We look forward to receiving your orders, which will receive our prompt attention.

Yours sincerely

John A Worthington

Take note

An example of a fuller business style letter is included to the rear of this booklet for guidance.

Leave a blank line after the Ref section, then insert an automatic date entry as follows: Open the Insert menu and select Date and Time. At the dialog box select the format '12 March 1999'. Tick the Update automatically box. This will ensure that each time the Form Letter is used, Word will insert the current date.

Note that when the **Merge Mail Helper** dialog box first opens you only have the one option available and that is the **Create** button. The other options buttons, **Data source** and **Merge the data with the document** will only become active as you progress through the mail merge process. This is to ensure that the process is completed in a logical order and that you do not overlook an important step.

- Click once on the **Create** button and a further box will open. At this, select **Form Letters** and the box shown below will open.

We have already produced the Form Letter, and it is open. Select Active Window.

Creating the Data Source

When you are returned to the Mail Merge Helper dialog box you will see that the **Get Data** button has become active.

- Click the **Get Data** button to drop down its menu and select **Create Data Source** to open this dialog box.

You will see that Word has already inserted a number of common **Fields**. You can remove any that are not wanted or add new fields if required. We will use some of the fields provided by Word for this exercise. Select each of these fields individually and when highlighted, click the **Remove Field Name** button: *Country*, *HomePhone* and *WorkPhone*.

- Once the unwanted fields have been removed, click the **OK** button. You will be prompted to save the Data Source, even though you have not entered any data yet.

Select **Yes** and save it as *Data Source1*.

- When the Data Source has been saved, a further box will open offering you a choice of **Edit Data Source** or **Edit Main Document**. Select **Edit Data Source**.

The **Data Form** dialog box will open. This is where we will fill in our client's details. Use the information contained in the document that you created earlier and saved as *Data Source Information*.

- When you reach the last field for a client, click the **Add New** button. Continue entering the clients' details until all have been entered, then click the **OK** button.

You are now returned to the Form Letter. Now look for the Merge Toolbar, it should appear adjacent to the Formatting Toolbar.

You will note that only nine fields are available, as the others were deleted.

Inserting the Merge Fields

We need to insert the address fields and the salutation fields in the appropriate places in the Form Letter.

Merge to new document

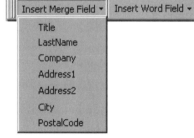

- On the Form Letter, place the cursor at the end of the Date line and press **[Enter]** twice.

- Locate the button **Insert Merge Field** and click on it to open its drop-down list.

- From the list, select the *Company* field. The field should now appear in the Form Letter as <<Company>>.

- Move down one line at a time, by pressing **[Enter]** and insert the four remaining address fields, each on its own line. When all fields have been entered, ensure there is a blank line between the address block and the salutation.

- On the Form Letter, place the cursor after the salutation starting 'Dear'. Insert a single space after it, or the words will run into each other.

- Click the **Insert Merge Field** button, and select the field *Title*, then the field *LastName*. These fields are to appear on the same line one after the other.

DO NOT enter spaces between field names, i.e. Title and LastName. The mail merge process will insert spaces as appropriate.

Once the necessary fields have been inserted, the top of Form Letter should look like this.

Ref: JAW/ct

Date

<<Company>>
<<Address1>>
<<Address2>>
<<City>>
<<PostalCode>>

Dear <<Title>><<LastName>>

We are now at the stage to carry out the actual merge. On the Mail Merge toolbar click the **Merge to New Document** button.

The completed merge

On releasing the Merge button, the box will close and the merge process will take place. Word has now produced a four-page document. This is, in fact, four different letters separated by page breaks between each letter.

This is the final product – the merged document. Save as *Merge* and close each document.

This was a simple merge involving only four records in the Data Source, and therefore this merge was easy to carry out, without any complications. To carry out a merge task accessing hundreds of records in the Data Source is more complex. You will have to select the clients that have an interest in the subject of the Form Letter. There will almost always be fields in the records that are surplus to requirement.

This section should be practised a number of times to gain confidence in using the facility.

Use the online Help to learn more of Mail Merge and how you can carry out more complex Mail Merge tasks.

Take note

You can also merge by using the menu option Tools > Mail Merge. The Merge dialog box will open and the default option is to Merge to a new document. Accept this option and click on the Merge button.

Using templates

A template is a pre-defined document that can be used time and time again. You can create templates of your own design and content. Word also comes with a series of templates already defined, which can be modified to suit your own specifications and requirements.

Good instances of templates would be:

- A document that has a company letterhead, with a logo at the top, while the remainder of the document is blank, ready for any text, etc. to be inserted.

- Forms, such as an order form that has certain standard text entries plus blank spaces, which the user would fill in.

A template is saved with a different extension. Instead of 'doc', templates use the extension 'dot' to denote that it is different from the everyday document, e.g. *Elegant Fax.dot.*

Open a template

To open a template you use a slightly different procedure, from that used for opening a standard document. Templates are stored in their own individual folders, one for each application.

To use templates follow this procedure:

- Select **File > New** to open the **New** dialog box. Click on the **Letters and Faxes** tab.

You will see a number of items – some are template documents and others are 'wizards'. We will return to the subject of Wizards later. Remember that Templates are identified by the 'dot' extension after the document name.

The templates are grouped into folders

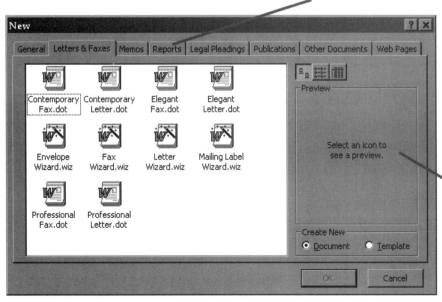

Some templates have previews to give you an idea of how they look

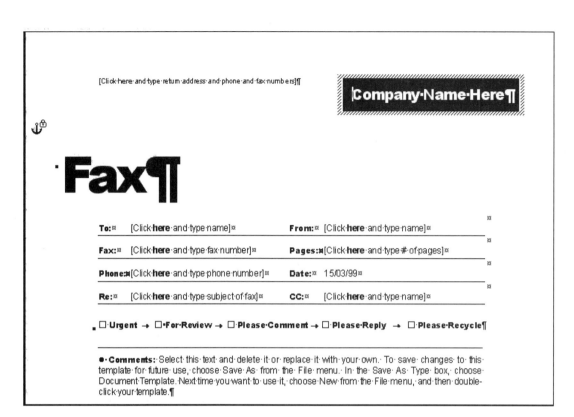

Using a template

Select the template *Professional Fax* either by clicking on it, then clicking **OK**, or by double-clicking on it.

When the template opens, you will see that a number of the items in the document require further action by you. See the example above.

Complete the instructions given on the template and fill in your own details as required.

When a template is opened for use, Word changes it to a standard document, thus preserving the template for further use. When you save the document Word will automatically assign a 'doc' extension to it.

You can modify the template permanently, i.e. insert your company name, address and telephone details and then resave the template under a different name, remember the 'dot' extension. The next time that you wish to use the Template, a high percentage of the detail is already complete.

Templates are extremely useful and can save you some considerable effort and over a period of time you will find more and more uses for templates.

Wizards

A Wizard is an automated process that creates documents, using a number of preformatted styles and layouts. It asks questions and uses the answers to automatically lay out and format a document, such as a newsletter or resume.

Wizards can be identified by the extension, wiz, which appears after the wizard name, e.g. *Fax Wizard.wiz.*

Styles

A Style is a named set of format settings that can be accessed from the Formatting toolbar. A Style can specify a font type and the size. In addition it may also specify indentation, line spacing and justification.

Applying a Style is a lot faster than manually applying individual Formatting adjustments to sections of text and assures consistency.

Word has several predefined Styles, and you can also create your own. Word predefines Styles as either paragraph or character:

Paragraph Styles are applied to entire paragraphs and may include all of the formatting elements listed above. Every paragraph, in a Word document, automatically has the default style, *Normal*, applied to it. This Style is based on your default selection of font and size.

Character Styles are applied to any section of text and can include formatting such as font type and size, underlining, embolden and so on. If you apply a character Style such as boldface to a section of text that is already formatted as italic, the text will then appear as both bold and italic.

Applying a Style

First select the text to be styled.

● To apply a Style to more than one paragraph, select them all.

● To apply a Style to only one paragraph, place the cursor anywhere inside it.

● To assign a character style, select the text you want the style to be applied to.

Now carry out the following:

● Click on the Style drop-down arrow on the Formatting toolbar. A list of Styles will appear, with the name in the Style's font.

● Select the required Style by clicking on its name. The Style will then be applied to the specified text.

To remove a Style

Select the text and from the Style drop-down list select *Default Paragraph Font* or *Normal* as appropriate to your requirements.

Tip

The online Help provides considerable scope to develop your skills in using Styles.

Integrating with other applications

Information stored within a Word document can very easily be copied or linked to any of the other applications in Microsoft Office.

Charts or data can be inserted in a Word document, an Excel worksheet or a PowerPoint presentation, and vice versa.

To exchange data between Word and Excel

To analyse the data from a Word table in Excel, you can copy and paste the data to a new Excel workbook. You can also import worksheet data into Word.

When you become proficient in using Excel, you could create a 'PivotTable' to analyse data from a Word table, just as you could from a data source such as an Access database.

Practice

It will only be possible to practise the following if you have already completed the module on Excel, so you might want to leave this for now and return to it later.

- Open the Word document *Data Source Information* and highlight the complete table.
- Open the **Edit** menu and select **Copy**.
- Open Excel with a new workbook.
- Ensure cell A1 is selected.
- Open the **Edit** menu and select **Paste**.

The table contents will now be pasted into the workbook and you may then format the worksheet to suit your requirements.

It is almost certain that the pasted version of the table will require some reformatting once within the worksheet. In particular cell lengths will require some adjustment to display long entries or field names.

You should, in time, learn how to use software integration to your advantage and reduce duplication in time and effort. Creating a table in Excel, which already exists in Word, or vis-a-visa, is wasteful. In the example above you copied the table, but you could have easily created a special link between the two applications, which will permit the table in Excel to be automatically updated when changes are made to the source table in Word.

Take note

The on-line Help system in Word is almost identical in style, appearance and operation to that of Excel (and all Microsoft applications). See page 137 if you need help with Help.

Sample paper 3: Word-processing

1	Explain how to highlight a section of text.	
2	Explain how you would insert the © symbol in a document.	
3	List two of the Views available to the user in Word.	1. 2.
4	Name the three parts of a mail merge.	1. 2. 3.
5	What is a template?	
6	List the two methods that can be used to re-size an image in a document.	1. 2.
7	Which item must be visible for setting or changing tabulations?	
8	You have just opened a new document, what is the first thing that you should do now?	
9	You have completed a document and require three copies of it printed. Explain briefly the sequence of events necessary to print three copies of the document.	

3: Word processing

4 Spreadsheets

What is a spreadsheet?

A spreadsheet is a tool for managing numbers and calculations. It is made up of columns and rows in which you record data or write formulas to perform calculations on it. Excel does not use the term 'spreadsheet'; instead it uses 'worksheet' (a single page), contained in a 'workbook' which may have up to 16 sheets.

Excel enables you to perform a wide variety of functions including sorting and selecting from lists. Automatic calculations mean that you will always have up-to-date results in your spreadsheet. Excel includes a feature that will produce charts from numeric data.

Excel also has a linking feature that allows you to enter data in one location and use it in other documents, which will be updated from source automatically. This speeds up and improves productivity, while reducing the likelihood of any errors being introduced by rekeying.

Excel allows you to experiment with the design and layout on the screen before actually printing the final product.

Below is an example of a simple spreadsheet.

The example is extremely simple in design and appearance. The calculations performed by it simply total up the sales figures, down by region and across by month.

Calculation operators

Operators specify the type of calculation that you want to perform on the elements of a formula. Excel includes four different types of operators: arithmetic, comparison, text, and reference.

Arithmetic operators perform basic mathematical operations such as addition, subtraction, division or multiplication; combine numbers; and produce numeric results.

There are specific rules when entering formulas in spreadsheets. Should you find that your results are not what you expected, first check how the formula was entered. If you have not used mathematics for sometime, this is an area where practice should make perfect.

If you combine several operators in a single formula, Excel performs the operations in the order shown in the following table.

Quarterly Sales				
Region	Jan	Feb	Mar	Area Totals
North East	50,985.00	45,987.00	48,755.00	145,727.00
North West	47,800.00	47,855.00	47,522.00	143,177.00
South East	51,200.00	46,585.00	52,456.00	150,241.00
South West	49,125.00	52,100.00	47,800.00	149,025.00
Monthly Totals	199,110.00	192,527.00	196,533.00	588,170.00

Operator	Description
: (colon) , (comma)	Reference operators
–	Negation (as in - 1)
%	Per cent
^	Exponentiation
* and /	Multiplication and division
+ and –	Addition and subtraction
&	Concatenation (connect strings of text)
= < > <= >= <>	Comparison

If a formula contains operators with the same precedence, e.g. both multiplication and division – Excel evaluates them from left to right. To change the order of evaluation, enclose the part to be calculated first in curved brackets.

The following produces two different results if the rules described above are not applied, i.e.

$(2+2)*3 = 12 \Rightarrow 2+2=4$, then $4 * 3 = 12$

$2+2*3 = 8 \Rightarrow 2 * 3 = 6$, then $6+2 = 8$.

Actual use of operators will be discussed later in the course.

Consult the online Help system for more information and examples of how to apply the various operators.

Starting Excel

In common with many Windows applications, you can start Excel a number of different ways. Here is one method. It is assumed that the computer has been switched on and that Windows is fully up and running normally.

- Click on the **Start** button to open its pop-up menu.

- Point to **Programs**. A further menu will open to the right. Click on **Microsoft Excel**.

Excel will open, and display a screen similar to that shown below.

Control buttons
Top 3 for Excel
Lower 3 for worksheet

Standard toolbar Formatting toolbar   Column header

Menu bar   Formula bar

Active cell

Row number   Worksheet number   Scroll bars

Starting a new workbook

In Excel, a workbook is the file in which you work and store your data. Because each workbook can contain many worksheets, you can organise various kinds of related information in a single file.

Use worksheets to list and analyse data. You can enter and edit data on several sheets simultaneously and perform calculations based on data from multiple sheets. When you create a chart, you can place the chart on the worksheet with its data or on a separate chart sheet.

The names of the sheets appear on tabs at the bottom of the workbook window. To move from sheet to sheet, click the sheet tabs. The name of the active sheet is bold.

Excel opens with a new blank workbook. For this section of the course we will close this workbook and open another new workbook.

This reason for doing this is to see where and how you can start a new workbook.

Basic steps

1   Close the blank workbook by clicking ☒ the Close button in the workbook controls.

2   If prompted to save the workbook, click the NO button.

3   Select File > New and the New dialog box will open.

4   Ensure that the General tab is selected.

5   Click on the Workbook icon.

6   Now click the OK button. A new workbook will now open, with the cursor in cell A1.

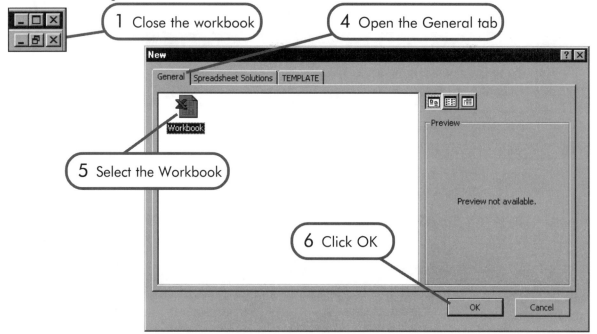

112

The number of sheets in the new workbook depends upon the default settings. You can change these to suit yourself.

● To change the default number, select **Tools** > **Options** and then the **General** tab. In the **Sheets in new workbook** area set the number and click **OK**. No changes will occur until you next open a new workbook.

Saving the workbook

We will now start entering text and figures in our worksheet. However, before we actually start we will save the workbook.

Basic steps

1 Select File > Save and the Save As dialog box will open.

2 Select a folder or disk to save the workbook in – in this instance select the 3½ Floppy (A:)

3 Click in the File name slot and type in the name *ECDL1*.

4 Click the Save button.

Take note

Excel set the following maxima:

32,000 characters in a cell

65,536 rows by 256 columns per worksheet

16 worksheets in a workbook

16 Undo actions.

Working with worksheets

There are a number of points worth mentioning before we actually start work.

Naming worksheets

By default, Excel names the worksheets as *Sheet 1*, *Sheet 2* and so on. It is often more practical to identify sheets by names rather than numbers and Excel allows you to do this.

● Double-click over the name tab and when it is highlighted, type in the name, then click on the worksheet to effect the change.

2 Select the folder or drive

4 Click Save

Click here to change disk

3 Enter the file name

Take note

When Excel saves a workbook, it assigns it the file extension, xls, to identify it as an Excel workbook.

113

Inserting worksheets

To insert an additional worksheet, select the last one in the workbook and from the menu bar select **Insert > Worksheet.**

Excel will allows you to place the new sheet in front of the selected one. For instances, if you select sheet 2 and then insert a new worksheet, it will appear between sheets 1 and 2.

The new sheet will be assigned the next sequential number. If there were six sheets in the workbook, the new sheet will be sheet 7. This will occur irrespective of where you insert it.

Moving worksheets

To move the position of a worksheet within a workbook, select the worksheet name tab and drag the sheet to the required location.

Moving within a worksheet

There are a number of methods that you can use to move the cursor from one cell to the next within a worksheet. The most common are:

Tab key

To move from one cell to the next, horizontally within the worksheet, press [Tab].

Shift-Tab keys:

Press [Shift] and [Tab] to move the cursor back to the previously selected cell.

The arrow keys

The four arrow keys will move the cursor in the direction of the selected key.

Mouse

Left-click in the required cell.

Entering data

Left-click in cell A1, which then becomes the active cell. The active cell is the one surrounded by a thick rectangle.

- Type the following text, then press **[Enter]**:
  QUARTERLY SALES FOR AUTUMN 1998

- Move to cell B3 enter '*October*'.

- Look closely at the active cell, particularly the lower right corner, where you will see a small square.

Drag on this point

- Place the mouse cursor over the square and the cursor will change its shape to a thin black cross when correctly placed over the small black square.

- With the cursor indicating a thin black cross, press and hold the left mouse button and carefully drag the cursor to the right, over the two cells C3 and D3.

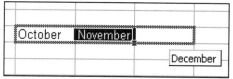

As you drag, you will see that Excel has recognised that you have entered a calendar month name. Because you are dragging the cursor to the right, Excel assumes that you require the following months, *November* and *December*, entered in the selected cells. This feature is called **AutoFill**. If you had dragged the cursor to the left, Excel would have inserted *September*.

Excel has a number of similar features, and you should investigate these features at a later date by going to the menu bar and selecting **Tools > Options > Customs Lists**. You can also create your own requirements within the Custom Lists. We will be using a number of these features in due course.

Continue to enter the following detail in the cells as indicated below, using Capital letters:

Cell location	Detail
A4	FOOTWEAR
A5	CLOTHING
A6	TOILETRIES
A7	MISC

	A	B	C	D
1	QUARTERLY SALES FOR AUTUMN 1998			
2				
3		October	November	December
4	FOOTWEAR			
5	CLOTHING			
6	TOILETRIES			
7	MISC			

Text may appear to run into adjacent cells

You may find that some of the text appears to have run into the adjacent cell. In actual fact the text remains in its respective cells. We will rectify the appearance of the display shortly.

Adjusting column widths

There are a number of ways to display the text correctly but we will investigate only one option at this stage. Do not carry out any actions yet, read the following first, then make the necessary adjustments.

- Point to the column headers, just between the headers A and B. The cursor will change to a double-headed arrow.

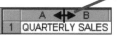

Drag to resize

- Left-click and drag the cursor to the right until you are satisfied with the positioning.

A quicker method, is to start as described above, and when the cursor changes to a double-headed arrow, double-click on the left button. Excel will automatically open out the column to the correct width.

If you adjust the width at this stage, you will not achieve the desired results. This is because there is a longer piece of text already in cell A1 and Excel will open the column to accommodate that text. The width will be excessive. To overcome this problem, we will first carry out some formatting to the text in cell A1.

- Place the cursor over the cell A1. It should resemble a fat white cross.

- Press the left button and select the cell A1.

- With the button held down, drag the cursor to the right and select the cells A1 to D1 inclusive, then release the button.

	A	B	C	D
1	QUARTERLY SALES FOR AUTUMN 1998			

- With all four cells selected, click ▦ **Merge and Centre** on the Formatting toolbar.

The cells will merge and the text become centred within the four. You will hardly notice any change, in respect of the text placement, but you will see that the four cells are enclosed in a bold rectangle without any highlight.

	A	B	C	D
1	QUARTERLY SALES FOR AUTUMN 1998			

We can now adjust the width of column A.

Point to the line between the headers A and B, as described previously and double-click on the left button when the cursor changes its shape. The column will be widened to accommodate the text contained in cells A4 to A7.

	A	B	C	D
1	QUARTERLY SALES FOR AUTUMN 1998			
2				
3		October	November	December
4	FOOTWEAR			
5	CLOTHING			
6	TOILETRIES			
7	MISC			

Before column width adjusted

	A	B	C	D
1	QUARTERLY SALES FOR AUTUMN 1998			
2				
3		October	November	December
4	FOOTWEAR			
5	CLOTHING			
6	TOILETRIES			
7	MISC			

After column width adjusted

Continue to enter the data as shown below:

Cell	October	November	December
B4	3980	3285	4120
B5	5740	5566	5990
B6	2541	3500	2654
B7	1500	1750	1458

This is what your worksheet should now look like after all the above data has been entered:

	A	B	C	D
1	QUARTERLY SALES FOR AUTUMN 1998			
2				
3		October	November	December
4	FOOTWEAR	3980	3285	4120
5	CLOTHING	5740	5566	5990
6	TOILETRIES	2541	3500	2654
7	MISC	1500	1750	1458

Formatting figures

When entering data into cells Excel will align text to the left and numbers to the right.

There is still considerable formatting to be carried out on the figures yet. The figures as they stand could mean anything, when in actual fact they are monetary sums. We will format them to show only whole currency, that is to say, not any denomination less than £1.

Here is a quick way to format all twelve cells together, rather than having to apply the formatting to individual cells.

Basic steps

1 Select the cells containing the sales figures. Click on cell B4, and drag the cursor down and to the right until all the cells B4 to D7 are highlighted, then release the button.

2 Right-click over the highlighted area.

3 At the pop-up menu, select Format Cells.

4 The Format Cells dialog box will open. Ensure that the Number tab is selected.

5 Select *Currency* from the Category list.

6 We will not be showing value less than £1. Click the down arrow next to the Decimal places slot to set this to 0.

7 Drop down the Symbol list and select *None*. We do not require the £ sign displayed in these cells at this time.

8 Click OK and the format will be applied.

The area will still be highlighted. To clear this, click in a blank cell.

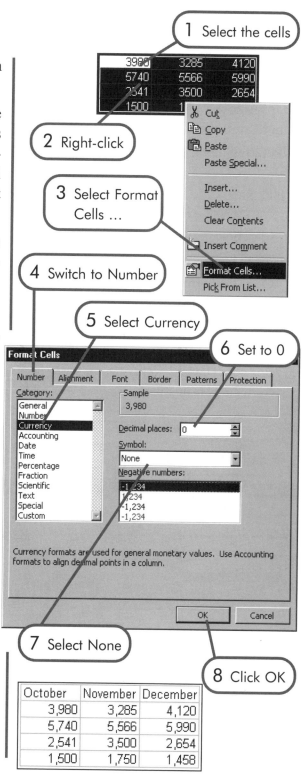

1 Select the cells

2 Right-click

3 Select Format Cells ...

4 Switch to Number

5 Select Currency

6 Set to 0

7 Select None

8 Click OK

October	November	December
3,980	3,285	4,120
5,740	5,566	5,990
2,541	3,500	2,654
1,500	1,750	1,458

Font styles and sizes

The title of this worksheet, in its current format, is not very eye-catching. We will increase the font size and add a little colour to it to make it more attractive. Naturally you will need a colour printer to gain the full effect of colour.

Basic steps

1 Click onto the cell A1 to select it.

2 Open the Format menu and select Cells.

Or

3 Right-click on the cell and select Format Cells from the pop-up menu.

✂	Cu̲t
🗒	Copy
📋	Paste
	Paste S̲pecial...
	I̲nsert...
	D̲elete...
	Clear Co̲ntents
🗐	Insert Co̲mment
🖻	F̲ormat Cells...
	Pic̲k From List...

4 Switch to Font

5 Set the size

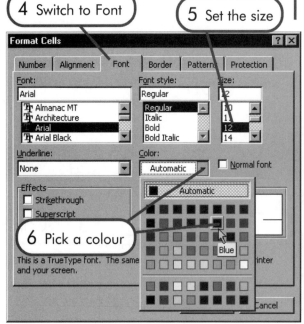

6 Pick a colour

Format Cells   ? ✕

Number | Alignment | Font | Border | Pattern | Protection

Font:
Arial

Font style:
Regular

Size:
12

Almanac MT
Architecture
Arial
Arial Black

Regular
Italic
Bold
Bold Italic

10
1
12
14

Underline:
None

Color:
Automatic

☐ Normal font

Effects
☐ Strikethrough
☐ Superscript

Automatic

Blue

This is a TrueType font. The same ... and your screen.

4 At the Format Cells dialog box, select the Font tab. The current settings are highlighted. We are going to set the size to 12 and the colour to blue.

5 Using the scroll bars if necessary, find and click on the figure 12 in the Font size list.

6 Click on the arrow next to the Color slot. A palette will appear. Select blue, and the palette will close automatically.

7 Click the OK button.

As you will see, the text is too large for the cell. We will rectify this problem in a moment.

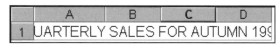

	A	B	C	D
1	UARTERLY SALES FOR AUTUMN 199			

We will now change the font size back to 10, but this time we will do it in a different way.

Basic steps

1 Select the title cell, A1.

2 In the Formula bar, click at one end of the text and drag to the other to select it all.

Tip

If you have a black and white printer, be careful with the use of colours and shades. Test print a page to determine the quality of its output and to ensure that the detail can be read.

1 Select the cell

3 Set the size

2 Select the text in the Formula bar

3 Click the Font size down arrow in the toolbar, and select 10.

4 Click on any part of the worksheet to activate the change. You will now be able to see all of the title text.

We are now going to format the text *October* through to *December*, to make it stand out from the rest.

Basic steps

1 Click onto cell B3, October, then drag across to highlight C3 and D3.

2 Click the Bold and then the Center icons on the Formatting toolbar.

3 Adjust the columns widths to compensate for the change in the text, i.e. bold occupies more space.

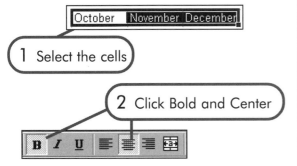

1 Select the cells

2 Click Bold and Center

Your worksheet should now look like the example shown below. Note how the names of the months stand out now that they have had the Bold format applied.

	A	B	C	D
1	QUARTERLY SALES FOR AUTUMN 1998			
2				
3		October	November	December
4	FOOTWEAR	3,980	3,285	4,120
5	CLOTHING	5,740	5,566	5,990
6	TOILETRIES	2,541	3,500	2,654
7	MISC	1,500	1,750	1,458

Close this workbook, making sure that you save any changes. We will return to this workbook later in the course.

Creating a second workbook

Create another workbook, saving it as *ECDL2*, on the floppy disk. Enter the data, and format it, as shown here.

	A	B	C	D	E
1		QUARTERLY SALES FOR WINTER 1999			
2					
3		January	February	March	
4	FOOTWEAR	2,976	2,367	2,989	
5	CLOTHING	4,356	2,340	3,452	
6	TOILETRIES	2,350	2,956	2,870	
7	MISC	1,300	1,456	1,299	

● The title, QUARTERLY SALES FOR WINTER 1999, goes in cell B1, but should be Merged and Centered across B1 to E1.

● For the months, enter 'January' and use AutoFill to write the others.

● The width of column will need adjusting to accommodate the descriptions.

Entering formulas

In the new sheet, add the following text – these will be the headings for our formulas.

    In cell E3, enter: *Quarterly Sales*

    In cell A9, enter: *Total*

    In cell A10, enter: *Monthly Sales*

Adjust the column widths to accommodate the newly entered text.

We will shortly enter the formula that will add together the sales for the months January to March, and display the result in cell E4. **Do not type anything yet** – just read the explanations.

When entered the formula will appear in the Formula bar as follows:

    =SUM(B4:D4)

Before we enter the formula, let's see how it is made up and the meaning of its components.

The syntax – the structure – of a function begins with the name, followed by its arguments, separated by commas and all enclosed in parenthesis (). If the function starts a formula, you need an equal sign '=' before the name:

    =SUM(B4:D4)

Function name   Arguments

The SUM function adds given values or the values in cells, or in ranges of cells.

The details contained within the parentheses are known as arguments and identify the cells that the calculation is to be based upon.

The formula =SUM(B4:D4) means: display the total of the values in cells B4, C4 and D4.

How to enter the formula

Click into the cell E4 and type in the equal (=) sign followed by the word 'SUM' and the opening parenthesis. **Do not** leave any spaces when entering the formula details.

- The formula should appear like this: **=Sum(**

- Click into cell B4 and drag the cursor over to cell D4. As you drag, a broken outline appears around the cells. The detail in cell E4 also reflects the movement of the cursor and inserts the cell references into this cell.

- When the three cells, B4, C4 and D4 have been selected, release the button. Your worksheet should look like this:

SUM	▾	✕ ✓ =	=sum(B4:D4	
	A	**B**	**C**	**D**	**E**
1		QUARTERLY SALES FOR WINTER 1999			
2					
3		January	February	March	Quarterly Sales
4	FOOTWEAR	2,976	2,367	2,989	=sum(B4:D4
5	CLOTHING	4,356	2,340	3,452	
6	TOILETRIES	2,350	2,956	2,870	
7	MISC	1,300	1,456	1,299	
8					
9	Total				
10	Monthly Sales				

- Type in the closing parenthesis to complete the formula and press **[Enter]**. The formula appears in cell E4 and in the Formula bar like this: **=Sum(B4:D4)**

Take note

Formula names and cell identifiers in formulas are not case sensitive – you may use uppercase, lowercase or mixed.

Re-select cell E4, move the cursor to the lower right corner of the cell and when the cursor changes to a thin black cross, left-click and drag the cursor down to cell E10 and then release the button. This action copies the formula down to the other cells and adjusts it accordingly.

Select cells E5, E6 and E7 in turn and you will see that Excel has adjusted the cell references relevant to each cell as it copied the formula.

	E10		▼	=	=SUM(B10:D10)
	A	B	C	D	E
1		QUARTERLY SALES FOR WINTER 1999			
2					
3		January	February	March	Quarterly Sales
4	FOOTWEAR	2,976	2,367	2,989	8,332
5	CLOTHING	4,356	2,340	3,452	10,148
6	TOILETRIES	2,350	2,956	2,870	8,176
7	MISC	1,300	1,456	1,299	4,055
8					0
9	Total				0
10	Monthly Sales				0

The example now shows all the calculations completed. There is a small problem however. Cells E8 and E9 display zero (0) values and their presence is an unnecessary distraction.

● Click into cell E8 and drag down to include cell E9 in the selection.

● Press [Delete] and the cells will be cleared.

The worksheet is not complete. The formula for the *Monthly Sales* has yet to be entered.

● Select the cell B10 and type in the formula: =Sum(B4:B7), then press [Enter].

● Point to the lower right corner of the cell. When the cursor changes to a thin black cross, drag it to the right to select cells C10 and D10. Release the button and the formulas will be copied into the cells, and the totals calculated and displayed.

Notice that as you dragged the cursor to the right, the zero value in cell E10 was changing

to reflect the increase in totals. Your worksheet should resemble the example shown below.

	A	B	C	D	E
1		QUARTERLY SALES FOR WINTER 1999			
2					
3		January	February	March	Quarterly Sales
4	FOOTWEAR	2,976	2,367	2,989	8,332
5	CLOTHING	4,356	2,340	3,452	10,148
6	TOILETRIES	2,350	2,956	2,870	8,176
7	MISC	1,300	1,456	1,299	4,055
8					
9	Total				
10	Monthly Sales	10,982	9,119	10,610	30,711

Save any changes to the worksheet and then close it by selecting **File > Close**.

Practical exercise

Re-open the worksheet *ECDL1*.

Select **File** and, provided that you have not opened many other worksheets since last working on it, you will find *ECDL1* in the lower area of the **File** drop-down menu. If *ECDL1* is shown in the list, click on it and it will open.

The aim is now to apply to this **all** the additional text and formatting that was applied to the worksheet *ECDL2*. Enter the new text and the formulas, complete with formatting, and carry out any adjustments if necessary.

When you have completed all the additions and adjustments to ECDL1, Save the changes. The worksheet should resemble that shown below.

	A	B	C	D	E
1		QUARTERLY SALES FOR AUTUMN 1998			
2					
3		October	November	December	Quarterly Sales
4	FOOTWEAR	3,980	3,285	4,120	11,385
5	CLOTHING	5,740	5,566	5,990	17,296
6	TOILETRIES	2,541	3,500	2,654	8,695
7	MISC	1,500	1,750	1,458	4,708
8					
9	Total				
10	Monthly Sales	13,761	14,101	14,222	42,084

Inserting rows and columns

At some stage you may need to insert a new row or column in a worksheet. Inserting rows and columns is quite simple.

Basic steps

1   Open *ECDL1*. Move to row 7, and right-click on the row number. The row will be selected and a pop-up menu will appear.

2   Select Insert. The worksheet will roll down one row and a new row 7 will appear. The old row 7 will be re-numbered as row 8.

3   Select cell E7. Notice that the Formula bar is empty. When a row is inserted, formulas in the old row are not copied over.

4   Point to the lower right corner of cell E6, and drag it down to cell E7. Release the button. Select E7 again and you will see that it now contains a copy of the formula.

In row 7, enter the following new details:

    Cell A7, HOSIERY
    Cell B7, 1256
    Cell C7, 1045
    Cell D7, 1145

Note that as you enter the *Hosiery* figures, the *quarterly sales* in E7 is updated automatically.

Inserting columns

We will now insert a new column in the ECDL1 worksheet. The new column will be used to display an Average Sales figure and is to be located between the column for December and the Quarterly Sales figures.

1 Right-click on the row number

2 Select Insert

4 Copy in the formula

Note that when a new column is inserted, the selected column and all those to its right will be moved one column to the right.

● The new column is to be inserted between the current columns D and E. Right-click in the header area of column E.

● Select **Insert** from the pop-up menu. Excel will insert a new column E and move the old one to the right, making it column F.

Place the cursor on cell E3 and type in: 'Average Sales', then press **[Enter]**. Format the new column title to match the others.

The formula that we will create will calculate the average monthly sales for each line of goods. It will be placed in cells E4 to E8.

- Select cell E4 and type in:
  =AVERAGE(B4:D4)

The AVERAGE function will add the contents of the cells, then divide by the number of cells. In this case:

(3980 + 3285 + 4120)/ 3 = 3795

- Use the drag method to copy the formula down to cell E11. Note that as you copy it down to each cell Excel carries out the calculation and displays the result in the appropriate cell.
- Highlight cells E9 and E10 and clear the cell contents by pressing **[Delete]**.

The completed sheet should look like this:

	A	B	C	D	E	F
1	QUARTERLY SALES FOR AUTUMN 1998					
2						
3		October	November	December	Average Sales	Quarterly Sales
4	FOOTWEAR	3,980	3,285	4,120	3,795	11,385
5	CLOTHING	5,740	5,566	5,990	5,765	17,296
6	TOILETRIES	2,541	3,500	2,654	2,898	8,695
7	HOSIERY	1,256	1,045	1,145	1,149	3,446
8	MISC	1,500	1,750	1,458	1,569	4,708
9						
10	Total					
11	Monthly Sales	15,017	15,146	15,367	15,177	45,530

Reformatting currency cells

It was decided when we first created the worksheets that we would not display any decimal places for any currency of a value of less than one pound. In other words no pence would be shown. Obviously this is somewhat unrealistic, so we will re-format the worksheet to show any pence that may be included in any calculations. We will also re-format the cells to display the pound (£) sign.

- Select the block of cells from B4 to F11, then right-click on the area and select **Format Cells** from the pop-up menu.
- At the **Format Cells** dialog box, ensure the **Number** tab is open, then select *Currency*.

Set the Decimal places to 2

Set the Symbol to £

The currency figures after reformatting

	A	B	C	D	E	F
1	QUARTERLY SALES FOR AUTUMN 1998					
2						
3		October	November	December	Average Sales	Quarterly Sales
4	FOOTWEAR	£3,980.00	£3,285.00	£4,120.00	£3,795.00	£11,385.00
5	CLOTHING	£5,740.00	£5,566.00	£5,990.00	£5,765.33	£17,296.00
6	TOILETRIES	£2,541.00	£3,500.00	£2,654.00	£2,898.33	£8,695.00
7	HOSIERY	£1,256.00	£1,045.00	£1,145.00	£1,148.67	£3,446.00
8	MISC	£1,500.00	£1,750.00	£1,458.00	£1,569.33	£4,708.00
9						
10	Total					
11	Monthly Sales	£15,017.00	£15,146.00	########	£15,176.67	£45,530.00

The reformatting may result in some cells not displaying correctly, as the new format may need more space than is available. The problem can be solved by adjusting the cell width.

Sorting data

There will be occasions where you may wish to present the data in a different order, for instance you may wish to display the sales data in ECDL1 in ascending order.

Basic steps

1   Highlight the block A4 to D8.

	A	B	C	D	E
1	QUARTERLY SALES FOR AUTUMN 1998				
2					
3		October	November	December	Average Sales
4	FOOTWEAR	£3,980.00	£3,285.00	£4,120.00	£3,795.00
5	CLOTHING	£5,740.00	£5,566.00	£5,990.00	£5,765.33
6	TOILETRIES	£2,541.00	£3,500.00	£2,654.00	£2,898.33
7	HOSIERY	£1,256.00	£1,045.00	£1,145.00	£1,148.67
8	MISC'	£1,500.00	£1,750.00	£1,458.00	£1,569.33
9					
10	Total				
11	Monthly Sales	£15,017.00	£15,146.00	£15,367.00	£15,176.67

2   Click ▲↓ the Sort Ascending button. The highlighted area will re-arrange to display the data as shown in the example below.

	A	B	C	D	E
1	QUARTERLY SALES FOR AUTUMN 1998				
2					
3		October	November	December	Average Sales
4	CLOTHING	£5,740.00	£5,566.00	£5,990.00	£5,765.33
5	FOOTWEAR	£3,980.00	£3,285.00	£4,120.00	£3,795.00
6	HOSIERY	£1,256.00	£1,045.00	£1,145.00	£1,148.67
7	MISC'	£1,500.00	£1,750.00	£1,458.00	£1,569.33
8	TOILETRIES	£2,541.00	£3,500.00	£2,654.00	£2,898.33
9					
10	Total				
11	Monthly Sales	£15,017.00	£15,146.00	£15,367.00	£15,176.67

3   Click in a blank cell to remove the highlight.

All the corresponding cells will automatically re-calculate their respective values in relation to the changes brought about by the Sort.

Copying data

Data and formulas can be easily copied from one worksheet to another. This is done by using the Copy and Paste features found in Excel. We are going to copy a row and a column.

Ensure that both ECDL1 and ECDL2 worksheets are open. There are a number of ways that you can move from one worksheet to the other. We will use the method described below.

● Ensure that the ECDL1 worksheet is active, i.e. the one that you can see. To confirm this, check the name in the title bar.

Cut, Copy and Paste
buttons

● Open the **Window** menu. In the lower section there are the file names of the two open worksheets.

The one with the tick alongside is the active worksheet.

We are going to copy the Hosiery row and the Average Sales column from ECDL1 to ECDL2.

Before we start, move to ECDL2, select the cells A4 to D7 and carry out a Sort Ascending on them. This will bring both of the workbooks in to a common presentation of data. If this is not done, the copied data, when pasted in, will not correspond to the correct data.

● Re-select workbook ECDL1.

Pasting a row

● Select row 6 and copy it, either by using the right-click menu option or by selecting **Edit > Copy**.

● Change to ECDL2 and select row 6 using the right-click menu option **Insert Copied Cells**.

Note that row 6 has carried over the formatting of row 6 in ECDL1, including the Average Sales figures in cell E6. The Quarterly Sales figure for Hosiery is now in cell F6.

Copying the row from one workbook to another has resulted in our worksheet displaying various figures in the wrong columns and this must be corrected before we proceed.

● Click in cell E6 and press **[Delete]** to remove the cell contents.

● Select cell F6, point to its lower edge and when the cursor changes to an arrow drag it into the empty cell E6. Release the button and the data will be transferred across.

Copying columns

When we created the workbook ECDL2 we placed the worksheet title, '*Quarterly Sales for Winter 1999*', in cell B1, whereas when we created the workbook ECDL1 the worksheet title was placed in cell A1.

The reason for changing the location was to highlight a problem often encountered when copying between workbooks or worksheets.

If you encounter difficulties when attempting to copy columns, re-check the overall layout of the worksheets – you will often find that there is a difference in the general layout of such items as titles, etc.

We will not be able to insert a new column because of the different locations of our title, but we can overcome this quite simply.

● Ensure that ECDL2 is the active worksheet.

● Select the cell B1, then right-click on it and select **Cut** from the pop-up menu. A dashed outline will now appear around the cell.

● Point to an area below the data and select an empty cell, e.g. A20. Right-click on it and from the pop-up menu select **Paste**. The title will now be moved to its temporary location.

We can now proceed and start copying the column from one workbook to another.

● Ensure that ECDL1 is the active worksheet.

● Select column E and using either the right-click or **Edit > Copy** method, copy it.

● Switch to ECDL2.

● Select column E, right-click on it and from the pop-up menu select **Insert Copied Cells**.

Take note

If you use Paste to copy in cells, the data will overwrite any existing data in the target cells.

The original column E will move to the right and become column F while the *Average Sales* figures column will now become column E.

We now want to move the title back up to the top of the worksheet, above the data. Select the title cell, Cut it from its current location and Paste it into cell A1.

There will now be some inconsistency in the overall formatting and appearance in the ECDL2 worksheet. Reformat as required for an overall consistency and in line with that of the workbook ECDL1.

Save the changes to the worksheet.

Review

This may have seemed a somewhat long and protracted method to insert data from one worksheet to another. However, consider the following facts:

- Our worksheets are on the small size and contain little data in comparison with that of Company/Corporate worksheets, which could, and do contain numerous columns and rows, so Copy and Paste would certainly save time.

- Most errors, if they are to occur, will happen as the user is typing in data. Copy and Paste facilities reduce the likelihood of error.

The exercises just completed, involved moving columns and rows. You should be aware that you can copy blocks of data as well as complete columns and rows.

The procedure is simple.

- Highlight the required range, right-click on the highlighted area and select **Copy** from the pop-up menu.

- Right-click over the appropriate cell, where you wish the copied data to appear, and from the pop-up menu select **Paste**. The text will appear in the appropriate cells.

Charts

'*A picture paints a thousand words*', and Excel gives you charts and graphs to help give figures more meaning. Charts make it easier to spot trends, highlight important changes and compare individual figures. Charts in reports and presentations will display numbers to your audience in a format that is easy to understand.

When you create a chart, each row or column of data on the worksheet makes up a *data series*. Each individual value within a row or column is called a *data point*.

The chart can include row and column headings. These are used as category labels and legend text. If the range does not include headings, Excel creates default headings.

You can either embed a chart in the worksheet you are currently working with, or create it on a chart sheet. When you want the chart and the worksheet data viewed or printed together, you should use an embedded chart.

A chart sheet is a separate worksheet in the workbook that contains only the chart. If you want to use the chart by itself (for example, in a presentation) you should use a chart sheet. Both kinds of chart are linked to the worksheet data and updated automatically if the data is changed.

The Chart Wizard

The Chart Wizard assists you in creating a chart by leading you through a series of dialog boxes that allow you to choose options. You can quickly learn the essentials of creating a chart using the Chart Wizard.

Basic steps

1   Open the worksheet ECDL1. Drag to select the range containing the data to be included in the chart – in this case, A3 to D8.

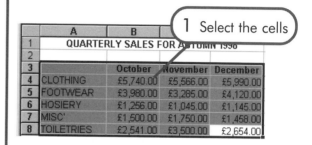

1 Select the cells

2   Click the Chart Wizard icon.

3   For the Chart type, select Pie, with the 3D Chart sub-type.

4   Click the Next button.

3 Choose Pie, 3D

Click for a preview of the chart

4 Click Next

5   Set the Series in option to *Rows*.

6   Click the Next button.

7   At the next stage, ensure that the Title tab is selected and type in '*Quarterly Sales Autumn 1998*'.

8   Click on Data Labels and select Show label and percent.

9   Click Next.

10 The next window will offer you two options as to where the chart should reside. Select: As new sheet.

11 Click Finish.

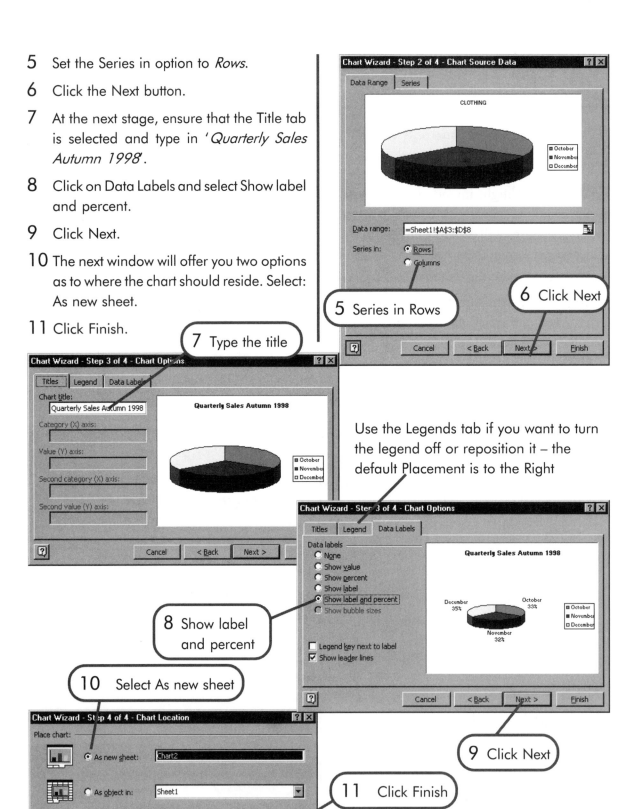

Use the Legends tab if you want to turn the legend off or reposition it – the default Placement is to the Right

128

That completes the chart building process using a Wizard. The chart should now appear as shown below.

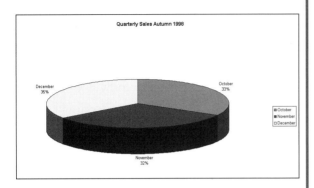

Creating a second chart

We are now going to create a second chart, this time using the ECDL2 worksheet. Close ECDL1 and save any changes if prompted.

This time we want all the figures except the *Average Sales* to be included in the chart. Open ECDL2 and follow the procedures below:

● Click into cell A3 and drag down to cell D8 to highlight this area. Release the button.

● Press **[Control]** and keep it pressed. Click on cell F3 and drag down to cell F8.

This will highlight the data within this range while retaining the previously highlighted data.

	A	B	C	D	E	F
1	QUARTERLY SALES FOR WINTER 1999					
2						
3		January	February	March	Average Sales	Quarterly Sales
4	CLOTHING	£4,356.00	£2,340.00	£3,452.00	£3,382.67	£10,148.00
5	FOOTWEAR	£2,976.00	£2,367.00	£2,989.00	£2,777.33	£8,332.00
6	HOSIERY	£1,256.00	£1,045.00	£1,145.00	£1,148.67	£3,446.00
7	MISC	£1,300.00	£1,456.00	£1,299.00	£1,351.67	£4,055.00
8	TOILETRIES	£2,350.00	£2,956.00	£2,870.00	£2,725.33	£8,176.00

The method is used to select scattered blocks and can be extremely useful when working with large worksheets.

Basic steps

1 Click the Chart Wizard icon.

2 At the first step, ensure the Standard Types tab is open. From Chart Type, select *Column* and from the Chart sub-type, click on the first image on the second row.

3 Click the Next button.

4 At Step 2, select the Series in *Rows* option and click the Next Button.

5 At Step 3, make the following selections.

On the Titles tab, type the Chart Title: *'Quarterly Sales Winter 1999'*.

On the Legend tab, tick Show Legend and select *Right* for the Placement.

On the Data Labels tab, select None, click the Next button.

6 At Step 4, Chart Location, select the option: As object in – the adjacent slot should show *Sheet 1*. Click the Finish button.

129

Handles

The components of the chart – the grid, axes, title, legend, etc., can be selected individually for moving, resizing or formatting

The Chart Wizard will now close and the chart will appear on the current sheet.

Moving a chart

You may find that the chart is not placed where you want it and it may be covering your data.

When the chart appears on the worksheet it should already be selected. You can confirm this by the presence of a dark outline, with 'handles' at the corners and mid-sides. Once the chart has been selected, it can be moved around the sheet or resized as required.

To move the chart, select it, then point up to the chart line until the cursor changes to a single arrow. When it does, click and drag in the direction that you wish to move the chart. The cursor will again change its shape, this time to a four-headed arrow pointer.

To resize a chart

It is possible to change the size of the chart. Select the chart, by clicking over an area that has no detail in it.

Point to the handle at the lower right-hand corner. The cursor should change to a double-headed arrow. Press the left button and hold it down. Drag the cursor in or out to change the size. Be careful at this stage – too much adjustment in either the horizontal or vertical planes may distort the chart.

To keep the chart in proportion, while changing its size, hold down **[Shift]** while dragging the cursor. When the desired size has been achieved, release both cursor and **[Shift]**.

Re-save the worksheet and then experiment moving and sizing the chart.

Also experiment with the components of the chart. For instance right-click over the Legend and a pop-up menu will appear from which you may Format the Legend…

Save the changes.

Tip

Charts can impart information, visually, extremely effectively. However, overloading the chart can defeat the objective.

Experiment with all aspects of the chart feature, to learn its versatility and which chart best suits the task and type of data.

Headers and footers

Before printing the sheet and chart we will first create a Header and Footer to contain descriptive text such as title and page numbers. Open ECDL2 and follow the steps.

Basic steps

1 Open the File menu and select Page Setup.

2 At the dialog box, click on the Header/ Footer tab.

3 Click the Custom Header button.

4 At the Header dialog box, type your name in the Center section, then click OK.

5 Back at the Page Setup dialog box, select *Page 1* from the drop-down Footer list to set the page numbering style.

6 When you have done click the Print Preview button.

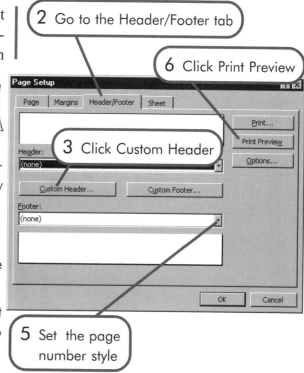

2 Go to the Header/Footer tab

6 Click Print Preview

3 Click Custom Header

5 Set the page number style

4 Type your name and click OK

Print Preview

This shows how the sheet, and its embedded chart, will look when printed. Use it to check that the layout is satisfactory and that the page contains all the elements you want to show.

The layout should be similar to the example overleaf. If the image is rather small, click once on the Zoom button to increase the view size. Clicking on the Zoom button again will reduce the view size.

After checking, close the Print Preview window, as we are now ready to print the worksheet.

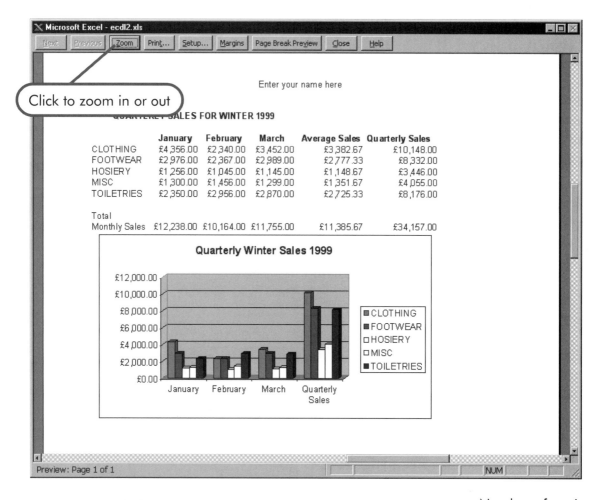

Click to zoom in or out

Printing a worksheet

Ensure that ECDL2.xls is open, and follow the procedures outlined below:

- Open the **File** menu and select **Print** to open the **Print** dialog box.

- Ensure that the **Active sheet(s)** option is selected.

- If more than one copy is required, set the Number of copies.

- Click the **OK** button to print the worksheet.

Experiment with the other aspects of the print output that can be altered in this dialog box.

Number of copies

Pages to print

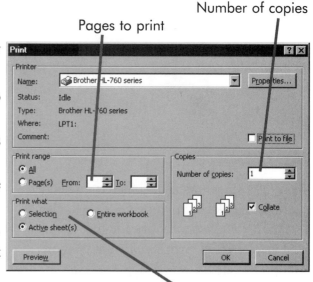

A selected block can be printed

Absolute references

When you enter cell references in a formula they are *relative* references. If you copy the formula, the cell references change relative to where the formula is copied. You saw this happening when we first entered formulas (page 120).

Absolute references do not change when used in formulas. The reference cell remains fixed because the value in that cell does not change when applied to other cells. Two examples of the use of an absolute reference are:

- Fluctuating currency exchange rates, where the rate changes after a period of time. When the rate is changed only the one figure, the absolute reference, has to be changed to reflect the overall change in holdings.

- Commission, usually awarded at a fixed rate for a given period of time. If the basic salary is increased, the commission percentage will usually remain the same, the absolute reference.

When entering an absolute reference in a cell the $ sign is used to fix the row and column identifiers, e.g. A15.

We are going to create an absolute reference in our worksheet ECDL1. The scenario is that it is company policy that each branch manager receives a 2.5% commission on sales.

Basic steps

1 Open the worksheet ECDL1.

2 In cell A13 type '*Managers*', then in A14 type '*Commission*'.

3 In cell A15 type: 2.5

4 Select cell B14 and enter the formula:
=B11/100*A15

5 Press [Enter] and you should now have the figure 375.425, or £375.43 if the currency format has been applied to this cell.

6 Copy the formula into cells C14 and C15 and carry out any formatting necessary, i.e. format cells to display the £ sign.

Tip

You can also use **Mixed References** — where only the row or column is fixed. This subject is beyond the scope of this book.

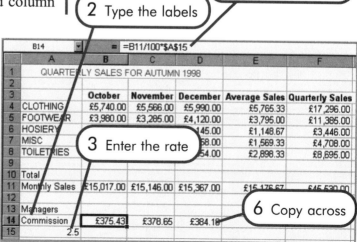

4 Enter the formula

2 Type the labels

3 Enter the rate

6 Copy across

	A	B	C	D	E	F
	B14		= =B11/100*A15			
1	QUARTERLY SALES FOR AUTUMN 1998					
2						
3		October	November	December	Average Sales	Quarterly Sales
4	CLOTHING	£5,740.00	£5,566.00	£5,990.00	£5,765.33	£17,296.00
5	FOOTWEAR	£3,980.00	£3,285.00	£4,120.00	£3,795.00	£11,385.00
6	HOSIERY			45.00	£1,148.67	£3,446.00
7	MISC			68.00	£1,569.33	£4,708.00
8	TOILETRIES			54.00	£2,898.33	£8,695.00
9						
10	Total					
11	Monthly Sales	£15,017.00	£15,146.00	£15,367.00	£15,176.67	£45,530.00
12						
13	Managers					
14	Commission	£375.43	£378.65	£384.18		
15		2.5				

Named cells and ranges

So far you have used cell addresses, e.g. A15, C15, etc. to refer to cells, and of course it works. There is however an often more convenient method of referring to cell addresses and ranges of cells. This method is known as naming.

Excel allows the use of named cells or ranges of cells and these can be moved, copied or entered in formulas, just like cells with ordinary addresses.

Picture this: you could give the absolute reference a name, such as *Commission* and use that reference in other worksheets. When an adjustment in the commission rate is called for, it only has to be made at the one located, in this case in the workbook ECDL1, worksheet 1, cell B15. The adjustment will automatically update all referenced worksheets.

Clearly one can see minor problems in this instance. Previous months' commission, which will have already been paid at the previous rate will be amended by the change and show an incorrect figure. There are ways and means of dealing with this situation, but this area is outside the realms of this book.

We have talked a great deal about naming cells or ranges of cells, so how do we do it? We will use the absolute reference recently created in the ECDL1 workbook.

Basic steps

1 Ensure that the workbook ECDL1 is open and that you are at worksheet 1.

2 Select cell A15, the one used in the absolute reference, then point to the Name box, to the left of the Formula bar. It will already have the cell reference A15.

3 Click into the Name box. The cell reference will be highlighted ready for you to overtype the existing name, in this instance A15.

4 Type in a name (up to 255 characters) – call it *Commission* – and press [Enter].

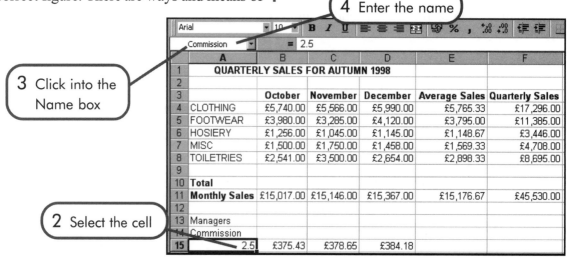

4 Enter the name

3 Click into the Name box

2 Select the cell

	A	B	C	D	E	F
1	QUARTERLY SALES FOR AUTUMN 1998					
2						
3		October	November	December	Average Sales	Quarterly Sales
4	CLOTHING	£5,740.00	£5,566.00	£5,990.00	£5,765.33	£17,296.00
5	FOOTWEAR	£3,980.00	£3,285.00	£4,120.00	£3,795.00	£11,385.00
6	HOSIERY	£1,256.00	£1,045.00	£1,145.00	£1,148.67	£3,446.00
7	MISC	£1,500.00	£1,750.00	£1,458.00	£1,569.33	£4,708.00
8	TOILETRIES	£2,541.00	£3,500.00	£2,654.00	£2,898.33	£8,695.00
9						
10	Total					
11	Monthly Sales	£15,017.00	£15,146.00	£15,367.00	£15,176.67	£45,530.00
12						
13	Managers					
14	Commission					
15	2.5	£375.43	£378.65	£384.18		

Name box shows: Commission = 2.5

Using names in formulas

You will recall that we used the absolute cell reference A15 in the formula for cells B14, C14 and D14 to calculate the commission due. The fact that we gave the Absolute Reference will have no bearing on this factor, the formula will still function.

We will now create a new calculation based on the absolute reference name and the Total Monthly Sales figure in cell F11.

Basic steps

1   In A17, enter *'Managers'*.

2   In A18, enter *'Quarterly'*.

3   In A19, enter *'Commission'*.

4   In B19, enter the formula:

=F11/100*Commission

Press [Enter] and you should have the result: £1,138.25.

Excel recognised that the name *Commission* was an absolute reference, and used it in the formula to perform the calculation.

Save the changes.

Take note

Valid names can include letters, numbers, periods, and underlines, but no spaces. A Name cannot begin with a number.

Take note

When creating named cells or ranges, Excel automatically changes the cell or ranges to an Absolute Reference.

You may have noticed that when you created the charts, earlier in the course, that the Chart Wizard step 2 dialog box, shown opposite, displayed the selected range as an Absolute Reference.

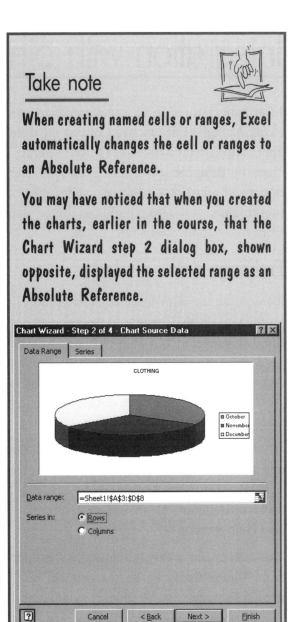

Integration with other applications

Information stored in an Excel workbook can easily be copied or linked to any of the other applications in the Microsoft Office 97 suite. A chart or data can be inserted into a Word document, an Access database or a PowerPoint presentation. It is also possible to import data from these applications into Excel.

Exchange data with Access

To analyse the data from an Access table in Excel, you can use features in Access to export the data automatically to a new Excel workbook. You can also import worksheet data into Access. If you want only a few records from an Access table, you can open the table and copy and paste selected records into Excel.

If you're working in Excel and have installed and loaded the AccessLinks add-in, you can convert a list to an Access database file. For more information about add-ins use the on-line Help system.

You can create a PivotTable to analyse data from Access just as you would from any external data source.

Practice

It will only be possible to practise the following if you have already completed the module on Access.

Basic steps

1 Open the Access database ECDL2 and then select, but do not open, the table ECDL Table2.

2 Open the Edit menu and select Copy.

3 Open Excel with a new workbook.

4 Ensure cell A1 is selected.

5 Open the Edit menu and select Paste.

6 The table selected in Access will be pasted into the workbook and you may then format the worksheet to suit your requirements.

It is almost certain that the pasted version of the table will require some reformatting once within the worksheet – in particular cell widths will require some adjustment to display long entries or field names.

Using the online Help system

The online help system in all Microsoft applications is similar in its style, appearance and operation. We are going to discuss the online help by accessing it using Excel. You should remember that the procedures discussed here are the same for Word, PowerPoint and Access though this latter has some special features.

We will look at only one avenue of the Help system, based on the Index tab.

Basic steps

1 Open the Help menu and select Contents and Index.

2 Select the Index tab if not already selected.

3 Type in one or more words relating to the subject that you want help on, e.g. type in 'Help' to find out more about the system.

4 Click the Display button.

5 The Topics Found dialog box will open, listing any relevant pages. Select a topic and click the Display button.

6 A dialog box will open, displaying the topic. Use the scroll bars to reveal more of the text, if appropriate.

7 To continue the search, or to locate another subject, click the Help Topics button, and you will be returned to the Index.

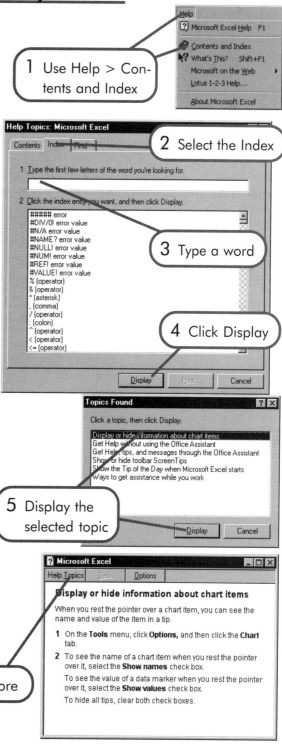

1 Use Help > Contents and Index

2 Select the Index

3 Type a word

4 Click Display

5 Display the selected topic

7 Go back for more

4: Spreadsheets

137

Printing the Help Topic

If you wish to print out the current Help topic click the **Options** button and select Print from the menu.

```
Annotate...
Copy
Print Topic...
Font           ▶
Keep Help on Top ▶
Use System Colors

Bookmarks...
Define Bookmarks...
```

Annotating Help pages

You can add your own annotations to the current Help topic.

Basic steps

1   Click Options and select Annotate.

2   Type in your comments, then click Save to save your annotations.

3   When you return you to the Help topic, you will note that a little green paperclip has been added, next to the topic title. To view an annotation, click the paperclip symbol.

4   To delete an annotation, open the Annotate dialog box and click Delete.

The F1 Help key

Help can also be obtained through the use of the **[F1]** key.

Place the cursor in any cell and press **[F1]** and the Office Assistant will appear.

Type in your question and Excel will attempt to match your question to its data bank. If successful, it will usually offer you a number of options.

This Help feature can be a little on the hit and miss. Keep your questions simple.

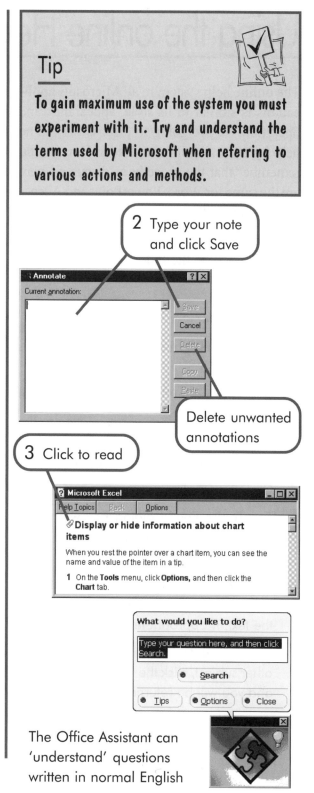

Tip

To gain maximum use of the system you must experiment with it. Try and understand the terms used by Microsoft when referring to various actions and methods.

2 Type your note and click Save

3 Click to read

Delete unwanted annotations

The Office Assistant can 'understand' questions written in normal English

Sample paper 4: Spreadsheets

1	How many worksheets are available when Excel opens a new workbook?	1. 1 2. 3 3. 16
2	How is an active cell indicated in a worksheet?	1. It has a label saying 'active'. 2. It has a thick black line around it. 3. It is a different colour to all the other cells.
3	In simple terms explain the formula: =sum(D2:D6)	
4	Access tables can be copied or imported into an Excel Worksheet, True or False?	1. True 2. False
5	List the two methods which will permit you access to the Format Cells dialog box.	1. The Edit menu 2. The Tools menu 3. Right -lick on cell 4. Format menu
6	To obtain Help when working in Excel, you can select Help on the Menu bar. What is the other way Help can be obtained?	
7	After opening a new workbook in Excel, what is the first thing you should do:	1. Type in the column headings. 2. Save the workbook. 3. Type in the row descriptions.
8	What information is shown in the Formula bar?	
9	Describe the quick method of adjusting the column widths.	

10	List the two sort options available in Excel.	1. 2.
11	Write the formula for calculating the average of cells B4 B5 B6 B7 B8.	
12	In the calculation 3*4+6/2, what is the answer? Show how it was reached.	

5 Databases

Introduction to Access

What is a database?

A database is a collection of information organised in such a manner as to make the information easily accessible. The structure of the database should be simple in order to make storage and retrieval equally easy.

Some examples of databases in everyday use, which people may not think of in terms of a database are:

- A telephone directory
- A dictionary
- A catalogue

In the business world, databases are used for such things as:

- Stock control records
- Customer accounts
- Personnel records

Within a database, related information is stored in tables, organised in *columns* and *rows*.

The columns have headings, known as *field names*, which relate to their content.

Each row contains items of data, known as *fields*, under the different column headings and makes up what is known as a *record*.

In the example there are five records of six fields. They are shown here with their field names.

Planning your database

Before you start creating the components of your database, it is worth spending some time thinking about the information that you are dealing with and how you will want that information handled and displayed.

Following on from this, you should spend some time designing the database on paper, planning the table and designing the layout of the forms and reports, before finally building the database within Access. This way you will identify your requirements and take away the hit and miss aspect, which would occur if you did not spend some time beforehand thinking out the design and layout.

Field name   Field data

Name	Surname	Tel	Fax	Town	Post Code
Michelle	O'Leary	01934 418261	01934 418261	Glasgow	G2 6YH
Keith	Champion	0171 548 7285		Hackney	NW12 7RQ
James	Bates	01705 293176	01705 293176	Portsmouth	PO3 2PL
Joe	Smith	01705 275193	01705 275213	Portsmouth	PO5 2DG
Peter	Bloggs	0181 329 1122	0181 329 1123	Richmond	TW9 1QP

Record

Primary and Secondary keys

During the course of creating the database covered in this book, you will encounter the terms *Primary* and *Secondary keys*. When you have created a table and attempted to save it, for example, Access will warn you that 'no Primary Key has been assigned'. This fact will have no bearing on the database that you will shortly build. It is worthwhile however explaining what the functions of these keys are and why they are used.

If you later progress to creating more complex databases, you will be building in ways to link different tables together, hence the term *relational database*. The linking of tables typically involves setting up each table with a field common to tables. Although this means deliberately duplicating some data in the database, it is better to duplicate a limited amount than have a long set of fields within the database.

The fields that are used to create the links, from one table to another, are usually described as Primary and Secondary keys.

Primary keys uniquely identify a record. A good example might occur in personnel database. Each person has a unique National Insurance number. This number would be in a field which would be assigned as the Primary key. This field would be used to link data to other records in other tables within the database.

If you want to link data from one table to another table you will need to include a field in the second table that corresponds to the Primary key in the first table. This field is then known as the *Secondary key*.

This screenshot of the Relationships display was taken from the *Northwind* example database which is supplied with Access.

There are three tables: *Suppliers*, *Categories* and *Products*. Two tables have Primary key fields: *Suppliers* is **Supplier ID** and *Categories* is **Category ID**. You will see that there is a link from each of these to the table *Products*.

The *Products* table has two fields with matching names, **Supplier ID** and **Category ID**, and these are the Secondary key fields.

Primary and Secondary keys provide the links within relational databases and one cannot exist without the other.

These keys are discussed solely as background information. While working on exercises in this book, if you are prompted by Access that no Primary key has been assigned, ignore it.

We do suggest that, at a later stage, it would be worthwhile investigating the Northwind database. It can be found in the Folder: Microsoft Office\Office\Samples.

Viewing and editing data

There are three ways in which you will work with data:

1 You need to enter records into the database and these records are stored within tables.

2 You need a means of editing or updating the data within the tables.

3 You require a means of searching and viewing the records found.

These tasks are performed using the following components of the database.

Tables are used to enter new data, edit existing data and to find data within the table. Tables enable you to view numerous records at once.

Forms are the usual method of entering or editing data contained within tables. You can create forms that combine data from one or more tables and each table may have more than one forms associated with it. Forms are normally used to view one record at a time. They are based and dependent upon tables.

Queries are used to sort or select data using a set of criteria. Once the data has been selected, it can then be edited using a Datasheet View of a table or Form View, or used to find data or to create other tables and forms.

Reports are outputs from the database – typically printed – with the information sorted, selected and organised into a useful form.

The report can be produced with the information displayed in a table format or as single columns, or the user can design the report layout completely.

A report can be set up to perform calculations and print out the results. It may have multiple tables associated with it.

Access is a powerful relational database which allows multiple tables and forms to be created and linked together according to a given set of criteria. See the example on the previous page relating to Primary and Secondary fields.

Starting Access

As with most Windows applications, you can start Access a number of different ways. Here is one method.

Click on ▒Start the **Start** button. Point to **Programs** to open its menu. Click on ▒Microsoft Access . You will be presented with this dialog box.

Make your choice – in this instance select **Blank Database** – then click the **OK** button.

Creating a database

The File New Database dialog box will open. Access automatically creates a name for you in the File Name slot. Note that the name is already highlighted, which means that when you type in your choice of name for the database, the name that Access prepared for you will be overwritten.

Basic steps

1   Click the down arrow by the Save In slot and select 3½ Floppy (A:).

2   Click into the File name slot and type the name *ECDL1*.

3   Click the Create button.

4   At the Database window, ensure that the Tables tab is selected, then click the New button to create a new table.

5   The New Table dialog box will open. Select Design View and click the OK button.

We left the database with the **Design View**

1   Select 3½ Floppy

3   Click Create

2   Type the File name

4   Go to Tables and click New

5   Select Design View

Views

Access databases can be viewed in several ways.

Datasheet View displays data from a table, form or query in a table format. In Datasheet View, you can edit fields, add and delete data, and search for data.

Form View displays one or more whole records. Form View is the primary means of adding and modifying data in tables.

Design View is used to design tables, forms or queries.

dialog box open, as shown below, and it is from here that you will create the relevant fields for this database.

An explanation of the three columns:

- **Field Name** is the column header that will appear in the table.
- **Data Type** defines and formats the type of column content. When the cursor is moved into this field a drop-down arrow will appear. Click on it to open up a list of options.
- **Description** is optional. It is there for you to include your comments to remind you, or others, at a later date, of the purpose and function of that particular field.

The Field Name and Data Type each have default and optional settings. For instance if the Data Type is Text, the default setting for the Field Name is 50 characters long. This can be increased to 255 characters or decreased as appropriate.

To learn more of these properties and their usage, consult the on-line Help, which is covered on page 137.

Entering the Field Names

Type in the following Field Names, with the Data Type options as indicated:

Field Name	Data Type
ID	AutoNumber
First Name	Text
Last Name	Text
Date of Birth	Date/Time
Salary	Currency
No of Children	Number

Field Properties

You may have noticed that as you selected the Data Type something happened in the lower area of the box, marked **Field Properties**. For the *Salary* and *No of Children* fields, click into the **Default Value** slot and delete the 0.

Once you have entered all the fields, click the **Close** button. You will now be presented with another dialog box, which will prompt you to save the table.

The completed table, in Design View

Most of the Field Properties should be left at their defaults at this stage

146

Click on the **Yes** button, which will open up the **Save As** dialog box. Enter the new name: *'ECDL Table1'* and click the **OK** button.

You will be warned that *'There is no primary key defined'*. We do not require a primary key, so click the **No** button. You will be returned to the database window.

The Database Window

Imagine that the database window as a flat-face filing card system with six items stored within it. These items are identified by the tabs located along the top of the window. All items that make up the database are stored in this window. For example, to locate a form, assuming that one exists, click on the **Forms** tab and that tab will open revealing any content.

This is where you must go to create a new table, form, report or other component. Open the appropriate tab and click the **New** button.

Select *ECDL Table1* in the Database window and click the **Open** button. The table will open in Datasheet View, so that you can now start to enter data into the table.

Click the tabs to see the other sets of components

Open existing item

Edit the design

Create a new one

Our new empty table

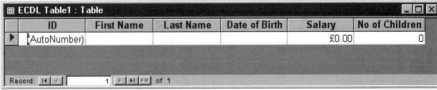

147

Entering data in a table

In the ID column you will see that Access is displaying word 'AutoNumber'. You will recall that this was the Data Type selected for this field at the design stage. As soon as any detail is entered into the File Name column, Access will automatically enter the ID number.

Access provides the AutoNumber data type to create fields that automatically enter a number when a record is added. Once a number is generated for a record, it can't be deleted or changed. AutoNumbers that increment by one are the most common kind and are a good choice for use as a table's primary key.

To enter the data press **[Tab]** and the cursor will move to the *First Name* field. Enter the name 'Simon'. Note that as soon as you typed the first letter, a new record appeared below the one that you are currently entering data in.

Moving between fields

To move to the next field, press **[Tab]** again and the cursor will move to the next field, *Last Name*. Continue entering the data relating to Simon Smith until you reach the last field, *No of Children*. After entering the number 3, press **[Tab]** again and the cursor will move to the ID field and start a new record. Continue entering the following data in the table, and ensure that you type the dates exactly as shown below:

Simon	Smith	12 Jan 71	£950	3
James	Bond	31 Oct 67	£1250	0
David	Jones	16 Aug 77	£1130	2
Angela	Mathews	18 May 70	£1180	0
Cherry	King	11 July 72	£1270	1

When you have finished typing in all the data, check the manner in which Access actually displays the date, which, for Simon Smith should be 12/01/71. You actually typed in 12 Jan 71, which is the way we want the date to be displayed in the table.

Changing the Data Type format

We will now ensure that Access displays the date the way we want it. To make any changes to the table we must revert to the Design View of the table.

Basic steps

1 Click the Design View icon .

2 At the Design View window, click in the *Date of Birth* field.

3 In the Field Properties area, select the General tab and click in the Format slot.

4 A drop-down arrow will appear on the right. Click on it and a list will appear.

5 Select the date style and format required.

6 Click the Datasheet View icon ▦ ▾ to return to the table.

7 You will be prompted to save the table. Click Yes to save your changes.

8 The table will re-open Datasheet View. Check the format of the date displayed and it should be as follows: 12-Jan-71.

Note the arrow beside the currently selected field

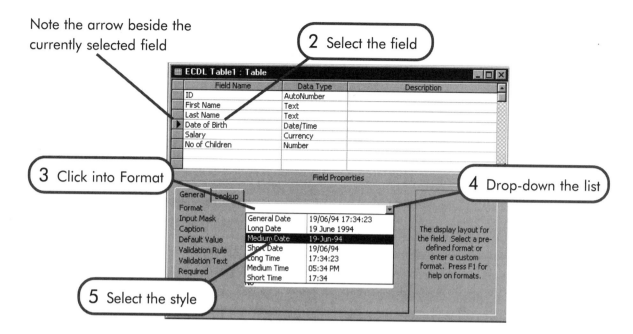

2 Select the field

3 Click into Format

4 Drop-down the list

5 Select the style

7 Save the changes

Adding records

We will now add a further three records to the table. Click once in the empty field as indicated, and type in the data shown below.

George Brown	13 Jan 55	£940	0
Joe Hopeless	01 Apr 81	£890	2
Peter Brown	31 Jul 79	£930	3

Tip

As you enter the data into fields, the table is automatically saved. Access does **not** automatically save changes in Design View, so when working in **all** Design views, periodically save any changes made to the item you are working on.

	ID	First Name	Last Name	Date of Birth	Salary	No of Children
	1	Simon	Smith	12-Jan-71	£950.00	3
	2	James	Bond	31-Oct-67	£1,250.00	0
	3	David	Jones	16-Aug-77	£1,130.00	2
	4	Angela	Mathews	18-May-70	£1,180.00	0
	5	Cherry	King	11-Jul-72	£1,270.00	1
*	(AutoNumber)					

Click here and add the new entry

Print Preview

Before printing a table, it is advisable to preview it.

To do this, open the **File** menu and select **Print Preview**. The preview window will open.

Check that the layout is similar to the example shown below. Should the document open up rather small, click on the Zoom tool (the magnifying glass icon). The cursor will now change to a magnifying glass. Point at the document and click.

- If the glass had a "+" sign within it then the image of the document will enlarge. If it had a "-" sign, the image will reduce in size.

- Select **Close** on the Print Preview toolbar and when the window closes, open the **File** menu and select **Print**. The Print dialog box will now open.

- Ensure the correct printer is selected, set the **Print range** and **Number of Copies** as required then click the **OK** button. The table will then be printed.

Print Properties

Various changes can be implemented from within the Print dialog box. We will not investigate these options at this stage, however you should, at a later stage, read the handbook relating to your printer and practise making changes to the way the document can be printed.

The Print Preview window

Click to zoom in or out

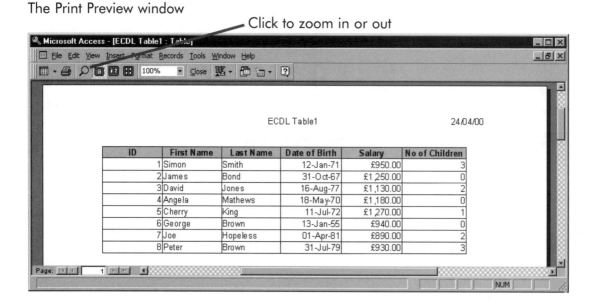

Saving a second copy of a table

You can export the table to another database or save a copy under a different name in the same database. To save the table in the same database, choose **Close** from the **File** menu, then **Save As/Export**, again from the **File** menu.

The **Save As** dialog box will open. Select the option **Within the Current Database as New Name** and the suggested new name will become highlighted.

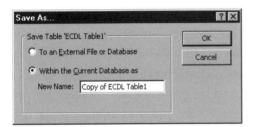

Access will offer you a name based on the current name of the table, preceded by 'Copy of'. In this instance the suggested new name is: *Copy of ECDL Table1*.

You may accept the suggested name, and it is recommend that you do because it is easier to identify the table. However, should you wish to change the name, you will have seen that it is already highlighted – simply type in the new name, and the suggestion will be over-written.

When you have entered the name, click the **OK** button. You will be returned to the Database window, which will now display, in the Tables pane, both copies of the table.

Renaming a table

You may wish to rename a table, or for that matter a Form, Query or Report, at some stage of your work. To do this Close the item and then select it in the database window.

- Right-click on the table and a menu will appear. Select **Rename**.

  Or select the file then use the menu command **File > Rename**.

- The highlighted item will now have a flashing cursor within the name area. Replace or edit the name as required.

In this instance, select the table *Copy of ECDL Table1* and then **Rename**.

- Enter the new name '*ECDL Table2*'. Press **[Enter]** for the change to take place.

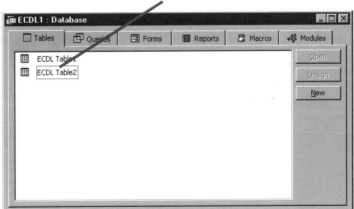

Right-click and select Rename

5: Databases

> ## Tip
>
> **Access remembers the last four databases that were used and stores their names in the File menu. Just click on the name and the database will open.**

151

Indexing records

An *index* is a pointer (an indicator) to a record. The index is placed on a field of a record. For instance if you had a database that was made up of addresses and you regularly run searches on the postal code, then you would place an index on the postal code field.

Indexing makes searches much quicker. The computer only has to read the pointers rather than each record in the database until it finds the required field.

Basic steps

1   Ensure that *ECDL Table1* is open.

2   Click on the Design icon 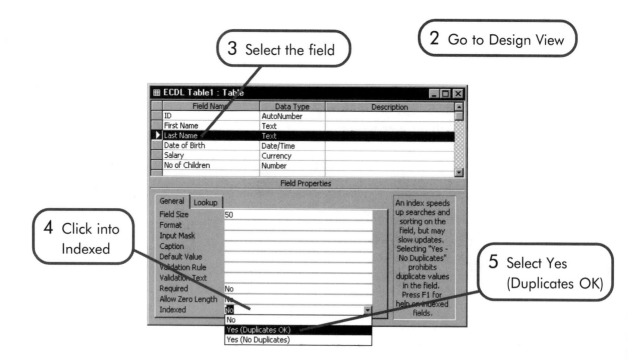 and the table will revert to Design View.

3   Select the field, in this case *Last Name*.

4   In the the Field Properties area, click in the Indexed slot and a drop-down arrow will appear on its right.

5   Select the option: Yes (Duplicates OK). The reason for selecting this, is that there may well be a number of people with the same surnames and had the other option been selected, you would not have been permitted to enter the same name twice. The Yes (No Duplicates) option should only be used where there will always be unique data in the indexed field.

6   Close the table, and save the changes when prompted. You will be returned to the database window.

3 Select the field

2 Go to Design View

4 Click into Indexed

5 Select Yes (Duplicates OK)

Deleting records

Though deleting records is quite a major action to undertake, and should be approached with caution, it is sometimes necessary.

Basic steps

1 If not already open, open *ECDL Table1*.

2 To select a record, click on the grey square at the left-hand side. In this case, select one relating to 'George Brown'.

3 Open the Edit menu and select Delete Record.

Or

4 Right-click on the record and from the pop-up menu select Delete Record. The record will be removed and the lower records rolled up to fill the gap.

5 A prompt will warn you that you are about to delete a record. Click Yes to confirm.

2 Select the record

4 Right-click and select Delete Record

3 Use Edit > Delete Record

ID field numbers are not adjusted when a record is deleted

5 Confirm the deletion

After a deletion, the record indicator shows the correct number of records in the database

153

Sorting records

An excellent feature of databases is that you can present the same information in a variety of ways. You may wish to display the information in the ECDL Table1 with the *Last Name* fields in alphabetical (or in Access terminology, ascending) order. Here's how to do this:

Basic steps

1 Select the field that you wish to sort by clicking on the field name. The column will be highlighted.

2 Click on the Ascending Order icon to sort the names into alphabetical order.

Insert additional records

To build the database up somewhat, we will now add a further two records. Enter this data into the table:

Gary Watson	20 Feb 76	£976	2
Linda Robson	19 Oct 78	£1100	1

Re-sort the table in Ascending order on the *Last Name* field.

1 Select the field to sort by

ECDL Table1 : Table					
ID	**First Name**	**Last Name**	**Date of Birth**	**Salary**	**No of Children**
1	Simon	Smith	12-Jan-71	£950.00	3
2	James	Bond	31-Oct-67	£1,250.00	0
3	David	Jones	16-Aug-77	£1,130.00	2
4	Angela	Mathews	18-May-70	£1,180.00	0
5	Cherry	King	11-Jul-72	£1,270.00	1
7	Joe	Hopeless	01-Apr-81	£890.00	2
8	Peter	Brown	31-Jul-79	£930.00	3
(AutoNumber)					

Record: 7 of 7

2 Click Ascending order

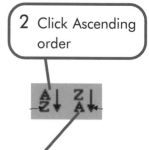

Descending order icon

The table with its additional records, sorted into ascending alphabetical order of the Last Name field.

ECDL Table1 : Table					
ID	**First Name**	**Last Name**	**Date of Birth**	**Salary**	**No of Children**
2	James	Bond	31-Oct-67	£1,250.00	0
8	Peter	Brown	31-Jul-79	£930.00	3
7	Joe	Hopeless	01-Apr-81	£890.00	2
3	David	Jones	16-Aug-77	£1,130.00	2
5	Cherry	King	11-Jul-72	£1,270.00	1
4	Angela	Mathews	18-May-70	£1,180.00	0
10	Linda	Robson	19-Oct-78	£1,100.00	1
1	Simon	Smith	12-Jan-71	£950.00	3
9	Gary	Watson	20-Feb-76	£976.00	2
(AutoNumber)					

Record: 1 of 9

Moving fields

After constructing a table you may realise that you would prefer to have two particular columns adjacent to each other. In this case we require *Salary* to be next to the *Last Name* column. Here's how to move it.

Basic steps

1 Click on the *Salary* header to select the column.

2 Keep the mouse button pressed. You will see a line appear to the left of the column and a small rectangle appear on the lower end of the cursor.

3 Drag to the left, towards the *Last Name* field.

4 As you drag, a black line will appear between the *Last Name* and *Date of Birth* fields. Release the button and the column will move next to the *Last Name* field.

At present, any time that we wish to view details of any of the personnel in our database we have to view this information in a table. The table has only six fields and is reasonably easy to view and use. Imagine if it included their addresses and the names of their wives and children. Not all of the detail would fit into the display window and we would be constantly using the scroll bars to see the detail.

There is an easier way to view the data and it uses *Forms*. We will be looking at those very shortly.

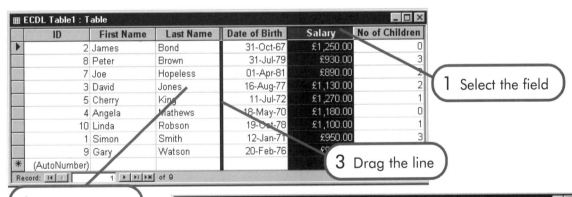

Salary is now next to the *Last Name* field

Modifying the database structure

Deleting fields

It is possible to modify the database structures long after the database was constructed. However such modifications should be carefully considered before being undertaken. This is particularly important when working with relational databases, where knock-on effects, from one table to another, may not have been considered or realised. Modification of smaller sized databases is somewhat easier but still require careful consideration and thought.

If the modification requirement is to remove a field, that is no longer required, select the relevant database table and go into Design View. Select the field and from the menu bar, click on **Edit > Delete Column**.

Access will warn you that deleting the field will result in a loss of data and allow you to either carry on and delete the field or to cancel the operation.

If you decide to carry on with the operation of deleting the field, the selected column will then be deleted. Close the Design View and when prompted save the changes.

If a form was based on the now modified table, if may be necessary to now modify the form and remove items relating to the deleted field.

Inserting fields

It is also possible to insert additional fields in an existing database. It is from the Design View of a table that additional fields are inserted, in a similar manner as when you were constructing the original table. Refer to page 146 if assistance is required. (Inserting additional fields will of course have knock-on effects on such items as Forms, Queries and Reports.)

Creating a form

Forms only display one record at a time, unlike tables, which display multiple records. They are all based on tables, and are not standalone items; therefore to create a Form a table has to be constructed first.

Forms can be constructed using a wizard or from the Design View mode.

Close *ECDL Table1* and save any changes. This will return us to the Database window. To create a form, follow these steps:

Basic steps

1 Click the Forms tab to open the Forms panel. It will be empty at present.

2 Click the New button.

3 In upper pane of the New Form dialog box, select Form Wizard.

4 Click the down arrow in the Choose the table slot and select *ECDL Table1*.

5 Click the OK button.

The Form Wizard

The next window to open will be one of the Form Wizard group.

A wizard is a semi-automated method of creating numerous items within Access and is an ideal way of creating a form for our database.

At various stages, the wizard will prompt you for information to assist with the design and construction of the form. You can often backtrack on a chosen option by clicking the Back button, which will take you back to the previous window.

Forms can be produced without the use of the wizard, by selecting Design View.

Selecting the form fields

At the first panel of the wizard, you select the fields required for the form from the list of those in the table, *ECDL Table1*. You may not want all the fields, though in this case we do.

Fields are selected and moved from the **Available Fields** to the **Selected Fields** pane. They can be handled individually or *en masse*. Fields in the **Selected Fields** pane will be included in the form.

To move a field, select it and click on this arrow.

The table that the form is based on – you can change it if required.

Fields available in the table

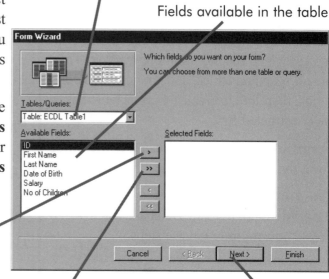

To move all the fields, click the double-headed arrow.

Click Next when you have done

Layout and style

The next two panels determine the layout and background style of the form. Select each option in turn and it check its appearance in the preview area.

● Select *Columnar* in this instance, then click the **Next** button.

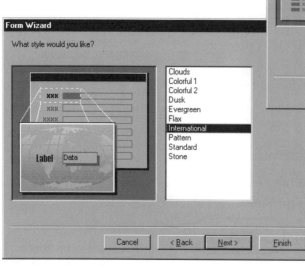

Use the preview to help you choose a background style – the example shows 'International'.

● Select Standard this time, and click the **Next** button.

The final stage of the Wizard prompts you for a name for the form.

- Call this form *ECDL Form1*.
- Do not change the options offered.
- Click once on the **Finish** button.

The wizard will now produce the completed form.

Navigating in Form View

The status line along the bottom of the form is for navigation through the database. It tells you where you are and contains arrow buttons that let you move between the records.

Using the guide outlined here, practise moving through the database and viewing different records. Remember what the various control buttons do, as they will save you considerable time with a large database.

Close the form window. The database window will remain open irrespective of whether you are using a table, form or query. At this stage you should only have the Database window open.

Form name
Record number
Field names
Total number of records
Add new record
First record
Last record
Back one record
Forward one record

5: Databases

159

Using Queries

Queries are used to extract information from the database. They can also be used to create new tables based upon the extracted information, and can perform a number of other tasks, which we will not cover in this book.

Queries are powerful tools and, during this book, we are only going to skim the surface of queries. You should, in time, use the on-line Help for further information on their use.

We will now create a query, which will extract from the database information that matches set criteria. The first stage is to specify the fields that define the criteria and/or are wanted in the results display.

Basic steps

1 Ensure all tables are closed and that the database window is displayed.

2 Open the Queries tab and click New.

3 At the New Query dialog box , select the Design View option and click OK.

4 The Query Design window will open, with the Show Table dialog box in front. Select *ECDL Table 1* and click Add.

5 Click the Close button.

6 Details of the table will appear in the Query Design window. In the Field name list, click on the *FirstName* field, drag it over to the first column and drop it in the Field row. The field's table will appear in the Table cell below.

7 Carry out the same action with the fields *Last Name* and *Salary*, placing them in the next two columns.

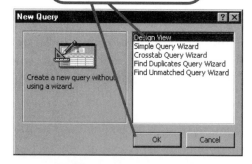

3 Select Design View and click OK

4 Add the table

5 Click Close

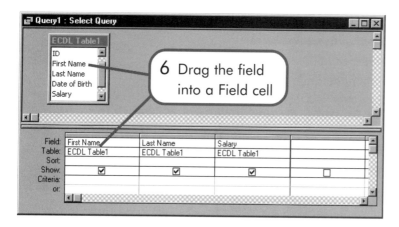

6 Drag the field into a Field cell

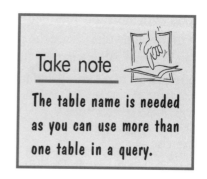

Take note

The table name is needed as you can use more than one table in a query.

As you progress and master Access queries, you may find that you have included a field in a query, which is an important element of the criteria, but you do not want the information, from that field, displayed in the query result.

In the example you will see that there is a check box in the *Show* row. By default Access always displays a tick in the box, but if you decide that the field should not be displayed in the query result, remove the tick. The field will still be used in the query but will not be displayed when the query is run.

- To remove the tick, click on the box. Click again on the same box to restore the tick.

We are going to define the criteria, using operators, to extract all the personnel who have a salary over £1000.

Basic steps

1 Click in the Criteria field under *Salary*.

2 Type a greater than symbol (>), then 1000 and press [Enter].

2 Enter '>1000'

4 Click the Run Query icon, [!], to run the query to produce the results.

Access will now search the database for all personnel with salaries over £1000 and present the information in a table format.

5 records met the criteria

The search was conducted extremely quickly due to the fact that there are only nine records. Access will still produce results very quickly even if it has to search several hundred records.

As we may want to run the query in the future, we will save it. Click the Close button on the top right of the window. You will be asked if you wish to save the query. Click **Yes**.

In the Save As dialog box, type a name for the Query, e.g. *Salary>1000*, then click **OK**.

You will now be returned to the Database window and you will see the query saved in the Queries tab. You may create any number of queries, each one saved under a different name.

Carry out the two short exercises below:

Exercise 1

- Create a query, in Design View, which will extract all the personnel listed in *ECDL Table1* who have 2 children.

  This time you should use the equals (=) sign, not the greater than (>) sign.

- Include the *First Name*, *Last Name* and *No. of Children* fields in the query as well.

- Save the query and call it *Children*.

The result table should look like this:

Exercise 2

- Create another Query, this time to extract all those personnel who were born after Jan 70 and have 3 children.

- Save the Query as Jan70.

The result table should look like this:

Reports

At some stage during the use of the database you will require some, or all, of the content to be printed for distribution. You could simply print a copy of the table but a table may be quite large and it does not lend itself to easy reading.

The best way to print data is to produce a report. You can created one using a wizard or do it yourself using the Design mode. In this instance we are going to create a report based on *ECDL Table1* using a wizard.

Basic steps

1 Close and open tables, forms or queries.

2 In the Database window, open the Reports tab and click the New button.

3 In the New Report dialog box, select *Report Wizard*.

4 Select *ECDL Table1* from the drop-down list of tables and queries, then click OK.

❑ The Report Wizard will start. The first stage is to select the fields which will constitute the report.

5 Ensure that the correct table name is displayed in the Tables/Queries slot.

6 Select *First Name* then click on the arrow to move it into the Selected Fields pane.

7 Repeat with *Last Name* and *Salary*.

8 Click the Next button.

9 The Wizard will ask you if you want to add any grouping levels. Experiment with this later. For now, ignore it and click Next.

The wizard will present you with a dialog box from which you may sort the records. We will only concern ourselves with the *Salary* field.

10 Select *Salary* from the drop-down list. The report will be sorted on the Salary field in ascending order.

11 Click Next.

The next step gives you options on the layout of the Report. Do you want the fields laid out in Columnar or Tabular form, the paper orientation set to Portrait or Landscape?

12 Leave the settings as Tabular and Portrait and click Next.

Leave the tick in the box. It will not affect us this time, but you should know of this facility.

13 The next step offers style options. Select *Soft Gray* and click Next.

At the last step there are a number of options:

● A report title. Access has already allocated it a name based upon the table name. Type in a new name, *Salary*.

● You can Preview the report. This is the default setting – select it.

● You can have the on-line Help displayed while working with the report. Do not select this option.

14 Having set the title, do not make any other changes. We want to see how the report looks before going any further. Click Finish and the Preview window will open.

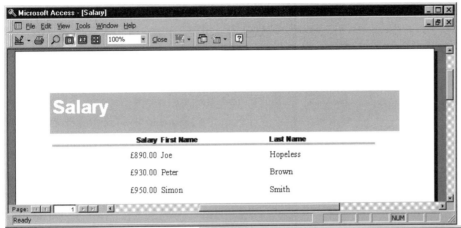

There is a problem with the layout. The *Salary* and *First Name* columns are too close and we need to make an adjustment.

Click the Design View icon to change to the Design View where we may make the changes. We need extra spacing between the *Salary* and the *First Name* fields.

2 Click on each field in turn

Both fields are selected

Basic steps

1 Hold down [Shift] – this will allow you to make multiply selections.

2 Click on the *First Name* field in the Page Header section, then click on the *First Name* field in the Detail area.

3 Release [Shift]. Both fields will be selected.

4 Point to the centre handle in either field. When the cursor changes to a double-headed arrow, drag it to the right for half a square then release the mouse button.

Resizing handles

4 Drag the handle to resize

Tip

Use the background squares as guides when moving and resizing objects.

5 On the Toolbar, click the down arrow to the right of the View icon.

6 From the drop-down list, select Print Preview.

6 Choose Print Preview

❑ The image will revert to Print Preview and you will see that there is a reasonable amount of space between the two fields.

Before spacing adjusted

Salary	First Name
£890.00	Joe
£930.00	Peter

Salary	First Name
£890.00	Joe
£930.00	Peter

After spacing adjusted

7 Close the Print Preview window and save the changes, then close the Salary report.

Printing the report

After previewing your report, you will probably want to print it.

Basic steps

1 Select the Reports tab on the database window and then select the *Salary* report. You can print the report without actually opening it.

2 Open the File menu and select Print. The print dialog box will now open.

3 Ensure that the correct printer has been selected. Your display will most likely be different to that shown here.

4 You can, if required, only print one page or all the pages within the report. As our report only has one page you need not make any changes in the Print Range area.

5 If you require more than one copy, you adjust the figure in the Copies area to that which you require. In this case leave it at 1 copy.

6 Click the OK button. After a short period of time your printer should start up and begin printing the report.

3 Select the printer

5 Set the number of copies

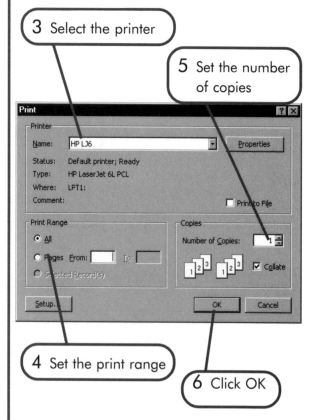

4 Set the print range

6 Click OK

Exporting a database

Earlier in the book we saved a copy of the *ECDL Table1* and renamed it *ECDL Table2*.

During the course of saving the table ECDL Table1 we were offered the opportunity to export it to another database. This is what we are about to do. We are going to use the existing database *ECDL1* and create a new database, which we will call *ECDL2*.

A table can be exported with data or as 'Definition Only'. 'Definition Only' means that just the table structure, without any data, is exported. A table structure may well be suitable for a series of tables, usually with just minor amendments. It is more logical to copy a table and make small changes to it rather than spend considerable time creating a new table from the beginning.

Basic steps

1 Close all tables, etc. then close the Database window.

2 From the File menu select New Database.

3 In the General tab of the New dialog box, select the Blank Database icon.

4 Click OK. The File New Database dialog box will open. Remember a database must be saved before you can start work on it.

5 If not already selected, in the Save In slot, select the *Floppy disk A:* drive.

❑ If you are using the same floppy disk that you saved the previous database on, you should now see *ECDL1.MDB* listed.

6 Type *ECDL2* in the File name slot.

3 Select Blank Database

5 Select the A: drive

6 Enter the name

4 Click OK

7 Click Create

7 Click the Create button.

8 The dialog box will close and the database window for the *ECDL2* database will open. We do not want this at the moment so close it, then select File >Open Database.

9 At the Open dialog box, ensure that the Floppy disk drive is selected, then open the database *ECDL1.mdb*.

10 At the *ECDL1* Database window, click the file *ECDL Table2*, then click the Tables tab.

11 Open the File menu and select Save As/ Export.

12 Select To an External File or Database

12 At the Save As dialog box, ensure that the option: *To an External File or Database* is selected and click OK.

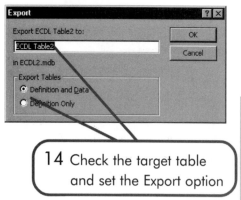

14 Check the target table and set the Export option

13 A further dialog box will open, offering you the option of which database to export the table to. As we only have two databases and the table is already part of *ECDL1.mdb*, the choice must be to export it to *ECDL2.mdb*. Select this by clicking Export.

14 At the Export dialog box , confirm that the target database is *ECDL2*, and select the option *Definition and data*. Access will now copy the table to *ECDL2.mdb*.

15 Close the *ECDL1* Database window, then select File > Open Database and choose *ECDL2.mdb*.

16 Go to the Tables tab and you should find a copy of the *ECDL2* table present.

17 Open the table *ECDL Table2* and add the following records :

Raymond Jennings	21 Mar 65	1350	3
Marie Rosenbloom	30 May 56	1175	2
Frank Robinson	25 Sep 57	1225	5
Richard Carson	15 Dec 60	1452	4
Clare Steine	21 Dec 61	1245	2
Rosemary Kline	15 Jul 59	1236	0

16 Go to Tables

17 Open the new table

Changing the table structure

You can add new fields to a database if necessary. In this case we want to be able to list personnel by gender. A simple way to do this would be to add another field to the table which we will call *Gender*.

Basic steps

1 With *ECDL Table2* open, select the Design View icon on the Toolbar.

2 Place the cursor in the blank line under the field *No of Children*. Type in '*Gender*' and in the Data Type column accept the default setting of Text.

3 Switch to the Field Properties pane , either by pressing [F6] or by clicking into the required item slot.

4 We are only going to enter a single letter in this field. Delete the default setting of 50 and type in '1', then close the window. Save the changes when prompted.

5 Back at the database window, open *ECDL Table2*. The new field, *Gender*, will appear after *No of Children*. You may have noticed that even though we set the field size to one, there clearly is more space in the field displayed.

6 Place the cursor in the *Gender* field for 'Simon Smith' and type in 'Male'. You should find that you will only be permitted to enter the first letter as the field size is controlled to one character only.

7 It would make more sense to have the *Gender* field after the *Last Name* field. Move it now – see page 153, if you have forgotten how to do this.

8 Fill in the *Gender* column appropriate to the names in the *First Name* field.

ID	First Name	Last Name	Gender	Date of Birth	Salary	No of Children
1	Simon	Smith	M	12-Jan-71	£950.00	3
2	James	Bond	M	31-Oct-67	£1,250.00	0
3	David	Jones	M	16-Aug-77	£1,130.00	2
4	Angela	Mathews	F	18-May-70	£1,180.00	0
5	Cherry	King	F	11-Jul-72	£1,270.00	1
6	George	Brown	M	13-Jan-55	£940.00	0
7	Joe	Hopeless	M	01-Apr-81	£890.00	2
8	Peter	Brown	M	31-Jul-79	£930.00	3
9	Raymond	Jennings	M	21-Mar-65	£1,350.00	3
10	Marie	Rosenbloom	F	30-May-56	£1,750.00	2
11	Frank	Ronbinson	M	25-Sep-57	£1,250.00	5
12	Richard	Carson	M	15-Dec-60	£1,452.00	4
13	Clare	Steine	F	21-Dec-61	£1,245.00	2
14	Rosemary	Kline	F	15-Jul-59	£1,326.00	0
*	(AutoNumber)					

ECDL Table2: Table

Record: 2 of 14

ECDL Table2 after the Gender field has been added and data entered

169

Exercises

1: Create a query to list all females

Create a query that will output a list of females in the table. Include these fields in the query:

- First Name
- Last Name
- Gender

The criteria should be on the *Gender* field.

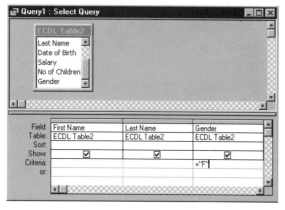

Run the query and you should find that it will return a table like this, with five females listed.

First Name	Last Name	Gender
Angela	Mathews	F
Cherry	King	F
Marie	Rosenbloom	F
Clare	Steine	F
Rosemary	Kline	F

Return to Design View and modify the same query to include the *No of Children* field. Run the query, and you should see this result.

First Name	Last Name	Gender	No of Children
Angela	Mathews	F	0
Cherry	King	F	1
Marie	Rosenbloom	F	2
Clare	Steine	F	2
Rosemary	Kline	F	0

Save the query as *Females*.

2: Create a query to list all males

Create another query showing all males with children, this time including the fields:

- First Name
- Last Name
- Gender
- No of Children

Click on the **Show** check box to remove the tick. Access will use the criteria set in the *Gender* field but will not display the Gender column in the query results table.

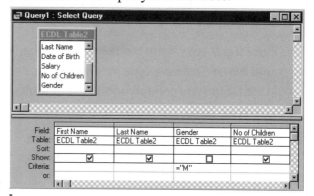

When run, the query result table should look like this:

First Name	Last Name	No of Children
Simon	Smith	3
James	Bond	0
David	Jones	2
George	Brown	0
Joe	Hopeless	2
Peter	Brown	3
Raymond	Jennings	3
Frank	Ronbinson	5
Richard	Carson	4

Save this query as *Males*.

170

3: Create a report based on a query

Close all the windows that may be open except for the database window. Select the **Reports** tab then click on the **New** button.

The new report is to be based on the query that you recently created and saved as *Males*.

Use the Report Wizard to create this new report. It should include all fields, with no grouping, but sorted on Last Name, and with the default layout and style settings. Accept the suggested name for the report – *Males*.

Preview the report, and make any adjustments if necessary, then print out a copy of it.

4: Delete some records

Open the table *ECDL Table2* and delete the records for the following personnel:

David Jones and *Frank Robinson*.

Close the table, re-run the *Males* report and then click on Preview.

Compare the print copy from the first time that the report was run – before any records were deleted – with the Preview copy now on screen. The screen copy reflects the changes as a result of the action of deleting the two records.

What this indicates is that the report will always run the query on which it is based, so that the information displayed is always current or as reflected in the database.

Integration with other applications

Information stored in an Access database can very easily be copied or linked to any of the other applications to be found within the Microsoft Office 97 suite.

A table can be inserted into a Word document, an Excel spreadsheet or a PowerPoint presentation.

It is also possible to import data from the above mentioned applications into Access.

Exchange data between Excel and Access

To analyse the data from a Access table in Excel, you can use features in Access to export the data automatically to a new Excel workbook. You can also import worksheet data into Access. If you want only a few records from a Access table, you can open the table and copy and paste selected records into Excel.

If you're working in Excel and have installed and loaded the AccessLinks add-in, you can convert a list to a Access database file. For more information about add-ins use the on-line Help.

You can create a PivotTable to analyse data from Access just as you would from any external data source.

Using the online Help system

You can use the normal procedures for Help, as described on page 135, with one major exception. Access has a much more interactive **[F1]** Help function.

This **[F1]** key will assist you in a number of circumstances when designing a database. Follow these steps to discover the differences between the Access **[F1]** key and that for the other Office applications.

Basic steps

1 Open the table *ECDL Table 2* in Design View.

2 Place the cursor in the *First Name* field and press [F1]. The Microsoft Access Reference dialog box will open and display details relevant to the selected field, in this instance the FieldName property.

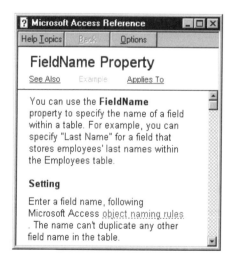

3 Close this box and you are returned to the Design View of the table.

4 Select the *Date of Birth* field.

5 Place the cursor in the Format slot in the Field Properties pane, and press [F1]. The Microsoft Access Reference dialog box will open again, this time displaying the Field Properties relevant to the *Date of Birth* Data Type, i.e. Date/Time.

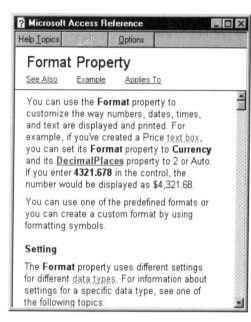

6 Close all dialog boxes.

Clearly the Access F1 online Help is much more interactive and does not require any input from you other than to select the appropriate field when in Design View.

Sample paper 5: Databases

1	Name three data types used in a database.	1. 2. 3.
2	What is meant by the term 'pointer' and what is the correct name for it?	
3	When running a query a certain field may be required for the query to function, but is not required to be displayed in the query result. What simple action will ensure that the field is not shown in the query result?	
4	What is the name of the view used to create the structure of a new table?	1. Datasheet View 2. Import Table 3. Design View
5	A field of the Text Data Type has a default length setting of 50 characters. What is the maximum length allowable in Access?	1. 100 2. 150 3. 200 4. 255
6	Describe the main difference between a table and a form.	Table: Form:
7	List the four main database components that the user can create and use.	1. 2. 3. 4.
8	If you decide that a certain field in a table has an incorrect default setting, what view would you use to change the setting?	1. Import Table 2. Datasheet View 3. Design View

9	When working in any of the Design views, Access automatically saves any changes made. True or False?	1. True 2. False
10	List the two sort options available in Access.	1. 2.
11	In simple terms, describe what a Wizard is?	
12	List two examples of a database in everyday use.	1. 2.
13	When viewing data, in Form view, what navigation controls does the user use to select different records within that database?	
14	You have completed a report and are ready to print the document. What feature is available to you to view the report before printing it?	
15	You see the following criterion in a query: =>250 In simple terms describe the condition the criterion has set.	

6 Presentations

What is PowerPoint?

PowerPoint is an application, in the Microsoft Office 97 suite, which is used to create presentations, also known as slide shows, to impart information to a wide variety of audiences.

- It can be used to produce a slide show on screen that will run unattended.
- PowerPoint has a number of preformatted templates to simplify the construction and design of presentations.
- PowerPoint has a range of coloured backgrounds and text formats that will suit most situations and presentations, but which can be easily adjusted to suit particular needs.
- You can also prepare a presentation that will be given using 35mm colour slides.
- PowerPoint can produce banners and overhead projector transparencies, both in colour and black and white.
- Sound and video clips can be incorporated into a slide show.

In this chapter we will create an on-screen presentation, and introduce some of the drawing and other tools to be found in PowerPoint.

Starting PowerPoint

There are a number of ways to start PowerPoint. In this book we will use the Start button method. You, in time, will develop your own preferred method of starting programs.

Basic steps

1 Click on the Start button on the Taskbar.

2 Click on Programs on the pop-up menu.

3 A sub-menu will open to the right. Click on Microsoft PowerPoint. The application will open and run. You will then be presented with the PowerPoint screen.

2 Point to Programs

3 Select PowerPoint

1 Click Start

A guided tour of the screen

When PowerPoint is first started, the opening display should be as shown below. The name of the presentation is normally displayed in the Title bar. As none is currently open, no name is displayed.

The PowerPoint dialog box opens on the initial start-up, and offers a number of options:

- **AutoContent wizard** brings up a number of templates from which you may select a topic suitable to your requirements.
- **Template** offers you a series of coloured background Presentation Designs.

- **Blank presentation** will open up another dialog box from which you may select from a number of slides with an outline structure, but no backgrounds or text. It is this selection which we will make shortly.
- **Open an existing presentation** will open a previously saved presentation.

The **OK** button will carry out your selection, whereas the **Cancel** button will close the dialog box without carrying out any action based on the selection.

Leave the dialog box open for a moment.

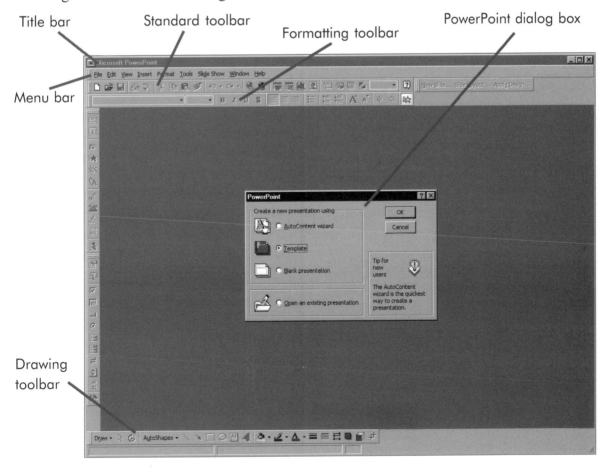

Title bar   Standard toolbar   Formatting toolbar   PowerPoint dialog box

Menu bar

Drawing toolbar

Slide show scenario

Our objective is to create a number of slides to introduce a new member of staff to a department within the company. This new member is in fact the new departmental head, hence the presentation to a particular department.

This company, *Tec-com*, specialises in computer training for companies and the general public, and recently underwent quite a major expansion investment. Previously *Tec-com* only ran courses on common applications, but have now started computer networking courses.

The original staff were not qualified in networking, and a whole new department was formed to teach these courses. This has resulted in an increase in trainers who specialise in networking, with back-up and support staff. The company has also invested a considerable sum in a number of different network systems, which will allow the students to install and run various types of networks during the courses.

Jonathan Morgan Richards is the new employee. He prefers to be known as 'Jon'. He is 38 years of age and is married to Katherine, known as Kathy, who works as a consultant website designer. They have been married for ten years and have two children, an 8-year-old son and a 6-year-old daughter.

Jon has a degree in Computer Sciences and went on to qualify as a Certified Novell Engineer, a Microsoft Systems Certified Engineer, and a Microsoft Certified Professional in a number of MS Office applications.

Jon completed a number of years' working in the field, designing and supervising the installation of various types of network systems, during which time he found himself instructing support staff on how the network was assembled and functioned.

Jon realised that he had a particular skill in teaching network subjects and then spent some time attending college to learn more of the art of instruction, and was later to gain the Microsoft Certified Trainer qualification.

Jon was initially employed in the UK with a large multinational company; Samson's United Systems as a systems engineer. During this time he was assigned to the company's US office, where a year later he was headhunted by an American organisation; Anglo-American International, who specialised in developing remote computerised control systems.

After two years Jon found he much preferred the hands-on experience of networking and people contact and returned to the UK where he joined the staff of one of the newly converted banks, Collins plc, as deputy systems engineer. It was during this time that his interest in teaching was re-awoken and he gained the Microsoft Certified Trainer qualification.

Jon was approached by a specialised recruitment agency and asked if he would be interested in a career divergence, retaining the network aspect but with an emphasis on training. Jon agreed to the offer and that brings us back to the current situation, the briefing.

Keep this information close to hand, as we will be referring to it within the presentation.

Creating the presentation

We are going to create the presentation using a number of the preformatted slides available in PowerPoint. Before we went into Jon's background we left PowerPoint open and displaying the dialog box.

Basic steps

1 Select the Blank presentation option and then click the OK button.

2 At the New Slide dialog box select the *Bulleted List* slide, then click the OK button.

3 PowerPoint will now open the slide, and we can edit the slide to our requirements.

❑ Before we proceed any further we will save the presentation.

4 Use the menu command File > Save. The Save As dialog box will open when saving the file for the first time.

5 We are going to save the presentation to a floppy disk. Click on the down arrow, and select the 3½ Floppy (A:).

6 Enter '*Jon's Intro*' into the File name slot.

7 Click the Save button.

Tip

You can often make a selection by double-clicking on an item, eliminating the need to click OK.

1 Select Blank presentation

2 Select a slide layout

Click to add title

• Click to add text

3 The slide ready for editing

5 Select the A: drive

6 Enter the name

7 Click Save

Editing the Slide Master

There are a number of sub-headings that we want on all the slides, and the way to do this is to edit the Slide Master. This is where you should put any graphics or text that you want on every slide. It also sets the default text formats and styles, colours and backgrounds.

We require the following on each slide:

● The company name: Tec-com.

● The date the presentation was created.

● The slide number.

Basic steps

1 Use the menu command View > Master > Slide Master to go into Slide Master View.

2 Double-click over the <date/time> text to highlight it, then from the menu bar select Insert > Date and Time.

3 At the Date and Time dialog box, select a date/time format and click OK.

❑ You will be returned to the Slide Master view. The last item that we wish to add to the slide is the company name.

4 Double-click on the <footer> text to highlight it. Type in 'Tec-com plc'.

5 Click on <#> in the Number area, then use View > Header and Footer.

6 At the Header and Footer dialog box, select the Slide tab.

7 Tick Slide number then click Apply to All.

2 Select then use Insert > Date and Time

Click to edit Master title style
Title Area for AutoLayouts

Click to edit Master text styles
– Second level
  • Third level
    – Fourth level
      » Fifth level

4 Type in the text

Object Area for AutoLayouts
Date Area   Footer Area   Number Area

5 Click then use View > Header and Footer

Date and Time

Available formats:
13/03/00
13 March 2000
13 March, 2000
March 13, 2000
13-Mar-00
March, 00
03-00
13/03/00 13:52
13/03/00 1:52 PM
13:52
13:52:24
1:52 PM
1:52:24 PM
Update automatically (insert as field)
OK
Cancel

3 Select a format

6 Open the Slide tab

Header and Footer
Slide | Notes and Handouts
Include on slide
☑ Date and time
  ○ Update automatically
    13/03/00
  ○ Fixed
☑ Slide number
☑ Footer
☐ Don't show on title slide
Apply to All
Apply
Cancel
Preview

7 Tick Slide number and Apply to All

❑ You will not be able to see the numbering until you return to Slide View. PowerPoint will insert a slide number in a similar way as Word does for page numbering.

8 Save the changes.

9 Select View > Slide to return to Slide View.

The detail that we have just entered on the Slide Master will now appear on each slide in the presentation.

Titles and bullet lists

We are now ready to enter the title for the first slide. At the top of the slide is the Title area.

> Click to add title

Click into here and the prompt will be replaced by a flashing cursor in the middle of the area.

Type 'Staff Briefing'.

Note that the font is Times New Roman, size 44 pt, and that the text is centred in the area. You can change any of these format settings if so desired. We will retain them at this stage.

Click anywhere on the slide, outside the title area and the display should change to that as shown below. Notice that title area no longer has an outlined box around it.

> Staff Briefing

We will now move on to the lower area of the slide where that we are going to type in the aims and objectives of the briefing. This section is preformatted as a bullet point list.

You can change the style of the bullet point from the deafult ● to that of an arrowhead, a hand and many other symbols.

> • Click to add text

The bullet points are formatted in font type and size – in this case Times New Roman at 32 pt.

Click at the prompt and type in '*Aims and Objectives*'. Press **[Enter]** and a new bulleted line will automatically be inserted.

'Aims and Objectives' is the title line for this area. Press **[Tab]** once and the cursor will be indented to the right and the text size reduced, in this instance to 28 pt. Type in '*Introduction of departmental head*'.

Press **[Enter]** to insert a new line. PowerPoint always inserts new lines at the same indent level as the previous one. Press **[Tab]** to further indent the text. Note that the bullet point has changed.

Type in: '*Jon M Richards*' and press **[Enter]**. PowerPoint has inserted a new line based on the previous line, but this time we want to return to that of the line starting '*Introduction*'.

On the Formatting toolbar are two icons which can increase ⬥ (promote) or decrease ◀ (demote) the indent. Click ◀ and the indent will decrease, moving one tab setting to the left.

Type in: '*Introduce Departmental Organisation*', and press **[Enter]** once.

Retaining the same settings type in: '*Instructional Programme*'. Do not press **[Enter]**, or you will end up with an empty bullet line.

Staff Briefing

• Aims and Objectives.
  – Introduction to departmental head.
    • Jon M Richards.
  – Introduce Departmental Organisation.
  – Instructional Programme.

23 March 2000   Tec-complc   1

That is all we are going to place on the first slide. Save the changes

Insert a second slide

We are now going to insert a second slide.

● Use the command **Insert > New Slide** and the New Slide dialog box will open.

● Select the *Text & Clip Art* slide. This slide is preformatted with a title area, a bullet area and a graphic placement box.

Tip

You can either double-click on the slide image or select it then click **OK**.

Click in the title area and enter '*Staff Briefing*'.

Click in the bullet area and type '*Jonathan Morgan Richards*'. This is too wide for the box and '*Richards*' will be automatically moved to the next line. We need to make the box wider.

● Select the Bullet list area and point to a resize handle.

Drag a resize handle

● When the cursor changes to a double-headed arrow, drag to the right until all the words fit on the one line. Release the button.

The frame for the bullet list may have overlapped the Clip Art frame. If so, adjust the left frame size for the Clip Art box in a similar way.

Carry on typing in the text, as shown in the example below. Ensure that you indent the relevant sections, as shown.

Staff Briefing

• Jonathon Morgan Richards
  – Prefers to be called Jon
  – 38, married with 2 children
• Qualifications:
  – Computer Sciences degree
  – Microsoft MSCE and MCP
  – Microsoft Certified Trainer
  – Novell CNE

23 March 2000   Tec-complc   2

184

Inserting a graphic

We should now to insert photograph of Jon, but as you won't have a copy of his picture, we'll cheat a little and use Clip Art.

Basic steps

1 Double-click on the Clip Art box on the slide.

2 At the Clip Gallery dialog box go to the Clip Art tab and find an image with more than one person in it. The one used here comes from the *People at Work* category.

3 Select the image and click on the Insert button.

2 Look in the Clip Gallery

Click on the name to switch category

3 Insert the image

4 If the image is too big or too small, right-click on it and from the pop-up menu select Format Picture.

5 Go to the Size tab

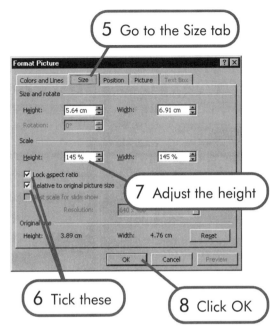

7 Adjust the height

6 Tick these

8 Click OK

5 At the Format Picture dialog box, click on the Size tab.

6 Tick the Lock aspect ratio and Relative to original size boxes.

7 Adjust the Height as necessary. The width will automatically adjust in relation to it.

8 Click the OK button to close the box.

6: Presentations

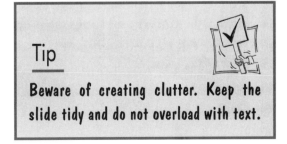

Tip

Beware of creating clutter. Keep the slide tidy and do not overload with text.

The Drawing toolbar

We are going to add a circle around the image to indicate which of the figures is Jon. The Drawing toolbar has the tools we need.

- If you do not have the Drawing toolbar visible, select **View > Toolbars** and click on **Drawing**.

Line — Circle/oval

- Click on the **Circle/oval** icon and the cursor will change to a thin black cross. Place the cross over the image. Hold **[Shift]** down, and drag the cursor down to the right to draw a small circle.

Holding **[Shift]** while drawing ensures that you to draw perfect circles every time. **[Shift]** also functions with other drawing tools. Experiment with these later.

You may now find that your image has been partially obscured by the circle. This is due to the fact that the circle has a *Fill* applied to it. This may be white or a colour, possibly green. If this is the case, we will now correct it so that we can see the image below it.

- The circle should still be selected – if not reselect it. Right-click and from the pop-up menu select **Format AutoShape**.
- At the Format AutoShape dialog box, ensure that the **Colors and Lines** tab is open.
- Click the **Fill Color** down arrow and select *No Fill*. Click **OK** to close the box.

You should now be able to see the image below the circle. Adjust the position of the circle to sit around your image tidily.

We need to draw a line from the end of the name 'Richards' to the new circle.

- Click on the Line icon. Place the cross cursor just behind the name 'Richards', click and drag the cursor to the edge of the circle. Release the mouse button.

Save the changes. The final appearance of the slide should resemble the example below.

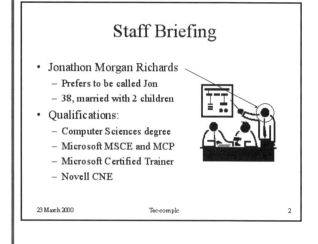

Insert a third slide

We still have to include Jon's employment history, so we will use a new slide. Select **Insert > New Slide** and select a *Bullet list* slide layout.

This slide has a title area and a larger bullet list area.

Complete the slide with all of the detail as shown in the example below.

Save the changes.

Staff Briefing

• Jonathon Morgan Richards
  – Employment History
    • 1987 - On leaving university, recruited by multi-national company: Samson's United Systems
    • 1993 - Joined Anglo-American International, worked stateside for two years
    • 1995 - Returned to UK and joined the newly converted bank: Collins plc
    • 1999 - Tec-com

23 March 2000   Tec-comple   3

Adjusting and editing objects

Graphics, list boxes, organization charts and other objects that can be inserted onto slides can all be handled in similar ways.

First click onto the object, selecting it. It will be given a grey outline with sizing handles at the corners and mid-sides.

● Move the mouse cursor over the object and the cursor will change to a four-headed arrow, which indicates that it can be moved around to a different position on the slide.

● Move the mouse cursor over any of the sizing arrows and it will change to a double-headed arrow, which indicates that it can be resized as appropriate to your requirements.

If you wish to change any of the detail on the object, simply double-click on it. You will be returned to the Clip Gallery, Organization Chart (see next page) or whichever other application was used to create the object. It can then be replaced or edited as required.

Organization Chart

We have now reached the stage of the presentation when the organisational structure is about to be discussed. PowerPoint has a slide layout designed to create organisation charts with the minimum of effort and fuss.

● Use **Insert > New Slide** and from the **New Slide** dialog box select the *Organization Chart* layout slide. You should be get a slide like this:

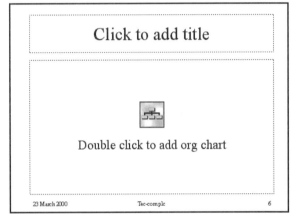

● In the slide title area type: '*Staff Briefing*'.

● Double-click on the icon and the Organization Chart window will open. Adjust it to a good working suitable size.

We are not going to make any changes to the existing chart at this stage, but will simply replace the '*Type name here*' prompts with other text.

To enter text into a box, click in it. The box will open out like this. We will only use the first two lines. 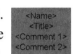 Ignore the remaining lines – they will disappear when the box closes.

To move from one line to another, e.g. from the *Name* to the *Title* line, use **[Tab]**.

Start by clicking on the uppermost box and type in the detail as shown in below. Continue until all the detail has been entered.

The Chart window

Add notes or headings

Change the Zoom level

Use these icons to add boxes to the chart

Inserting additional boxes

In retrospect, it would be advantageous to inform the staff of the changes and additions to the company, so we will add another two boxes. These are both at subordinate levels.

- Select the **Subordinate** icon on the Chart Toolbar. The cursor will change to ⊏⊐.

- Point to the box that you want to attach it to, in this case, the *Jan Meinard* box and click. The new box will attach itself as shown here.

- Click into the new box and when it opens out add the detail as shown below.

Repeat to add a box beneath *Colin Brooks*.

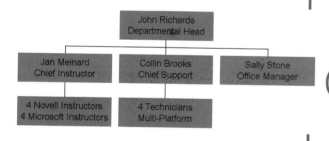

Deleting boxes

If you place a box on the chart and later decide that you do not want it, you can delete it easily by selecting it and pressing **[Delete]**.

Saving the chart

The chart will be saved as part of the presentation, but it is also possible to save it as a separate file, which can be used in other applications, for example Word or Excel.

Basic steps

1 On the Organization Chart menu bar select File >Save Copy As.

2 At the Save Chart dialog box, click on the down arrow and select the 3½ Floppy (A:)

3 Type in the name: *Tec-com Chart*.

4 Click the Save button.

5 Reselect File and click on Update Jon's Intro, then close the chart window. You will be returned to the normal PowerPoint window, with the chart on display.

Save the changes to the presentation. This is particularly important at this stage. **Do not** save any changes from this point onwards unless specially instructed to do so.

Experiment with resizing, moving and re-opening the Chart window. **Do not** save any changes that you may make. Close the presentation and click **No** when prompted to save changes.

Slide Sorter View

We are now going to re-open the presentation. You may recall that Office applications remember which files were used recently. Open the **File** menu and you will find the presentation listed. Click on the name to open it.

The presentation will open up at Slide 1. We want to move to Slide 4 and this is the ideal opportunity to introduce the Slide Sorter View.

In the lower left-hand area of the presentation window is a set of icons.

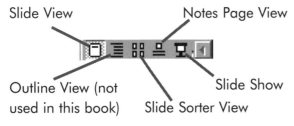

Slide View

Notes Page View

Outline View (not used in this book)

Slide Sorter View

Slide Show

Click on the Slide Sorter View icon.

Slide Sorter View displays all of the slides in a miniature format. It is here that you can change the position of slides or insert a new slide in the appropriate position within the presentation.

First save the presentation, then practise the following.

- Select Slide 4, that is the one that contains the chart. When selected, the image will have a thick border surrounding it.

- Place the mouse cursor over the image, left-click and hold. The cursor will change to an arrow with a small rectangle attached to it.

- Keeping the left button depressed, drag the cursor to the left until it is between the first and second slides, then release the button.

Slide 4 will now be Slide 2.

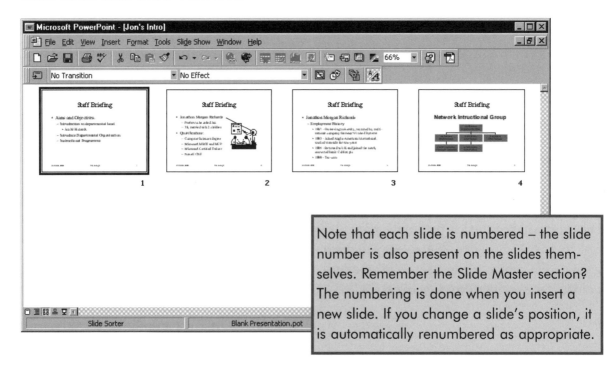

Note that each slide is numbered – the slide number is also present on the slides themselves. Remember the Slide Master section? The numbering is done when you insert a new slide. If you change a slide's position, it is automatically renumbered as appropriate.

You may have noticed that as the cursor was dragged to the left and when it arrived between the various slides, a vertical line appeared between the slides. This indicates that you may, if so desired, release the button and the slide will be moved to that location.

Practise the above actions, but **do not** save any changes at this stage.

When you feel confident moving slides as described above, Close the presentation but **do not** save the changes when prompted.

The reason for not saving the changes at this stage is that we wish to retain a common presentation throughout the book, and there is still more to be done.

- Re-open the presentation and move to the fourth slide, then double-click. So that we may modify the chart, double-click on it to open the Organization Chart.

- With the chart window open, highlight the chart title and type in 'Network Instructional Group'.

- Reselect the chart title then use **Text > Font** to open the Font dialog box.

- The Font Size is only 14, rather small for our requirements, so change the Size to 36 and Font style to Bold.

- When the selections have been made, click on the **OK** button. Select **File > Update Jon's Intro**, then select **File > Exit and return to Jon's Intro** for the changes to be implemented. You are now returned to the Slide View of the chart slide. Save the changes.

Tip

You can return from Slide Sorter View to Slide View simply by double-clicking on the appropriate slide image.

Running a slide show

At this stage it would be well worth checking the overall appearance of the presentation when run as a slide show. A slide show is the combination of all the slides assembled in the presentation, shown in full screen size, without any of the menu bars, toolbars, etc. being visible.

Slides can be either manually changed or set to run automatically. We will use the manual method during this presentation.

Click the Slide Show icon. The show will start at Slide 1. It is now up to the presenter to decide when to move onto the next slide.

To move onto the next slide, either:

· click the left mouse button, or

· click the icon in the lower left of the screen. A pop-up menu will appear and it is from here that you may control the slide show.

Practise both methods.

If you want to stop the show before reaching the end, you can select End Show from the pop-up menu or simply press **[Escape]**.

Now that we have previewed the show we realise that we have forgotten to include any details of Jon's family. Also the slide background was rather plain – just white. We can improve this easily because PowerPoint has a number of preformatted background designs.

Before we proceed, use **File > Save** to ensure the file is completely up to date. Another reason for saving at this stage is that we are going to experiment with a background design, but we will not retain it, as this book is published in black and white and some of the designs are rather dark and would not print particularly well.

Click to open the control menu

192

Applying a design

Go to Slide 1 of the presentation.

To apply a design use **Format > Apply Design**. The **Apply Design** dialog box will open. It is here that the design selections are made.

We will only to discuss the basics in respect of selecting a design. Experiment later to learn the other features and options available.

In this instance select *Dads Tie.pot*, and click the **Apply** button. This design will give you a good idea of the colour aspects. Remember **do not** save any changes.

If your slide show is to be run from an overhead projector, practise the show on the projector.

Projectors usually have a background colour, and this colour, often blue, may cause colour clashes with your display. Practice may not always make perfect, but it will help eliminate embarrassing moments for the presenter.

Formatting individual slides

It is possible to format individual slides with different colour displays and though we are not going to cover this option here, you should be aware of it. To format an individual slide, select it then use **Format > Slide Color Scheme...** Experiment with this at a later date.

We are now going to close the presentation and when prompted **do not** save the changes, because we want to return to the stage before any designs were applied.

Re-open the presentation and move on to the next page where we will insert the slide relating to Jon's family and make some changes to the font, font size and apply some colour.

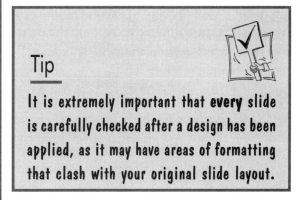

Tip

It is extremely important that every slide is carefully checked after a design has been applied, as it may have areas of formatting that clash with your original slide layout.

The folder in which PowerPoint stores all the default designs.

Design names – the currently selected design is *Dads Tie.pot*. The *.pot* extension identifies a file as a presentation design.

Miniature display of the design

Inserting a Text Box

Change to the Slide Sorter View – it is from here that we will insert the additional slide.

The new slide is to be inserted between Slides 3 and 4. Click between them and a thin vertical line will appear.

Use **Insert > New Slide** and at the **New Slide** dialog box select the *Bulleted list* slide.

Double-click on the new slide to return to Slide View, where we will start entering the family details (see page 180).

In the slide title area type '*Staff Briefing*'.

We want an additional, separate text box, but where will it fit without overlapping the existing two areas? At the moment it cannot fit without overlapping, so we are going to resize the bullet list area first.

● Click anywhere on the bullet list to select it – the resizing handles will appear around it.

The easiest way to change the size is to use the handles. As we only want a little more space between the two existing areas, point to the top, middle handle. When the cursor changes to a double-headed arrow, drag it down to just below the words '*Click to add text*' and release the button.

> • Click to add text

This is the level to which the box should be re-sized.

We will now insert a new text box between the two existing areas.

● Select ▤ the Text box icon from the Drawing toolbar. The cursor will change its shape to a thin inverted cross, ⊥.

● Place the cursor roughly mid-way between the two existing boxes and then press and hold the left mouse button. Drag the cursor down and to the right to create the additional text box, as shown in the example below, and then release the mouse button.

Be careful at this stage not to click outside the text area just inserted, because if you do, the text area will simply disappear. This is due to the fact that there is no text inside it, and PowerPoint thinks that it is no longer required and deletes it.

Staff Briefing

> • Click to add text

Tip

Use the spellchecker regularly.

194

Fonts and borders

When you insert a new text box, PowerPoint will automatically format it as left justified, i.e. with the text in the extreme left of the box. You can confirm this by the location of the flashing cursor.

The font type and size is the same as that used throughout the presentation, i.e. Times New Roman, at 24 pt. We will return to this shortly.

Type in '*Jon's Family*'.

If you investigate the three text boxes, you will find that each has the same font type, i.e. New Times Roman, but each is a different font size.

The slide title is set to 44 pt, the new text box is set to 24 pt while the bullet list is set to 32 pt. It is convention that the slide title is the largest of the three. However, the new text box font size is too small. We want it to be the same size as shown in the bullet list.

Changing font size and type

- Click and drag over the text '*Jon's Family*' to highlight it.
- Right-click on the text and from the pop-up menu, select **Font**.
- At the **Font** dialog box change the size to 32
- To change the font type click on the **Font** down arrow and select a new type.
- Click the **OK** button when you have done.

Changing the alignment

With the text still highlighted, click on the **Centre** icon, on the Formatting toolbar. The text will now change its location and become centred in the text box.

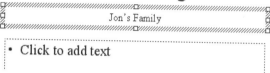

There is still more to do to this text box. Highlight the text again and this time click on the **Bold** icon on the Formatting toolbar.

Borders

You can, if you wish, include Borders around the various types of boxes used in PowerPoint. We will include a Border around the text box that we recently created. Follow the sequences outlined below:

Select the text box by clicking in it. Remember that when a text box is selected, a hatched outline appears around it.

With the text box selected, right-click over it and a pop-up menu will appear.

Select **Format Text Box**.

The Format Text Box dialog box will open. Ensure that the **Colors and Lines** tab is open.

Adjust the settings in your dialog box to match those shown above. Click the down arrow besides **Color** and select *Automatic*.

When you have done, click the **OK** button.

You will be returned to Slide View. The text box should still be selected – click anywhere on the slide to deselect it. You can now clearly see the border surrounding the box.

The box is too wide for the amount of text it contains. We will now re-size it.

Staff Briefing

Jon's Family

• Click to add text

Click once within the box area. The outline will change and the resizing handles appear.

Point to the middle handle on the left border of the box. When the cursor changes to a double-headed arrow, drag the cursor to the right. The box will shrink as you drag. Continue to adjust the size until you are satisfied with the way the text appears within the box – leave a little space at each end of the text.

The box appears to have moved to the right side of the slide. It has not actually moved – it was simply resized.

The box should at this stage still be selected. Move the cursor up and over the lower border line of the box. When it changes to a four-headed arrow, drag it to the left until the box appears central below the slide title.

Staff Briefing

Jon's Family

• Click to add text

Save the changes. Select the bullet list and enter the text, complete with all formatting, as shown in the example below.

Once you have completed typing in all the text, Save the changes.

Staff Briefing

Jon's Family

- • Katherine, prefers to be called Kathy
  - – Consultant Web Designer
  - – Married to Jon for then years
    - • Two children
    - • Richard 8 years of age
    - • Hazel 6 years of age

23 March 2000   Tec-compk   4

Practice slide show

We are now at the stage to do a re-run of the slide show to check the layout and presentation of the slides. This time use the menu command **Slide Show > View Show** to run the show.

On viewing the slide show, we see that the chart, on Slide 5, appears rather small, so we are now going to increase its size somewhat.

- Ensure that the chart slide is on display.
- Select the chart by clicking over it and the resizing handles will appear around it.
- Point to the top left handle, and drag up to the left. Release the button when the border is about 3cm from the slide's left edge.
- The chart is still not quite large enough. Repeat the same actions, only this time drag the lower right handle to the lower right of the slide.
- Release the button when the handles are about 1.5 cm from the right slide edge.
- Re-run the Slide Show to ensure that you are happy with the final size and positioning on the slide.

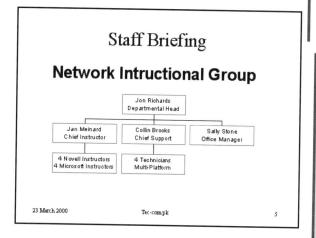

The fourth slide, with Jon's family details, has an oddity on it. The first bullet item has the text '*Katherine, prefers to be called Kathy*'.

The name 'Katherine' is okay size-wise, but the rest of the text should be in a smaller font.

- Highlight the text '*prefers to be called Kathy*' and change the font size to 24 pt.

Save the changes to the presentation.

That completes the overall presentation. However, to practise one or two other procedures, we are going to insert a sixth slide.

Insert a new slide after Slide 5. Select the *Title only* slide.

In the slide title type '*Practice Slide Only*'.

Switch to Slide 2, which has the image that we used to identify Jon to the audience.

Select the image and Copy it, either by clicking the **Copy** icon on the Standard toolbar, or by right-clicking on the image and selecting **Copy**.

Switch to Slide 6 and click the **Paste** icon on the Standard toolbar. The image will be placed on Slide 6. Practise moving and sizing it.

Save the changes to the document.

Tip

If you wish to run the complete presentation, as a Slide Show, always ensure that you are looking at the first slide in the presentation, otherwise PowerPoint will start the Slide Show from whichever slide is being displayed at that time.

Integration with other applications

Information in a PowerPoint presentation can easily be copied or linked to any of the other applications in the Microsoft Office 97 suite.

Data can be inserted in a Word document, an Excel worksheet or an Access database.

It is also possible to import data from the above mentioned applications into PowerPoint.

Exchange data between Word and Powerpoint

This is provided as an 'interest only' section. You do not have to carry out the exercise if you don't want to. You should, however, be aware that it is quite easy to use existing data, from other applications, in a PowerPoint slide show.

You can use text created in other programs to make a new presentation or add slides to an existing one. The text you import is in Outline format. This format is beyond the scope of this book – use the on-line Help to learn about it.

When you import text, PowerPoint uses the outline structure from the styles in the document. Heading 1 becomes a slide title, and heading 2 becomes the first level of text, and so on. If the document contains no styles, PowerPoint uses the paragraph indentations to create an outline. In plain text documents, tabs at the beginning of paragraphs define the outline structure.

Practice

It will only be possible to practise the following if you have already completed the module on Word.

To insert a Word table:

● In Slide View, display the slide you want to add a table to.

● Click the Word Table icon, on the Standard Toolbar, then drag to select the number of rows and columns you want.

● Enter the data in the table cells.

● Use the Word tools and menus to format the table. For example, to add borders to the table, use **Table > AutoFormat**.

● Click outside the table to return to PowerPoint.

Take note

You can easily create a presentation from an existing Word outline. In Word, open the document, point to **Send To** on the **File** menu, and select **Microsoft PowerPoint**.

Tip

PowerPoint comes with a slide layout that includes a placeholder for a table. To use this layout, look for the Table slide in the New Slide dialog box.

Sample paper 6: Presentations

1	Explain how to add the date to the Footer of a slide so that it appears on each slide.	
2	List three examples of preformatted slides	1. 2. 3.
3	List two of the PowerPoint Views	1. 2.
4	You have created a chart in PowerPoint, the chart can be used in Microsoft Word and Excel. True or False?	1. True 2. False
5	You are about to insert a new slide. What is the quickest method of selecting a slide from the New Slide dialog box?	
6	List the two methods that can be used to resize an object on a slide.	1. 2.
7	List the two methods, discussed in the book, to move from one slide to another while running a slide show.	1. 2.
8	Briefly describe what a Design is when applied to a presentation.	
9	Once a Design has been applied to a series of slides, it is impossible to change the design for an individual slide. True or False?	1. False. 2. True.
10	When a chart has been created and placed on a slide, it cannot be modified. True or False?	1. True. 2. False.
11	List three examples of any AutoShapes.	1. 2. 3.
12	The drawing tools found within PowerPoint are common to other Microsoft applications, such as Word or Excel. True or False?	1. True. 2. False

7 The Internet

The Internet

This module will introduce you to the Internet and the World Wide Web and demonstrate a number of key features and uses of both.

The module has been split into two sections: *The Internet*, which will show you how to navigate the World Wide Web to find information and Web sites of interest; and *Electronic Mail*, which will demonstrate how to send and receive mail using your computer.

The Internet section has been designed using Internet Explorer versions 4.0 and 5.0. If you are using a different browser, you may find some differences between the screenshots in the exercises and what you see on your computer. However, the concept of the exercise and results should be the same.

Similarly, the Electronic Mail module has been designed using Outlook Express version 4. If you are using a different version of Outlook Express or different e-mail software you may find some differences.

If you are unsure what software version you are using, please seek advice.

The background

Although the Internet has only become popular in recent years, it was designed back in 1969 by the US Department of Defense. For many years it remained an academic and military network, but in the 1990s people started to realise its commercial potential. As we enter the new millennium it has approximately 100 million users worldwide, and this is increasing exponentially.

The Internet actually consists of many networks round the world passing data to each other using a protocol called 'TCP/IP'.

- **TCP/IP (Transmission Control Protocol/Internet Protocol)** – developed in 1974 by Kahn and Cerf and allows computers to communicate over the Internet.

No single organisation manages or polices the Internet, and any individual can access, and post information to the Internet as long as they have the necessary equipment.

The Internet is changing the way we live – the way we communicate with each other, the way we find information, the way we shop and the way we do business.

Information delivered via the Internet can be current and dynamic. For example, a Web site dedicated to news, sport or weather can be updated every few minutes providing information as it happens, unlike traditional media.

But taking your first steps on to the Internet can be a puzzling experience. You will have heard all about Web sites on TV and in magazines telling you how simple the Internet is to use. There are now many journals and magazines dedicated to the Web, along with many guidebooks. But for the first-time user it can be difficult to cut through the technical jargon.

This module will show you how to take your first steps on the Internet, and prepare you for making the most out of its services. However, the best way to find out what is available over the Internet will be for you to explore it.

Getting Started

Before we discuss what the Internet can do for you, let us establish *how* you get on the Internet. Internet access these days is much simpler than it used to be, but you will still need these:

A computer – this would seem obvious, but we are now seeing the introduction of Internet-compliant televisions, allowing you to connect your television to your telephone line, and 'surf' the Internet via this medium.

A modem - this will enable your computer to 'talk' over the Internet via your telephone line. Modems are available at different speeds and prices, so when deciding which to buy you need to balance the cost of the modem, against the cost of telephone calls that may be longer when using a slower modem.

- **Modem (MOdulate/DEModulate)** – converts digital data into analogue signals to pass down the telephone line, and then back into data at your PC.

A telephone line – note that most lines will not allow you to make voice calls while you are logged on to the Internet, so you may wish to consider having a separate telephone line, for use with the Internet. An alternative is to install an ISDN line, which can handle both voice and data and can communicate at a far quicker rate.

- **ISDN** (Integrated Systems Digital Network) – a digital telephone line.

An account with an ISP (Internet Service Provider) – this allows you to connect to the Internet via the ISP's communication equipment. Some ISPs charge a monthly fee for the service, but many offer a free dial-up service where all you pay for are the costs of the telephone call – usually at Local Rate charges. A new breed of ISPs is emerging offering a totally free service using a 'Freephone' telephone number. When deciding which provider you wish to use you need to balance level of service against the cost.

Once you have all the items above, and have decided upon which ISP to use, access is simple. Your ISP will either provide you with all the information you require to set-up your Internet connection, or more likely will supply you with a disk that will automate the whole process.

Take note

You will find that on occasions the Internet may be a little temperamental, or appear to run slowly. This may be due to the site you are visiting, or the volume of traffic, so patience is also required during your early days of exploration.

Surfing the Internet

The most popular part of the Internet is the World Wide Web (WWW) – which allows people to publish pages, or Web sites, from anywhere in the world. A Web site can be read at any time by anybody, anywhere.

The phrase 'surfing the Internet' is generally used to describe an undirected type of Web browsing in which the users jumps from page to page on the WWW whimsically, as opposed to searching for specific information.

The best-known Web sites are large-scale professional services packed full of information, entertainment and with the capability to purchase items on-line – anything from buying flowers, to booking a holiday, to ordering concert tickets. However, anyone can be a publisher on the Internet. Many Web sites are the work of small groups or individuals talking about their hobbies or interests.

So how do you get to these sites? The Web is viewed through a '*browser*'. These are free, and if your PC was not supplied with one you can easily obtain one on a disk from your ISP.

● **Browser** – the software you use to view the World Wide Web. We are using Internet Explorer in this book, but other browsers are available, such as Netscape Navigator.

Logging on to the Internet

You connect, or *log on*, to the Internet via your ISP. To log on you need to open your browser by clicking on Internet Explorer's icon 🅔 or by selecting it through your Programs menu.

If your browser is configured to automatically connect to the Internet upon opening, you may be asked for a *Username* and *Password*. These will have been supplied by your ISP when you first registered with them.

HitWeb – a new company with new solutions for business

You can configure your computer to save your Username and Password, so that every time that you log on you do not have to type them in. There are security implications though and anyone who has access to your computer, can use the Internet without your permission.

During logon, a dialog box displays the progress while your Username and Password are being verified. Once your computer has successfully completed this, you will be on-line and able to access the Internet and the World Wide Web

Interflora – a established organisation, but one that is making excellent use of the Internet

The Tate Galleries – old masters, new masters in a slick, modern setting

Finding a site

Web site addresses (or URLs) are everywhere these days – in newspapers, on television adverts and even on your breakfast cereal packets. Although addresses may look daunting, you will soon get the hang of reading and remembering them.

- **URL** (Uniform Resource Locator) – the address of a Web site.

Addresses usually begin with '**http://www**' followed by more letters, dots and slashes. Most browsers do not need you to type in the '**http://**' part; you can just start with the '**www**'.

- **HTTP** (HyperText Transfer Protocol) – the method used by browsers to view and download Web pages. That's why Web site addresses begin with 'http://'

Following the 'www.' you will then usually find the name of the organisation or company which publishes the site. For example, you would expect IBM computers to start '**http://www.ibm.**', or the Wembley site to start '**http://www.wembley.**'.

The end of the URL indicates the type of organisation that publishes the site. For example:

- International businesses end with '**.com**' (commercial)
- Non-commercial organisations end '**.org**'
- Network and Internet specialists use '**.net**'

These are referred to as *global domains*.

Where sites are country-specific the extension is followed by an international country code. For the United Kingdom this is '.uk'. Other examples include '.de' for Germany, '.us' for USA, and '.fr' for France. Every country has their own international country code.

Therefore within the United Kingdom

- Commercial sites end '**.co.uk**'
- Government sites end '**.gov.uk**'
- Academic sites '**.ac.uk**'
- Non-profit sites use '**.org.uk**'

Sometimes the URL will have a further part that works in the same way as a sub-folder in Windows Explorer. For example, at the Hitweb site '**www.hitweb.co.uk**' there are a series of pages with information about a company called Perkins Slade. These pages can be found by going to the Hitweb site and using the site navigation to find the appropriate pages, or alternatively and much simpler, the address '**www.hitweb.co.uk/perkins-slade**' will take you directly to the required pages.

Take note

Web sites are constantly being updated and changed. If at any time, you are directed to a site, and when that site opens you find that the first page is different, don't worry. Some organisations change the appearance of their sites every couple of months.

Practice session

The best way to understand the Internet is to explore it. Let's get on-line.

Basic steps

1 On your desktop, double-click on the icon that connects you to the Internet. This is probably 'Internet Explorer', but may be 'Netscape' or some other, depending on which browser you are using.

2 Your computer will now connect to the ISP, and open the default home page.

3 In the address line at the top of the browser type 'www.bmw.com', and hit [Enter].

4 There will be a slight delay while the computer searches for this site. When the page opens, select English and you will be taken to BMW's English section.

5 The page will load a bit at a time with text being downloaded first followed by the images. If the images are big it may take many seconds, or even a few minutes to complete. You will know when the page has finished downloading, as the message 'Done' will appear in the Status line of your browser.

Exercises

● Find the Web site of Hitweb, a UK based business.

● Find the Web site of the ECDL foundation, an international business.

● Find the Web site of the RNIB, a UK based charity.

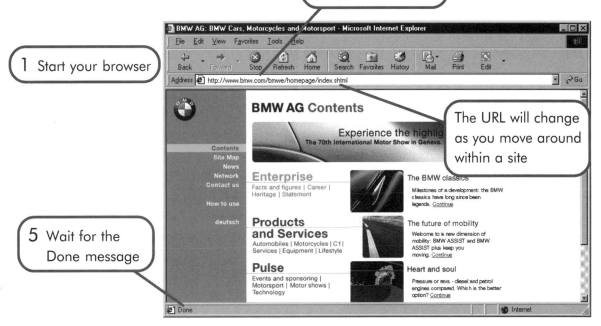

3 Type the address

1 Start your browser

The URL will change as you move around within a site

5 Wait for the Done message

7: Communications

Home Page

Every time you start your browser, it will head for your 'home' page. This is the Web site you have chosen as your regular starting point. When using Internet Explorer, the default home page is '**www.msn.com**', but you can change this to a page of your choice.

If you get lost on the Internet, click the **Home** button in your browser to go to your home page.

Basic steps

1 Go to 'www.bcdtraining.co.uk'.

2 When the page opens, open the View menu (I.E. 4.0) or the Tools menu (I.E. 5.0) and select Internet Options.

3 At the Internet Options dialog box select the General tab.

4 In the Home Page area, click Use Current. BCD's URL will appear in the Address slot.

5 Click OK.

❑ The BCD site is now your home page and will appear every time you start your browser or click its 'Home' button.

Exercises

● Set 'www.hitweb.co.uk' as your home page.

● Visit another site, and then return to your home page using the 'Home' button.

3 Select General

1 Go to BCD

4 Click Use Current

5 Click OK

2 Select Internet Options

The BCD Group

★ ECDL ★

Introduction
Syllabus
FAQ
Log Books
BCD
Course Demo

presents the ECDL - the international standard of competence for computer users

BCD is an accredited ECDL Test Centre and accredited IT for All partner. ECDL is promoted in the UK by the British Computer Society and supported by the European Commission via the European Fund.

Favourite sites

As you start to use the Internet on a regular basis, you will want a quick way of getting to your favourite sites without having to remember their addresses. One of the most useful browser tools is 'Favorites' (or 'Bookmarks' in Netscape), which stores site addresses.

When you arrive at a site you want to bookmark, add it to your Favorites. When you want to return to it, you can then simply click it in the Favorites list. If your list starts to get out of hand, you can organise it into folders – one for news, one for your hobby, and so on.

Note: The screenshots are from Internet Explorer (IE) 5. If you are using IE 4, you will find that the dialog boxes are slightly different, but still allow you to carry out the instructions and complete the exercise.

Basic steps

❏ Adding Favorites

1 Find the Web site of 'madesimple.co.uk'.

2 Open the Favorites menu and click Add to Favorites'.

3 At the Add Favorite dialog box, enter *'Made Simple books'* in the Name slot and click OK.

❏ Organising Favorites

4 Open the Favorites menu again and select Organize Favorites. The Organize Favorities dialog box will open, listing your folders and favourite sites.

5 Click on *'Made Simple books'*, then click the Move to Folder button.

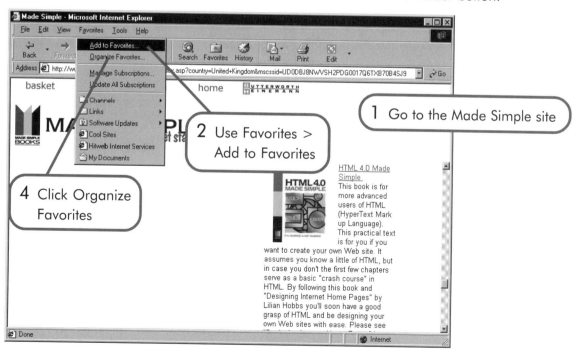

209

6 At the Browse for Folder dialog box, select the '*Cool Sites*' folder, then click OK.

7 Back at the Organize Favourites dialog box., click on the '*Cool Sites*' folder. When the folder opens, you will see '*Made Simple books*' is now in it.

❑ Using Favorites

8 The next time you wish to visit this site, click on Favourites, select the '*Cool Sites*' folder, then double-click on '*Made Simple books*'.

Exercises

● Go to the Website 'www.itforall.org.uk' and add it to your list of favourites, named 'IT for All'

● Organise your list of favourites so that 'IT for All' is kept in the 'News and Weather' folder.

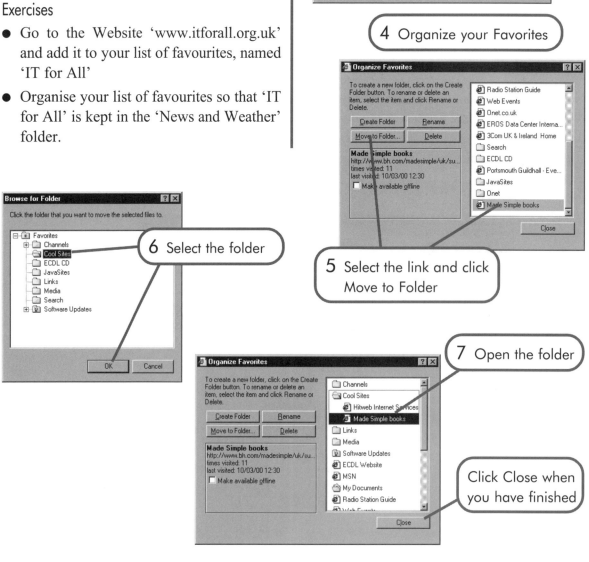

3 Enter the name

4 Organize your Favorites

6 Select the folder

5 Select the link and click Move to Folder

7 Open the folder

Click Close when you have finished

Surfing

You need to get to know your browser buttons to become more proficient in your surfing.

- **Back** takes you to the Web page you were looking at last. You will be surprised how often you want to retrace your footsteps.

- **Forward** use this if you do go back, then want to return to where you just came from.

- **Stop** click this if you wish to stop downloading a page that you selected either by accident, or are having trouble loading.

- **Refresh** will download the current page, all over again. This is useful if some images have failed to load properly, or if the page is likely to be updated frequently.

- **Home** as we discussed in the last section, takes you to your home page.

- **Favorites** open your Favorites list in the same way as the Favorites menu command.

- **Search** opens the default search engine within your browser window. We shall discuss search engines later in this document.

- **History** provides a listing of all the sites you have visited over a set period of time, allowing you to click on the URL and be taken directly there.

In addition you can return to a site you visited the last time you were on the Web by clicking on the arrow at the end of the box containing the current Web site address. This will drop-down a list of the Web sites you have looked at most recently. You can click on the one you want, to go directly there.

Most browsers have many other tricks you can use to help you navigate the Net – experiment with the controls to find out extra features.

Your browser may have other icons to open related applications

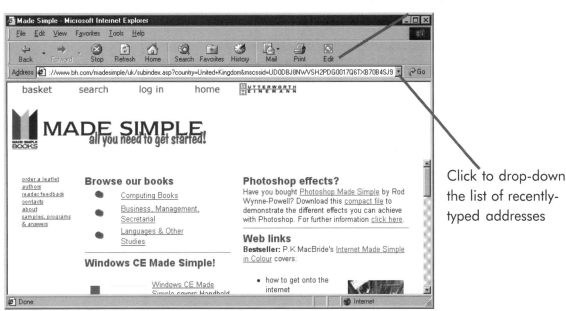

Click to drop-down the list of recently-typed addresses

Search engines

Many newcomers to the Internet worry about how they are going to find the addresses of Web sites that might be of interest to them. There is no equivalent of a phone book for the Internet – but you will find it remarkably easy to find what you are looking for.

The nearest you will get to a telephone book is one of the major search engines. These have indexed millions of Web pages to allow you to track down topics by typing in keywords.

Try it out on the Ask Jeeves search engine that features on the Hitweb site.

- Go to **www.hitweb.co.uk** and when the page is loaded, click on '*Links*' then on '*Help Me*' to reach the page shown below.

- Type into the search box some relevant words to describe what you are looking for.

- Ask Jeeves will return a long list of Web sites that match your criteria, with the closest matches at the top of the page.

Now you can surf to your heart's content.

You may find that you get too many results, or that you are not getting the information you require. It is important that your search is specific as possible, for example:

- If you require information about your nearest branch of Boots the Chemist, don't simply type 'Boots' as this will return boot and shoemakers from around the world! Instead you should use keywords such as 'Boots', 'Chemist'', Pharmacy', 'UK', etc.

- Most search engines have an 'Advanced' feature, which will allow you to include and exclude certain criteria, or search with strings of words, e.g. 'Boots the Chemist'.

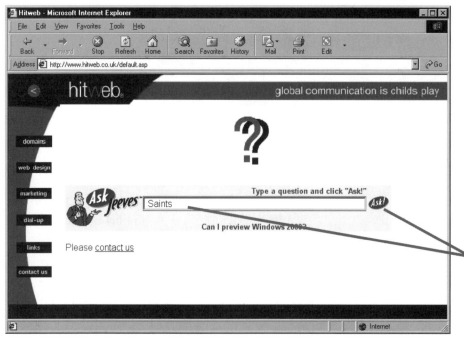

Type one or more relevant words and click Ask

Retrieving information from the Internet

On occasions you may find information on a Web site that you wish to save to your computers hard disk for future reference. This can be achieved in a number of ways.

Download

There are thousands of sites on the Internet offering all sorts of files you can download. Popular examples would be the MP3 music files, movie trailers and the latest games demos. You can download files from any Web site simply be finding the file and following the instructions contained on the Web page. When you start to download, you will usually encounter this dialog box.

After you have made your selection and clicked the OK button, this dialog box will appear.

You can stop a download at any time, simply by clicking the **Cancel** button.

● Create a folder and call it '*Download*' and always save your downloads in it.

Downloading files can take some time and transfer rates can vary widely. Try to download during off-peak hours, that is early in the morning or late at night.

If you are interested in attempting a download, try the following Web sites:

> http://www.download.com
> http://www.shareware.com

Take note

Files downloaded from the Internet may contain computer viruses. See Chapter 1 for further information on viruses.

Save an image

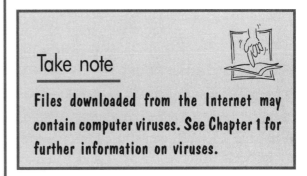

To save an image that is on a Web page, simply right-click on it and select **Save Picture As** from the pop-up menu.

You will need to specify which folder on your hard disk you wish to save the image to.

It's easy to copy just about anything from the Internet, but sometimes it may not be legal.

Before you copy any text or images, which you intend to use on your own Web page, make sure that you have permission from the original author. If you fail to do this, you could find yourself with a costly legal problem.

Save a Web page

To save the Web page you are currently viewing, first click the left mouse button on the page – this is known as 'anchoring' – then open the **File** menu and select **Save As**.

The page will be saved in HTML format and can be viewed at a later stage using your browser. It should be noted that this would not save any graphics on the page.

Print a Web page

To print the Web page you are viewing you again need to 'anchor' the page, then open the **File** menu and select **Print**.

Note that many sites are constructed using 'frames', so that what appears to be a single Web page is actually constructed from several components. After selecting 'Print' you may be asked whether you want to print all the frames, or just the one that you 'anchored' to.

Exercises

- Go to the www.hitweb.net site, anchor on the home page, and then print the page.

- Go to the www.bcs.org.uk site, anchor on the home page, and then save in your download folder or on your 'A:' drive. Using Windows Explorer, find the saved page, and then by double-clicking on the file name, view the page.

Hyperlinks

As you move from Web site to Web site, you will get used to clicking on text, pictures and graphics to link through to more information or other Web sites. These links are known as 'Hyperlinks'.

- **Hyperlinks** are connections between Web pages, or different parts of the same page, and provide a shortcut method of navigating around the Internet.

Links are usually designed to stand out from the rest of the page. A text link will be highlighted in some way – often in <u>blue underlined text</u> when the rest of the text is black. Links might also take the form of graphics, or even pictures. With practice, you will soon work out how to spot a link.

When you have discovered a link on a page, the 'Cursor' on the screen will change, as it moves over the link, from an arrow into a little hand, with the finger pointing upwards. Click the mouse button, and the browser will whisk you off to another site or page.

Exercises

- Go to the Ask Jeeves search engine at www.hitweb.co.uk, as described previously, or the Yahoo search engine at www.yahoo.com
- Enter a keyword of your choice relevant to a subject you are interested in
- Select the result most appropriate to the topic you are interested in from the list returned.

Five sites of interest

Going online is an adventure to start with. Surfing the Web is great fun and can be very informative. But you will soon discover that the practical uses of the Internet will make it increasingly central to all aspects of your life.

Communicating with family, friends and business associates by e-mail is quicker, cheaper and easier than writing letters.

Online shopping is taking off as companies prepare to do more and more of their business over the Internet. If you want you can do all your Christmas shopping from the comfort of your home. Sometimes, with such as CDs, books or even a new computer, you will be offered extra discounts for buying online.

Your children will use computers at school and can use the Internet to help with homework and make e-mail pen-friends in other countries.

Detailed below are our top five sites to visit, showing you what the Internet can do for you. Take the opportunity to visit the sites, and also search for a few of specific interest to yourself.

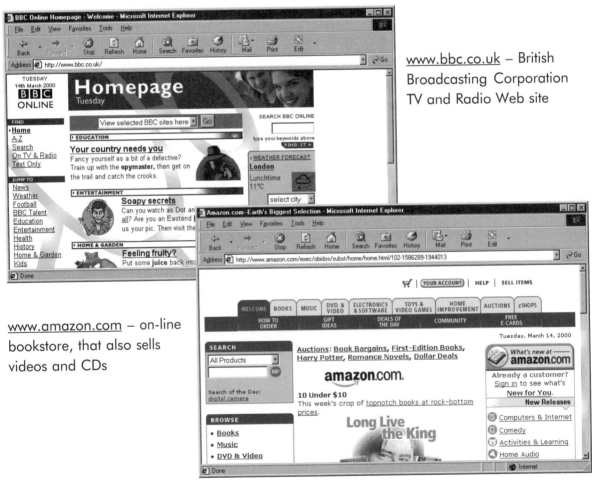

www.bbc.co.uk – British Broadcasting Corporation TV and Radio Web site

www.amazon.com – on-line bookstore, that also sells videos and CDs www.itforall.org.uk – DTI 'IT for All' initiative with information for the beginner

www.hants.gov.uk – a local government Website, as recommended by Bill Gates!

www.virgin.com – a commercial site, the Virgin company's Website

217

Web site development

Once you have spent a few hours looking at other people's Web sites, you might decide you want one too. The following pages will show you how to build a very basic Web page. *Note that you will not be required to know this as part of your test.*

Large, commercial Web sites that have good design and complex functionality are usually designed by professional Web development companies. It is recommended that if you require a Web site for a professional organisation, that you approach one of the many Web development companies that specialise in all aspects of site design.

However, most ISPs these days provide you with free Web space so that you can create your own personal Web site.

Web pages are created using a system called HyperText Mark-up Language, or HTML.

To make best use of your free Web space, you will need to learn the basics of HTML. It is simple to learn and with practice you can create Web sites quite easily.

HTML works by inserting tags into text. So an HTML file can be written entirely in a normal word processor or text-editing program, like Word, Notepad or Wordpad.

Each tag is surrounded by angle brackets like this < >.

Browsers display Web pages by reading through the text of an HTML file, and obeying the formatting commands given in the tags.

We are going to create a Web page in Notepad. Click onto the **Start** button and then select **Programs**, **Accessories** and **Notepad**.

You will be presented with a blank page ready to beginning typing in your HTML code.

Before we start, we will save the file. Open the **File** menu and select **Save As**. When the Save As dialog box opens, switch to the download folder and type the filename '*My web page.htm*'. It is important to include the extension '*.htm*' as this specifies the file is HTML and tells your computer that it should be viewed via a browser.

Using Notepad, enter the following text:

```
<HTML>
<HEAD>
<P><TITLE>My first web page</TITLE></P>
</HEAD>
<BODY>
<P><H1>Welcome to my home page</H1>
</P>
<HR>
<P>There's not much here at the moment, but
I am busy learning more HTML so that I can
create the web site <I>of my dreams.</I></P>
<P>You can e-mail me by <A HREF=
"mailto:me@myaddress.com"> clicking here
</A></P>
</BODY>
</HTML>
```

You can now view the Web page you have just created in two ways.

Using Windows Explorer, locate the file '*My web Page.htm*' in the folder you have just saved it to, and double-click on the file name.

Alternatively, open your Internet Explorer window, and in the Address bar type the full path of where your file is, e.g. *C:\My Documents\Exercises\My web page.htm,* and hit **[Enter]** on your keyboard. You should now be viewing the Web page.

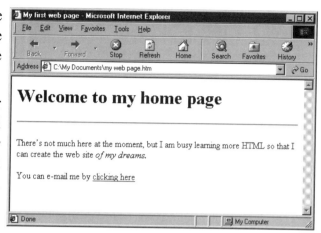

HTML tags

You will see that most tags have to be opened and closed. The closing tag has a forward-slash inserted before the word, so it looks like this: </HTML>.

A Web browser will format everything between two matching tags in a particular way.

Each tag in the exercise on the previous page has a function.

<HTML> shows this is an HTML document.

<HEAD> identifies the document header – it will not appear in the display, but gives each page an identity.

<TITLE> gives the page a name. The title will appear at the top of the browser, and will identify a page in Favorites lists.

<BODY> is the main part of the document – the part that will appear in the browser.

<H1> is a heading, size 1 – the biggest text the browser will display. Everything between the <H1> and </H1> will be displayed as a large title on the page.

<HR> draws a horizontal line across the page. It does not need a closing tag.

<P> is to show the start of each paragraph.

<I> </I> makes text between them *italic*.

<A...> creates a hyperlink to another page or e-mail address. Note that after the 'A' is more code that tells the browser to make a link to a specified e-mail address.

Exercises

- Build a new Web page with a file name of 'ECDL.HTM', saved to the temp folder.
- It should have:

    the heading, 'My exercise page';

    a title of 'ECDL exercise site';

    and the text 'This is my completed ECDL exercise Web page. To congratulate me, mail me at', followed by a hyperlink to your mail address of 'yourname@acme.co.uk'.

There are many guides on the Internet to help you learn HTML and assist with Web site design. Remember to keep things simple and add to your knowledge slowly over time.

Web design software

There are many Web authoring tools which allow you to build Web sites in a simpler manner than coding in HTML. Users of Windows 95 and 98 have an application called FrontPage Express, which is ideal for building simple Web pages.

- FrontPage can normally be found at **Start > Programs > Internet Explorer > FrontPage Express**.

Shown below is FrontPage Express, displaying the first page of the BCD Group ECDL CD course.

FrontPage Express is a cut-down version of the full product and you will not have full access to all of the software facilities. Practise and learn how to use FrontPage Express and don't forget to use the online Help, provided as part of the application.

Uploading to the World Wide Web

Uploading is the opposite of downloading – transferring files from your computer to a site on the Internet, e.g. your ISP Web computer.

Having successfully built your Web page(s) you may wish to consider putting your site on to the World Wide Web so that your friends, colleagues and the whole world can see your work! Your ISP has probably allocated free Web space to you, if not, Business Communications Development Limited have teamed up with Hitweb Internet Solutions to enable you to do this free of charge, as follows:

- Complete the form at www.onet.co.uk/hitweb and you will be instructed on how you can upload your site onto the World Wide Web making it visible to 100 million plus Internet users around the world.

Special tools for creating forms

Formatting tools – almost identical to those in Word

Browsing tools

Estimated download time for the page – keep an eye on this, as visitors prefer fast-loading pages.

Electronic mail

Electronic Mail or e-mail is a method of sending and receiving messages, from or to a computer or specialist telephone, via the Internet.

Sending and receiving e-mail is very cheap and is very fast.

The most commonly used program for sending and receiving e-mail is Outlook Express which is distributed with the Windows operating system. Double-click on the Outlook Express icon on the desktop to start it. Depending on which version of Outlook Express you have, your screens may appear a little different from those shown.

Basic steps

❑ Composing a message

1 Click the Compose Message (or New Mail) button.

2 The New Message window will open. If it is too small, click on the Maximise button.

3 Enter the e-mail address of the the recipient in the To box., e.g. *info@bcdtraining.co.uk*

4 In the Subject line, type a subject, e.g. *'Next meeting of the Wine Drinkers Appreciation Society'*.

5 Type your message.

6 Click Send.

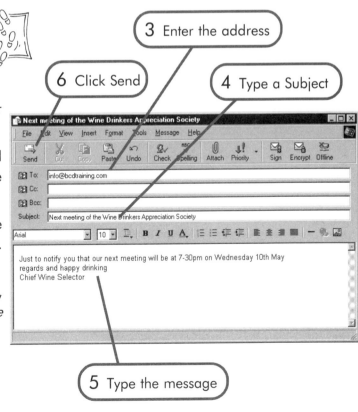

Attaching a file to a message

Files such as Word documents or Excel work-books can be attached to e-mail.

Basic steps

1 Click the paperclip icon.

2 At the Insert Attachment dialog box, select the file(s).

3 Click the Attach button.

❑ A new slot will appear below the Subject line, showing the attached file .

4 Click the Send button.

1 Click the paperclip

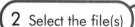

2 Select the file(s)

4 Click Send

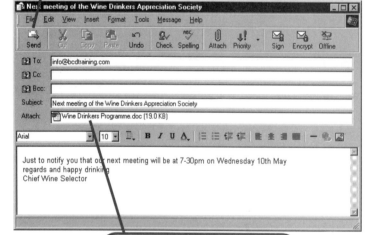

3 Click Attach

Cc and Bcc

Cc as shown in the example to the left stands for Carbon Copy and is sent as information to a third party.

Bcc stands for Blind Carbon Copy. Only the sender will be aware that the person shown in the Bcc address line has received a copy.

Attached files are listed here

Incoming mail

Click a header to open the message in the lower panel

To receive e-mail

To receive e-mail click ![Send/Recv] the **Send/Recv** button. If you are not connected to your ISP, you will be prompted to connect and when online, your e-mail will be sent to you.

Whenever you send an e-mail, Outlook Express checks your mail box at your ISP, to see if there is any mail waiting, and to collect it, if there is.

Received messages are stored in your **Inbox**. You can tell how many unread messages there are by looking at the Folders list. The number of unread messages is displayed next to the **Inbox** label.

Copying a message

To copy a message to another application highlight it, then open the **Edit** menu and click on **Select All**.

The entire text will then be highlighted, as shown here.

From the **Edit** menu select Copy, and the message will be stored in the Clipboard ready for further use.

The copied text can then be imported into a second application, such as Word. With the application open and a new or existing document open, right-click in the appropriate area of the document and select **Paste** from the pop-up menu. The message will appear in the document and you can, if so required, edit it.

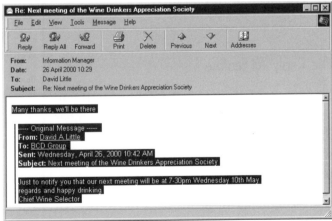

Replying to mail

The Reply feature has the option to copy the original message into your reply. The default setting is for this to be on, and it can be very useful. Imagine the scenario, you wish to respond to an e-mail, and include the original message. Do you re-type the entire message? No, you use Reply.

This copied message feature means that there is little room for error or misunderstanding, on the part of any of the recipients, if the original text is included in the response. The recipients can easily refer back through the messages at any time and re-read them.

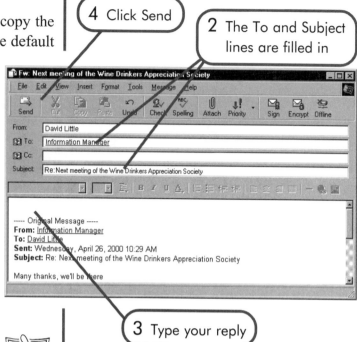

4 Click Send

2 The To and Subject lines are filled in

3 Type your reply

Basic steps

1 Select the message that you wish to respond to and click Reply.

2 At the Compose window, note that Outlook Express has completed the To: and Subject lines for you.

3 Type in your response.

4 When finished, click Send.

The Reply All feature

Another Reply feature is the Reply All. If you receive an e-mail, which was sent to a number of people, and you wish to respond to it and you want all of the recipients to see your responses, you can use the Reply All feature.

● Select the message and click the **Reply All** button.

● The Reply All dialog box will open and you will find that all the addresses from the original message have been copied into the 'To' slot for you.

In the message section, type in your responses and when finished, left-click on the Send. Outlook Express will send the message to all the addresses listed in the 'To' slot of the message. You do not have to send each of the message addressees an individual message. A real-time saver.

Forwarding a message

You can send a message that you have received on to another person. This feature is very useful and a time saver.

To forward a message, first select it then click on the **Forward** button.

The Compose window will open.

Enter the mail address of the recipient in the 'To' slot.

Add your own message, and amend the Subject and the original message if required.

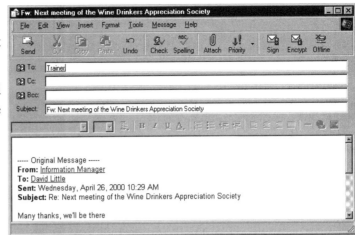

Filing e-mail

The more e-mail you get – and keep – the more important it is that you store it in an organised manner. Filing is simple, and should be done regularly.

Basic steps

1 Open the Inbox, and highlight the message to be filed.

2 From the Edit menu select Move to Folder. The Move dialog box will open

3 If you need to create a new folder, click the New Folder button.

4 At the New Folder dialog box , type a name for the folder and click OK.

5 When you return to the Move dialog box, select the new folder then click OK.

❏ The dialog box will close and the message will be moved to its new folder.

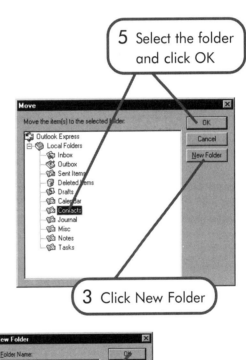

5 Select the folder and click OK

3 Click New Folder

4 Type a name and click OK

Sample paper 7: Communications

1	Apart from a computer name two things you require before being able to access the Internet?	
2	In what format does an ISDN line transmit data:	1. Analogue 2. Digital
3	What does 'HTTP' stand for?	
4	What extension to a URL (Uniform Resource Locator) is a UK based company likely to have?	
5	What is the name given to the first page your browser opens when logging onto the Internet?	1. Index Page 2. Favourites Page 3. Home Page
6	In Internet Explorer, the navigation toolbar allows you to perform a number of tasks. 'Search', and 'Stop' are two, name a third.	
7	What function do 'Hyperlinks' provide?	
8	Before saving or printing a Web page you first need to click onto the page. What term is used to describe this process?	
9	Name three practical uses of the Internet or World Wide Web?	1. 2. 3.
10	When developing a Web page using HTML, formatting commands are written in angle brackets – '< >'. What name is given to these commands?	1. Tags 2. Brackets 3. Prompts
11	When sending an e-mail, what does Cc mean in the address section?	

12	You wish to respond to an e-mail. To avoid any confusion as to which e-mail you are referring to, what facility of Outlook Express would you use?	1.	Copy
		2.	Edit
		3.	Reply to Author
13	You have received an e-mail and wish to use the content in a Word document. What facility would you use rather than retype the message?	1.	Move
		2.	Copy
		3.	Forward Message
14	You wish to send an e-mail to a number of people, but you do not want everyone to know that it was sent to a particular person. Which address line would you use for this person?	1.	Cc
		2.	To
		3.	Bcc
15	You have received an e-mail and you wish to send it to another colleague who was not on the original mail address listing. Which facility would you use?	1.	Reply to Author
		2.	Forward
		3.	Send and Receive

Index

BCD
PO Box 404
Portsmouth
Hants
PO5 2YW

BCD
PO Box 404
Portsmouth
Hants
PO5 2YW

TESTING

In order to obtain the ECDL Certificate you have to undergo the tests for each module. In order to arrange tests please complete and return this card to BDC.

Name: _____

Company (if applicable): _____

Address: _____

Telephone: _____ Fax: _____

Email: _____

SUPPORT

To claim your 30 days of free ECDL support please fill in your details below and return to BCD. You will also receive news on the ECDL.

Name: _____

Company (if applicable): _____

Address: _____

Telephone: _____ Fax: _____

Email: _____

NICOLAS DE OLIVEIRA

NICOLA OXLEY

MICHAEL PETRY

installation art
in the new millennium

the empire of the senses

TEXTS BY NICOLAS DE OLIVEIRA

with 317 illustrations, 269 in colour

contents

page 1 Oswaldo Macia, *Memory Skip*, 1995
The Colombian artist Oswaldo Macia's
work straddles the visual and the
olfactory. In it smell becomes a physical
object. Here, the skip held pine essence
and its scent acted as a memory aid,
though pine soap is generally used as a
cleaning agent and for evacuating noxious
odours. The liquid was bound by its solid
container, but its odour evaded such fixed
parameters and pervaded the entire
space. *Memory Skip* was partnered by an
audio work entitled *The Sound of Smell*,
recorded in a sound studio and consisting
of the mechanical grinding and manual
chopping of pine needles. This lasted the
length of time as it took for the sealed
room to be filled with scent.

pages 2–3 Andrea Zittel, *Raugh Furniture:
Lucinda*, 1998 (see page 74).

First published in the United Kingdom in 2003 by
Thames & Hudson Ltd, 181A High Holborn,
London WC1V 7QX

www.thamesandhudson.com

© 2003 Thames & Hudson, Ltd, London

First paperback edition

British Library Cataloguing-in-Publication Data
A catalogue record for this book is available from the
British Library

ISBN 0-500-28451-2

Printed and bound in China by C+C Offset

Over the past decade the position of Installation art has shifted from a relatively
marginal practice to achieving mainstream status within contemporary visual
culture. Its hegemonic presence has given rise to new terms which redefine the
art form and impact on a range of other disciplines.

Artists and works that mark this shift include: Ann Hamilton (USA), Stan
Douglas (Canada), Stefan Brüggemann (Mexico), Steven Pippin (UK), Barbara
Kruger (USA), Hans Op de Beek (Belgium), Rodney Graham (Canada), Michael
Landy (UK), Tomoko Takahashi (Japan), Ilya Kabakov (Russia), Chris Burden (USA)
and Francesc Torres (Spain).

The new 'immersive' Installation reflects desire for sensual pleasure. It provides
a 'total artwork' which envelops the viewer in a hermetic and narcissistic space.
The location of the installation is in the realm of the imaginary, stimulated by
the need for escape.

Artists featured include Doug Aitken (USA), Per Barclay (Norway), Olafur
Eliasson (Denmark), Bruce Gilchrist and Jo Joelson (UK), Ann Veronica Janssens
(UK/Belgium), Kazuo Katase (Japan), Jaume Plensa (Spain), Ugo Rondinone
(Switzerland), Børre Sæthre (Norway), Andrea Zittel (USA), Lee Bul (Korea) and
Pierre Huyghe (France).

While artists desire autonomy, their installations often require collaborators in
the form of museums and curators. The resulting relationships provide a platform
for discussion and collaboration. The outcome of this process is the project:
Installation as an open-ended experiment which transforms the art institution
into a cultural laboratory.

Artists in this section include: Barbara Bloom (USA), Martin Creed (UK), Henrik
Plenge Jakobsen (Denmark), Mischa Kuball (Germany), Micah Lexier (Canada),
John Newling (UK), Tobias Rehberger (Germany), Navin Rawanchaikul (Thailand),
Elmgreen & Dragset (Denmark/Norway) and Thomas Hirschhorn (Switzerland).

exchange and interaction 106

Installation has been defined by its refusal to accept fixed boundaries.
Its experimental edge has led artists to examine the boundaries of other
disciplines. Practitioners are looking to forge relationships of exchange with
other artists on a global level, through the ability of fast travel, information
technology and the media. In addition, Installation artists have found opportunities
to collaborate with specialists in areas such as anthropology, science and
technology, opening the field to experimental strategies beyond the traditionally
visual. Installation is thus seen as moving beyond the physical boundary of a
single space into a realm of negotiated interactivity and simultaneity.

Artists are drawn from a broad spectrum of Installation practice and
include: Atelier van Lieshout (Netherlands), Jose Dávila (Mexico), Alicia Framis
(Spain), Carsten Höller (Belgium), the duo Muntean/Rosenblum (Austria/Israel),
Carsten Nicolai (Germany), the Scandinavian group N55, Paola Pivi (Italy),
Mark Povell (UK), Allan Wexler (USA) and Keith Tyson (UK).

time and narrative 132

In a rapidly changing world, time and memory are key concerns for contemporary
artists. Though borrowing from existing methodologies, Installation artists prefer
to construct their own spaces of memory. The singular term 'history' is under
constant threat from the emergence of multiple 'histories'. Artists have used
this concern with remembrance by focusing on official and unofficial means
of retrieval in an attempt to question existing systems through more private and
individual ways.

Examples are drawn from the works of: Christian Boltanski (France), David
Bunn (USA), Damien Hirst (UK), Tadashi Kawamata (Japan), the French duo
Loriot/Mélia, Mike Nelson (UK), Jason Rhoades (USA), Bob & Roberta Smith (UK),
Jane and Louise Wilson (UK), Eija-Liisa Ahtila (Finland) and João Penalva (Portugal).

the body of the audience 166

Following an examination of the conditions of contemporary viewing, it is argued
that the audience has become the key site of the Installation. This chapter
concludes that Installation returns us to the body of the spectator, a space that is
sentient and active: The Empire of the Senses.

Artists include: Vanessa Beecroft (Italy), Carlos Amorales (Mexico), Thomas
Eller (Germany), Gary Hill (USA), Christian Jankowski (Germany), Aernout Mik
(Netherlands), Santiago Sierra (Spain), Roman Signer (Switzerland), Christine Hill
(USA), Mariko Mori (Japan) and Sylvie Fleury (Switzerland).

foreword
by Jonathan Crary

For the last several centuries, the most compelling forms of Western visual art were often works by artists who critically engaged with the experience of human perception, who tested its limits and expanded its possibilities. The Scientific Revolution accelerated the search for workable explanations for understanding the interplay of vision and appearance, and the empirical study of perception became a recurring part of the modernization of European thought. With the models of artist-researchers like Leonardo and Brunelleschi available, innovative art has frequently taken shape within an awareness of the double-sidedness of perceptual experience: that it is formed both through external techniques and practices and through the subjective capabilities of the observer's own body and nervous system. For many centuries, representational techniques like perspective and printing exemplified the standardization as well as the replication, storage and circulation of perceptual experience, while devices such as the telescope or microscope functioned as prosthetic amplifications and extensions of human sensory capabilities.

Up until the mid-1800s the artist operated within conditions of relative equilibrium between the imperatives of external rules and techniques (e.g. academic codes and studio practices, optical instruments like the Claude Glass, and perspectival systems) on one hand and the autonomy of subjective visual experience on the other. But beginning in the late 19th century, intensified technological development triggered the erosion of this reciprocity between individual experience and exterior processes and instruments. The last 125 years have seen a dramatic transfer of human capabilities to machines, especially capabilities involving vision, thought and memory which continues unabated today, in terms of tools for information storage, communication and visualization. We are now in a material environment where earlier 20th-century models of spectatorship, contemplation and experience are inadequate for understanding the conditions of cultural creation and reception. If the diverse artists featured in this volume have anything in common, it is a recognition of this shift and a realization that art must reconfigure itself in relation to transformed modes of cognition and experience. Their work is linked, directly and indirectly, with the activity and imagination of new groups, subjectivities and communities in a conflict-ridden global environment. Taking place in both art and in diverse cultural arenas are experiments with perceptual and cognitive experiences outside of the dominant possibilities offered by contemporary media and technology. Some of this experimental activity involves the creation of unanticipated spaces and environments in which our visual and intellectual habits are challenged or disrupted. The processes through which sensory information is consumed become the object of various strategies of de-familiarization.

The continuing proliferation of techniques of perception and information is tied to one of the crucial paradoxes of global present: the greater the technological capacity for connection, speed, for exchange and circulation of information, the more fragmented and compartmentalized the world becomes. Much of our intellectual heritage from the Enlightenment supported the opposite belief: that universal access to knowledge and communication tools ought to have been the basis for conditions of freedom and participatory democracy for example. For those working in the visual arts and new media, there is a particular awareness that the current spread of communication networks is not generating a trans-national community with a shared set of aesthetic and perceptual foundations. Instead, there has been the spread of relatively self-sufficient micro-worlds of affect, meaning and experience, between which intelligible exchange is less and less possible.

The unfathomable amount of information available today works powerfully against the possibility or even the ideal of shared knowledge. Instead, electronically accessible data can be used in the service of any point of view, regardless of how extreme or absurd. But it is within this generalized epistemological crisis that some of our most important contemporary artists, grouped here under the term 'Installation art', are rethinking the nature of research, challenging hegemonic uses of media and testing out new ways of assembling and presenting information. We encounter here strategies of materializing knowledge through concrete procedures of bricolage, as well as unexpected awakenings of communal memory within a culture dependent on historical amnesia. This is a far cry from the appropriation art of the 1980s when it was fashionable to present virtuoso demonstrations of endless chains of simulation, of the cynical play of signs and images that supposedly no longer referred to anything.

As the authors of this volume recognize, the appellation 'Installation art' is a paradoxical one in that it too can imply a sense of position and a spatial homogeneity which is alien to most of the examples of work represented here. For, in fact, Installation art directly engages the patchwork, composite character of contemporary experience and it does so with a stunning diversity of materials and practices. In a related sense, 'Globalization' is also a misleading term in that it seems to connote spatiality or territory, albeit on a large scale. But as we well know, the workings of capitalism now are increasingly independent of actual territory. There is more and more disconnection of economic circulation from physical space, as abstract forms of wealth have a mobility and fluidity unrelated to what we used to think of as location. This should not lead us to hyperbolic theories about the disappearance of space or the ubiquity of instantaneous speed and so on. We must begin to understand the strange kind of dislocations and associations that now constitute subjective reality. Unavoidably, our lives are divided between two essentially incompatible milieus; on one hand, the spaceless electronic worlds of contemporary technological culture and, on the other, the physical extensive terrain on which our bodies are situated. Much Installation art affirms that experience (and art) is constituted out of the paradoxes and discontinuities of this mixed heterogeneous zone.

Many of the Installation artists seem to be working with the awareness of how the tangible 'real' world can seem dilapidated in comparison with the infinite phantasmagoria of images and data available on-line or on-screen. The potential decrepitude of our physical surroundings and all the cosmetic, genetic imperfections (not to mention the mortality) of our own bodies are a permanent humiliation in the face of dematerialized digital phenomena. It is of course entirely logical now that immense corporate industries are relentlessly trading upon the fragility of the body to expand a central arena of consumption: bio-engineering, cosmetic surgery, psycho-chemicals ever more available for diverse emotional and behavioural needs (e.g. an anti-shyness drug now being marketed), anti-aging procedures, and the patenting and commercialization of the human genome, to name a few. But these are some of the issues out of which artists are generating counter-models of the body and its dynamics, which disclose its political volatility and which might work against its fraudulent domestication.

The cultural changes now underway, however, are not analogous to previous historical transformations. The rise of typographic culture did not suddenly occur after the 15th-century invention of the printing press and moveable type. It took place slowly over several centuries and its effects were not fully in place until the late 18th or early 19th centuries in terms of an extensive diffusion across a social field. Perhaps most significantly though, we are not witnessing so much a change in technological conceptions from one dominant arrangement of machinic systems to another, as the emergence of an unprecedented dynamic of continual innovation and obsolescence. It is not as if we are in a transitional period of adjustment to a new set of tools which will all seem quite mundane in another generation, like the telephone or radio. For the vast majority of people, our perceptual and cognitive relationship to communication and information technology is and will continue to be estranged, because the speed at which new products appear and reconfigurations of technological systems take place precludes the possibility of ever becoming familiar with a given arrangement. What we habitually refer to as photography, film, video, television no longer has a stable identity and is now subject to increasingly frequent mutations as part of larger technological transformations. Whatever is currently touted as essential to our practical needs is always disquietingly close to obsolescence. Perception itself is so closely aligned with these rhythms of change that one of its primary characteristics is continual permutation. In this context, aesthetic debates dependent on the notion of 'medium' are out of touch with contemporary actuality. Much of the work documented here consists of provisional counter-strategies of integrating technological tools into plural zones of creative activity, and of inventing flexible models of imagination and narrative outside of the enforced routines of cultural consumption. It establishes a perceptual field which simultaneously engages periphery and centre, continually revealing multiple routes of entry and exit. Perhaps most importantly, the work is often frankly utopian in its ambitions: it provides a rough outline of alternate forms of living, creating and thinking which might become hopeful anticipations of a highly variegated but more egalitarian global future.

Tomoko Takahashi, *Line Out*, 1999
Referring to an unprejudiced
exploration of selection and
classification, a cheerful celebration
of human organizing tendencies,
Takahashi focuses on the retrieval
and redeployment of materials in
order to integrate the detritus of
consumer society into an artistic
practice. She creates chaotic tableaux
of redundant equipment which can be
interpreted as fantasies of neurotic,
urban landscapes.

introduction

In February 2001 the British artist Michael Landy re-opened the disused C&A department store in London's Oxford Street. Over a period of two weeks all his belongings were publicly destroyed for his installation *Break Down*. In the catalogue of the show Landy provided an inventory of his posessions: 'Artworks, Clothing, Electrical, Furniture, Kitchen, Leisure, Motor Vehicle, Perishable, Reading Material, Studio Materials'. He described the work thus: *Break Down* is a bit like a Scalectrix version of a material reclamation facility with all my possessions circulating on

Michael Landy, *Break Down*, 2001

a roller conveyor until they are taken apart. I'm building an audit of my life. Objects that have been classified into different categories...are numbered, weighed and detailed on an inventory.... The conveyor is like a plinth in a way, it-er-conveys what's going on.'

Break Down provides a useful departure point for reconsidering the nature and form of the artwork at the beginning of the 21st century as it raises important questions about the current position of the artist, material culture, exhibition practices and the role of the audience in Installation art. This book aims to present the diverse practices that have today come to redefine the term Installation art.

The final decade of the 20th century saw the passage of Installation art from a relatively marginal art practice to the establishment of its current central role in contemporary art. 'These days installation art seems to be everybody's favourite medium,' wrote the influential American critic Roberta Smith in 1993. She was also critical, stating that 'installation has become a series of conventions' (Smith uses the terms 'installation' and 'installation art' interchangeably). However, as we shall see, in the intervening years Installation has moved from what the American art theorist Hal Foster describes as 'medium specific' to 'debate specific', a form of art that is not defined in terms of any traditional medium but in terms of the message it conveys by whatever means.

Earlier attempts to define Installation art by medium alone failed because it is in the nature of the practice itself to challenge its own boundaries. This questioning process constitutes a discourse which investigates the relationships between the artist and the audience. Installation is therefore defined by this process, something that has led artists to work with materials and methodologies not traditionally associated with the visual arts. Roberta Smith's assertion that Installation was governed by conventions has been challenged since the publication of her article. Current practice suggests that a more fluid and open approach has taken over from the conventions that attempted to bind Installation art to the medium. This idea of fluidity was already being discussed in relation to Postmodern practice in the 1980s. Moreover, it is in the current period that these earlier theories have become fully integrated into art practice. As the French philosopher Jean Baudrillard noted: 'The medium is no longer identifiable as such, and the confusion of the medium and the message (McLuhan) is the first great formula of this new era.' The Canadian theorist Marshall McLuhan was one of the key theorists writing in the early 1960s to address the impact that information technology would have on global culture. This formula predicts the shift from objective critique towards a new subjectivity which emphasizes uncertainty and brings both artist and viewer together in a discursive environment.

The practice of the Russian artist Ilya Kabakov has been emblematic of this move from objective knowledge to subjective experience. His *Palace of Projects* (1998) presented a vast range of proposals from the

Ilya Kabakov, *The Palace of Projects*, (detail), 1998

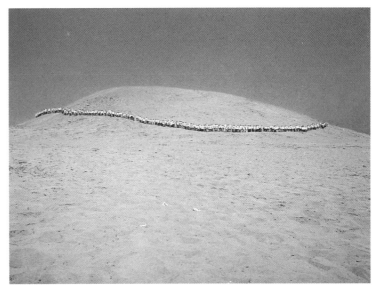

Russian people, which were then turned into maquettes and drawings. These proposals were the flights of fancy of ordinary people faced with the breakdown of ideological certainties in the wake of the collapse of the Soviet Union. Kabakov goes so far as to state that Installation will take the place of 'the icon, the fresco, and the painting'. He affirms that Installation 'is not a movement in art, not a new or fashionable style' but rather 'a new genre which is still in the very beginning of its development.' Kabakov sees Installation as a genre entirely directed towards the viewer, though the audience's reaction is anticipated by the artist. In generating the work, the artist instills a sense of familiarity in the viewer, directing them to their own everyday experience. Moreover, the demystification of art's content in Kabakov's work is a concern shared by many artists.

While referring to the content of Installation art, Rochelle Steiner, curator of the Saint Louis Art Museum, writes that 'museological critique, world and identity politics, and the position of the viewers tend to be preconditions rather than battlegrounds.' These terms, suggested by Steiner, are no longer the subject of installations but constitute a

Francis Alÿs, *When Faith Moves Mountains*, 2002
The Belgian artist Francis Alÿs' work crosses over between performance, painting, photography and web projects. On 11 April 2002, five hundred volunteers were given shovels and asked to form a single line at the foot of a giant sand dune in Ventanilla, an area outside Lima, Peru. This human comb pushed a quantity of sand a specific distance, thereby moving a 16-foot-long (4.8 m) sand dune roughly 4 inches (10 cm) from its original position. The piece functions as a social allegory, infiltrating local history and mythology with the aim of de-romanticizing Land Art.

right Renée Green, *Between and Including*, 1999

opposite left Meschac Gaba, *Museum Shop*, 2001
The Benin artist Meschac Gaba diagnoses how art history and the museum culturally, ethnocentrically and selectively assimilate non-European cultures. The piece Project for the Museum of African Contemporary Art was made in Amsterdam in 1997 at the Rijksakademie. This museum, organized in twelve different departments or installations (Museum Shop, Museum Restaurant, Museum Discotheque, etc.), was reconstructed and temporarily staged for exhibitions. Gaba playfully confronts his work with the defined mechanisms of business and the rules of the global contemporary art market.

common ground between artist and audience upon which the work is based. Installation is therefore not specifically charged with addressing the issues mentioned by Steiner, as artists and viewers already understand these concerns as *given*. In the many contemporary installations that recognize the reality of an information culture the issues are implicit.

Many artists appear to give credence to Steiner's argument; as the issues are implicit in the work, they can remove the need to remind the audience of their presence. The American artist Renée Green constructs video-lounges and libraries which act as information centres in which the viewer becomes a 'browser' who picks from the available material. Similarly, Meschac Gaba from Benin provided a reading area and a shop entitled *Museum Shop* (2001), which invited visitors to browse through books and magazines. Both these artists' installations propose informal settings which encourage spectators to relax and enjoy the work without being pressurized by overt messages or ideological stances. The perceived absence of apparent control mechanisms or the lack of an explicit message in these works suggests an understanding shared between the artist and the audience. The audience is encouraged to choose its own interpretation without relying on that of the artist. Artists and curators are indeed motivating spectators to experience works in an open-ended manner and become authors and generators of their own meanings.

The relationship between the artist and the audience is closely linked to the continuing debate around 'theatrical space'. If the gallery or site is likened to a stage, the question then arises of how and why the viewer participates in the work. The American curator Robert Storr's exhibition '*Dis*locations' at the Museum of Modern Art in New York in 1992 helped to pave the way for the recognition of Installation art as a mainstream discipline. His article 'No Stage, No Actors, But It's Theatre (and Art)', published in 1999, observed that installations have become 'complete immersion environments'. Refering to installations by artists such as Ilya Kabakov and Ann Hamilton, he asserts that 'the experience they provide is much like wandering onstage and picking up loose pages from a script,

above right Bik Fillingham Van der Pol, *The Bookshop Piece*, 1996
This was a recreation of the theory section of the ICA Bookshop in London at the Museum Boijmans van Beuningen, Rotterdam.
One of the characteristics of the ICA Bookshop is that the main stock consists of theory-related literature, including sociological, cultural, historical and philosophical works. The Dutch artists Liesbeth Bik, Peter Fillingham and Jos van der Pol, who work collaboratively under the name Bik Fillingham Van der Pol, wanted to create a link between the different collections, which operate in discrete areas such as modern art, classical art, prints and design. The reconstruction of the ICA Bookshop was based with the original architect's plans and included all titles on a sale-or-return basis.

right Barbara Kruger, *Power Pleasure Desire Disgust*, 1997
The American artist Barbara Kruger no longer attacks the public's attitudes towards advertising and mass propaganda but their zones of intimacy which create claustrophobic spaces. Her signature texts and aphorisms are projected all over the gallery's surface, while on the rear wall, three large-scale video projections of changing heads voice her confrontational texts, based on snatches of dialogue overheard by the artist.

overhearing bits of recorded dialogue and trying to figure out what the setting is...and what actions might still be taken.' He implies that the proscenium arch has been removed and that the division between actors and audience is no longer clear. The removal of the frame that separates stage from auditorium brings together the spheres of making and viewing. The 'theatricality' of the work, once seen as a weakness because of the reliance on entertaining the audience, has become a virtue. Rochelle Steiner goes so far as to state that 'theatricality paradoxically outlined the conditions that would come to define installation art.'

Yet, while the idea of the theatre still provides one of the paradigms for today's installations, its rhetoric has been superseded by other concerns. In *Double Bind* (2001), the last major work by the Catalan artist Juan Muñoz, the idea of the stage remains present through repeated use of framing devices. The installation at Tate Modern, London, provided a labyrinthine architecture of several levels and chambers and introduced *trompe l'œil* effects which encouraged multiple perspectives. Placed strategically, a series of cast figures, painted the same shade of grey as

opposite Juan Muñoz, *Double Bind*, 2001

the entire work, stood watching. The Turbine Hall, a cavernous and dramatic space combined with the monumental scale of the work to curtail intimacy and to remove the possibility of a single perspective for the static viewer. However, the theatricality of this installation was placed at the service of a dysfunctional play with the conditions of viewing which emphasized the alienation of the audience.

The British collective Blast Theory have moved away from the constrictions of traditional performative spaces by engaging with the possibilities offered by new technologies. Their 1998 project, *Kidnap*, followed the popular format of Reality-TV where individuals were invited to compete for their own abduction. Two winners were selected and kidnapped by the group then taken to an undisclosed location where their captivity was filmed and could be watched as a live webcast. This project parallels the shift from static notions of space and time towards multiple spaces and simultaneous events, a move closely associated with the development of 'telematic media'. This term is used to describe the range of new tele-technologies that enable us to instantaneously and simultaneously transmit sound and vision to any number of locations. This simultaneity has a disorienting impact on our experience of space and time and has become an important issue in the development of Installation. Moreover, in recent years we have witnessed the arrival of digital technology, as well as the availability of new means of production and reception based around the processing power of the personal computer as a virtual studio. The virtual studio offers new working tools for artists, and encourages a nomadic and heterogeneous practice. The Mexican artist Stefan Brüggemann stated, in conversation with the authors, 'Who needs a studio? All an artist needs today is a computer and a phoneline.' Thus, these technologies have been instrumental in changing the role of the artist from that of a generator of original or primary materials, to that of an editor of existing cultural

left Stefan Brüggemann, *Opening*, 1998
Brüggemann's work challenges the institutional framework, which is continually used for the presentation of visual art. The Mexican artist removed the plate-glass window of the exhibition space from the street elevation, allowing the audience to step through. The window that usually provides the first visual contact with the museum and its contents loses its function as a looking glass, while acquiring a new status as an exhibit.

opposite Wendy Bornholdt, *Subspace SE8 3NU (Relay)*, 2001
The installation by the New Zealand artist Wendy Bornholdt consisted of a walkway of scaffold poles and thin strips of mirror. A cycle of hissing white noise imposed itself on the space, only to be counterpointed by moments of pristine silence. The noise plundered one's ability to concentrate or complete a thought, while the silence was accompanied by an acute awareness of the moment of anticipation when thought could be resumed.

objects to be inserted into new contexts. This argument is echoed in the book *Postproduction* by the French curator and theorist Nicolas Bourriaud who likens the activity of the artist to that of the computer programmer or the DJ. 'This recycling of sounds, images, and forms implies incessant navigation within the meanderings of cultural history, navigation which itself becomes the subject of artistic practice.

The British author J. G. Ballard has extensively explored the shifts in cultural experience as we adapt to new technological landscapes. In an interview with the Italian journalist Lorenza Pignatti he stated: 'Our homes are slowly turning into TV studios, full of electronic equipment – camcorders, VCRs, advanced stereo systems – designed to make us the star, script-writer, director of our own continuing mini-drama. Reality is turning into a home movie, in which an infanticized version of ourselves runs across a garden of artificial grass.' However, though the technologies to which Ballard refers are having a deep impact, transforming the private representation of individual identities and the

below Ann Hamilton, *Salic*, 1995

environment of the home, the cinematic experience continues to dominate the public language of visual culture. Therefore, in spite of the proliferation of home entertainment, the resurgence of cinema-going since the 1980s reveals a continuing desire for immersion in a communal activity with repetitive conditions. The 'immersive condition', discussed more fully in Chapter 1 (Escape) clarifies why the cinema has been crucial in the development of Installation. Cinema provides the dominant cultural experience that Installation must explore. Film has been instrumental in setting the viewing conditions and expectations for today's audiences, as it envelops the spectator in an overwhelming spectacle of narrative, sound and vision. Despite the escalation of 'special effects', along with the improvements in sound technology and viewer comforts which have helped to fill cinemas, watching films still relies on the traditional division between screen and audience. This separation provides, on the one hand, a practical viewing solution, while on the other, it allows the audience to focus on the narrative or the unfolding of the plot. Installation, through its use of cinematic techniques both quotes and deconstructs the experience of film: its viewing place and conditions, its narrative sequencing and its use of represented space. To this end, artists such as the American Ann Hamilton and the Canadian Stan Douglas have used the effects of early cinema in their installations.

Stan Douglas, set for *Der Sandmann*
(The Sandman), 1995

Jonathan Hernández, *Everything is OK*, 2001
The Mexican artist Jonathan Hernández confronts the viewer with a glittering statement about existence. His work elicits responses from his audiences, asking them to reflect on his statements, which are paradoxically banal and profound.

Hamilton's *Salic* (1995) was staged in a disused passenger carriage and used the pre-cinematic device of the Zoetrope to arrive at flickering projections which simulated the train's movement. Douglas's *Der Sandmann* (1994–97), used two film projectors to create a split-screen effect. Douglas built two identical filmsets of a civic garden, one showing the garden in contemporary times, the other as it would have been in the 1970s. These were filmed using the same 360-degree rotation in a continuous pan and then projected to form two halves of a screen so that one image always appeared to wipe out the other. The resulting installation uses this complex technique to represent the return of repressed memory and history which the Austrian psychoanalyst Sigmund Freud describes in his essay *The Uncanny* (1919). Artists are using the physical apparatus of film-making, the language of cinematography and the subject matter of filmic narrative as a means of exploring the conditions of viewing when film is taken out of the cinema and installed in the gallery context. The British artist Sam Taylor-Wood makes multi-screen films, often casting well-known actors and celebrities, in which the camera is used as a static eye and the action unfolds in front of it. The use of recognizable personalities echoes the position of the film star in cinema. In Taylor-Wood's work the viewer remains unsure as to whether the celebrities are playing a part or are simply themselves. In so doing, the artist reveals the way in which life seeks to imitate film. In contrast, the Swiss artist Ugo Rondinone constructs atmospheric filmic installations which immerse the spectator in a repetitive and purposefully nostalgic dream-state.

The work of the American artist Matthew Barney is emblematic of this confusion of boundaries between disciplines, as he fuses film, installation, theatre and set-design. His epic film cycle *Cremaster* is characterized by lush backdrops, slick art direction and labyrinthine narratives. On questioning one of his actors, Steve Tucker, guitarist

in the band Morbid Angel about *Cremaster 2* (1999), Tucker said:
'Dude, it's unbelievable...I could watch it a thousand times, frame
by frame and never tire of watching it, but still never know completely
what the fuck it was about.' In Barney's work, which operates between
film and installation, the theatrical element is always present. 'Character,
for Barney,' writes art critic Neville Wakefield, 'is sculptural material.'

While Installation was seen as an emerging practice, many attempts
were made to define its ever-growing remit. In the current period,

Matthew Barney, *Cremaster 2:
The Drone's Exposition*, 1999

however, artists and curators make use of the term to describe a wide area of related activities across a range of media. Installation art has come to encompass other terms such as 'intervention', 'interaction', 'interior art', 'ambient', 'event' and 'project'. Within the field of Installation, such terms have equal standing and may even be interchangeable. They are used by artists, curators and critics to further define specific activities. The practice of Installation, then, is increasingly characterized by its multifariousness and polyphony. Some voices have been raised announcing the demise of Installation, or at least the possibility of it splitting into, or being replaced by, one or other of the terms mentioned above, though, crucially, Installation is seen to be moving from a position of homogeneity to one that stresses its heterogeneous nature. The process, execution and display of works now demonstrates a variety of emphases, each informed by a different context or enquiry. Faced with these changeable manifestations, the British artist Keith Tyson, the Turner Prize winner in 2002, suggests that the encounter with a work of contemporary art should not make the viewer ask 'what is it about, but how do I feel?' Tyson asserts the need for subjective readings as a means of dealing with unstable realities.

One of the evolving facets of Installation was pointed out by the Canadian art historian Johanne Lamoureux who indicated a change in artists' attitudes towards the idea of site over a decade ago. The relationship between a work and its location, its 'site-specificity', was once the crucial focus for artists and audiences. Lamoureux stated that 'Installations today are often movable pieces, not the least ephemeral, transported from exhibition to exhibition, sometimes with slight, timely adaptations to fit a more peculiar context.' Lamoureux foresaw the need for installations to function as packages, to be adapted to the needs of given exhibitions, rather than being dominated by the demands of a non-art environment. The idea of the installation package

Alexandra Ranner, *Basement*, 2001
By transforming elements of photographs or stills from films into three-dimensional works, the German artist Alexandra Ranner re-creates spatial arrangements. These artificial, model-like replications are often reminiscent of the anonymity of cheap hotel rooms and furnished apartments. The atmospheric suggestion of the photographic or pictorial view is transformed into a bodily encounter.

Carl von Weiler, *Matrix*, 1998
In this work by the British artist
Carl von Weiler, television sets were
installed in a low dark space, clinging
to the ceilings and emitting feeble
sounds and light levels from their
hanging screens. The images on the
monitors were of the artist actually
hanging upside down like a bat.

or module can also be likened to the term 'interior art', suggested by
the Dutch art historian Camiel van Winkel. Interior art is discussed as a
symptom of the loss of public art by the Dutch theorist Dieter Roelstraete
who refers to Van Winkel's term, arguing that 'the individualisation of
spatial experience (or privatisation of space) by...young artists results,
at a deeper level, in the privatisation of art *tout court*.' Roelstraete mourns
the loss of public space, a place once closely associated with culture, and
productive of stable meanings and truths. The move from exterior to
interior is typified by the rise of interior art, itself a hybrid between art,
fashionable design and lifestyle culture. Furthermore, the focus on
internal space allows artists to sidestep the demands for universality
inherent in the use of public, or external space.

Though compelling, the arguments for the return of Installation to the
protected and internal space of the gallery, do not invalidate a continuing,
often parallel connection with public locations. The American art historian
Miwon Kwon perceives a change in the fixed reading of the site whether
gallery or public space. In her influential book *One Place After Another* she
calls this move away from a fixed reading 'site oriented', suggesting that
place is not about fixity, nor the extraction of a definite meaning from a
site. Rather, the move gives rise to artists whose practice is 'nomadic,
fluid and sometimes even virtual rather than restricted to a geographical

above Bruce Gilbert, *Cross over*, 1998
The British artist Bruce Gilbert
combines digital technology and
experimental sound in his installations.
For *Cross over* he dug up the gravel in
his drive which had a depression in
it and was collecting rainwater. The
puddle was transferred to a showcase
with a soundtrack of dripping water.

below Sarah Sze, *Everything that Rises
Must Converge*, 1999
Sarah Sze uses the detritus of everyday
life, brought together into organic-like
structures which expand vertically
and fill the entire exhibition space.
These fragile, meticulously arranged
constructions are adaptable to large-
scale sites, merging space and material.

place or institution.' If the site is no longer a precondition for the work,
it follows that the content of the work is not necessarily generated by
the location. On the contrary, it is negotiated by the artist through the
dialogue engendered by the project. The context, once a marker of site,
has thus been superseded by the notion of mobility, as described by,
among others, Ilya Kabakov and the Russian theorist Boris Groys.
The current idea of art as a 'project' requires a pliable time-frame and
a flexible or portable site. The freedom to travel without boundaries does
have its problems, however. The endless international displacement of
artists is likened by the American theorist Hal Foster to the activities
of an ethnographer: 'one selects a site, enters its culture and learns its
language, conceives and presents a project, only to move to the next site
where the cycle is repeated.' The problem of the location is echoed by
the Swiss artist Thomas Hirschhorn:

> It is a provisional location, since the construction will be
> dismantled after the exhibition. But it is a location which
> is unequivocal – unequivocal because I am invited to...a city
> I don't know and whose history and inhabitants I know nothing
> about. But I come with the desire to make sculptures and show
> them to the residents and visitors of this city. And so I don't want
> to make reference to anything that has to do with the city; that
> would be pretentious.... So I selected a location which is a non-
> place, i.e. a place where people can or must go for reasons that
> have nothing to do with the geography or history of the place.

Hirschhorn correctly identified the problem of immersion in a context
provided by a location or site, and Foster's comparison between the
artist and the ethnographer was indeed recognizable in the installations
by many artists throughout the 1980s and the first half of the 1990s.
As the context of the site became the content of the work, the artist was
cast in the various roles of tourguide or archivist. This position proved to

Olav Westphalen, *E.S.U.S.,*
Extremely Site-Unspecific Sculpture, 2000

be unenviable, since it did little to 'reveal' what was not already known. Hirschhorn's position is by no means unique among contemporary artists. Eschewing local habits, histories and politics has allowed artists to move from objective knowledge to the subjective and personal. This reliance on subjectivity impacts upon how artists perceive the exhibition context.

The writer James Meyer echoes Miwon Kwon's earlier point by coining the term 'functional site'. This site, he argues, is 'a process, an operation occurring between sites, a mapping of institutional and discursive filiations and the bodies that move between them (the artist's above all). It is an informational site, a locus of overlap of text, photographs, and video recordings, physical places and things.... It is a temporary thing; a movement; a chain of meanings devoid of a particular focus.' Kwon's reading of site states that 'it is now structured (inter)textually, rather than spatially, and its model is not a map but an itinerary, a fragmentary sequence of events and actions through spaces, that is, a nomadic narrative whose path is articulated by the passage of the artist.'

The creation by the German artist Olav Westphalen, *E.S.U.S., Extremely Site-Unspecific Sculpture* (2000), a lunar pod-like structure, provides an ironic take on this 'nomadic' tendency. 'The *E.S.U.S.* – friendly but indifferent...acknowledges any given site and adapts to it.' The work refutes local context as 'being nostalgic, at times even picturesque', preferring mobility above the stasis caused by the overemphasis on local knowledge. The American artist Spencer Tunick uses the mobility of an idea from one place to another. The recurring motif is that of hundreds of bodies lying prone at selected locations, as in *Maine* (1997). These temporary events are then documented in photographs and video. A salient feature of these displays is that all the participants are presented entirely naked, arranged in rows, piles or waves. Tunick's human subjects vary from one location to another. As bodies are replaced by new ones, the body itself is transformed into a mere component of the artwork.

The idea of the public site has become increasingly important to 'regenerative urbanism', which seeks to reanimate post-industrial city spaces. According to the writer Suzanne Lacy, this creates an uneasy relationship between the concept of the public monument and 'new genre public art', with its emphasis on temporary installations and interventions. While the prospect of maintaining relationships with spaces beyond the gallery appears attractive to artists, the latter often seem reluctant to enter into a dialogue with the civic authorities and agencies that traditionally commission such works. However, the art historian Walter Grasskamp persists in arguing the case for public art, since it moves the emphasis from the gallery to the city. Under modernism we see an increasing trend towards an internalization, that is, a return to the physical and institutional sphere of the gallery and the museum. It may therefore be argued that, 'as cultural end sites, museums reinforced the demand for the high degree of protection which art now demanded.'

opposite Spencer Tunick, *Maine*, 1997

right Keith Wilson, *Puddle*, 1999

opposite above Rodney Graham, *The King's Part*, 1999

This position clearly privileges art of a permanent nature housed indoors over one of a temporary nature in the public sphere.

It remains to be seen whether these state-sponsored approaches to public space, disguised as sculpture projects or sculpture trails, are a significant alternative to the strictures imposed by the museum, or whether it simply moves the institution outdoors. The British artist Keith Wilson's *Puddle* (1999) provides a useful counter-argument to this reading of public art. The artist simply created a depression in a path and filled it with water, creating an artificial puddle. The work caused much debate and consternation at the time and illustrates the way in which a growing number of artists are approaching public commissions. It also serves to demonstrate that the internalization referred to by Grasskamp can also be seen as a rediscovery of the artist's and spectator's subjectivity and not simply as institutional pressure. In this instance, both models – public space and the museum – are replaced by privacy and introspection.

Subjective models of space have played an important part in the visual arts throughout the 20th century. Salient examples include Piet Mondrian's studio, Kurt Schwitters' house, Marcel Duchamp's exhibition arrangements and Brian O'Doherty's description of the 'white cube'. All of these have provided readings of spatial concepts which have been of great significance to Installation art. In each case, we find a conflation of real space with the concept of an ideal model. The German art historian Oskar Bätschmann argues that one of Installation's key characteristics is the ability to form a perceivable space, modelled or arranged towards the presence of the viewer. The above examples are then reminders of the difference between lived space and experienced, or represented space.

The King's Part (1999), a mobile installation by the Canadian artist Rodney Graham, provides a complex model for art in which the mechanism is revealed rather than the intended result. The installation

below Janet Cardiff, *The Missing Voice (Case Study B)*,1999
This work by the Canadian artist Janet Cardiff is based on a soundtrack recorded on the streets of London's East End. The work lasted for fifty minutes, tracing a route through Spitalfields and towards the City of London. Part urban guide, part fiction, part *film noir*, Cardiff's audio walk engaged the listener in a narrative which shifted through time and space. Intimate, even conspiratorial, Cardiff's work created a psychologically absorbing experience.

right Carsten Höller/Rosemarie Trockel, *Ein Haus für Schweine und Menschen* (A House for Pigs and People), 1997

opposite above Maurice van Tellingen, *Shadowman*, 1999
The Dutch artist Maurice van Tellingen creates models which include photography and video. In this work Van Tellingen uses miniature scenes in which the illusion of space is heightened by the combination of the two media. The effect makes the three-dimensional image more real and the action of the drama is rendered atmospheric and filmic as the viewer remains unaware of the plot. Van Tellingen deliberately leaves the main action outside the frame of the work, thus building tension.

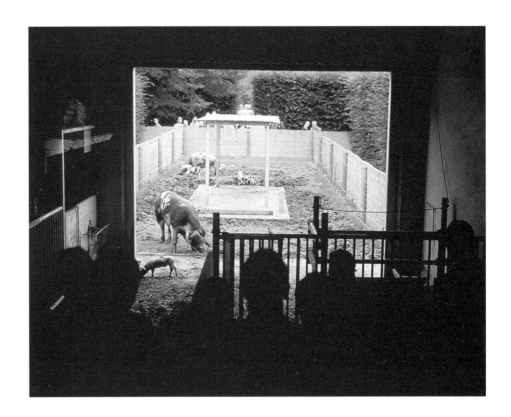

presents a soundproofed box in which the audience can listen to the third flute concerto of Frederick II, King of Prussia. However, no music can be heard since the flute is not blown, the only sounds is the percussive clicks of the instrument's keys performing the work.

Ein Haus für Schweine und Menschen (A House for Pigs and People,1997), a collaboration by the artists Carsten Höller and Rosemarie Trockel, combines a minimalist building with a pigsty. The building is split in half by a glass screen, separating the audience from the animals. The architecture of the work proposes an ironic model for the genetic coexistence of animals and humans. Each of these two examples presents a particular model which questions the viewer's perception of their own presence. The viewer's sensation is heightened by the artwork's ability to propose an altered relationship between the individual and their social environment (Höller/Trockel) and the actual bodily experience through the muting of sound

(Graham). In each case the model creates artificial conditions and provides an environment separate from the external world. At the same time, it is a functioning environment which offers a parallel experience in real time.

By contrast, in architecture, models and computer-generated images serve primarily as future projections for buildings, as in the case of the designs for the new Turner Museum in Margate by the Norwegian practice Snøhetta. Only the actual building provides the user with a tangible spatial sensation. In Installation, as we have seen, the model supports a particular way of addressing the viewer's experience and ceases to be merely a tool. The Dutch artist Maurice van Tellingen maintains that the scale-model, though a traditional genre, can be a miniature installation which challenges viewers' perceptions of space. The space of the installation need not be

below Snøhetta AS, Animation for *Turner Centre, Margate, England*, 2001

above Hans Op de Beeck, *Exercising the Nowhere (2)*, 2000

opposite above Sven Påhlsson, Stills from *Sprawlville*, 2002
This computer animation examines what is at the heart of American society and culture. Through the use of computer-animated images, he reveals the connection between the 'non-place' of the suburban landscape and the Virtual Reality world. Påhlsson's use of generic architectonic models comment on a society in which virtual, electronic experience replaces the actual, physical experience.

opposite below Martin Dörbaum, *Schwimmen mit Vater, de: 'Banana Yoshimoto'* (Swimming with Father), Tsugumi 2000

below Martin Dörbaum, *Microviseur 2200/H*, 2000

entered to be perceived and enjoyed. Accordingly, the painstakingly assembled works by the Belgian artist Hans Op de Beeck and the Russian artist Alexander Brodsky operate on the principle of drawing the viewer into their reduced, yet highly effective theatrical spaces. The model offers an alternative dimension to the activity of Installation art: the viewer cannot enter it other than by virtue of the imagination, albeit by reducing their own scale. This activity of translating scale, from the large to the tiny, and vice versa, provides an invaluable insight into the nature of the viewing experience.

This experience is further challenged by the development of Virtual Reality and Mixed Reality, that is, totally or partially simulated environments. This advanced use of computer technology has brought about the simulation of sites and situations, allowing us to experience different spaces at will, and additionally has called into question our perception of what is real and what is not. The idea of the virtual model differs in many aspects from the 'real' miniature, yet both could be designated as 'heterotopias', a term associated with the French philosopher Michel Foucault. Heterotopias are 'something like counter-sites, a kind of effective enacted utopia in which the real sites, all the other real sites which can be found within the culture, are simultaneously represented, contested and inverted. Places of this kind are outside of all places, even though it may be possible to indicate their location in reality.' The Swedish artist Sven Påhlsson creates entire virtual cities, while the German artist Martin Dörbaum presents private spaces drawn from the domestic. Dörbaum's spaces are achieved without the aid of photographs. They only exist in the digital realm, rather than being modelled on the basis of photographic representations. Similarly, the British artist Paul Noble's *Unified Nobson* (2001), an animated video installation, is entirely conceived in the artist's imagination. No pretense of realism

right Paul Noble, *Unified Nobson*, 2001

opposite Damían Ortega, *Cosmic Thing*, 2002
The central component of the Mexican artist Damían Ortega's work was a disassembled Volkswagen Beetle. The different car parts were suspended in the manner of a three-dimensional diagram. Beetles are still made in Puebla, Mexico, to this day, and carry notions of national identity for Mexicans, while also playing a role in the country's burgeoning globalization.

is made, and the projection reads like a black-and-white drawing, which is charming yet carries an undercurrent of menace. In his book *Being Digital*, the media theorist Nicholas Negroponte states: 'Computers and art can bring out the worst in each other when they first meet. One reason is that the signature of the machine can be too strong...the flavor of the computer can drown the subtler signals of the art.' Though technology has become an integral part of Installation art, it is the way in which artists have appropriated these advances that is important. These 'techniques' have been integrated into their work by artists, often highlighting the artificiality of the medium. Påhlsson and Dörbaum's rendering of space has nothing to do with perceived reality; on the contrary, the digital medium is exposed for what it is. The artists revel in the artificiality of their environments, pointing out that the parallel and simulated worlds of gaming are of greater interest than their real counterparts. Negroponte's argument is thus reversed, making the centrality of the computer's signature desirable.

These spaces, like the real miniatures discussed above, might be described as simulations of elsewhere. The real site may indeed exist, but it is replaced by another version, as recalled in the painstakingly accurate scale models of the Dutch artist Frank Halmans entitled *The bedrooms in which I still wake up* (1996–2002). These installations in miniature, as the artist prefers to call them, are purported to be facsimiles of spaces in which the artist has dwelled. The intimate detail provided by the spaces (individual books on shelves, evidence of tiny hands on distressed paintwork) gives the viewer a sense of familiarity making them almost believable. Their attraction resides in the fact that the viewer is confronted with simultaneous sites: the visible simulation and its real counterpart.

The French theorist Gilles Deleuze maintains the need to reconcile these two positions: the real and the copy. He suggests that each real thing exists in different formats, including that of the simulacrum. In her book on Deleuze, the writer Claire Colebrook claims that 'each unique work of art...is a simulation.' On the basis of this statement, it might be argued that the virtual is the precondition of the real; the real, argues Deleuze, is an image first, before fulfilling its promise of becoming.

Frank Halmans, *The bedrooms in which I still wake up* (studio detail), 1996–2002

'The idea of "copy" presupposes some original model and Western thought has been dominated by the idea of the copy.' An example of this theme can be seen in Micha Ullman's installation *Empty Library* (1995) in Berlin, which marks the burning of books by Nazi students, 10 May 1933. The subterranean rectangular room filled with empty shelving can only be glimpsed through a small glass pane inserted into the cobblestones of the Bebelplatz. Here, the temporary installation has given way to a permanent monument which exhibits a 'paradoxical dysfunctionality'. The paradox resides in the fact that the installation is actually an anti-monument, it is inaccessible and difficult to view. In addition, it does not attempt to celebrate an event, preferring instead to act as a sombre

Chris Burden, *Mexican Bridge*, 1998–99
The American artist Chris Burden created a room of Meccano-like bridges, among them a model of an 19th-century bridge designed, but never built, for a gorge in Mexico and another which replicated the 1928 Tyne Bridge in Newcastle for the first round of shows at BALTIC. Standing back, the large-scale models appeared to be the same size as the Tyne Bridge which could be seen through a panoramic window.

above left Francesc Torres, *The Repository of Absent Flesh*, 1998
In this work twenty objects were displayed on separate identical steel tables in a darkened, warehouse-like space. As the viewer approached each table, a beam of light abruptly illuminated the object and a disembodied voice told the story of the display. Each one referred to a fictive character, acting as metaphors of their memory. The Catalan artist Torres created a vast archive of narrations on memory and modern identity, a portrait of our age, composed as a Proustian history.

above right Francesc Torres, *El continent de cristall* (The Crystal Continent), 1993–94
This monumental work combines a vast field of 48,000 glass bottles with a steamroller apparently making its way towards a glass house at the opposite end of the space. The installation refers to the fragility of civilization in the face of social history and political power.

warning. Ullman's installation provides a model of a library, but not of any particular one, thus eschewing the quest for authenticity.

As new forms of Installation move into the mainstream, questions of value are inevitably raised and addressed. Museums, commercial galleries and collectors have been instrumental in this change. Since more Installation art has found its way into large-scale exhibitions and, subsequently, into major collections, the relationship between the artist, the curator and the collector has been altered. While questioning exhibition practices, Installation has been central in changing the display and collection activity of institutions. The Swedish curator Maria Lind states, 'It is about scepticism and enthusiasm, affirmation and critique all at the same time. As the older generation, so to speak, "broke the ice" with their confrontations and polemics it is easier today to be more nuanced, smart and sensitive.' Installation art now combines a flexible approach to display, while insisting on interaction and discussion with the audience as an integral part of the work itself. Though the collection 'remains the key to the museum', according to the curator Hans-Ulrich Obrist, the question arises about its nature and contents. Obrist makes the distinction between objects and 'life-works'. The latter term refers to artworks involving installations, events and actions in a close relationship with the viewer. Although objects provide the backbone of the institution, it is arguable that new forms will continue to be added to collections which challenge the format and direction of the museum. These new forms may be seen as positively disruptive influences operating within the body of the collection, undermining the educational status of the museum, a development that the British writer Richard Sennett sees as beneficial. He also offers a note of caution, suggesting that participation should not

below Steven Pippin, *Addendum*, 1994 The gallery picture project of the British artist Steven Pippin is made by dividing the space so that one half acts as a camera, recording the other half as its subject. The artist's preoccupation with turning spaces into photo machines, e.g. laundromats converted into pinhole cameras, explores the issue of the self-sufficient machine, which loses its former function and takes on a personality of alienation.

opposite page Monica Bonvicini, *Plastered*, 1998
The Italian artist Monica Bonvicini opposes uncompromising and aggressive actions with the expected reverential behaviour inside the whitewashed gallery. The artist herself can be seen kicking holes in walls or demolishing spaces. In this piece the audience was invited to walk on a fragile plaster surface which covered the entire gallery floor. In one single action, the spectators destroyed the artist's work, while also disrupting the perfection of the gallery space.

substitute for interpretation, leading to the collapse of critical thinking. However, the establishment of new types of audience interaction proposes a different form of interpretation. Interaction is then not simply an opportunity to ensure the audience's participation, but instead suggests a creative engagement with the content of the artwork which directly impacts on the evaluation of the museum itself.

These developments and discussions are well under way in many contemporary institutions and have introduced new forms of display. A curious example of these changes can be found in an unlikely setting: the One Picture Gallery in Penza, Russia, can be seen as an institution unwittingly dedicated to the techniques of Installation art. Paradoxically, it shows no installation whatsoever, instead displaying a single painting at a time. Before viewing the painting, the visitors are given a slide-show that contextualizes the work. Finally, the curtain is drawn back to reveal the single painting. The artwork is framed by a theatrical set. In this instance the experience of the work is mediated by the addition of a further frame, the frame of the proscenium arch. This setting points to the problem of attention commonly experienced in museums, as we are distracted by too many works on display. Though showing only single paintings, the museum makes use of the techniques of Installation in creating a setting for the work, thus turning the work into an environment.

In a discussion between the critics Jeffrey Kastner and Mary Jane Jacob, we are made aware of a paradigmatic shift which has taken place in the art of recent years, suggesting that 'less emphasis was placed on creating an artifact in the traditional sense, and more on exposing and challenging the processes that create cultural activity, whether or not they create art as an object.' According to Kastner's and Jacob's argument, the creation of objects becomes optional. The nomadic artist leaves no physical trace behind and simply moves on. It is arguable that Installation art, with its shift in emphasis from site to open-ended projects, leads to a 'belonging-in-transience' for artists, a state that is neither dependent on lasting objects nor on fixed locations. Accordingly, Michael Landy's installation proposes the wholesale removal of the object: the destruction of the belongings that make up the artist's material life presents a vast installation as a process culminating in dust. *Break Down* suggests a last futile stand of the idea of the *Gesamtkunstwerk*, the 'total artwork'. By confronting us with our own conspicuous consumption, Landy suggests that after art's demise there is always shopping. As Landy writes, 'This project is a kind of luxury in one respect. I don't want the work to be seen as purely negative, as a sacrifice. In a sense, it's the ultimate consumer choice.'

opposite page staatsbankberlin, *Einstein on the Beach*, 2002
For this opera/installation at the staatsbankberlin, artists from various fields as well as scientists were included in the cast. All installations assumed functions traditionally assigned to the theatre. Operatic action became sculptural, the installations provided content for the action, and the music interacted with the artworks and the architecture. During the performance – which lasted four and half hours – the spectator was free to move around in the various halls and levels of the building and explore it as an exhibition. The live music was heard throughout the space and video transmissions allowed for constant monitoring of what was happening in the other rooms. The performance space as a whole was considered as a zone of interaction between the operatic action and artistic and scientific 'intervention strategies'. The participating artists and scientists focused their research either on the relationship between private life and science or on the spectators' attitude towards the music.

escape

If a place can be defined as relational, historical and concerned with identity, then a space which cannot be defined as relational, or historical, or concerned with identity will be a non-place. The hypothesis advanced here is that supermodernity produces non-places.

Describing the sumptuous installations of the Norwegian artist Børre Sæthre, the critic Ina Blom uses the term 'immersive mode...a type of experience in which the subjective awareness...appears to merge with the artwork, so as to create a sensation of a new, more powerful, experience of totality.' Experience is mediated through the body: the degree to which our sensory faculties are stimulated is linked to the impact that an experience has on us. An 'immersive' work may be described as a mixture of sensory and narcissistic pleasure offered to the viewer. Sæthre's 'non-places' are part interior design and part filmset. We are cocooned in the lush experience of the work and identify with its retro-futuristic chic, recognizable from film and television. The artwork's aim to elicit sensual pleasure through sensory manipulation is significant as it mirrors developments in contemporary life; the theorist Frederic Jameson states that 'We are submerged...to the point where our postmodern bodies are bereft of spatial coordinates and practically incapable of distantiation.' Jameson uses the term 'submerged' to describe a space that leaves the individual in a state of confusion. This lack of orientation returns the audience to a reliance on sensation and subjectivity. The critic Paul Virilio suggests that perspectival geometry, in which space is ordered and stable, has given way to 'the relativity of an accidental, discontinuous and heterogeneous space'. These shifts mark important changes in the development of Installation in recent years, as sensation itself appears to have replaced the traditional art object. The 'immersive mode', referred to above, has become a key condition of viewing: it appears to indicate a withdrawal into the self, to a place of bodily sensation. It allows artists to propose an escape from perceived reality which no longer offers stable boundaries.

The Chinese writer Sze Tsung Leong suggests that the term 'space' has been superseded by the idea of 'control space'. Space, in other words, no longer exists as a three-dimensional construct, but instead 'enables the packaging of total environments – the total engagement of the senses – where sights, smells, sounds, feelings are engineered, refined... and deployed for maximum effect. Control space,' Leong continues, 'can be anywhere.' Leong's idea of space provides a useful example for the new interpretation of Installation art. The loss of 'site', discussed in the Introduction, can be linked to changes in our urban experience: the city is no longer perceived as an entity or object, nor is it based on traditional human relationships. In other words, the city is now marked by discontinuity and uncertainty, it has become a 'non-place'. The way we think about space is therefore wholly experiential and is reliant on a series of stimuli, which renders our perception of it much more fluid and transient.

The American artist Andrea Zittel's installation *Raugh Furniture: Lucinda* (1998) provides an ironic look at how we inhabit public and private space. It is a living-room setting in which nature merges with the man-made environment. The gallery in which the installation is presented is occupied by large rock formations of foam rubber, which double as seating and sleeping arrangements. The outside, usually unforgiving and hard, is transformed into a comfortable and relaxing interior fit for human enjoyment. The same artist's *A–Z Escape Vehicles* (1996), designed like minimalist survival capsules, extend the artist's concern with containment and comfort. While their very mobility alludes to and elicits a sense of nomadism, the displacement also acknowledges a desire for solitude, for withdrawal into the self.

The themes of privacy and contemplative withdrawal are echoed in the works of artists such as Gregor Schneider, Lee Bul and Absalon. Absalon, from Israel, foresaw the audience's fascination with intimate spaces in the early 1990s. His installations,

each carrying the title *Cellule* (1991–92), took the form of white cardboard and plaster structures, tailor-made for the artist. These minimal cells displayed a monastic quality which lent itself to contemplation. 'By modifying the architecture, I compelled the visitors to be aware of themselves inside my space,' says Absalon. 'Thus, through his vision of a few items meant for his own use and adapted for rest and peace of mind, the artist describes the domestic universe.' By contrast, the Korean artist Lee Bul presents shiny plastic shells which are highly engineered. Rather than inspired by architecture, they are derived from cutting-edge product design. The futuristic pods, cocoon the individual within environments made for single persons.

If the audience in the work of Absalon and Bul is reduced to the individual, it could be argued that the German artist Gregor Schneider requires no public at all. His work *The Dead House Ur*, (1985–) often related to Kurt Schwitters's celebrated *Merzbau*, consists of the endless remodellings of his house in his native town of Rheydt. The work is 'solitary and secretive' and involves covering the interior with a separate layer by copying or doubling what is beneath. The actual work receives few visitors, but, occasionally, Schneider rebuilds sections of it in museums and galleries. His *Ur* appears to be a celebration and excavation of a specific site, yet on closer examination it is revealed to be a simulation, a situation in which all semblance of the original is lost. As states the

French theorist Jean Baudrillard, 'It is no longer a question of imitation, nor duplication, nor even parody. It is a question of substituting the signs of the real for the real.' The house, its history and function are obliterated by the installation which mimics the original. Although ostensibly the same, the artwork shares none of the house's characteristics and functions, leading to a clear separation between what is real and what is not. The French writer Bernard Marcadé writes of a certain utopia that is 'situated in the non-place of the world'. These are 'locations which of themselves constitute universes provided with an autonomous economy and an autonomous imaginary realm'. Marcadé's notion of a 'non-place' utopia might be shared by the Swiss artists Biefer/Zgraggen, whose work entitled *God* (1998) proposes a parody of a space of worship in the shape of a vast styrofoam dome construction. Lit from within, its surface, rather than being perfectly finished, is roughly constructed in the manner of a stage set. A changing room is provided for viewers to remove their clothes before confronting *God*. The artists stated:'When you look at something beautiful, you also feel as if you are being observed by what you are observing.' The viewer is 'scrutinized' by the work and by other viewers, who themselves are also naked. Although the idea of the 'immersive' may be represented ironically in Biefer/Zgraggen's work, the notion of immersiveness indicates the broadening of references and attitudes towards space and its

relation to the spectator's body. In the Belgian artist Ann Veronica Janssen's work *Blue, Red and Yellow* (2001), steam is released into a specially constructed plexiglas space. The external walls are coated with transparent coloured film, which allows natural light to infuse the room. Unable to see the confines of the space, the audience is enveloped in dense fog which generates shifting patterns of coloured light. As the American artist and writer Robert Smithson has argued, museum and gallery spaces could thus become venues for new forms of entertainment, like 'discotheques'. Janssen's work borrows the sense of euphoria generated by the use of light and sound made in night clubs. *Blue, Red and Yellow* generates an atmosphere that is reliant on the audience's ability to 'let go' and become 'lost' in the work.

The connection between club culture and Installation is no accident. The writer Aldo Bonomi characterizes club culture as 'the quest for outer limits and the realisation of fantasies' which 'are at the heart of existential experience...a smooth space where lived time pursues a glimmering trip-hop of impulses and emotions.' The ambience in clubs is at once introspective, immersive and social; these spaces provide compelling examples of human activity which may cross over into the production and reception of art. In galleries and museums we are now witnessing the rise of a new conviviality brokered by the desire to communicate with others. This activity of spending time in the public space provided by art ranges from interaction and conversation to simply sharing the place with others, while witnessing an event, a familiar occurence for any theatre, concert or cinema-goer. The installation is therefore a focal point for the viewer's attention, as well as a meeting place.

The work of the American artist Doug Aitken exemplifies the change in audience's expectation and attitude. In his exhibition 'New Ocean', at the Serpentine Gallery in London (2002), he showed a wide range of large-scale video projections. The interior of the gallery was remodelled to house 360-degree projections of waterfalls, melting glaciers and other natural phenomena. Eschewing the usual formality of the gallery, the audience was invited to sit or lie on the floor in the darkened rooms to enjoy the spectacle. The work created a viewing environment that was part cinematic and part 'chill-out lounge'. Works such as *New Ocean* are indicative of certain types of installations as 'ambients', relaxed spaces that envelop the viewer while stimulating their senses. Such places are not unique to Installation art, however, and find their counterparts in design and music developments, as well as in 'lifestyle culture'. Other examples of this tendency are found in work by the American partnership Diller+Scofidio whose media pavilion for Swiss Expo 2002 entitled *Blur Building* (2002) – a platform rising from a lake, and shrouded in an artificial cloud – promotes a harmonic relationship between the architectural space, the surrounding landscape and the audience. Viewers are cocooned in high-tech rainmacs which keep them dry as they negotiate the pavilion, and eventually end up in a bar. Diller+Scofidio made use of extensive sensory stimuli to immerse their audiences in environments that fostered sociability through shared experience.

A different approach to immersivity was given in the collaboration of the British artists Bruce Gilchrist and Jo Joelson entitled *Polaria* (2002), the result of a research project in Greenland. On site, over several weeks, the artists recorded natural light conditions. The final work consisted of a white booth with a perspex ceiling which hid an arsenal of fluorescent lights. Viewers entered the space one at a time wearing an insulated white coat and sat in a clear perspex chair. By resting their hands on copper transmitters in the armrests of the chair, the electrical circuit was closed. The lights overhead came on and their luminosity could be controlled by the amount of pressure exerted on the copper pads. The experience of the arctic light was enhanced by the low ambient temperature in the booth. Although the installation referred to a specific site in the sub-polar region, the white booth at its centre merely proposed a space that enveloped the spectator, allowing the individual to explore the changing light conditions. Greenland thus ceased to be a real site and was replaced by the spectator's imagination. The roots of works such as *Polaria* are arguably to be found in the 'sites' and 'non-sites' of Minimal artists of the 1960s, which traced the relationship between

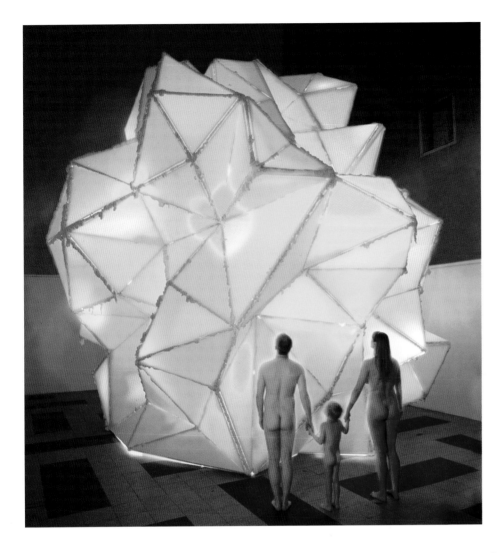

Marcel Biefer/ Beat Zgraggen
God, 1998

outdoor and gallery spaces as a means of critiquing 'display'; yet a crucial change in current artists' attitudes has emerged: no critique of the exhibition system is intended, instead, the focus rests with the viewer as a sentient being.

The immersive space remains fundamentally an experiential and sentient place, though it is also a means of escaping our everyday conditions. Often departing from the artist's body, needs and imagination it succeeds in disconnecting the spectators from their everyday surroundings and transporting them to a place of contemplation. This is not a direct contemplation of the world first and foremost, but a viewing of the self contemplating the external world. As Franz Kafka wrote:'It seems to me that I am not in front of my house, but in front of myself, in front of myself sleeping, and that I at the same time have the joy of sleeping profoundly and of guarding over myself as a sentry.'

Per Barclay

right *Pas de deux*, 2001
In this work two chainsaws 'performed' a violent dance, choreographed to the sound of the destruction of the space. The human figure was physically absent, but potentially threatened. The Norwegian artist creates spaces of palpable tension. He confronts the viewer with the absence of comfort, pointing out issues of sublime and 'terrible' beauty.

below *Untitled*, 1999–2000
This installation by the Norwegian artist consisted of two inflatable structures of parachute silk, powered by motorized fans. The envelopes changed form as the supply of air varied, resembling a giant organism. While gently billowing, the structures were nonetheless perceived as invasive and suggestive of coerciveness. Though the audience perceived no threat, its freedom of movement became restricted.

above and left Lee Bul, *Gravity Greater Than Velocity II*, 1999
The work of the Korean artist Lee Bul consisted of three 'karaoke pods', installed with a video and corresponding song list which addressed a specific theme. In the privacy of the soundproofed, highly designed car-pods the viewer was provided with an opportunity to indulge in a solo performance. The work referred to the significance of karaoke in contemporary Asian cultures.
Bul's work also includes funky street performances, outlandish installations and interactive sculptures. Monstrous and grotesque goddesses are mixed with science-fiction manga characters which interact with cyborgs and sexually predatory living dolls.

above Ann Veronica Janssens, *Blue, Red and Yellow*, 2001
The Belgian artist Ann Veronica Janssens confronts the visitor
with an empty translucent space filled with mist. Coloured

film covers the external skin of the room. Referring to the
tradition of colour field, the artist confronts the beholder
with an immersive non-site without boundaries.

below Bruce Gilchrist and Jo Joelson, *Polaria*, 2002
Returning from their research trip in Greenland, the British
artists Bruce Gilchrist and Jo Joelson created a simulated
daylight chamber. One visitor at a time, wearing a white overall,
entered the immersive chamber. By placing their hands on

two copper plates the audience triggered virtual daylight
responses. The chamber makes explicit the nature of the
body as a technology in itself. The body is both the source
of the data and its receptor, both recorder and transmitter
of phenomena.

below Jaume Plensa, *Love Sounds I-V*, 1998
The viewer opened a small metal door to enter each of the five cubicles made of alabaster bricks and illuminated from within. Once inside, the isolated viewer heard amplified sounds, which were recordings of five different points on Plensa's body. The Spanish artist recorded the fluid passing through his body, creating an inner world of sounds normally inaccessible to our perception.

opposite page Ernesto Neto, *Walking in Venus blue cave*, 2001
Ernesto Neto creates worlds between the body and architecture. His work articulates the spaces of buildings while simulating bodily membranes. These structures are constructed from polyamide, shaped by being pulled across architectural spaces or gorged with substances like powdered turmeric or lead shot. The process is always intrinsic to the form. Neto has created entire rooms out of polyamide material suspended from existing ceiling structures. The corners are weighted and looped over beams or rings to create a semitransparent cube with concave walls. These walls are disturbingly skin-like, an association that the artist sometimes highlights by embroidering small orifices into the membrane. Other polyamide objects are arranged in clusters, taking the form of soft standing tubes, like fungi or crowds of amorphous figures. In every case the works are highly sensual, an experience heightened by the aroma of turmeric or cloves, which strikes visitors long before they see the installations.

above Pipilotti Rist, *Sip My Ocean (Grossmut Begatte Mich)*, video still, 1994–96
The Swiss Video artist Pipilotti Rist understands the impact of pop culture on audiences and she has appropriated the style of music videos with their fast pace and message-induced content. *Sip My Ocean* provides an example of this with its music track and ambient mood.

left (above and below) Absalon, *Cellule nr.6,* 1992
The Israeli-born artist Absalon made a series of works entitled *Cellules.* These were mock-ups of architectonic spaces he planned to install in major cities around the world. They were intended to be his home, like stations in a nomadic life. Based on combinations of the square and the circle, every *Cellule* was self-contained and painted pristine white. Combining elements from the ideals of Le Corbusier with the rigours of the Bauhaus, he produced models of mental and physical spaces. The interiors were cramped, the proportions of the spaces exclusively fitted the artist's body.

opposite above Børre Sæthre, *MY PRIVATE SKY, unit1/trauma white,* 2001
The spatial creations of the Norwegian artist Børre Sæthre focus on our permanent and innate desires for comfort, relaxation and luxury. His artificial, aesthetically perfect environments, echo retro or futuristic filmsets, as might be found in style magazines. Though appealing seductively to voyeuristic and narcissistic needs, the interiors of the artist leave the viewer powerless and isolated. Sæthre's work simulates the experience of a fake totality, trapping the viewer in the construction of a virtual reality environment.

right Siobhan Hapaska, *Here,* 1995
The Irish artist's work was exhibited at Documenta 9 in 1995. The visitor lay on a sheepskin-covered bed, inhaling oxygen from a cylinder to the sound of water trickling all around. The work had a futuristic feel, luxurious and seductive. Hapaska creates works that evoke feelings of escape and travel. This piece also contained sound, fragmented narratives oscillating between hyper-reality and evocations of strange road movies.

right Gregor Schneider,
Ur12 Total isoliertes Gästezimmer
(Completely Insulated Guest Room)
Rheydt, 1995
For the German artist Gregor Schneider
the house acts as a mirror, a thin barrier
between the world as it is, and the world
as he would like it to be. In Schneider's
terms the house is a space of reclusion,
a shrine for anxieties, needs and
aspirations. In the late 1980s the artist
started transforming his house into a
projection of his thoughts. Constantly
assembling, excavating, constructing
and deconstructing, he has rebuilt
walls, added rooms, corridors and
wells, turning his house into a labyrinth.

The house takes on its own personality
and life, claustrophobic and silent, a
totally hermetic environment allowing
the artist to act out, unseen, his
imagined desires and fears. Schneider
reconstructs the house from the
original as a series of public
installations. He meticulously takes
apart the original and reassembles
parts in public museums and galleries.
The overall game of reconstruction,
display of the real, or fake, fuses
together into a blind Borgian play
with no beginning or end.

below Mischa Kuball, *'Believe/ Disbelieve'*, 1999
Kuball's installation focused on blurring the boundaries of built space. Two large motorized mirror-balls spun in the space, while projectors beamed slides with letters from the alphabet onto their surfaces. The room, lit by moving specks of light, appeared to be spinning simultaneously in two opposed directions, producing an effect which was both vertiginous and unnerving.

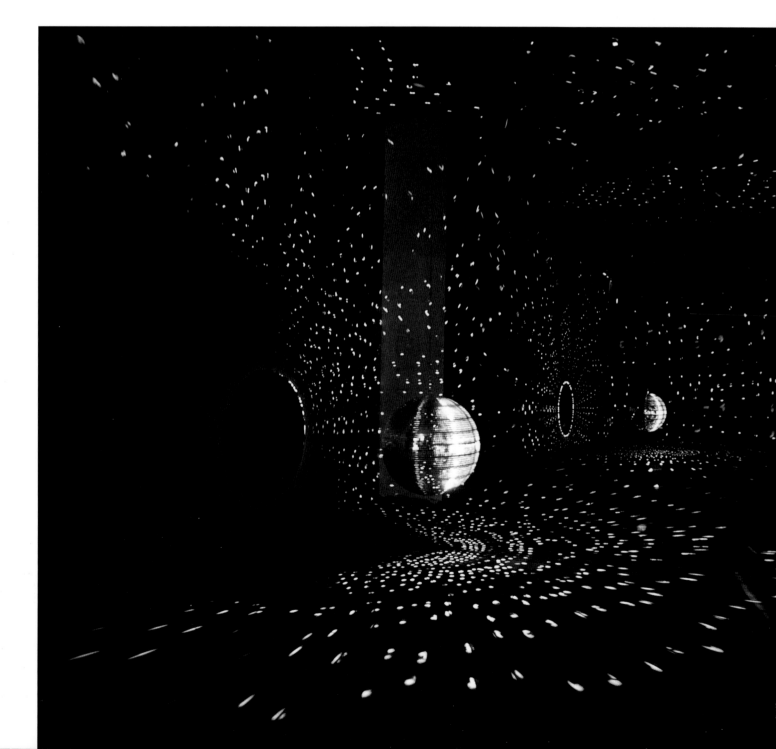

below right Kazuo Katase, *Winterreise*, 1998
The installation of the Japanese artist Kazuo Katase made use of elementary geometries and the play of light and shadow. It was built around the Zen concept of *koan-chaos-satori*, meaning 'the way', a term associated with Japanese sites and ritual. He extends this theme to other situations, through contemplation of Western philosophies and an involvement with theatrical elements – stage sets and spatial dramatization. His work points out that the meaning of being cannot be grasped rationally, only experienced.

opposite above Pierre Huyghe, *L'expédition scintillante, a musical, Act 1, Act 2, Act 3* (The Glistening Expedition) 2002
The French artist Pierre Huyghe set up an imaginary journey to Antarctica as a musical, using spatial stagings which included ice, water, rain, fog and snow. A large ship made of ice slowly melted in one of the galleries, while elsewhere a black skating rink served as the stage for the musical. The entire building was programmed so that light, weather, music and action followed a filmscript.

opposite below Yayoi Kusama, *Dots Obsession*, 2000
This work was presented at the Consortium in Dijon in 2000. Fifty years of involvement in contemporary art has established her as a phenomenon. Her work, as she describes it, is a reflection of her inner life; it includes poetry, novel writing, sculpture and painting and constitutes a body without limits or boundaries. She has taken up residence in a psychiatric hospital where the calm and solitude allow her dreams to travel.

right (above and below)
Jon Lockhart and Tom Cox-Bisham, *Jon Thomas: Together in Electric Dreams*, 2002
The British artists John Lockhart and Tom Cox-Bisham's work entirely transformed the exhibition space, covering every surface with pink and white vinyl, producing a mock-minimal 1980s look. Blue grids covered the white surfaces, alluding to the banal computer aesthetic of the minor classic film *Tron* (1981), in which the hero is imprisoned in a virtual space. Semitransparent plastic sheeting covering the walls hid endless

banks of old audio appliances of which the operating lights flickered and flashed intermittently. The movement and sound generated in each space was monitored via microphones which gave an overall atmosphere of claustrophobia and entrapment. The installation gave the participators total sensory overload as if they were physically immersed in the computer game. Finally, they were offered an exit through a false escape hatch smelling of cherries.

above Julian Opie, *Imagine that you are moving*, 1997
This work was installed at Terminal 1, Heathrow Airport in 1997. In a secure enclosure, designed by the architect Richard Rogers to cater specifically for transit passengers making connections with international flights, Opie's commission presented a stylized vision of the British landscape on four massive lightboxes which ran the full length of the atria and dominating the whole space. This encounter with Britain was inverted in the second part of Opie's work; dispersed around the transfer lounge waiting area were a series of closed circuit monitors. These showed the same stylized landscape, but the images travelled across the screens. The viewer was static but the landscape moved on.

left and below Ugo Rondinone,
It's late and the wind carries a faint sound as it moves..., 1999/2000
Inside a room flooded in blue light, six large-format, black-and-white video projections with twelve loops showed women and men performing simple acts – walking, lying down, dancing. Using atmospheric material from retro feature films combined with his own film material and a soundtrack, the Swiss artist Ugo Rondinone created a performative situation of sustained action and enclosed space.

below Doug Aitken, *Thaw*, 2001
During the exhibition 'New Ocean' by the American artist
Doug Aitken, the viewer entered the exhibiting space through
the basement, descending into the darkness of its utility
spaces and resurfacing in the central body of the Serpentine
Gallery's dome. The overall effect of the work gave the feeling
of being submerged, like swimming in a weightless space.
Surrounded by projections and swallowed by the play of
shadows and colour, the disoriented viewer tried to find
their own intimate order in this apparently fragmented vision.
Literal space was transformed into psychological space.

opposite far right Dalziel+Scullion, *Rain*, 2000
The structure of this work by Scottish artists Dalziel+Scullion
was conceived as a temporary pavilion for the contemplation
of rain. A tin roof amplified the sound of rain, and channelled
it into a collecting pool at the rear. The pavilion was entered by
a long wooden ramp, and a bench was provided for visitors.
The walls of the structure were clad in a cellular plastic
material, which reflected light during the daylight hours.
In the evening the structure was lit by an animated 'gobo'
system which created a stylized pattern of rain on the walls.

opposite above left Ann Lislegaard,
I-You-Later-There, 2000
The Danish artist Ann Lislegaard's
work challenged the viewer's
sensory perceptions. Her use of
logical connections of sight and sound
were contrasted with aggressive shifts
between light and dark.

opposite below Ron Haselden,
Maid of The Mist, 1994
The British artist Ron Haselden divided
the exhibition space into two parts
through a large white screen suspended
at a 45-degree angle across the space.
Two projections using a theatrical
device projecting fire and clouds
alternated on either side of the screen.
Live sounds were relayed from different
areas inside and outside the space.

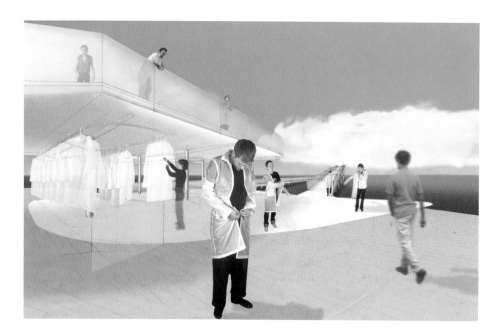

Diller+Scofidio, *Blur Building*, 2002
Diller+Scofidio is a collaborative, interdisciplinary studio which fuses architecture, visual and performing arts. The team is primarily involved in thematically driven experimental work

which takes the form of temporary and permanent site-specific installations, multimedia theatre, electronic media, and publishing.

Blur Building, a media pavilion created for the Swiss Expo 2002, was situated

at the base of Lake Neuchâtel in Yverdon-les-Bains, Switzerland. A fine mist sprayed through thirteen thousand nozzles created an artificial cloud 300 feet wide (91 m), 200 feet deep (70 m) and 65 feet high (20 m). A built-in weather station controlled the fog output by responding to the shifting climatic conditions, measuring the temperature, humidity, wind direction and wind speed. The public approached the *Blur* via a bridge. The 400-foot long (122 m) ramp deposited visitors at the centre of the fog mass on a large open-air platform. Visual and acoustic references were erased when entering the fog, leaving only an optical 'white-out' and 'white noise' of pulsing water nozzles. Entering the cloud, each visitor was asked to respond to a

questionnaire and received a 'braincoat' (smart raincoat).
The coat was used as protection from the wet and for storing
the personality data of the audience communicating with
the cloud's computer network. Using tracking and location
technology, the position of each visitor could be identified,
and as they passed one another, the coats compared profiles
and changed colour indicating the degree of attraction or
repulsion, much like an involuntary blush. The system allowed
interaction among four hundred visitors at a time. Visitors
could climb another level to the Angel Bar at the summit.
The final ascent resembled the sensation of flight as visitors
pierced through the cloud layer to the open sky.

this page and opposite above Olafur Eliasson, *Die Dinge die du nicht siehst* (The Things You Cannot See), 2001.
The Danish artist Olafur Eliasson is primarily interested in a simulation of natural phenomena as art, while at the same time revealing the technique used to recreate it. His ultimate aim is to question our very perception of reality. The entrance to the exhibition was turned into a cardboard tunnel. When visitors walked through it, an optical illusion occurred which made it appear to rotate on its own axis. A machine produced a fog spiral in a side space that contorted and changed shape as the visitors progressed down the tunnel. The fog was expelled into the courtyard where, according to atmospheric conditions, it became more, or less, visible.

left Louise Sudell, *Ascensor Negro* (Black Lift),
1998
The British artist Louise Sudell often
uses magic tricks and entrapment in her
installations. In this work she was influenced
by the famous escapologist, Harry Houdini.
When spectators inside the lift pressed a
button to open the door, instead they became
trapped inside. At the same time a video link
was activated so that viewers outside could
see the panic on the faces of the people inside.
Sudell is well aware of the potential for control
which exists in the relationship between the
artist and the viewer.

below Carl von Weiler, *Nest*, 1993–96 The installation by the London-based artist was a long-term project involving the excavation of earth from the disused basement of a London studio complex. Out of a journey governed by hand digging and exchanging earth for wooden planking, a subterranean 'container' comprising two rooms at different levels and a long connecting corridor began to emerge. The climate was regulated according to body temperature using small heaters and a cooling fan.

Andrea Zittel
above *A–Z Homestead Unit*, 2001
left *Raugh Furniture: Lucinda*, 1998
Though the American artist Andrea Zittel's chairs do not actually provide the most comfortable position for the body. *Raugh Furniture*, inspired by the habits of a dog, which daily changed its resting places, is a form of environmental furniture which can be carved or sculpted continuously as the need in the space changes. This attempt to discover new ways in which to position the body both spatially and socially focuses on Zittel's preoccupation with the nomadic state of human beings. *A–Z Homestead Unit* plays on the concept of ideal spaces for contemporary living, which cater for individuals' needs.

above Lee Bul, *Live Forever*, 2001
This futuristic installation involved video projection and three
soundproofed karaoke booths, pod-like capsules in which
visitors could give a solo performance. Bul first created a
karaoke booth for *Gravity Greater Than Velocity II*. The pods
in *Live Forever* continued the artist's exploration of the
significance of karaoke in contemporary Asian culture.

Doug Aitken
left *Blow Debris*, 2000
This video installation depicts the lives of people living in a deserted landscape (the Mojave Desert, Salton). They appear as nomadic squatters moving restlessly in a post-industrial age.
below *New Skin*, 2002
Aitken's multi-screen Video installation addresses the relationships between man and his contemporary surroundings. It follows a young woman in a Tokyo apartment who is losing her sight and is consuming images for her subjective archive. The narratives reveal themselves in ambiguous windings in which the viewer is engaged: physically by passing through the space, and mentally as the images prevent a single linear viewing.

author and institution

The relationship between art and the institutions in which art is displayed, such as museums, came to play an increasingly important role in the production and reception of art from the 1960s onwards. By the early 1980s, the questioning of the relationships of power between authorship and institutions was seen by many critics as necessary for a postmodern practice, as argued by Hal Foster: '...just as the conceptual artists extended the minimalist analysis of the art object, so too...later artists have opened up the conceptual critique of the art institution in order to intervene in ideological representations and languages of everyday life.' Progressively, artists have come to resist the centrality of the institution in their work. They now tend to move away from projects displayed inside museums, even when given license to critique internal power structures, thus showing their reluctance to participate in arguments formulated by and for museum professionals.

Although artists acknowledge the importance of the gallery space as a means of disseminating their work, the idea of fusing the exhibition with the concept of the gallery has gained ground. In so doing, Installation artists are able to circumvent the agenda of the institution, albeit by appropriating its language and organizational structures. An ironic example of this appropriation strategy can be seen at the Leytonstone Center for Contemporary Art. This organization, launched in 2001, is run by the British artist Bob & Roberta Smith and the American artist and curator Jessica Voorsanger. Leytonstone, a London suburb, houses no significant arts venues. The grandly named Center contains a single skylit exhibition space in a purpose-built shed at the end of the artist's garden. The space may be viewed as a complete artwork or as an art centre in name only, which parodies existing modes of display. It follows that the 'white cube', synonymous with the idea of display, may be removed from the museum or the gallery and reappear in the context of an artist's suburban garden. The Thai artist Navin Rawanchaikul provided an alternative to the standard gallery. His I [love] TAXI (2001) was an exhibition space in which the emphasis was on its reduced scale and portable nature. Artists were invited to create installations in the back of the cab for future passengers. Thus, the audience was reduced to small numbers of individuals who hailed the taxi for the purpose of transport while witnessing an art event.

Though alternative display spaces have been instrumental in the presentation of new and challenging works, their strategies have also been adopted by mainstream galleries. Michael Elmgreen and Ingar Dragset, from Denmark and Norway, install Modernist white cubes in galleries, museums and public spaces. These architectural interventions betray an ironic return to Modernist, functional design principles and simultaneously act as spaces for 'cruising', that is for sexual encounters. Their exhibit *Taking Place* (2001–2002) at the Kunsthalle in Zurich, on the other hand, literally tore down the walls of the galleries, disrupting the workings of the institution. Nothing was completed, rather, it was the upheaval generated by destruction and rebuilding that constituted the work. Elmgreen & Dragset's installation echoed the ideas of the architect and urbanist Cedric Price who proposed that buildings should not be long-lasting, but should disintegrate after a few years. Price also argued that the 21st-century museum should use uncertainty and incompleteness as a catalyst for change.

However, according to Maria Lind, curator at the Moderna Museet in Stockholm, the museum continues to be 'thought of as a place of display, a showroom, and exhibitions are taken for granted as the natural way of dealing with art.' Lind goes on to describe a type of work that 'is oriented towards the everyday. It generally wants to avoid the solemnity and the static quality that often embody institutions, when it is not downright critical of them.' Lind argues that the institution is not dismissed or rejected by these projects, but is 'problematised'. The Swiss-born curator Hans Ulrich Obrist has suggested a shift in the culture of museums, to transform them into 'laboratories'. He states that 'the idea of embracing contradictions is very important.... The laboratory is

about leaving the museum, is against the museum.' Obrist is known for innovative exhibitions and concepts which have travelled to cities worldwide. These include *Cities on the Move* (with the Chinese curator Hou Hanru) in London, Bordeaux, Humblebæk, Helsinki, Vienna and Bangkok (1997–99), *Unbuilt Roads* (1997) with Guy Tortosa and *Do It* (1994–2001), an exhibition format presented in numerous different cities. Obrist advocates flexible exchange with artists, curators and architects. Influenced by Obrist's working methodology, a group of 105 artists, working under the rubric *Morphing Systems* took over a former hospital in Zurich (1998) and began to intervene and interact with each other's works over a period of six months. The hospital site provided in the first place a point of reference for the artists, only to be replaced as the focus for subsequent interventions.

It remains significant that these projects are always accompanied by a publication. Once simply described as 'exhibition catalogues' which complemented the exhibitions, these publications have come to alter, add to, and indeed challenge the perception of the work. The photograph, as a means of documenting a work of art, has had an important role in preserving temporary installations. Indeed, it might be argued that the photograph (in books, magazines and on the internet) has become a major means of viewing Installation art, and that it has superseded witnessing the actual work in situ. Walter Benjamin and André Malraux wrote extensively about the photograph's power to change our perception of art. The result of this technique of reproduction was a waning of uniqueness. While Installation art, through its temporal nature and reliance on place, does not require uniqueness per se, it nonetheless depends on the viewer's experience. The photograph may serve as an aide-mémoire, but it can only offer a view, without transmitting the experience of the work. The display of an installation via a photograph certainly alters its reception as we move from the position of the viewer to that of the reader or browser.

The art theorist Brian O'Doherty refers to the perception of the viewer by stating: 'Avant-garde gestures have two audiences: one which was there and one – most of us – which wasn't.' O'Doherty goes on to argue that the original audience completes the work through memory after seeing the work. 'We from a distance know better. The photographs of the event restore to us the original moment, but with much ambiguity.' Ilya Kabakov, who arguably wrote the most detailed 'manual' in existence for Installation art, argues that 'any installation is incredibly, impossibly sensitive to the place where it is constructed.' To Kabakov, firsthand experience of the work remains crucial. Although we have become used to the documentary value of the photograph (and video) in communicating installations to wider audiences, rarely do we question how our experience is altered by the shift from presence to reproduction. By placing the work in the context of a

publication, the viewer's perception of the work is irrevocably altered. The publication is not simply a means of extending the exhibition's visibility, but it allows curators, artists and designers to rework the context in which the work is shown. This has resulted in innovative ways of displaying installation projects, while allowing the artistic and curatorial processes involved in the work to become revealed. Salient published examples include Rem Koolhaas/Hans Ulrich Obrist's *Mutations* (2001), *Morphing Systems'* eponymous catalogue, Damien Hirst's *I want to spend the rest of my life everywhere, with everyone, one to one, always, forever, now* (1997). The key difference between the traditional catalogue and these examples, is that the more innovative publication extends the possibilities for dialogue and the remit of the installation itself. The publication has thus replaced the importance of site to become the place and meaning of the work. Countless catalogues and magazines have aspired to present 'exhibitions' on the printed page, as predicted by Malraux, in his *Musée Imaginaire*: 'A museum without walls has been opened to us, and it will carry infinitely farther that limited revelation of the world of art which the real museums offer us within their walls: in answer to their appeal the plastic arts have produced their printing press.'

The 're-presentation' of Installation art through a range of different formats confirms its position as a versatile and even unpredictable activity. In his book

From Subject to Project (1994), the Czech cultural critic Vilém Flusser suggested that the notion of the 'project' defined our identity, as it is engagement in some activity that gives us our place in the world. Similarly, installations have come to be increasingly referred to as 'projects', suggesting a greater emphasis on a work's process, while keeping the production of a work more flexible and open-ended as well as stressing its collaborative nature. Such works now require a range of skills, significant financial input and negotiations to secure a location. Thus the project begins as a collaboration, that is to say that 'interaction' is built into the work from the very start. Funding agencies and institutions need to be secured from the outset, rather than solicited later on out of necessity. Such partnerships are not without their problems and they do impact on the work. As Kasper König, director of the Museum Ludwig in Frankfurt suggests: 'The art museum can act as a producer concerning contemporary art...I think this is an important task.' On the other hand, Jerôme Sans, co-curator of the Palais de Tokyo in Paris, continues to question whether the 'museum is really a place for experimentation'. Sans's position is echoed by a growing number of innovative arts organizations which attempt to elude the grasp of the institution. Locus+, founded in 1993, is an organization with networks of artistic centres in the UK and Canada. Its commissioning policy is centred on the artist instead of the institution, 'thus opposing the norm accepted on the UK art scene,' writes Àgnes Ivacs. While artists struggle for acknowledgment of their authorial credentials, institutions have moved away from being solely collectors to being also producers of new works. However, conflicts of ownership may arise between artists and commissioning institutions. 'The work is indivisible from the persona of the artist,' argues Miwon Kwon, 'the intricate orchestration of literal and discursive sites that make up a nomadic narrative requires the artist as a narrator-protagonist.' Having built up the artist's voice, as a means of reaching new and active audiences, the institution will not benefit from its silence.

left Mischa Kuball, *Private Light/Public Light*, 1998
In this project Kuball gradually replaced public lights on the streets of São Paulo with domestic fixtures. In the *Private Light* phase of the project, Kuball moved to the interior site. Standardized lamps replaced private fixtures, which had been removed from different homes and exhibited; in a certain way they thus represented their owners. The private settings, before and after swapping light sources, were documented in photographs. As private tastes gave way to standardized lighting, one language to another, individuality and identity were brought into conflict with civil society.

left Kendell Geers, *Poetic Justice*, 1999
The South African artist's work was concerned with the political heritage of the apartheid regime in South Africa. His work uses television sets and packing materials, pallets, cables, plugs, etc. The themes of the short video loops were intentionally disturbing. Geers wished to evoke the uncanny and a feeling of danger.

Beat Streuli
above *Portraits*, 2002
below *Billboard Sydney*, 1998
Streuli's work is concerned with erasing history and difference, changing images into a flat universalism. The work deliberately uses the language and techniques of advertising. Duraclear images are usually placed in main urban shopping areas or on building concourses. The works consist of larger-than-life portraits of anonymous passers-by who are depicted in a state of deep introspection and juxtaposed with their actual surroundings.

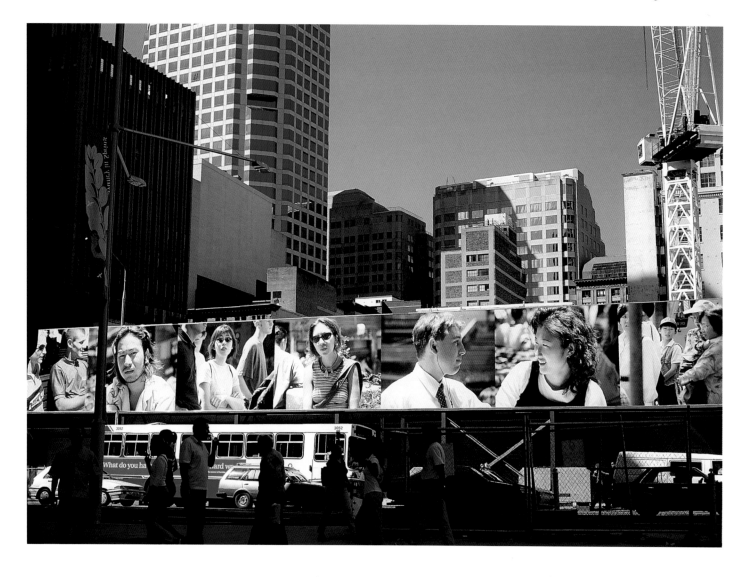

right Tobias Rehberger, *Brancusi*, 1997
Rehberger combines art, architecture and design, focusing
on creations for immediate consumption – instantaneous
works that paraphrase the dogma of modernistic actuality
and question issues of commercialization. The artist designed
an advertisement for a Berlin gallery, which appeared in art
magazines. He then presented the advertisement to a textile
designer, who used it as a pattern for garments worn by
gallery staff during an art fair. Subsequently, the gallery
used the same advertisement as a model for the exhibition
'Brancusi' in 1997. The two-dimensional layout was translated
onto three-dimensional surfaces, which could be interpreted
as 1970s-style furniture or as autonomous sculptures. In this
work Rehberger renounced his authorship, concentrating
like a manager on co-ordinating different processes, thus
reducing hierarchies, but also focusing on the variability
of interpretation and content.

right Françoise Bassand, *3D*, 1998
A number of artists (105 in total) were invited to modify
the interior and exterior of a former private clinic in Zurich,
Switzerland. These works were then 'morphed' by other
artists. One of the participators was the Swiss artist Françoise
Bassand, who created a room inspired by the 1970s wall
decoration in the staircase of the building. Bassand then
invited five more artists, who had been working on the
project, to interact with the existing installation.

Fabrice Gygi
right *Sans nul titre*, 1998
below *Tribunal*, 1999
The Swiss artist Fabrice Gygi fabricates portable structures such as platforms, constructions of metal and plywood, tarpaulins, tents made from foam rubber padding and inflated, oversized airbags from industrially produced materials. The notion of displacement is aimed at the institution destined to host the pieces. Gygi has acquired a keen awareness of the workings of authoritarian power, the ways in which freedom and control, security and threat interact. His installations communicate a deep-seated mistrust of any form of finality where the meaning of the work emerges from an exchange with the physical and mental context in which they are made.

left Luchezar Boyadjiev, *Gazebo*, 1996
Boyadjiev placed four cinema chairs
on a stone platform of local stone from
a cleared site, hired from the farmer
who owned the land. Vegetation
between two private fields was cut
down to create an opening revealing a
view towards the city. This construction
evoked a metaphor of the cinematic
frame and revealed the artificiality of
perception, thus allowing for the
contemplation of landscape to appear
as a culturally constructed utopia.

opposite below Bob & Roberta Smith, Jessica Voorsanger, *Joe Amrhein at the LCCA*, 2001
Bob & Roberta Smith inaugurated the Leytonstone Center for Contemporary Art in his back garden with the artist and curator Jessica Voorsanger. The garden shed acts like a parody of the modernist art gallery, the so-called 'white cube'.
A series of conferences, actions and exhibitions have been held in the equivalent of a garden shed from which they deliberately comment on the institution and undermine its authority .

below Michael Smith and Joshua White, *The QuinQuag*, Arts and Wellness Centre (touring exhibition), 2002
Combining the irreconcilable language of corporate entrepreneurship and New Age spiritualism, the New York based artists Michael Smith and Joshua White created an elaborate installation about a fictional art colony. The installation took the form of a travelling exhibition, displaying apparently authentic photographs, craft objects , self-help videos and artworks. Through the use of elements familiar from news stories and historical narratives, the viewer was immersed in a fictional world.

below Jorge Pardo, *Pier*, 1997
In many of his works the Cuban artist Jorge Pardo makes explicit reference to the exhibition site, combining the exhibition venue, the artwork and the conditions of its reception. In Münster, Germany, in 1997, Pardo constructed a 131-foot-long (40 m) pier, which led to an open pavilion and a viewing platform with steps to a lake. Pardo often highlights the utilitarian aspect of his installations, making furniture and arrangements in order to focus on a distinction between art and design.

above Mark Dion, *Alexander Wilson Studio*, 1999
The American artist Mark Dion has been involved with the history of collection, classification and display as practised by scientific institutions such as natural history museums or pre-museum archives (*Wunderkammern* and Cabinets of Curiosity), often collaborating with museums like the Tate, London. Using the strategy of imitation, the artist assumes the role of a scientific researcher and explorer in order to analyze the ideological foundations and the myths of objectivity and neutrality of such institutions. His environments include 'realistic facts' which are theatrically exaggerated and fictionalized.

opposite Ayşe Erkmen, *Sculptures on Air*, 1997
Antique sculptures from a museum collection were carried by helicopter from the museum's storage place, located some distance from the main building, to the roof of the museum. Each time, the helicopter carried a new sculpture and took away the previous one. A sculpture stayed on the roof until the next one arrived. This action of the Turkish artist Ayşe Erkmen was repeated once or twice a week at Münster Sculpture Projects, 1997.

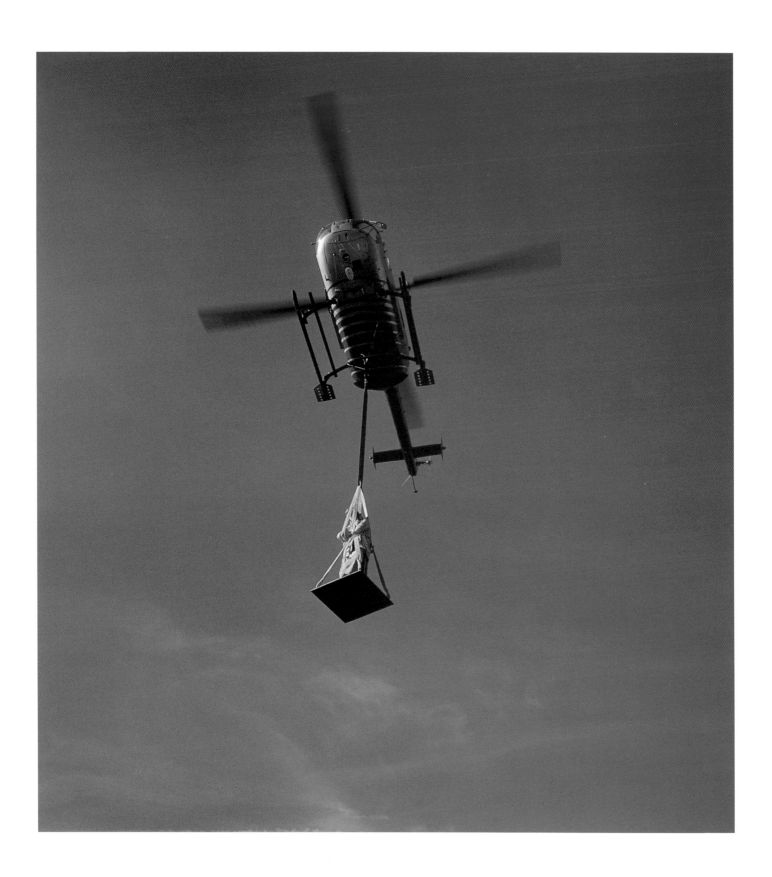

below Hans Haacke, *Der Bevölkerung (To the Population)*, 1999–2000
The work consisted of an installation in the northern open-air courtyard of the Berlin Reichstag (German Parliament building) and a web site. At the invitation of the Bundestag the artist invited the 669 members of the German parliament to fill an oblong wooden trough with 100 kilogrammes of earth from their respective electoral districts. The dedication *Der Bevölkerung* was chosen to contrast with the words on the portal of the Reichstag, *Dem deutschen Volke* (To the German People). The dedication was designed with the same typographic font and size. Haacke interpreted the writing *Dem deutschen Volke* as 'nationalistic' because it failed to take into account people from other countries. The project sparked debate between the political parties in the German parliament, with 260 voting for the project, 258 against it and 31 abstaining. All the Conservative parties rejected the project.

above and opposite Christo and Jeanne-Claude, *Wrapped Reichstag*, Berlin, 1971–95
In 1945, after the battle for Berlin, the Reichstag was in ruins. It was restored however between 1957 and 1971. After the fall of the Berlin wall in 1989, the Reichstag regained its status as the seat of the German parliament. Already in 1961 Christo had created a collage with photographs and a text, entitled *Project for a Wrapped Public Building*. The idea of the *Wrapped Reichstag* was developed between 1971 and 1995, during which time the Christos spent many months lobbying in Bonn, talking personally to 352 MPs, to convince the German parliament to grant permission for the wrapping of the building. Permission was refused three times, in 1977, 1981 and 1987. Finally, the

Bundestag voted to grant permission on 25 February 1994. On 18 June 1995 at 5 a.m. the unfurling of the fabric began simultaneously on the four façades. Custom-made cushions placed between the cages supported the rolls of fabric, keeping them in a horizontal position and facilitating the unrolling. For safety reasons, every panel was temporarily roped tight in case of a sudden wind. The entire roof and both inner courtyards were wrapped with 100,000 square metres of 70 recyclable, aluminum-coated, fabric panels. The rooftop wrapping was secured by blue ropes which in turn were attached to 270 anchors on the roof and weighted on the sidewalks around the building. The Reichstag remained wrapped for fourteen days.

Christo and Jeanne-Claude have completed many projects, including wrapping buildings, surrounding islands with floating fabric skirts and fencing in miles of coastline and inland hills. All these have taken years of planning. The sale of early works of the 1950s and 1960s, as well as the preparatory drawings, fund their projects. In fact, drawings and collages add to the development of ideas and serve as pre-documents which can be compared with actuality. The whole process is part of the work, be it meetings with town planners, site owners, court hearings, bureaucratic redtape and the installation of the work. All Christo and Jeanne-Claude's projects are site-specific and time-based (often only being up for a few days or weeks) and can be looked upon as large-scale site installations.

below Anish Kapoor, *Tarantara*, 1999
Anish Kapoor's installation at the
BALTIC, Newcastle, in 1999 was part of
of a programme of commissioned works

entitled 'B4B' in collaboration with the
region's cultural organizations. The new
Art Centre was still under construction
and would only be completed in 2002.

opposite above Thomas Hirschhorn,
World Airport/ Flugplatz Welt, 1999
The Swiss artist Thomas Hirschhorn's
works are epic and detailed displays.
He chooses disposable materials,
cardboard, tape and tin foil, which he
uses as umbilical cords to connect the
environments. The deliberate use of
crude materials coupled with the
monumental subject matter produces
a metaphorically fragile world which
questions the hypocrisy of political
power structures and the museum
as an institution. Hirschhorn deliberately
employs what he himself describes as
cheap tricks and stupid things in order
to humorously undermine power.

opposite below Micah Lexier,
*Ampersand: A Project for the
Sheppard/Leslie Subway Station*, 2002
Every wall of the new Sheppard/Leslie
Subway Station was covered with one
of 17,000 custom-printed tiles. The
tiles bore the handwriting of different
members of the public, spelling the
words 'Sheppard' and 'Leslie'. During
May 1997 the public were invited to fill
out ballots which were then enlarged
and turned into individual tiles. A total
of 3,500 different samples where
selected and made into an edition of five
tiles. The work played off the dichotomy
between community and individuality
and was a homage to the unique yet
anonymous contribution of those
who participated.

right Daniel Pflumm, *Ohne Titel* (Untitled), 1998
In the early 1990s the Swiss artist Daniel Pflumm set up
a series of lifestyle spaces, like clubs, creating fashionable
forums for art as action. He renegotiated the idea of corporate
identity, appropriating visual indicators, symbols from the
world of the media, logos, spear points of image production
in a live situation. Using the elevations of various venues
around the world Pflumm installed illuminated signs of his
logo. This underlines the artist's mission to include a corporate
symbol which lives on after the exhibition is over and leaves
a permanent brand on each institution.

below Barbara Bloom, *Pictures from the Floating World*, 1995 Hundreds of male and female oriental masks of stone-coloured plaster were arranged in pairs on a red floor painted the colour of Chinese lacquer. A vitrine was placed in the middle of a carved wooden bridge spanning the whole space. Six magnifying lenses were mounted into the glass top of the vitrine and positioned over six grains of rice which each bore a miniature erotic Japanese image. The installation focused on the theme of scale, composed as it was of elements both extremely large and small. The beauty of the forbidden, censored erotic Japanese Shunga prints contrasted with the large field of masks on the floor.

right and below Tatsurou Bashi (alias Tazro Niscino), *Villa Victoria*, 2002
Bashi's *Villa Victoria* was a hotel room, built around an existing monument of Queen Victoria, which could be hired for the night. It was commissioned by the International 2002 exhibition for the Liverpool Biennial. The exterior resembled a building site, but it concealed a highly finished and comfortable interior. The scale of the monumental sculpture in a domestic setting drew attention to the difference between public and private space.

left Micah Lexier, *The Hall of Names*, 1996

The work by the Canadian artist Micah Lexier consisted of one thousand laser-cut stainless steel names which were hung in a series of chains in the 800-foot-long (244 m) Grand Concourse of the National Trade Centre in Toronto. From a submission of 6,435 names from over 65 communities across Canada, the Canadian artist randomly drew 1000 names to be included in the work. Lexier's work is preoccupied with the audience's participation through anonymous processes.

above Stefan Brüggemann, *Capitalism and Schizophrenia*, 2003

The Mexican artist Stefan Brüggemann's work makes an ironic reference to the writings of the French philosophers Deleuze and Guattari. The vast styrofoam letters were produced and shown at the same factory in Puerto Rico, thus combining the activities of making and exhibiting in one site. Brüggemann's work employs techniques of quotation to comment on the history of ideas.

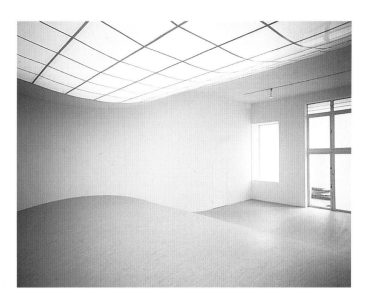

right Elmgreen & Dragset, *Powerless Structures*, *Fig. 111*, 2001; below *Taking Place*, 2001–2002
In their work the Scandinavian duo Michael Elmgreen and Ingar Dragset created a series of white cubes, which were displaced, fragmented and manipulated. The artists had staged unexpected clashes between the aesthetic of the white cube and that of sites of gay sexuality. The work showed not only the powerlessness and flexibility of all structures – white walls do not have to carry the kind of transcendental significance they are sometimes assigned – but also a gay 'infiltration' of modernist aesthetic.

Miguel Leal
right *Bunker Project (1996–99), Museum of Modern Strategy — International Department Room*, 1999
below *Bunker Project (1996–99), Museum of Modern Strategy – Frozen objects: Producing Contents; Showcases and Institutional Objects*, 1999

The *Bunker Project* of the Portuguese artist Miguel Leal is an ongoing work which has been shown in different locations around the world, varying its configurations at each site. The *Museum of Modern Strategy* (*MOMS*) was set up by the artist as a critique of the museum and its power base. It was planned on the basis of a fictional and heterodox structure, seeking to use its ambiguous status to largely justify its existence. *MOMS* is part of a vaster project with the generic name of *Bunker*. The first classification of *Bunker* included the *Analytical Department*, the *Art Department*, the *International Department*, the *Digital Department* and also the *Revolting Museum Project*; the second category included the projećts *Bird's Eye*, *Night Watch* and *Warin Theory*.

above and below Joëlle Tuerlinckx,
*In Real Time, Space Parts/ Night
Cabin/Solar-room*, 2002
An announcement is heard as the
spectator enters this space. A female
voice draws attention to the 100 per

cent natural daylight conditions in the
gallery and assures the audience that
any changes are due to bad weather and
climatic conditions. The Belgian artist
Joëlle Tuerlinckx comments on gallery
decorum and manners, where art ends
and the everyday begins. Everything in
her work is in transit, between display
and stockpile, gallery installation and
skip. Tuerlinckx's work is not a
commentary on art, but more on small
perceptual shifts that change our
understanding of reality.

opposite above and below
Dutton/Peacock, *Apocotropes*, 1996–97
The British artists Steve Dutton and Percy Peacock began collaborating on projects in 1996. Much of their work had involved the use of large-scale, often inverted or revolving photographs. Three 6-foot-square (0.5 m square) photographs on MDF proposed the artist's studio as an artwork in various stages of production. The photographs effectively documented the processes of their own production, within which the location of the 'work' is difficult to define. The status of photographs as props, complex artworks, or factual documents is here problematized.

left above and below Michel François, *Bureau Augmenté* (Enlarged Office), 1998
The work of the Belgian artist Michel François transformed the gallery into a chaotic office: computers, empty bullet casings and capsules, a heap of metal coins spilled onto the floor, stacks of newspapers littering the carpet, primary coloured numbers and letters seeming to float on the walls, loose wires dangling from the ceiling. The busy effect of clutter and excess was accentuated by the incessant flashing of a white fluorescent light and several videos perpetually playing in various corners of the gallery. The sound of frogs emanated from hidden speakers, objects came apart, spilled over, scattered and separated in a series of gestures that explored chaos, order, dispersion and restoration. The installation mirrored the disintegration of the gallery as an inert white cube, revealing the tension and deadening repetition of our daily working lives and finally reflecting a Kafkaesque view of corporate life.

below Dutton/Peacock, *Europe*, 1999
In this work Dutton and Peacock threw
the contents of a vacuum cleaner into
the air at their studio and a series of
photographs documented the event.
These sequences were concerned with
the use of the studio as a space of
ambiguous production. One photograph
was chosen to be inverted and made
into a postcard. The resulting card was
then widely distributed around Europe.

below and right below John Newling, *Weight*, 1998

This work by the British artist John Newling examines the relationship between literal and metaphorical value by revealing human traces extracted from coins. Ten laboratory assistants weighed and cleaned fifty thousand two-pence coins at the gallery, which had been transformed into a well-equipped laboratory. As part of this pseudo-scientific method, tents erected on an adjacent roof acted as evaporation sites for the cleaning chemicals. All the residue of human touch was removed from the coins and stored in jars placed on ten laboratory tables in the gallery and could be viewed at the end of the experiment. Calculations demonstrated that the dirt on the coins had a measurable value, equated to the weight of seven pence, a magic number. Newling's work offered an intriguing exploration of the relationships between people and objects of financial and cultural worth and consequently questioned value systems.

below right Henrik Plenge Jakobsen, *Diary of Plasma*, 1995–96
Experimental science as an ecstasy of limits is the subject of this ongoing video/publication/installation project. The installation uses fake scientific elements and real laboratory materials, such as a urine reactor. The core of the piece is the text, of which the plot mirrors Mary Shelley's Frankenstein story, a young scientist who works with an undefined biotech product and has been deadlocked in a blind alley of psychosis. The work counters the utopian expectations of experimental science. Jakobsen's art constitutes a tenacious intervention in the structures that determine systems. It throws doubt on the human body as matter and on its relation to authority and the social context.

right Martin Creed, *Work No 270 'The Lights Off'*, 2001
The spectator's gaze is directed through the darkness of
the empty space to a sales certificate on the gallery wall.
'The Lights Off' perfectly expresses the conceptual position of
the British artist and Turner Prize Winner, which is marked
by sublime humour and an often paradoxical pragmatism.

below Renato Niemis, *[;]*, 1994
The British artist Renato Niemis built a wooden catwalk, an
isolated, floating path, on which visitors were allowed to walk
and stand. The piece frames the setting of the exhibition space
by focusing the viewer's attention on the relationship between
the viewer and the viewed.

left and below Hew Locke, *Cardboard Palace*, 2002
This was a vast architectural construction which investigated
the traditions of British culture and heritage, resonating
with issues surrounding the nation's monarchy. Locke created
an apparently chaotic structure, in which visitors negotiated
loosely defined areas. As viewers passed through this
fantastical maze, they witnessed a series of cardboard
images of the British royal family, delicately intertwined
with cut-out texts alluding to packaging, export and
commodity culture.

exchange and interaction

In the seventies and eighties, we lived in a society of spectacle, in the nineties in the society of participants, and we are now developing a 'society of interactors'.

It is necessary to explore the assertion that the spectator, the viewer of an artwork, is now an interactor and the ways in which this affects the artist and their chosen forms of address. What strategies do they employ to facilitate the desired interaction and exchange, and in what way does new Installation work address such issues?

The opening of the Palais de Tokyo in Paris in 2002 was welcomed as a new 'site of contemporary creation'. Nicolas Bourriaud, joint project director, put forward his idea about 'relational aesthetics', which sees art's response to an ever more regimented society to introduce 'interactivity, conviviality and relationality'. He proposed an art in which objects are catalysts generating communicative processes.

Rirkrit Tiravanija, from Argentina, is one such artist. According to Paolo Bianchi, co-curator of the exhibition *LKW* (from *Lebenskunstwerke*, 'life artworks'), held in Bregenz, 2000, Tiravanija 'mistrusts objects, putting his faith into that which takes place between people, in communication.' Tiravanija's collaborative installation *Bon Voyage, Monsieur Tiravanija. Opel Blitz* with German artist

Franz Ackermann consisted in a remodelled truck containing a library of guidebooks, together with a series of monitors showing videos by the two artists on their travels. 'The truck provides new, more open, more flexible and more spontaneous structures,' stated the artists. Elsewhere in the exhibition, the Danish Collective N55 constructed sleeping arrangements, a kitchen and a waste-disposal system. The work focused on the economics and activities of everyday lives and needs.

A different approach to alternative lifestyle culture is taken by the Dutch group Atelier van Lieshout, who rely on a factory-like environment to generate their projects. Their catalogue raisonné, *A Manual* (1997), shows their full range of artistic products, along with detailed instructions on their manufacture for the audience. The large, glass fibre, reinforced polyester environments are often portable. The vehicle subject appears frequently and provides an art that makes a virtue of its mobile nature.

Tiravanija and Ackermann's collaboration focuses on the 'nomadic' element of place, as the site of the work changes continuously and each location visited by the truck relies on a different audience, offering alternative readings of the installation. Van Lieshout's modules also eschew the notion of a fixed site through their utopian living spaces which prioritize human activity. The location becomes simply the place the same time appear as if they do not quite belong anywhere. In this way, their restlessness is underlined by the suspicion that they are 'non-places', totally mobile yet essentially rootless.

The questions of mobility and exchange with different audiences have come to dominate the practice of Installation. The two terms are linked, since the mobile or flexible site enables artists to reach a greater diversity of viewers. The works of Spanish artist Alicia Framis and Mexican-born Jose Dávila provide examples of these developments by involving their audiences in activities and exchanges, which in turn raise questions about the institutionalized behaviour patterns of viewers towards art. Framis's *Blood Sushi Bar* (2000) invited visitors to partake of food in a highly designed environment, while Dávila's *Open Studio* (2000) included discussion on the nature of artistic production in the open air. The installation was a set resembling an artist's private working space. The studio, or indeed its absence, had become the exhibit, as it generated nothing beyond itself, other than a critique or discussion of the traditional studio which has provided a crucial focus for artists over centuries.

Many contemporary Installation artists today have abandoned the studio, preferring to work on a 'project' basis whenever required. If artists are invited to make installations for a gallery, the given space

is produced is compounded by the spread of electronic communication and international mobility. The result is the production of an increasingly restless kind of artwork.'Thus, if the artist is successful,' writes Miwon Kwon, 'he or she travels constantly as a freelancer, often working on more than one site-specific project at a time, globetrotting as a guest, tourist, adventurer, temporary in-house critic, or pseudo ethnographer.'

As Installation has moved into the centre of artistic practice and with it, embraced its constant mobility, it has reached new types of audiences, resulting in different modes of audience participation. Installation provides places for exchange in which the audience becomes an integral part of the work, as shown in these examples. The artist, as a rule does not perform to the audience, rather it is this open-ended interaction with the potential of the real-life situation that mark the viewer's experience.

This theme of exchange may also take the form of commercial activity. The British artist Mark Povell's exhibition *Supply & Demand* (2001) at the Museum of Installation, London, invited visitors to make drawings on computer terminals, which were then turned into three-dimensional cardboard objects. The transition from drawing to object was cemented by the filling out of a contract between the artist and the interactor and on receipt of the object the interactor was asked to pay an appropriate sum to the artist. Here art became a non-essential 'service provision' to the spectator. According to Kwon, 'The artist as an overspecialised aesthetic object maker has been anachronistic for a long time already. What they provide now, rather than produce, are aesthetic, often "critical-artistic" services.' This absence of art objects can be seen in the work of the British artist Simon Moretti. *A Space For Conversation* (2000) consisted of circular carpets laid on the access-ramp of the Tate Modern museum in London. The installation created an intimacy in a busy thoroughfare, as visitors were invited to sit on the carpets and participate in a drawing project devised by the artist. While Moretti asked viewers to participate in producing, the level of public interaction required in Surasi Kusolwong's *Happy Berlin (Free Massage)* of 2001, was simply to submit to the free service provided by the artist's professional crew: a massage. Kusolwong, from Thailand, promotes an egalitarian and inclusive art, while looking after his visitors' needs. The participation in a form of 'game' in Moretti's Installation led participants to indulge in seemingly open play which stimulated inventiveness. The media theorist Marshall McLuhan had predicted the growing desire within post-industrial culture for playing games, an argument which he extends into the world of scientific research: 'The world of science has become quite self-conscious about the play element in its endless experiments with models of situations otherwise unobservable.'

It is through the shared mode of 'play' that artists and scientists have found perhaps the most intriguing partnerships. The depth of research provided in this field has attracted a number of artists to form new relationships and collaborations. In particular, the absolute necessity of process and play in scientific research provides a useful parallel for artistic practice.The Belgian-born artist Carsten Höller initially trained as a scientist. His installations combine the rigorous language of science with playful experimentation. Wim Delvoye, also from Belgium, shares Höller's engagement with research, culminating in what is arguably his most provocative work *Cloaca* (2001) shown at the New Museum of Contemporary Art in New York and in Switzerland. The work was a complex machine which commented both on the methods of manufacture, as well as on our revulsion towards bodily effluvia. The machine replicated the human digestive tract and was fed a careful diet of food prepared in the adjacent kitchen. This passed through several chemical stages of 'digestion', each part clearly visible to the audience, until the apparatus produced perfect examples of stools. The work also played with the idea of participation, in that it needed to be continually fed to produce editions which the audience could take away. The audience was offered the very thing it does not want as a by-product of the artistic process. While *Cloaca* uses scientific methods and manufacturing technology to his own ends, *Polar* (2000), a collaboration between Marko Peljhan and Olaf Nicolai, sought to utilize science as a means of disclosing new relationships between art and technology. Exhibited in Tokyo, it was represented by an installation that revealed the internet in real time. The artists compared it to the sentient sea in the Stanislav Lem story which became the basis for *Solaris* by Andrej Tarkovsky. Peljhan, from Slovenia, and Nicolai, from Germany stated: 'We wanted to create an interface between the matrix and the human senses and body.'

To those who would believe that social interactivity might provide an unproblematic solution for the future of art, Bourriaud offers a word of caution: 'Now that the ideology of the internet links and continuous contact has come to pervade the globalised economy...how much critical radicality is left to work based on sociality and conviviality?' He champions instead a type of exhibition that addresses 'a new problematic, that of the coexistence of humans, objects and forms, which generates a specific meaning.' The exhibition is not simply a means for conviviality, but to Bourriaud it acts as 'a cognitive tool', a way of generating meaning and content.

The German artist Christian Jankowski's installations appears to bear out Bourriaud's argument. The encounter with others leads to a series of dialogues which transform the outcome of his works. In *Mein erstes Buch: Inszeniertes Schreiben* (My First Book: Staged Writing, 1998) Jankowski sits in a gallery and invites a range of specialist consultants to aid him in writing his first novel. The artist is not 'performing', instead he is absorbed in the process of writing or in discussions.

The question of process as a form of dialogue between artists, collaborators and audiences is of paramount importance to many contemporary installations. What is intended here is to suggest that the form of the artwork has become secondary to its journey and duration. Fluidity has become a buzzword in the new millennium and is indicative of a lack of boundaries. It is unsurprising that artists are keen to work with flexible boundaries, a desire that begins to explain the rise of the art-project which can take any form, occur anywhere and, as Rirkrit Tiravanija states, include 'lots of people'. Moreover, the development of the audience as a site, that is, the centre and meaning of the work, has resulted in a shift from aesthetic and art-historical issues to a concern with the social integration of the installation. The cross-fertilization between disciplines, the exchange between curators and artists and the interaction with audiences as a means of generating the work itself have all been instrumental in shaping Installation art. The Chinese curator Hou Hanru states that 'we are contributing, directly and jointly, to the development of situations'. Such 'situations' based on exchange and interaction bear witness to the open-ended and inclusive approach to Installation art in the new millennium.

above and right Cai Guo-Qiang, *Cultural Melting Bath*, 1997
The Chinese artist transported 30 tons of rock from Diangsu in China to New York. Using traditional *feng shui* on the site, the massive Taihusu rocks were each carefully selected for their characteristics of stimulating the flow of energy in the space, and bestowing beneficial *qi* on the museum and its visitors. The clusters of rocks also contained a Chinese medicinal herbal bath. Cai sees his therapeutic *Cultural Melting Bath* as a metaphor for social healing. In his work he used the term 'melting pot', inviting individuals from disparate backgrounds to bathe together, fusing East and West.

opposite page Carsten Nicolai and Marko Peljhan, *Polar*, 2000
This collaborative piece by the Slovenian artist Pelijhan and the German artist Nicolai was produced by Canon Art Lab in Tokyo; they were awarded a golden Nica at Ars Electronica for their work. *Polar* works as a tool to experience the network in real time. It is a machine that translates and makes visible not only the information flow, but also the meaning of data that is found in the networks. Peljhan described the work as follows: 'We envisioned the space as totally connected, as a complex tactile – matrix.' This enables the audience to experience the data in the global and local networks in a completely immersing yet cognitive way. The work was inspired by the notion of the sentient ocean in Stanislaw Lem's novel and the film *Solaris* by the director Andrej Tarkovsky. 'We wanted to create an interface between the matrix and the human senses and body.'

above and below N55, *Hygiene System Extended*, 1999
This collective WC, an object referring to a kind of minimalism with social consciousness, was created by N55, a Danish artist collective, founded as a group in 1994. The experiments focused on an examination of social conventions and issues of power, which influence the audience's perception. This social experiment in the everyday included confronting people in a combination of leisure and work environments.

above ECM 323, *Test Sites*, 1999
The group of artists ECM 323 created a set up which surveyed and analyzed experimental sound, virtual imagery and individual perceptions. The primary theme of the project was how sound can influence form and vice versa. The piece focused on the investigation of an audience's response to Binaural brain frequencies, the manifestation of wave forms as visual information, and the production and evolution of acoustic signals realized as electronic feedback.

opposite above Rirkrit Tiravanija, *Untitled, (He Promised)*, 2002
This Argentinian-born artist was brought up in Thailand, Canada and Argentina. His work fuses art and life, from music to cooking. The performative and interactive projects pursue cultural boundaries and themes such as nomadism, global art and the internet. He has been working on a democratic art magazine in which contributors can publish their own work around the world, without editorial restrictions.

opposite below Carlos Amorales, *Producion/Calidad*, 2002
The Mexican artist Amorales created a metaphoric *maquiladora*, a cost-saving business venture which seeks to attract corporations, usually American, to bring manual jobs to Mexican border towns. Amorales's work suggested a warehouse by a geometric grid marked on the museum floor, using famous artworks from the permanent collection, some in boxes for shipping, others on view for the public. The work raised socio-political questions about production and consumption and explored the issue of the museum as a storage area but also as a participant in the globalization of the art trade.

above Keith Tyson, *Supercollider*, 2002
The exhibition title by the British artist Keith Tyson, was derived from the slang name for the CERN particle accelerator in Geneva. A giant glowing sphere, two metres in diameter, gradually changed colour as it reacted to heating and cooling elements inside. *Field of Heaven Long Shot Magnet* presented a motorized model which made real pieces of planets and meteorites, including a chunk of the moon. These rotated around each other in an orbital arrangement that would never occur in reality. Tyson's ongoing fascination with scientific ideas and philosophical arguments leads to a desire to experiment with information, drawing objects and devising systems that question our existence.

Carsten Höller
above and right *Glück*, 1996
opposite above *Skop*, 1996
opposite far right *Riesenpsychotank*, 1999
The Belgian-born artist's work is based on his training as a biologist and explores theories of evolution which regard human sentiments, such as love, primarily as strategies for the reproduction of genetic material. Formally, his installations remind us of laboratory structures in which it is possible to fly around in a circle, immerse one's head in an aquarium or to speed down a slope in a soundproofed

sledge. *Glück* features an experimental obstacle course in which visitors see themselves as subjects and conductors of experiments at the same time. For the 'Sanatorium' exhibition, he created *Riesenpsychotank*, a large, semi-transparent container, offering the audience the chance to bathe in public.

above Alicia Framis, *Blood Sushi Bank*, 2000
'Art can occur anywhere; it is not the space that makes the event but the event that creates the space,' states the Spanish artist Alicia Framis. *Blood Sushi Bank* was an interactive and highly stylized bar which offered food for thought to the audience. The service provided by the artist gave visitors an experience in which they could participate, thus questioning their perception of artistic production.

left and below Mark Povell, *Supply and Demand*, 2001
British artist Mark Povell devised a computer programme which generated templates for a system of simple three-dimensional objects; these templates were designed to be customized by the visitor to produce new objects. The *Supply and Demand* team undertook to manufacture versions of these objects over the course of the exhibition period as part of a 'contract' with the visitor. The visitor was asked to offer an 'interpretation' in exchange for the object and equivalent to their estimation of its value.

below left Surasi Kusolwong, *Happy Berlin (Free Massage)*, 2001
In the 2nd Berlin Biennale, Kusolwong used Thai silk curtains
to divide the museum space and opened it as a massage salon.
Almost every day during the two-month show, museum goers
were invited to have a free traditional Thai Massage. While
waiting, they could relax on comfortable mattresses watching
the film *The Mask of Zorro*.

below right Surasi Kusolwong, *Emotional Machine (VW)*, 2001
The Thai artist Surasi Kusolwong focuses on creating spaces
for exchange. He is well known for his large-scale market
installations where Thai products are sold at low prices.
He describes his work as 'Poor Minimal' and juxtaposes
free massages, lottery games, dismantled parts of cars,
classic design furniture and vending machines offering drinks.
Visitors to his exhibitions enjoy relaxing, humorous scenarios.
In this work, commissioned for the 2002 Gwangju Biennale,
'Pause', Kusolwong displayed a stripped-down Volkswagen
Beetle which was hung upside down from the ceiling, turning
it into a swing. Inside the car a wooden floor was built up with
soft mattresses and pillows providing the visitors with a bed
to lie on. The visitors were able to watch the film *Harry Potter*
in comfort. The floor was covered with a green carpet and
potted plants, creating an artificial city garden, vending
machines provided free soft drinks and chocolate and a bank
of computers gave free internet access.

above and opposite Navin Rawanchaikul, *I [love] TAXI*, 2001
The Thai artist Navin Rawanchaikul used the universal space
of the taxi as the physical container for his mobile gallery.
The audience of the work was literally transported to the
destination of their choice. This dialogue between the taxi as
the art receptacle and the driver as the willing artist-host finds
its partner in the fare-paying participant. Rawanchaikul adopts
a new strategy for art production by taking a common activity
and appropriating it as an art strategy.

right Alexander Pilis, *Architecture Parallax: Blind Date*, 1998
The image expresses the discourse underlying *Architecture Parallax: Collective Intelligence*. According to the Brazilan artist Pilis, embedded within a frozen moment of love and dependency are positions in motion, with no discernible fixed point of reference. From here, an architectural conversation emerges to articulate differences and impossibilities where the depth of field has collapsed.

top right Maywa Denki, *Hall in Love*, 1999
Maywa Denki combines exhibitions, live stage performances, music, videos, writing, merchandising toys, stationary and electrical devices. This work was a live sound performance using their products. Each one was stylishly designed and modified as a toy to be mass-produced in the marketplace. They became so popular among young people that some of Japan's major toy stores set up Maywa Denki departments.

119

left Chris Grottick, *New Clear Days*, 1998
In 'Turbulence' (1998) by the British artist Chris Grottick, a sequence of scans made from air pressure charts taken by a satellite over Northern Europe every six hours over a period of a year were erratically reanimated using an apparatus measuring gusts of wind from the street outside the exhibition space.

above Henrik Håkansson, *Tomorrow and Tonight*, 1999–2000
The Swedish artist Henrik Håkansson uses video and closed-circuit surveillance systems to record the behaviour of wild life. He incorporates the incompatible combination of club music, youth culture and ritualized entertainment with the natural sciences, and ends up with a visual mix which is at once utopian and dystopic. The environments of this modern-day Doctor Doolittle establish the possible mixing of the characteristics of one subculture with another. In this work the artist proposed the proliferation of roof gardens as 'landing-strips' for insects and other wildlife.

below Carsten Nicolai, *Model zur Visualisierung von Sound* (Model for Visualizing Sound), 1999
The German artist Carsten Nicolai has developed a keen interest in the psychological and physical effects of sound. The artist's work for the Liverpool Biennial in 1999 was an extension of his research on the possible bodily effects of vibration. Sampled tones, modem beeps, and telephone clicks were organized into loops to produce minimalist cycles of abstract sound. This resulted in a manifestation of the invisible energy of electricity: the acoustic trace of an intangible commodity.

below Paola Pivi, *E*, 2001
The Italian artist Paola Pivi's interactive installation simultaneously triggered both attraction and repulsion. The construction was a cylindrical metal structure, made of innumerable vertical nylon wires to which nails were attached, the points turned towards the visitor. When these were approached, sensors became activated which made all the tips shift in one collective, threatening movement. The fragility of the structure and the delicacy of the movement itself, however, seemed to restrict the action and thus negated the potential aggression of the piece.

left Adriano Guimarães and Fernando Guimarães, *The Theatre of Installation*, 2000
This work by the Brazilian theatre directors Adriano and Fernando Guimarães dealt with presentation strategies of the stage and the gallery. Their interactive elements of their staging add an immersive dimension to their work.

left Angela Bulloch *'Macro-World': One Hour3 and Canned*, 2002
The complex pixel works of the Canadian artist Angela Bulloch, such as *'Macro-World'*, uses digitally controlled light boxes to probe the interactive relations between the production and reception of visual images. The artist uses the pixel patterns of selected scenes out of films and television programmes. The basic idea behind these works is that the pixel, normally the smallest component of digital image information, is massively enlarged. Through the exaggerating shift of scale, the grid system of the pixel boxes controls the viewer's visual and kinaesthetic experience, submerging the viewer and the space in a dynamic, coloured luminous space.

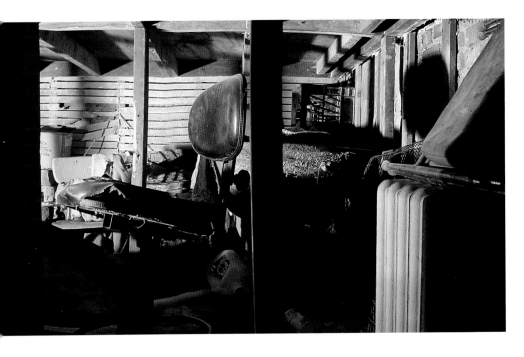

Christoph Büchel, *Untitled*, 2001
For the inaugural exhibition at
Maccarone Inc., 2001, in New York City,
the Swiss artist Christoph Büchel made
an installation that took over the entire
2152 square feet (200 m²) of the gallery
space. The artist created a labyrinth
of rooms ranging from a waiting room,
kitchen, bomb shelter, schoolroom and
jail cell which visitors had to crawl
through to experience.

Atelier van Lieshout **above** *Compostopia*, 2002
opposite below right *Maxi Capsule Luxus*, 2002
The Dutch artist collective Atelier van Lieshout employ
standard industrial measurements to produce and create
series of modular objects and constructions, which offer
practical, adaptable solutions to everyday problems, focusing
entirely on the client and his desires. Behind modernity's
clarity and rationality, these objects and interiors offering
optimum physical comfort, are exercises in self-reliance and
self-provision; artifacts are intended to facilitate the survival
of the fittest. They are objects of personal obsession, buildings
and implements, which represent the materialization of hidden
but basic drives of society, such as eroticism and power.

opposite above Wim Delvoye, *Cloaca – New and Improved*, 2001
The Belgian artist Wim Delvoye has always been preoccupied
with materials of fabrication used in industrial design. The title
of his installation, *Cloaca*, means a cavity in the pelvic region
of most invertebrates, or a sewer. Delvoye created a perfect
reproduction of the human digestive tract. The machine was
fed three times a day in order to excrete once. The final product
was wrapped and sold as an edition with a certificate listing
the ingredients. The installation included a fully equipped
kitchen in which a sponsor provided food for the machine.
Delvoye plays with the balance between high and low culture,
the works are both highly crafted and functional, as well
as absurd.

above Sissel Tolaas, *It must be the weather, Part 1: Dirty 1*, 2001
The Norwegian artist Sissel Tolaas operates on the margins
of traditional perception. Her work appears in the guise of
experiments which use fire, water and air. By delving into the
world of the ephemeral, the artist explores the conventions
of space which are activated through the bodily experience
of the audience. Following a process of extensive research
in Deptford, London, which utilized sophisticated 'Headspace'
technology, a process developed by the perfume industry,
Tolaas was able to extract specific smells which prevailed
in the area. In collaboration with a Perfume House in Paris
she produced a perfume of the area entitled 'Dirty 1'. A video
accompanied the exhibition showing the view through a camera
attached to a dog exploring the area, while a soundtrack
provided local weather reports and recordings of the local
Salvation Army band.

right Lili Fischer, *Meute im Museum* (Mutiny in the Museum), 2001
In *Meute im Museum* the German artist Lili Fischer focused on concerns with natural phenomena, mediated through social role-play. Her work demands that viewers 'act on each other in a two way transfer of information'. In this installation, a transfer of identity took place between the animal characters and the audience, as visitors were asked to wear rat costumes to view the exhibition.

right Simone Michelin, *Bonjour Bonsoir Adieu Tristesse* (Good morning Goodnight Farewell Sadness) 2001
The installation of the Brazilian artist Simone Michelin was an interactive, three-dimensional structure. The system operated a jukebox, which was set in motion through a plug-in and -out telephone line. The participant could select between eight different sequences of video, featuring popular love songs and interviews recorded from public radio. An LCD (flat-screen) monitor displayed animated images of mouths, noses, eyes and tiny vulvas.

left Maywa Denki, *Uke-TEL (NAKI-U1)*, 1998
This installation consisted of a fish cage containing a special device. Hanging needles fell from the roof when the spectator dialed the telephone time signal. The fish swimming at the bottom was at risk from the falling needles.

below Jeroen Offerman, *Silent Boatman*, 2000
The installation by the Dutch artist Jeroen Offerman addressed questions of evidence and proof provided by the site. Paper casts of debris found on a dry riverbed functioned as a link between the original site and the gallery. The British artist Simon Moretti collaborated in the work, and added his own *Cover-Versions*, small felt copies of Offerman's casts.

above Jose Dávila, *Open Studio*, 2000
The Mexican artist's installations deconstruct architectural spaces. At Oxford in 2000, the artist's answer to the working site was to reconstruct his studio in the open air. Visitors coming to view new work were instead confronted with a makeshift studio in a field. No work was made in this space, but the artist led informal discussions on the nature and site of art production.

above Veronika Witte, *Institute for socio-aesthetic research (ISF)*, 2001–2002
This installation was a work in progress in times of genetic engineering. It presented a pseudo-scientific questionnaire about the image that visitors had of their body. Using multiple-choice questions and drawings of their ideal physical appearance, it confronted the viewers with fictitious possibilities of genetic manipulation.

above left and right Allan Wexler, *Vinyl Milford House*, 1994
The American artist constructed this piece too small to contain a bedroom, bathroom, kitchen and dining room all at once. The furniture and equipment necessary for these arrangements were stored in crates integrated into the four exterior walls. They bulged out, leaving the interior empty, but were pulled in when required. This project was a suburban backyard survival kit.

right Christian Jankowski, *Mein erstes Buch: Inszeniertes Schreiben* (My First Book: Staged Writing), 1998
German artist Christian Jankowski created an exhibition consisting of six different installations which changed from week to week. Following the expert advice given by important publishers who were invited to meet the artist in the exhibition, the artist produced his first book.

below Renée Green, *Between and Including Partially Buried in 3 Parts*, 1999
The American artist Renée Green's work poses questions on the nature of art production. Through her pieces, she demonstrates how work and leisure activities cross between different cultural domains. Green's work is interactive, combining video-lounges with films, soundworks and web pages, enabling the audience to use it for the purpose of social interaction, or simply as a means of gathering information.

right Ana Miguel, *I love you*, 2000
In this work the Brazilian artist Ana Miguel used knitted
fabrics, velvets and silk to create a bed on the gallery floor
for visitors to lie on and rest their head on the heart-shaped
pillows. The visitor relaxed beneath a series of spider webs
containing teeth and a love song soundtrack was triggered
by the weight of the head on the pillow. Miguel's work lures
the visitor into a trap of ambiguity, leaving the audience
unsure whether the experience is pleasurable or sinister.

below Simon Moretti, *A Space for Conversation*, 2000
The installation by the London-based artist consisted of five
circular carpets placed in the Turbine Hall of Tate Modern,
London. A simple communication exercise ensued among the
museum public. They were given a pen and a piece of paper
and asked to communicate without spoken language, only
through drawings. They engaged in a process of negotiation,
which generated a number of images produced collaboratively.

above Muntean/Rosenblum, *Where else*, 2000
The Austrian artist Markus Muntean and the Israeli artist Adi
Rosenblum have collaborated since 1992. In *Where else* they
transformed the gallery of the Vienna Secession into a generic,
non-functional cafeteria. Elevator music was piped into the
room and a series of urban youth portraits hung on the walls.
The images were derived from popular culture magazines.
On the opening night live performers in colour-coordinated
outfits posed motionless as cleaners. The performance was
videoed and replayed throughout the duration of the exhibition.

left Jiri Kratochvil, *Joseph*, 1998
The Czech artist Jiri Kratchovil's installation, *Joseph*, was
based on a mathematical formula. The display contained
fish tanks and movement sensors connected to a bank
of computers which monitored the passage of the fish
between the three different coloured, interconnected aquaria.
A soundtrack was also generated by the activity of the
monitoring devices. His investigation into neurology and
psychiatry and the effects of electromagnetic radiation on
living cells, led to the 'Hive', a construct used by both
scientists and appropriated by artists through history.

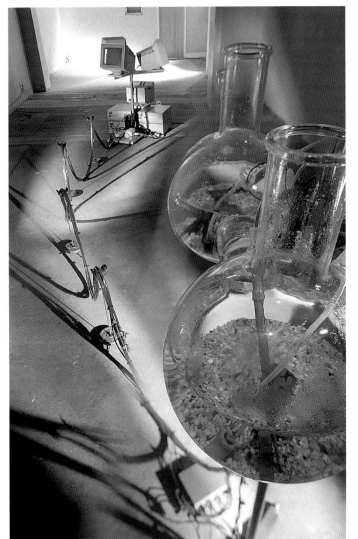

time and narrative

Despite yourself...you're impressed by the fact that you're going to completely disappear.

In a rapidly changing world, time and memory are key concerns for contemporary artists. Though borrowing from existing methodologies, artists depart from personal experience to construct their own spaces of memory. The singular term 'history' is under constant threat from the emergence of multiple 'histories'. Many artists have shied away from commenting on grand narratives, preferring to focus on the story of the everyday. They have used this concern with memory by focusing on official and unofficial means of retrieval, in an attempt to question existing systems through more private and individual means.

The exhibition 'Deep Storage – Collecting, Storing, and Archiving in Art' (held in Munich, Berlin and Düsseldorf, and subsequently at P.S.1 Contemporary Art Centre, New York, and at the Henry Art Gallery, Seattle, 1998) concerned itself with an examination of memory. It brought together a wide range of artists and works on the theme of archive and storage, a concern usually confined to museum specialists.

One of the key exhibitors in 'Deep Storage' was the German artist Karsten Bott. His project, *Archive of Contemporary History*, is an archive in progress, which has been growing for well over ten years, and contains thousands of everyday objects. A selection is displayed at each site and new objects are added to the collection. When constructing installations such as *One of Each* (2001), the artist chooses objects for temporary display from this vast archive and lays them out in specific configurations. Visitors are prevented from touching the items, as they can only view the exhibition from a raised walkway straddling the space. Once the installations are dismantled, all the objects are carefully wrapped and placed in cardboard banana boxes. Duly catalogued, they are stored on racks in a room dedicated to the collection. This room provides a second site, but one to which neither curators nor audiences have access. The artist has thus appropriated archival strategies, while dealing literally with 'rubbish'. He has turned collector, affording himself the privilege of the museum: to gather, catalogue and selectively display.

Such displays owe a debt to the celebrated works of the art historian Aby Warburg, *Mnemosyne Atlas*, and the theorist Walter Benjamin, *Arcades Project*. Though different, both are linked by a concentration on archiving knowledge and the philosophical readings to which they lend themselves. As the critic Geoffrey Batchen writes in the catalogue for 'Deep Storage', 'Exchange rather than storage has become the archivist's principal function, a shift in orientation that is evidenced in the flurry of networked projects that are under way all around the world.'

The theme of exchange forms the basis for the installation *I feel better now, I feel the same way* (1996) by the American artist David Bunn, who uses the discarded card catalogue of the Los Angeles Central Library, which was replaced by an electronic database. Bunn includes the archive in his work to create a poetic narrative from the endless readings provided by the display of the cards themselves. 'The artist as archivist' might be an appropriate way of describing the activity of the French artist Christian Boltanski. His incessant scavenging and collecting has resulted in displays of encyclopaedic proportions. In *Les Abonnés du Téléphone* (2000), Boltanski displayed thousands of international telephone directories which visitors were invited to browse, while a soundtrack played the list of twelve thousand registered voters living within a ten-minute radius gallery.

nski's activities find an echo in the er Vilém Flusser's assertion that we live in of recycling. By this he means that our lives tuated by objects, feelings and ideas that are sly retrieved and re-used. He thus aligns commercial waste recycling with psychoanalysis, both activities that aim to regenerate and to rebuild by sifting through and reinstating discarded and forgotten material. A number of artists have turned to personal recollections and anxieties as material for public displays. The British artists Bob & Roberta Smith, Mike Nelson and the French duo Loriot/Mélia

have all, in different ways, produced this kind of work, in which Installation becomes a means of gathering objects that evoke personal feelings and ideas to be displayed alongside one another. Loriot/Mélia's fragile reflections are arrangements made from broken toys, glass and plastic shards, a world of pathetic cast-offs. Bob & Roberta Smith's *Paint it Orange* (1997) was based on a childhood memory in which the artist's mother decided to use orange paint on all the furniture. The action was reprised in the gallery which was filled with the adult artist's various belongings, including his car, all of which were painted in the same luminous colour. Mike Nelson creates atmospheric installations in interlocking rooms, sparsely filled with objects from his own storerooms. These claustrophobic spaces give an impression of recent abandonment and melancholy. Such works are not archives in the institutional sense, nor do artists who use archiving methods aim to parody them. It is the emphasis on personal narratives that marks such work, the narrative of objects that have deep, personal associations. Individual memory is thus turned into a disrupted and discontinuous archive of history. Contemporary culture is so saturated with the idea of its historical authenticity that it has become fascinated with endless speculative re-interpretations of episodes in the near or distant past. Subjecting history to constant analysis and counter-analysis has contributed to a mistrust of any unifying historical explanation governing issues of identity, politics and culture and to a mistrust of any value systems which provide clear frameworks for moral or aesthetic judgment. Instead, each object, each experience, each incident, each image must be evaluated according to its own particularities and itself constitutes evidence, so that the image becomes as real as the event it portrays. 'There is no higher order of experience or material form that aesthetic practice can offer or separate cultural space in which it can dominate. The real,' states the theorist Peter Osborne, 'now coincides with its image'. The conflation of the real with its images provides the central argument in the installation *Garden* (2000) by the British artist Marc Quinn, which featured a large glass tank containing a flower garden. The plants were real and were prevented from wilting by the temperature-controlled formaldehyde in which they were immersed. Taken from their original context, they were preserved in the exhibition in what appears as 'archival suspension'. Drawing on the ideas of the French philosopher Michel Foucault, art historian Irit Rogoff writes that 'accentuating the performative aspect of the archive has allowed us to move away from solid sites of accumulated knowledge to a series of "archive effects".' While we may understand archives as a 'technology of control', it has also given rise to 'the perception of archives as the construction site of fantasmatic fictions.'

The work of Jane and Louise Wilson might be viewed in this context. Their video installation *Stasi City* (1997) was made in a former East German secret service headquarters. The secret police files once represented the dream of the perfect record of a nation's private activities and, as such, provided fertile ground for the artists' video works. 'We became focused on the meaning embedded in buildings, that certain sites represented,' the artists stated. And yet, the installation did not seek to reveal hidden historical truths; instead, the spaces served as memory triggers for the audience to imagine what remains invisible. The techniques employed by Jane and Louise Wilson are closely related to developments in current film-making, in which the image has become progressively unstable and unreliable. 'Cinematographic and videographic techniques – the artisanal invention of dissolves, feedback, slow-motion and time-lapse, zoom, live and decayed broadcast – now appear to have been premonitory signs, symptoms of a de-realisation of sensory appearances,' writes the theorist Paul Virilio. Location as such has disappeared, since our traditional visual link with place has been broken. The separation between location and viewer is due precisely to the acceleration of contemporary living and the establishment of tele-technologies. Virilio's position is borne out by the contemporary practice of Installation art in which the certainty of location is replaced by the restlessness of the artist and viewer. However, the

Mike Nelson, *The Coral Reef*, 2000
British artist Mike Nelson creates
labyrinthine, large-scale architectural
installations. *The Coral Reef* was a
collection of shabby and disquietingly

vacant reception rooms where viewing
became an act of storytelling as the
spectator picked a way through the
curious amalgam of identities and
histories. Nelson fuses encyclopaedic,

though idiosyncratic references – which
are often defined through the irony and
kitsch of his materials – into three-
dimensional narratives.

continuing popularity of projects based on personal
memory, dependent on the artist's ability to
recombine familiar elements in unusual ways,
points to the need for private worlds with their own
logic. In these, the artist's imagination provides
stability and purpose.

The pursuit of memory through archival
techniques is invariably a melancholic activity.
The current fascination with archives for artists
represents a desire to internalize and divert the
narrative, rather than a need to critique such
structures employing its own methods. It is the
'archival effect', as Rogoff argued earlier, that
remains the key for the artist, along with an
engagement with the 'slowness' and introspection of
such an activity in which the work searches for its own
boundaries. The French philosopher Jean-François
Lyotard explains:

A Postmodern artist or writer is in the
position of a philosopher: the text he writes,
the work he produces is not in principle
governed by pre-established rules. (These)
rules and categories are what the work of art
itself is looking for. The artist or writer, then,
is working without rules in order to formulate
the rules of what will have been done.
Hence, the fact that work and text have
the characters of event.

In this way, artists working with the retrieval of
memory through found or invented narratives, are
creating 'events' in which the work searches for its
own context and boundaries; it is time itself that is
revealed and experienced as the central subject.
Since all narratives reference time, the artist uses
these techniques to remind the viewer of their
own story and experience of time.

right Jane and Louise Wilson, *Stasi City*, 1997
The images were projected simultaneously on four screens in the gallery, depicting a journey around abandoned secret service intelligence headquarters in East Berlin. Long corridors with identical offices, desolate spaces and decontamination chambers were revealed. The work was not explicitly political, rather it was concerned with powerlessness and horror. A soundtrack of static interference and clanking added to the drama and the twin artists were filmed keeping guard. This repetitive mirroring and doubling occurred throughout this installation, as well as in other works by the British artists.

right David Bunn, *I feel better now, I feel the same way*, 1996
As libraries replace their card catalogues with on-line databases, the cards themselves, obsolete, bulky and worn, are usually thrown away. For his work, the American artist David Bunn rescued two million cards from the Los Angeles Central Library. Using them as raw material, he directed the viewer's attention to the poetic trace. The work returned the obsolete artifact to the world as a living archive of reverie.

below Christian Boltanski, *Les Abonnés du Téléphone* (The Telephone Subscribers), 2000
Christian Boltanski transformed the exhibition space into a library of three thousand telephone directories from around the world. Spectators were invited to look through them and scan for familiar names. The exhibition included a specially commissioned sound piece in which the names of twelve thousand registered voters living within a ten-minute radius from the gallery were read out from different points. This archive of the whole world in the gallery space was fundamentally flawed and incomplete. Over the past four decades, Boltanski has explored archiving and the loss of the individual identity in the midst of collective experience and memory.

above Amanda Wilson, *Mirror*, 1997
Conceived as part of the 'Mirror' exhibition in 1997, the work of the British artist Amanda Wilson returned the viewer's attention to an investigation on the construction of individuality. In the basement of the space she constructed a series of wooden, backlit vitrines, which contained traces taken from her newborn child.

left Teresa Serrano *Vanishing City*, 2001
Small cacti gardens were placed inside three 'stroller' suitcases in the Programa gallery in Mexico City. Audiences were invited to move at will within the gallery space.

opposite below Darren Almond, *H.M.P. Pentonville*, 1997
Almond's work addresses concerns with duration and time. *H.M.P. Pentonville* was a live broadcast of limited duration. Television cameras relayed the interior of a deserted cell in Pentonville Prison, London, to the Institute of Contemporary Art, London, in real time. The tiny cell was projected onto the gallery wall, oppressive and bleak. Almond wanted to picture a space impossible to imagine, dead and inert, sparse and institutional. Nothing moved or changed, except time and sound. In the frame, the video digital counter rattled through the seconds, while the incidental acoustics of the prison were amplified to an unbearable degree.

Maurizio Cattelan
below left *Lift*, 2001
below right *Lift*, 2001 (detail)
Cattelan always incorporates a sense of the absurd and humour in his work. Punchlines of laconic narratives suspend story endings, as he deliberately shows the spectator only a clue or an out-of-context iconic figure. He describes his work in relation to theatre, for 'theatre, like art, is a biological function. It's just like everyday, every minute'. Life-size and miniature scenes are presented in which Cattelan is both director and character in his schizophrenic reality. His purpose is to dethrone authority and to play with the notion that in his world, art is condemned to tell untruths while maintaining its sense of the ironic.

left David Allen, *Thames Piece*, 2001
On entering the basement of the
exhibition space, visitors of the
project *Thames Piece* were exposed
to underwater sounds. These were
transmitted live through a hydra
microphone in the nearby river Thames,
and relayed via an antenna, through
two mobile telephones.

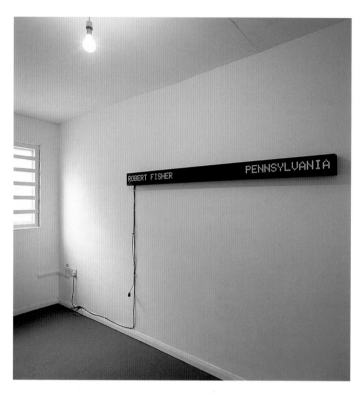

right David Davies *Row 01, 2001
The British artist David Davies researched the precise schedule of ongoing state executions in the USA and tracked the population on Death Row. *Row 01 relayed information concerning all significant decisions related to appeals, stays, commutation and the execution itself, onto an LED messaging system installed in the rear room of the space. At the start of the year there were over 3,700 prisoners waiting on Death Row.

left Massimo Bartolini, *Zwei Horizonte (particolare), (Two Horizons, detail),* 2002
The work of the Italian artist Massimo Bartolini deals with the effects of light and space and is filled with visual boundaries and illusions. This piece plays with an experience, both visual and corporeal, which is shared by the viewer. The installation for Manifesta 4 consisted of a series of domestic rooms bathed in intense light. Visitors entered one of the rooms, climbed on top of a drawing table and put their heads through a trapdoor in the ceiling. A recurring motif in his work is the spectator's ability to observe, while being denied access to proceed.

opposite below 'Archive', *Group Exhibition,* 1995
The exhibition 'Archive', 1995, coincided with the Museum of Installation's move to another location in London, and represented five years of projects. Conceived and designed by the organization's curators, in association with architects Simon Miller and Alain Chiaradia, it featured over thirty artists who were asked to exhibit works, prepared and previously shown at the Museum of Installation, as archive versions. In addition, all other parts of the museum were systematically catalogued and displayed, including its entire office and contents, as well as the walls of the space. The show represented an attempt to present a living and interactive archive of Installation art.

left Juan Cruz, *Driving Back*, 1999–2000
This sound installation featured two
loudspeakers in an empty gallery
space. A resonating soundtrack of the
artist related a car journey into the
countryside. As the topographical
details accumulated, a mental map
formed in the listener's mind. *Driving
Back* presented Cruz's own account as
a mediated process of communication.
First, it was a recollection, filtered
through the artist's memory; next, it
was performed, with diversionary
rhetoric and idiosyncratic tangents;
and finally, it was presented to the
listeners, who created yet another
layer of meaning through their own
memories of similar excursions.

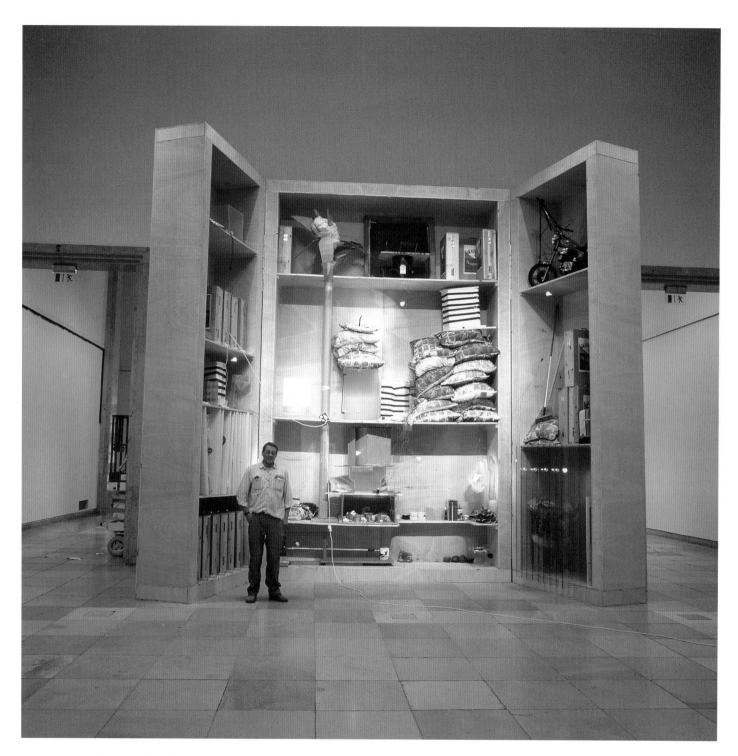

above Jason Rhoades, *The Great Sea Battles of Wilhelm*, 1994–95

The assemblage artworks of the American artist Jason Rhoades are random collections which, though arranged with great deliberation, have gone beyond control. His work deliberately accumulates trash of everyday consumerism, found objects or items, some of which are still in their packaging, creating visual archives out of the reminders of the sites of everyday life. Picking up on biographical data *The Great Sea Battles of Wilhelm* recreated a fictional portrait of a collector's life. Beyond the biographical frame of reference, the installation followed an intuitive and imaginary concept derived from the artist's idea of life on the move – most spectacularly suggested through the giant suitcase structure that housed the piece.

right Tracey Emin, *My Bed*, 1998
The British artist Tracey Emin exhibited *My Bed* unmade
and rumpled after a week's illness, complete with all the
paraphernalia she had used in it, books, bottles, cigarette
butts, condoms and handkerchiefs. In an era of superficiality,
this private and autobiographical emblem of the artist's
everyday life was exhibited as an authentic statement about
herself and her relationships.

below Liza Lou, *Trailer*, 1999–2000
Liza Lou's dazzling beaded tableaux transform the most
familiar settings of American domestic life into exuberant
spectacles. At the same time, by hand-stringing the millions
of tiny glass beads which go into such scenes as this, the artist
describes the labour-intensive activity as elevating, repetitive
'women's work', almost a form of meditation.

above Ann Hamilton, *Mattering*, 1997
An undulating canopy of red-orange silk divided the gallery space in half laterally and visitors shared the territory with five male peacocks. Barely audible were the recorded sounds of an opera singer giving lessons to a student – and of the student mimicking the teacher. A wooden pole rose through a large circular hole in the silk and a figure sitting on a seat attached to the pole drew an endless thin blue line from a small white porcelain ink-pot on the ground, wrapping the inked ribbon around one hand until it formed a dense ball. The binding was then cut and dropped to the floor, only for the process to begin anew.

opposite below left David Wilkinson, *Untitled*, 1999
A rotating projector showed a forty-five-second film loop. The progress of the image around a cylindrical screen was synchronized to follow a 360-degree camera pan, filmed in the nearby Charlton Park, where, thirty years earlier, Antonioni shot scenes for the film *Blow Up* (1966).

opposite below right David Wilkinson, *Untitled*, 1996
The beam from a video projector was split through a system of mirrors to cover the surface of a latex weather balloon suspended from the gallery ceiling.

right Dermot O'Brien, *Untitled*, 1995
The installation by the artist Dermot O'Brien dealt with language and its sensory support structures. A pattern of small, coloured air fresheners installed on the wall of the gallery, made reference to written language which remained indecipherable to the sighted but was 'visibly' encoded in braille for the blind. The powerful and sweet smells overwhelmed the space. The discs provided the audience with an olfactory reference to these sample smells, which are usually employed to mask noxious household odours.

left Sam Taylor Wood, *Third Party*, 1999
Seven films were shot simultaneously on seven motor drive cameras, a deliberate use of multiple images to deconstruct traditional film techniques. Over ten minutes, this process broke down the usual chronological sequences of film.
In *Third Party* the London-based artist Sam Taylor-Wood directed each projection as a finite, unedited sequence of its own. The cameras shot whatever was in front of them. As a theme, the party is a much used motif in cinema. From Antonioni and Warhol to Kubrick, they are places of alienation, seduction and jealousy, places for quick sex, oblivion and unexpected encounters, places of intoxication, light and darkness; places of endless tedium. While choosing a familiar theme, Taylor-Wood unsettles the audience through her narratives and unconventional cinematographic techniques.

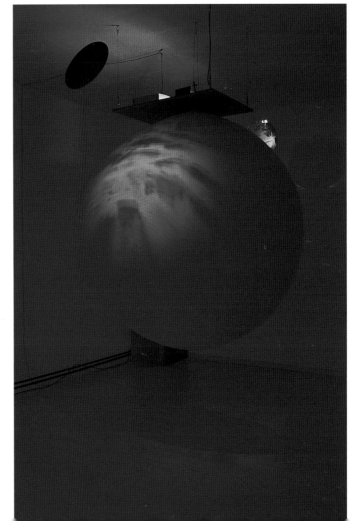

right and below Damien Hirst, *Love Lost (Large River Fish)*, 2000
Hirst's preoccupation with dissecting animals, revealing their insides and suspending them in formaldehyde, challenges the ideas of inertia and beauty. Within this theme of preserving and freezing motion, the work of the British artist is extended to the play with animate and inanimate objects. He used the form of the enclosed space to capture objects in a large museum vitrine for this work, creating an estranged and claustrophobic environment from which the viewer was excluded.

left Phyllida Barlow, *Depot*, 1995
This work by the British artist Phyllida Barlow related to the gallery as a storage space of lost or forgotten objects and referred to a state of incompleteness and dislocation. Large timber structures were brought together with pliable shapes, which were placed near or attached to them. This created a narrative of remaking and appropriating the originals, which then only functioned as bad copies.

below Mona Hatoum, *Homebound*, 2000
A sparse, 1950s living room and bedroom was dimly lit and fenced off by cables, reminiscent of high-security borders. Kitchen utensils were distributed across the furniture and wired to each other and small light bulbs glowed intermittently. The Lebanon-born artist experimented with the alienation of everyday objects, in order to speak of her ambivalent relationship to home and family.

above Knut Åsdam, *Psychasthenia (5)*, 1998
Working with the 19th-century notion of Heterotopias, Utopian Sites, The Norwegian artist Knut Åsdam writes that 'Cinematic space is a notion of space as narrative, a space as an unfolding of a certain idea of the unconscious'. In this sense he is more interested in looking at and working with space as a 'temporality of unfolding intensities...of different velocities; so it becomes a space of velocity, a space in which to fall in love, have adventures or dream.' This is, however, the space in which people experience restriction, suppression or defeat – a political space, which is also one of fantasy and memory.

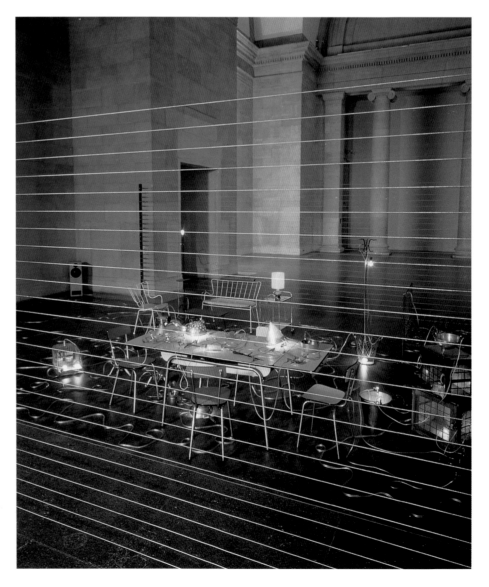

below Alexander Brodsky, *Coma*, 2000–2001,
For *Coma*, the Russian artist Alex Brodsky created a miniature city of houses and skyscrapers made of clay and attached to intravenous feeding tubes, which nourished the town with a continuous drip of crude oil. His evocative work reflects the idea of a society that has stopped believing in progress and has been captured in a coma-like state of ghostly inertia.

opposite below Marc Quinn, *Garden*, 2000
Garden was described as a kind of homage to the 16th-century artist Hans Holbein. Impressed by Dutch art of the period and its preoccupation with the representation of nature and the human figure, Quinn commented: 'it's like the last judgement of the vegetable world'. A perfect image of eternity was provided by the display of flowers, frozen in silicon oil, controlled at a temperature of -20°C. The artist's main preoccupation was with the process of prolonging the lives of plants in an attempt to freeze and immortalize time and beauty.

right Hans Op de Beeck, *Border*, 2001
The spectator enters a vast, darkened room in which a moving image of a small group of people in a confined and abstract space is projected onto one wall. Their strange, whispered, but strongly amplified conversation, is hard to situate, but intriguing. Gradually, the group is surrounded by a life-size, X-ray image of a loaded truck and it becomes clear that these people, refugees, are locked in a box in the depths of a cargo lorry. Their conversation takes on another meaning.

left Hans Op de Beeck, *Location I*, 1998
The Belgian artist's scale model of
crossroads in a deserted landscape,
deliberately set up at shoulder height,
was installed in a darkened space
illuminated with blue light simulating
night time. Op de Beeck's miniaturized
replicas of anonymous public spaces
make the spectators feel as though
they are inside the models, a moment
shared between the artist and the
audience. These still and quiet places,
which represent a kind of timeless
nowhere, carry an atmospheric mood
without offering any story.

opposite Tadashi Kawamata, *Les Chaises de traverse* (The Shortcut Chairs), 1998
A double installation by the Japanese artist Kawamata connected two buildings of important historical significance – the Synagogue in Delme and the Hôtel Saint-Livier in Metz, France. Kawamata decided to reuse two thousand old chairs and erected a vertical structure into an imposing wall in the yard in Metz. This corresponded to the height of all the chairs laid out horizontally, separating the two floors in the Delme Synagogue. The artist also placed single chairs next to the plastic seating in thirty bus shelters along the route between Metz and Delme. Kawamata is preoccupied with the concept of contemporary chaos theory and issues of urbanism. He also chooses the locations of his works carefully, researching the city, collecting necessary materials and involving local communities.

below Rosemarie McGoldrick, *What Katy Did* in 'Day for Night', 1999
As part of the exhibition 'Day for Night ' organized by the Museum of Installation, London, the British-born artist Rosemarie McGoldrick installed miniature cages in a Portacabin. The metal cages contained speakers which were connected to a computer programme. As listeners approached, the shrill sound of crickets was switched from one cage to another.

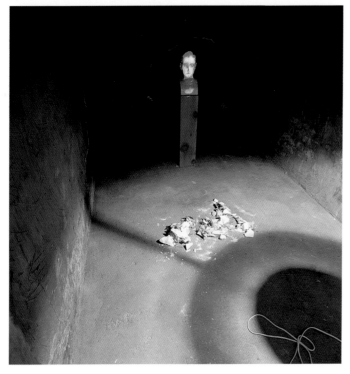

Loriot/Mélia
above *Le Leurre et l'agent du leurre*
(The Illusion and the Illusion's Agent), 1994
above left *Ready Made in China*, 2000
left *Le Diable Probablement* (Probably the Devil), 1993–2000
The French artists Loriot/Mélia create optical illusions and tricks of light to achieve cinematic images. Carefully sifted debris is used as material for the production of images which are caused by bouncing light through the meticulous arrangement of the debris. The original material appears as if removed from an archaeological dig, while the resulting images take the form of a cinematic light show. The concept of landscape was addressed in *Ready Made in China* which featured a spinning mountain range diorama, achieved by illuminating a bicycle wheel studded with glass shards. The illusion of a distant aeroplane, which appeared to be heading towards this mountain range, was glimpsed in an adjacent work. The resulting overall panorama triggered the memory of a classic cinematic moment where the plane either crashes into the rock or disappears into the distance.

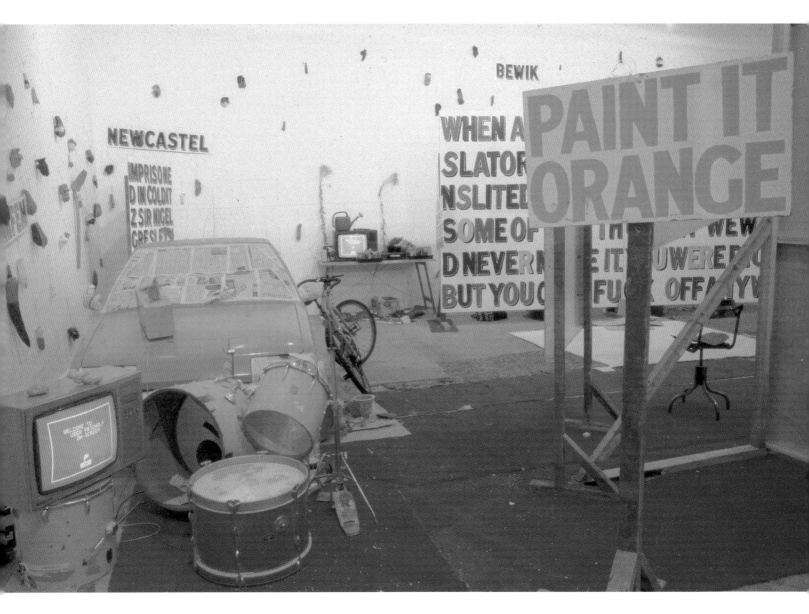

above Bob & Roberta Smith, *Paint it Orange*, 1997
Paint it Orange was based on an autobiographical event of the
British artist Bob & Roberta Smith. As the artist's mother
painted items of furniture with a coat of bright orange gloss,
she ruined a set of Windsor chairs and devalued her son's
bicycle. Smith recalls: 'As a five year old I was instantly taught
how art could liberate and emancipate whilst also destroying
and humiliating.' The work points to sincerity through failure,
to a genuine, obsessional desire to make something, eventually
leading to misconstrued notions of value or usefulness.

below Sarah Lucas, *Chuffing Away to Oblivion*, 1999
The British artist Sarah Lucas is known for her large-scale collages consisting of photocopies and cuttings from newspaper articles. The artist creates claustrophobic environments, which communicate an often aggressive directness in her handling of themes, such as sexism or violence through abstruse or outrageous images, as in this installation.

above and opposite page João Penalva, *From R.*, 2001
The Portuguese artist João Penalva transformed the Palazzo Vendramin in Venice into a sequence of improvised theatres, archival displays, video projections, photographs and vitrines.

Throughout the installation *From R.*, the audience was confronted with competition scenarios acted out on video and through sound. The Eurovision Song Contest contrasted with a conversation in Esperanto in which a couple failed to understand each other. Penalva

juxtaposed winning and losing with the fallibility of human nature and its susceptibility. The context and setting of the work within the Biennale commented on its competitive agenda.

above Miquel Angel Ríos, *Si me buscas...no me encuentras* (If you look for me, you will not find me), 2001
This work by the Argentinian artist Miguel Angel Ríos was a three-screen piece depicting the artist's journey through the desert. The synchronized projections showed the artist collecting hallucinogenic plants available in the location. His experience was altered by the effect of the powerful drug, resulting in a series of surreal visions.

opposite below Markus Wirthmann, *The Twentieth Century. Chapter V: The Total Eclipse*, 2000
The beam of a theatre headlight hit a turning mirror ball installed in the centre of the room, which cast a shadow on the wall opposite the headlight. The movement of the video camera enabled the apparent passage of the moon's shadow across the viewer's field of vision, and at the same time, the simulation of a total solar eclipse could be observed on a monitor. Simulating the telematic experience of a natural phenomenon, this work by the German artist challenged the clichés of the Western perception of the 'dark continent', ironically negotiating issues of Afro-centrism.

left Jeremy Wood, *The Map of Hope and Other Improbable Locations*, 2002
The British artist Jeremy Wood plays with and modifies existing artistic strategies. For this installation, Wood arranged furniture and lighting in a room, taking as reference original archival photographs of its 1960s interior. Visitors were invited to spend time in this retitled *Waiting Room*, either to wait indefinitely or to watch a short film essay, compiled from the application of Fluxist games of chance to the artist's own home-video footage. An exterior projection window was also set up for the theatre building showing an animation loop derived from Piet Mondrian's *Broadway Boogie-Woogie* (1942–43). This pseudo-advert would 'hopefully' catch the eye of people on the train passing in front of the theatre.

left Joe Banks, *Soundproofs*, 1998
In his work for *Soundproofs* the British
sound artist Joe Banks used the live
frequency of the national electricity
grid. The resulting compression of
sound was amplified through a series
of sensitive nodes and produced a
loud tremor, which vibrated throughout
the building.

left Diana Thater, *Broken Circle*, 1997
The work of the Californian artist Diana Thater avoids the comparison with cinema, deliberately ignoring the possibilities of technical perfection. Her coloured projections bleed over the walls and the images look as if they have been projected on top of each other. Her large-scale, overlapping projections juxtapose images portraying animal behaviour in man-made parks and zoos. Her intention is to show that both of them have been artificially appropriated by mass culture.

opposite above right A. K. Dolven,
Stairs, 2002
The work of the Norwegian artist
A. K. Dolven deals with stillness,
whether in her paintings or her video
installations. In her films, actions are
slow and deliberate and the camera
often records the precise duration of
a movement. As in *Stairs*, time is
measured in relation to the unfolding
of everyday processes.

Eija-Liisa Ahtila
above *Anne, Aki and God*, 1998
opposite below *Tuuli/The Wind*, 2002
The three-screen DVD installation
entitled *Tuuli/The Wind* by the Finnish
artist Eija-Liisa Ahtila charted a
woman's deteriorating grip on reality as
she fell prey to psychosis. A violent wind
entered the room, leading the woman to
turn her apartment upside down,

breaking furniture and destroying
objects. This gradual mental breakdown
was paralleled by the intricate and fluid
choreography of the projection.
Simultaneous yet different views of the
apartment and a disrupted flow of linear
time, along with the de-synchronization
of events, contributed to the eventual
dismantling of the familiar logic of
screen narration.

this page Michael Petry, *Contagion*, 2000 Blood-red, hand-blown, human-heart-sized shapes hung from the gallery's ceiling in this work by the American artist Michael Petry. Each heart was suspended on steel wire at the height of the artist's heart, forming a large curved rectangle (modelled on the architecture of the room) which could be entered at any point and, like cell walls, the object was permeable. The gallery was floodlit with red light both day and night, but incoming sunlight meant that, slowly over the day and into the evening, the room dramatically changed colour. Petry had ascertained that the gallery was mainly visited at dusk (for theatre and cinematic performances) when the transition would be most obvious. *Contagion* was evocative of blood-related images, AIDS, hospitalization, transfusions, birth and death. As viewers approached the work they were suffused with red light, and appeared to other viewers as 'contaminated'. Once marked, as through a ritual, like blood brothers, they crossed over the threshold altered.

below Catrin Otto, *Full House*, 1998
Using the traditional techniques of assemblage, collage and photomontage, Otto appropriates domestic plastic objects, which she reforms, remodels and then re-photographs from different angles. These photographs are cut out and reassembled among the original objects in the space. The suggestive play between the real and its photographic record immerses the viewer in a tactile environment. The artist's compulsive use of red and beige is employed as a metaphor for the visceral and corporeal illusions created by the work. The resulting effect is both obsessive and uncannily erotic.

above Gabriel Kuri, *Momento de importancia* (Moment of Importance), 2001
This installation by the Mexican artist Gabriel Kuri adapts the temporality and significance of the event in which it is

exhibited. For this occasion, the piece served as a conference table for a talk about space and time, in which four academics and one cloud of cold steam participated. This confined the time the piece was on display to the duration of the talk.

left Teresita Fernández, *Bamboo Cinema*, 2001
American artist Teresita Fernández created this work from acid green poles arranged in a maze of concentric circles. As visitors walked between the poles, they experienced a flickering effect like the opening and closing of a camera shutter. The further viewers entered into the work, the greater became the effect of distortion of the surrounding landscape. The artist was concerned with the cinematic view arrived at by the movement and placement of the audience.

left Bodys Isek Kingelez, *Ville Fantôme* (Ghost Town), 1996
This self-taught Congolese artist constructs vibrant and meticulously ornate phantom cityscapes made out of paper and other materials. Models of corporate and public buildings in bright, flamboyant colours, hotels, stadiums, parliaments and other pieces of urban architecture, are integrated into a phantasmagoric and luxurious architecture of everyday travel and consumption. These 'architectonic simulations' place relationships of signs and representational systems under the command of a playful and utopian order of social, political and economic equilibrium of wealth. On the other hand, the artist presents a critique of the naïve and patronizing attitude of Western visionaries and planners towards the so-called 'primitive'.

opposite above right Daniel Guzmán,
Untitled, 2000
Guzmán creates highly idiosyncratic
space models using drawings which he
juxtaposes with found objects. He
also creates networks which connect
scattered objects, sounds, images and
activities. In *Prestano* (Loan, 1997), a
one-day show, Guzmán reconstructed
his sitting room in the exhibition space
and made several of his treasured
goods (books, records, videos) available
for the audience to borrow indefinitely.

below Karsten Bott, *Von Jedem Eins*
(One of Each), 2001
Since 1986, the German artist Karsten
Bott has obsessively collected,
categorized and documented objects of
life in the present, founding an 'Archive
of Daily Life'. His work consists of three
closely related areas: the archive, the
installations – which display selections
from the archive, such as this piece –
and films documenting people's lives,
traces and routines.

below Do-Ho Suh, *Seoul Home/L.A. Home/New York Home/Baltimore Home/London Home*, 1999
This piece hung from the ceiling like a spectre, swaying with the air currents in the space. Made from green silk, its transparency allowed light to shine through, creating the illusion that it not only floated, but also allowed the surrounding space to be reflected in the work. The Korean artist Do-Hoh Suh's installation was an exact replica of his childhood home in Seoul, and each time the work travelled to another city, the name of the host city was incorporated into the title. For Suh, this is a way of symbolizing his experience of transcultural travel. His work is a compelling statement on his identity and displacement.

Bill Viola, *Going Forth By Day*, 2002
opposite above *The Deluge*, panel 3
above *The Voyage*, panel 4
right *First Light*, panel 5
The work of American artist Bill Viola investigates the tension between stasis and motion, consciousness and the unconscious. It is described as an anachronistic 'suspension zone'. These transient records of duration, captured by monumental projections, act as a series of metaphors for the time in-between. *Going Forth By Day* was a five-part projected digital-image cycle which explored themes of human existence: individuality, society, death and rebirth. The five-image sequences were synchronized on a continuous loop and projected directly onto the walls, giving the work the epic character of moving frescoes. The story told by each panel was embedded within the larger narrative cycle.

the body of the audience

Western modernity since the nineteenth century has demanded that individuals define and shape themselves in terms of a capacity for 'paying attention', that is, for a disengagement from a broader field of attraction, whether visual or auditory, for the sake of isolating or focusing on a reduced number of stimuli.

Though audiences have come to expect a level of interaction and entertainment in Installation, other entirely different artistic strategies are emerging. The Mexican artist Carlos Amorales's event, *Funny 13* (2001), confronts the spectator with the figure of a 'devil'. The masked devil is dancing to disco music and attempts to entice the audience to participate; but the conventions of the gallery forbid it, making the spectator unsure about what action to take. Simply viewing might be seen as churlish, though dancing along might lay one open to ridicule. Caught between action and stasis, the viewer is effectively trapped. The trap is all the more effective because the viewers are lured towards a physical activity that promises pleasure. The ability to walk around the space occupied by the work and the possibility of close examination are no longer seen as being sufficient as an experience: the audience expects to play a significant part in the work, in its creation and reception. The artist's promise of participation, and its subsequent withdrawal, create anxiety in the audience. The work of the Spanish artist Santiago Sierra consists in paying groups of people to inhabit his creations. His subjects are often individuals, such as migrant workers, the unemployed or asylum seekers; some of his installations even involve voluntary incarcerations. However, he does not seek to expose the vulnerability of his collaborators, or turn them into performers, but instead focuses on the impotence of the observers, who are unable to alter the participants' predicament.

The work of the Italian artist Vanessa Beecroft has similar aims: tightly choreographed groups of photographic models, hired especially for the occasion and often naked, are displayed motionless in the gallery. Unlike Sierra's figures, Beecroft's models are at the other end of the social spectrum, their work glamorous, their bodies desirable. The photographic model here can be said to represent the ultimate simulation of a human being: it appears like one, yet its removal from everyday reality is absolute. Such installations have a finite timespan and, during their exhibition, no interaction from the public is welcomed. This lack of engagement is significant in the work and may be seen as its *raison d'être*. It would be natural for the public to wish to help the unfortunate asylum seekers, or to touch the beautiful models, yet it is their very proximity or palpability that renders them forbidding. The subjects, immensely real, remain achingly beyond the audience's grasp.

This position is confirmed by the art historian Jonathan Crary: 'Spectacle is not primarily concerned with a looking at images but rather with the construction of conditions that individuate, immobilise, and separate subjects, even within a world in which mobility and circulation are ubiquitous.' Moreover, as the viewer looks at the objects that make up the installation in a given space, a perspectival shift occurs. Whatever the spectator can see constitutes one point from which he could be seen. The mirroring between the viewer and the viewed becomes endless. The French psychoanalyst Jacques Lacan stated: 'I see myself seeing myself...I see outside, that perception is not in me...it is on the objects that it apprehends.' Lacan's statement pinpoints the predicament of the viewer: one cannot see without being aware of being seen. The desire for a secluded viewing experience is always accompanied by the self-conscious thrill of being caught in the act.

The video installations of the American artist Gary Hill aptly illustrate the point made by Lacan. *Viewer* (1996) shows a tableau of people engaged in looking. They are lined up side by side, but are entirely isolated and unaware of one another. Instead, their gaze is directed outside the frame, ahead of them. They are looking at us, the viewers, as we look at them. Here, the wall of the projection acts as a hinge

between two worlds; what intrigues and unsettles the viewer is the lack of engagement or identification usually found in the cinematic experience. Instead we are confronted with an endless mirroring between the individuals and ourselves. Installation challenges the aesthetics of frontality, that is, the paradigm of cinematic screen and monitor. This engagement with frontality is expressed in the relationship between viewer and artifact to the extent that the audience participates in the work by becoming fused with it. Here, what is important is not the audience's ability to circulate round the figure or an object, but, on the contrary, the challenge to spectatorship by focusing on the viewer's frozen immobility. It may be argued that such installations act like surfaces, endlessly returning our gaze, rendering viewer and viewed the same. Similarly, the authorship of the work passes from the artist to the viewer.

From the Renaissance onwards, the position of the 'I' is central to perspective, and is privileged above all others. The world then becomes a picture or object to be viewed from a single angle. Thus, perspective suggests that the world circulates around the eye of the observer. Gilles Deleuze argues that cinema provides the opportunity to disrupt our self-centered perception, by providing competing viewpoints. The moving image challenges a view of the world that is entirely arranged around each individual. The filmic installations of the British artist Tacita Dean serve to illustrate Deleuze's point. *Fernsehturm* (Television

Tower, 2001) shows a view from the observation deck of a television tower in Berlin. The camera appears to turn in a panoramic sweep, but it is the room that is turning slowly on its axis. The camera's viewpoint remains static, but the space provides the movement through its rotation. In *Fernsehturm* the world rotates around the individual spectator, eliminating the need for movement.

The works of the Canadian artist Stan Douglas also require a static viewer. Stillness is conducive to 'paying attention', as argued by Jonathan Crary. However, Douglas's film projections hide intricate spatial arrangements and camera settings. The apparent simplicity of his footage is only made possible because of complex sets specially built for the works. As in Dean's work, the position of the spectator is questioned: the viewer is seduced by the film, yet has difficulty in working out how the scene is shot. These artists' installations require patient and concentrated viewing.

Writing on films and panoramas, the American academic M. Christine Boyer asserts that 'we begin to be faced with the absent-minded viewer who is uncritical of conventionality yet slates any innovation since it changes the format of endless repetition.' The waning of the unique artwork comes about through processes of replication and repetition of images. Repetition has become ubiquitous in contemporary art; indeed, it has become an essential condition of production and reception. The filmic

installations of British artist Douglas Gordon disrupt the inertia generated by repetition in works such as *Twenty-Four Hour Psycho* (1993) which slowed the classic Alfred Hitchcock film down to occupy a whole day. The installation *Feature Film* (1998–99) showed the same director's *Vertigo* (1958), along with footage of Bernard Herrmann's celebrated soundtrack of the movie being conducted by James Conlon of the Paris Opera. The conductor's actions were projected onto an enormous screen while the music surrounded the viewer in a wall of sound. The spectator was literally immersed in sumptuous sound and vision and the public's critical distance is eroded by the spectacle, sweeping away the viewer's bodily resistance.

Stanley Kubrick's 1968 film *2001: A Space Odyssey* provides a final example of the viewer's predicament. In the culminating scene, the spacepod of the astronaut Bowman, played by Keir Dullea, is transferred from outer space to an interior. The dwelling has no windows but is lit by an opaque glass floor, an arrangement usually found in suspended ceilings in museums which filter sunlight: the museum space is turned upside down. This reference to the museum is important, since it turns everything within the space into an exhibit. As the

Carlos Amorales, *Funny 13*, 2001
The Mexican artist Carlos Amorales works between 'decors', static installations and 'performances', actions undertaken by himself and other collaborators. In 'Funny 13', 2001, Amorales was dressed as a masked devil and exhorted the public to dance with him.

character appears in the room, dressed in a red spacesuit, he is confronted with his alter ego, albeit as a much older man, who, in turn sees himself as an ancient bed-ridden figure facing a floating, black, stone wall. The film set combines the aesthetics of the museum, that is, the past, with the technology of the future through the spacepod. Furthermore, the viewer's attention is directed from one viewpoint to another in a linear progression, a technique also used in the 19th-century museum, in which the spectator's attention is handed from one character to another as in a relay-race. The progression of shifting viewpoints follows the ageing process towards death and rebirth.

In Jean Baudrillard's description of 'private telematics' the author explains that 'each person sees himself at the controls of a hypothetical machine, isolated in a position of perfect and remote sovereignty, at an infinite distance from his universe of origin. Which is to say, in the exact position of an astronaut in his capsule, in a state of weightlessness that necessitates a perpetual orbital flight and a speed sufficient to keep him from crashing back into his planet of origin.' In *2001: A Space Odyssey* the space-shuttle turns into the museum. The figure in the set replaces the viewer, who thus witnesses his own self in stages of progressive disintegration. The end of the viewer's journey is the realization of his own disappearance. The more we look, the less we see ourselves: the Empire of the Senses masks our own vanishing.

this page and opposite above Christoph Draeger, *Apocalypso Place*, 2000
For the past decade the Swiss artist Christoph Draeger has commented on and documented the sites of both natural and manufactured disasters. Draeger approaches the distressing subject matter through strategies such as the re-enacting of thrillers or action films. He creates photographs, video installations and complex gallery environments which replicate ruined sites, destroyed houses or burned trailer parks. All involve a resounding critique of the preponderance of mass-media coverage of catastrophic events.

right Aernout Mik, *Piñata*, 1999
Inside a small space a video projection
was purposefully staged at floor level,
allowing the spectator to participate
with the protagonists. Within a domestic
setting, the actors destroyed anything
and everything. The concern of the
Dutch artist Aernout Mik was to provide
a platform on which the body became
the situation or site, acting out a game
plan of interaction and passivity.

right Douglas Gordon, *Feature Film*, 1999
For his installation the British artist Douglas Gordon filmed
the conductor James Conlon leading a performance of
Bernhard Hermann's musical score for Alfred Hitchcock's
film *Vertigo*. The conductor's movements were synchronized
on screen with the soundtrack. The artist addressed issues of
guilt and fear, exploring them through repetition, enlargement
and slow motion. The memory of the classic film, which was
screened separately from Gordon's, conflicted with the
actuality and scale of the conductor's image.

below Terry Smith, *Marking Time*, 1999
The video work by British artist Terry Smith was developed
in Rome and filmed in London, and focused on the time when
Casanova was alive. It was projected onto the walls of the
Ca Rezzonico Museum, Venice, before its temporary closure.
One screen depicted a game of poker in progress, the second
showed a portrait of a woman's face, and each of the screens
was shot to resemble a Caravaggio painting. The voice-over
narrative consisted of a man describing the rules of poker,
and a second voice stood in for the audience, asking questions
about what was represented.

left Eric Steensma, *Roadmovie*, 2002
The Dutch artist Eric Steensman uses computer-generated video projections which are transformed using the theatrical illusion called 'Pepper's Ghost'. In *Roadmovie* a sheet of glass was placed between a number of monitors and the space, creating the illusion of miniature figures. The protagonists in this magical environment walked around and interacted with actual toy cars and other objects, while appearing suspended in mid-air.

below Abigail Lane, *The Inspirator*, 2001
This playful work by the British Artist Abigail Lane features the surreal projection of a panda playing a trumpet in the depths of a forest. A poster declared, 'Her mind was a wilderness, her world a wasteland and then from nowhere he returned'. This whimsical and unexpected spirit smiled fleetingly before disappearing, leaving only the outline of a grin. Derived from her long-standing fascination with late-19th-century theatrical phenomena, such as seances, freak shows, circus and magic acts, Lane created a funhouse of absurd narratives.

left Eric Duyckaerts, *How to draw a square*, 1999
The Belgian artist Eric Duyckaerts has a background in both law and philosophy and his work contains a humorous play between art and pseudo-scholarly discourse. He is interested in the fusion of reality and fiction and uses the device of the lecture as an ironic critique of the authority invested in the speaker. In his video lectures he takes on the character of the professor or logician. Duyckaerts's works explore the rhetoric of experimentation and pedagogical discourse.

below Nicolas de Oliveira and Nicola Oxley, *Burg Weogaran Dyreby*, 1996–98
Based on Wheatstone's 19th-century stereoscope, this work examined the relationship between the space and the audience. Two identical viewing devices were set up opposite one another and viewers were encouraged to interact with them. The mirrored tables allowed viewers to transform their perception of the space, culminating in their own visible removal.

opposite below Santiago Sierra, *Trabajadores que no pueden ser pagados remunerados para permanecer en el interior de cajas de cartón* (Six workers who cannot be paid for sitting inside cardboard boxes), 2000
This Spanish artist's work deals with political and social comment and the gap between the 'first' and Third World. His work challenges issues of employment, health, nationality and social origin, examining different political and economic systems and their consequences for individuals. During the project, asylum seekers volunteered to sit in narrow cardboard boxes for four hours daily for the duration of the exhibition. The boxes were closed and hid the participants from the viewer's gaze. The invisible silent presence was a shocking reminder of the predicament of asylum seekers, who are powerless because of the official restrictions imposed by the state on their ability to work and travel.

left Besnik and Flutura Haxhillari,
Die Gulliver Träumen (Gulliver's
Dreams), 1999
Besnik and Flutura Haxhillari's work is
concerned with their Albanian culture:
the constant upheavals of migration
have influenced the production of
pieces based on the literary figure
of Gulliver. Like Gulliver, the artists
are caught up in new contexts
and territories. The work is
autobiographical and acted out
with ironic humour, playing on the
estrangement and nostalgia of their
nomadic life.

opposite page Michael Landy, *Break Down*, 2001
Michael Landy's work explores aspects of contemporary consumerism. Three years in the making, *Break Down* is the British artist's most extreme project. He made an inventory of his life, of everything that he owned: pieces of furniture, records, articles of clothing, his car, books, gadgets and works of art. Over five thousand individual items were drawn up and catalogued. During a two-week period, Landy and his team of workers, installed on public view in a disused department store on London's Oxford Street, proceeded to systematically number, dismantle and weigh every item. These were then placed onto a specially constructed conveyor belt –

a production line of destruction. What was left at the end of the elaborate process was powder, which the artists intends to bury in a capsule under a shopping precinct. The only physical evidence that survived the process was an artist's book which acted like an inventory and included the complete list of contents and an accessible public database. Landy described the work as an audit of his life. He is fascinated by the common currency of marketing information which profiles and classifies individuals through 'data mining'. Left with nothing, Landy escaped consumerism, only to admit ironically that he is now the perfect person to sell to – the ultimate consumer.

opposite Christine Hill, *Volksboutique Organizational Ventures*, 2002
The American artist Christine Hill dissects the institution of work, both in and outside the art context, appropriating daily influences to which an artist is constantly exposed. Hill portrays herself as living a variety of identities. She does not role-play, but performs in order to make a living, taking jobs that are often poorly paid and exploited (masseuse, shoeshine, striptease dancer). This project exhibited and sold the production of the work that took place in it, while attempting to create a space of discussion and a situation of exchange with the audience.

opposite and above Stan Douglas,
Journey into Fear: Pilot's Quarters 1 and 2, 2001
This work is based on two feature films of the same title, one from 1942 and a 1975 remake. The Canadian artist Stan Douglas recreated the setting of the films in which the characters were cramped in an ocean container ship. While the actions remained the same, the dialogue (co-scripted by Douglas and Michael Turner) kept changing as it was dubbed onto the endlessly revisited scenes. The piece lasted for over six days, and was impossible to view in its entirety. In this work the narrative chronology became a mathematical conundrum of infinite possibilities, constantly dislodging the intricate plot.

right Olaf Nicolai, *Portrait of the Artist as a Weeping Narcissus*, 2000
The German artist Olaf Nicolai's sculpture depicts himself gazing at his reflection in a pool, in the manner of Oscar Wilde's Dorian Gray. Frozen in time, Nicolai's likeness sheds a tear.

opposite below John Bock, *Lombardi Bängli*, 1999

The German artist John Bock chooses the form of the lecture as his artistic medium. His aim is to transform simple structures and artistic tasks into abstract and absurd scenarios, which function as models of society. In his lectures, Bock combines language, dramatic elements and sculptural objects. He acts on 'stages' built from tables, cupboards or multilevel wood constructions. The objects are handmade or re-modelled accessories of the lecture, made out of clothing, electrical equipment, such as hoovers and mixers, or 'plastic diagrams' illustrating his mathematical explanations. After the lecture, they are left on the stage to form 'theatrical collages'. The lectures are structured through different scenes in which Bock sometimes works with (non-professional) actors. Frequently he plays pop songs or classical pieces from a record player. The lectures are mostly recorded on video and later integrated into the installations.

below Christian Jankowski, *Rosa*, 2001

The artist's narrative video installations play a central role in his strategy of setting up complex scenarios around encounters with 'normal', mundane behavioural patterns (supermarket shopping becomes a hunting expedition, the exhibition becomes a magician's act), transforming the ordinary into filmic fantasies. Documentation and magic, reality and fiction can hardly be separated. He observes life as an open-ended set of adventures – which can have absurd consequences – and is narrator and observer, a commentator and prankster. Despite its hilarity, *Rosa* had a dark side, dwelling on the cruelty of seemingly normal situations. Set deliberately in the business world of art, the burlesque situations provided built-in-failure elements, although the bittersweet ending ultimately gave the spectator a feeling of redemption.

below Patrick Tuttofuoco, *Walkaround*, 2002
The Italian artist found inspiration for this work in a trip
to East Asia. The installation consists of a group of ten
skyscrapers made of wood, plastic, painted metal and neon
lights, each 6 feet tall and mirroring human scale. The high-
tech city centres with their Utopian architecture, hybrid forms
and atmosphere of futuristic kitsch were parodied in the work.
The constructions were like a children's building game, a
comment on how useless design can be when confronted
with an irrational and playfully anarchic vision.

opposite above Sylvie Fleury, *Bedroom Ensemble II*, 1998
The Swiss artist Sylvie Fleury has focused her art on the world
of fashion and consumerism, copying luxurious products and
developing branding techniques. *Bedroom Ensemble II*
stimulated the senses and created objects of desire as fetishes
of an affluent society. At the same time, the installation
criticized the cultural legacy left by them.

below Ana Laura Aláez, *Prostibulo* (Brothel), 1999
The Spanish artist Ana Laura Aláez confronts the viewer with
an interior resembling an oriental boudoir. In this profane
ambience the viewer was invited to act out their own fantasy.

THE BODY OF THE AUDIENCE

below and opposite above Hans Weigand, *Cotton*, 2001
Cotton is a combination by the Austrian artist Hans Weigand
of two structures built in the exhibition space. While one of
them shows video sequences of a modern version of the
Jerry Cotton story in the form of a photo-novel, the other
is an imitation of a design element from Stanley Kubrick's *2001:
A Space Odyssey*. The avant-garde Utopias of late-1960s design
in Kubrick's idealized sci-fi fantasy are combined with a story
steeped in the dime novel and pulp fiction.

left Roman Signer, *Kabine*, 1999
Much of the work of the Swiss artist Roman Signer exists only as the trace of an action. His materials are ordinary and infused with practical experience, yet in the context of his performances they take on a life of their own, flowing and forming responsive patterns. In *Kabine* the artist exposed himself to an explosion inside a specially constructed shelter. The remains of the event became part of the subsequent exhibition. Signer describes his work through a feeling 'for tragedy, for the absurd, the senseless and the useless that we humans inflict.'

opposite above Patrick Tuttofuoco, *Velodream*, 2001
For Tuttofuoco's work, the SMAK galleries in Ghent, Belgium, were turned into a Velodrome. The exhibition featured a series of vehicles designed by the artist as portraits of his close friends which viewers were able to take for a spin. Tuttofuoco's work is concerned with play, entertainment, youth culture and sport.

opposite below Chinese Cartoon, *We Are the Kids Who Never Grow Up*, 2001
The work of the collaborative artists' group Chinese Cartoon takes its inspiration from the artificial world of computer animations, games and toys. In this installation the Chinese artist Huang Yihan refers to the conflict of the younger generation who remain physiologically immature in spite of being socially grown-up.

Charles Long and Stereolab
right *The Amorphous Body Study Centre*, 1995
right below Charles Long, *Holidays Situations*, 1999
The American artist Charles Long has collaborated with various artists and musicians to complete a series of complex pieces. *The Amorphous Body Study Centre* consists of a series of pod-like, organic forms with headsets for the viewer to listen to the songs of the British pop band Stereolab. It revealed the importance of the tangible in the emerging information-based reality. For *Holidays Situations*, Long created a tableau of male and female mannequins in the window of the Saks Fifth Avenue store in New York. These acted as stand-ins for the viewer and posed in attitudes of fashionable boredom in opulent living rooms invaded by snow drifts. The work exuded humour, but masked a darker mood. One of the scenes referred to the claustrophobic landscapes of Stanley Kubrick's film *The Shining*. In another window, a snow globe, reminiscent of Orson Wells's *Citizen Kane*, was perched on a baroque foam structure. The tension between the mimetic shapes and posed figures was heightened by the electronic, upbeat mantra of the audio artist Mark Mothersbaugh, which included laughing, purring and ringing bells.

Mariko Mori, *Beginning of the End,
Shibuya/Tokyo*, 1995
Mori's work presented a series of
photographs showing her suspended in
a plexiglas body capsule in urban public
spaces all over the world. Mori believes
in the necessity of Utopias, conveyed in
works that are neither ironic nor naive.
The implication is that we already live in
a world where the machines are on the
whole more colourful, lively and
interesting than people.

right Mariko Mori, *Body Capsule*, 1995
The Japanese artist Mariko Mori
celebrates herself as an art product,
as a star born out of the world of image
streams, who cleverly succeeds in
mixing visions of fashion and
architecture transforming them into
virtual environments. She appears in
her photographs dressed as a futuristic
comic book figure or a sweet and
harmless cyborg. For her work
Beginning of the End (above), Mori
encased herself in a Body Capsule to
express a transcendence over space-
time.

Thomas Eller, *THE Human Re-entering Nature*, 2000
The work of the German artist Thomas Eller responded to the problems of the Japanese location in which it was exhibited. Extreme seasonal conditions – an average of more than two metres of snowfall in winter – and the pull of the big cities, led to an increasing depopulation of the area. The artist symbolically repopulated it with three figures mounted on aluminium sheeting. These were covered in snow in the winter and overrun with plants in the summer.

below Momoyo Torimitsu, *Miyata Jira*, 1997
The Japanese artist Momoyo Torimitsu describes her work
as focusing on the tension between reality as perceived
through the senses and physical or objectively real experience.
The crawling robot *Miyata Jira* looked exactly like an ordinary
Japanese businessman. Torimitsu, dressed as a nurse,
assisted it as it crawled along the pavement. The work was
a statement on the predicament of the Post-1960s economic
boom, when individual identity became subsumed into a
uniform collective. The artist takes general themes highlighted
by Japanese culture and comments on the difficulties
experienced when a society is so over stimulated by commerce
and fantasy that common values and reality are overlooked.

above Vanessa Beecroft, *VB46.026.ali*, 2001
Since the mid-1990s the Italian artist Vanessa Beecroft has
displayed a succession of scantily clad or naked women.
All the women are made up and dressed in a similar way,
resembling shopfront mannequin or models in fashion shoots.
Standing before the public like living pictures, these set-ups
are not performances; the figures do not move, they only take
up a position. Neither the models, nor the public show any
emotion and no comment is made. Derived from media
images of commodified beauty, these ensembles suspend
human communication, emasculating the charm of the
erotic interplay.

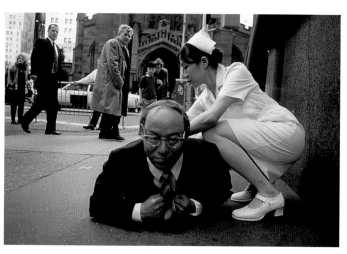

Gary Hill, *Viewer*, 1996
Slightly larger-than-life colour images of seventeen labourers facing out from a neutral black background were projected onto a 45-foot-long wall. For this, five laser discs were synchronized so that the figures appeared to be standing side-by-side in a line. The men stood almost motionless, their movement limited to involuntary stirring – an incidental shifting from foot to foot, slight movements of the hands, and almost imperceptible changes in facial expression. There was no interaction among them, each man stood alone and gazed out from the plane of projection towards the viewer.

this page Tacita Dean, *Fernsehturm* (Television Tower), 2001
The British artist Tacita Dean's work is a 16-mm film made on location in Berlin, several hundred metres above ground level in the rotating room of the old East German television tower. Dean used the slow pan of the tower turning full circle as a metaphor for the reunification of Germany, a meeting of both cultures, old and new establishing a new world order.

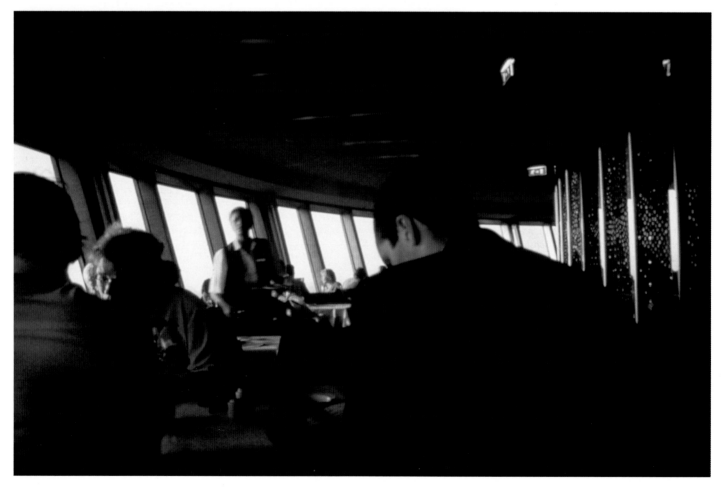

notes on the text

Numbers in bold refer to pages on which quotations appear.

introduction

13 Michael Landy, *Breakdown*, exh. cat., London, 2001, p. 107.

13 Roberta Smith, 'Installation Art, a Bit of the Spoiled Brat', *New York Times*, 3 Jan. 1993.

14 Hal Foster, 'The Un/making of Sculpture' in Ferguson et al. (eds), *Richard Serra: Sculpture 1985–98*, Gottingen and Los Angeles, Calif., 1998.

14 Jean Baudrillard, *Simulacra and Simulation*, Ann Arbor, 1994.

15 Ilya Kabakov, *On the 'Total Installation'*, Ostfildern, 1995.

15 Rochelle Steiner (ed.), 'Spaces for Wonder', *Wonderland*, exh. cat., Saint Louis Art Museum, Miss., 2000, p. 36.

17 Robert Storr, 'No Stage, No Actors, But It's Theatre (and Art)', *New York Times*, 28 Nov. 1999.

18 M. Fried, 'Art and Objecthood', *Artforum*, Summer 1967. Quoted in Storr *op. cit.*

18 Steiner, *op. cit.*, p. 34.

22 Nicolas Bourriaud, *Postproduction*, New York, 2002, p. 12.

22 J. G. Ballard, interview by Lorenza Pignatti in *Tema Celeste*, 85, May/June 2001.

27 Neville Wakefield, 'The Passenger', *Frieze*, issue 67, May 2002.

28 Keith Tyson on *The News at Ten*, BBC, 28 October 2002.

28 Johanne Lamoureux, 'Exhibitionitis: A Contemporary Museum Ailment' in Chris Dercon (ed.), *Theatergarden Bestarium: The Garden as Theater as Museum*, London, 1990, p. 124.

29 Dieter Roelstraete, 'Sonsbeek 2001, A Place Odyssey' in Dieter Roelstraete (ed.), *Sonsbeek 9: Locus Focus*, Arnhem, 2001, p. 27.

29 Miwon Kwon, *One Place after Another*, Cambridge, Mass., 2002, p. 1.

30 Ilya Kabakov and Boris Groys, *Die Kunst der Installation*, Munich, 1996, p. 23.

30 Hal Foster, *The Return of the Real*, Cambridge, Mass., 1996.

30 Thomas Hirschhorn, *Contemporary Sculpture Projects Muenster*, Ostfildern-Ruit, 1997, p. 216.

31 James Meyer, 'The Functional Site', *Platzwechsel*, exh. cat., Kunsthalle Zurich, 1995, p. 29.

32 Kwon, *op. cit.*, p. 29.

32 Suzanne Lacy, *Mapping the Terrain: New Genre Public Art*, Seattle, Wash., 1995.

32 Walter Grasskamp, 'Art and the City' in K. Bussmann et al. (eds), *Contemporary Sculpture: Projects in Münster*, exh. cat., Ostfildern-Ruit, 1997, p. 10.

35 Oskar Bätschmann, *The Artist in the Modern World*, Cologne, 1997.

38 Michel Foucault, 'Of Other Spaces', in *Diacritics 1*, 16, Spring 1986. Quoted in *Politics, Poetics: Documenta X – The Book*, Ostfildern-Ruit, 1997, p. 265.

40 Nicholas Negroponte, *Being Digital*, London, 1996, p. 223.

42 Claire Colebrook, *Gilles Deleuze*, London 2002.

42 Colebrook, *op. cit.*, p. 100.

43 Sergiusz Michalski, *Public Monuments*, London, 1998.

44 Maria Lind, 'Learning From Art and Artists', in Gavin Wade (ed.), *Curating in the 21st Century*, Walsall, 2000, p. 94.

44 Hans Ulrich Obrist, in Gavin Wade (ed.), *Curating in the 21st Century*, Walsall, 2000, p. 54.

45 Richard Sennett, 'The Museum as an Anarchic Experience' in Chris Dercon (ed.), *Theatergarden Bestarium: The Garden as Theater as Museum*, London, 1990, p. 136.

47 Jeffrey Kastner, interview with Mary Jane Jacob, in *Public Art*, London, 1996.

47 Michael Landy, *Breakdown*, exh. cat., London, 2001, p. 109.

escape

49 Marc Augé, *Non-places: Introduction to an Anthropology of Super-modernity*, London and New York, 1995, p. 77.

49 Ina Blom, *Børre Sæthre*, exh. cat., Galleri Wang, Oslo, 2001.

49 Frederic Jameson, *Postmodernism, or, The Cultural Logic of Late Capitalism*, Durham, N.C., 1991, p. 87.

49 Paul Virilio, *Lost Dimension, Semiotext(e)*, New York, 1991, p. 35.

49 Sze Tsung Leong, 'Control Space' in R. Koolhaas et al. (eds), *Mutations*, Bordeaux, 2000, p. 187.

50 Jean-Pierre Bordaz, 'The World As It Should Be' in Idit Porat (ed.), *Absalon*, exh. cat., AFAA Tel Aviv Museum of Art, 1992.

50 Laurence Bosse, *Gregor Schneider*, exh. cat., Musée d'art Moderne de la Ville de Paris, 1998.

51 Jean Baudrillard, *Simulacra and Simulation*, Ann Arbor, 1994, p. 167.

51 Bernard Marcadé, 'Absalon's Monadology' in Idit Porat (ed.), *Absalon*, exh. cat., AFAA Tel Aviv Museum of Art, 1992.

51 'Biefer/Zgraggen' in H. Griese, E. Schmidt, (eds), *Do All Oceans Have Walls?* exh. cat., Künstlerhaus Bremen, 1998, p. 18.

51 J. Flam (ed.), *Robert Smithson, The Collected Writings*, Berkeley and Los Angeles, Calif., 1996

51 Aldo Bonomi, 'Smooth Space' in R. Koolhaas et al. (eds): *Mutations*, Bordeaux, 2000, p. 451.

53 Franz Kafka, 'The Burrow' in *Metamorphosis and Other Stories*, Harmondsworth, 1981, p. 128ff.

author and institution

78 Hal Foster, *Recodings*, Seattle, Wash., 1985, p. 100.

79 Cedric Price, 'Survey', *Tema Celeste*, 90, March/April 2002.

79 Maria Lind, 'Learning From Art and Artists', in Gavin Wade (ed.), *Curating in the 21st Century*, Walsall, 2000, p. 88.

79 Hans Ulrich Obrist in *The Producers: Contemporary Curators in Conversation (2)*, BALTIC, Gateshead, 2001, p. 34.

80 Brian O'Doherty, *The Gallery as Gesture*, 1981. Quoted in Yves Aupetitallot (ed.), *Wide White Space*, exh. cat., Palais des Beaux-Arts de Bruxelles, Düsseldorf, 1995, p. 7.

80 *Ibid.*

80 Ilya Kabakov, *On the 'Total Installation'*, Ostfildern, 1995, p. 271.

80 André Malraux, *Museum Without Walls*, London, 1967, p. 12.

81 Vilém Flusser, *Vom Subject zum Projekt: Menschwerdung, Schriften 3*, Düsseldorf, 1994.

81 Kasper König, 'Survey', *Tema Celeste*, 90, March/April 2002.

81 Jerôme Sans, 'Survey', *Tema Celeste*, 90, March/April 2002.

81 Àgnes Ivacs, *Locus Solus*, Book Review, Artpool Library, 2002.

81 Miwon Kwon, *One Place after Another*, Cambridge, Mass., 2002, p. 51.

exchange and interaction

106 Alicia Framis, *Blue Dogma*, exh. cat., Berlin Biennale, 2001, p. 87.

106 Nicolas Bourriaud quoted in Jemima Montagu, 'Site de création contemporaine', exhibition review, *Frieze*, 67, May 2002.

106 Paolo Bianchi, *LKW Lebenskunstwerke*, exh. cat., Kunsthaus/Kunstverein Bregenz, 2000.

106 *Ibid.*

106 Rirkrit Tiravanija and Franz Ackermann, *LKW Lebenskunstwerke*, exh. cat., Kunsthaus/Kunstverein Bregenz, 2000, p. 112.

107 Miwon Kwon, *One Place after Another*, Cambridge, Mass., 2002, p. 46.

108 Kwon, *op. cit.*, p. 50.
108 Marshall McLuhan, *Understanding Media*, London, 1964, p. 264.
109 Nicolas Bourriaud, 'Berlin Letter About Relational Aesthetics', *2. Berlin Biennale*, exh. cat., Berlin, 2001, p. 40.
109 Hou Hanru, 'On the Mid-Ground', *Timezone 8*, Hong Kong, 2002, p. 15.

time and narrative

132 Marcel Duchamp quoted in Pierre Cabanne, *Dialogues with Marcel Duchamp*, New York, 1987, p. 106.
132 Geoffrey Batchen, 'The Art of Archiving', Ingrid Schaffner and Matthias Winzen (eds), *Deep Storage – Collecting, Storing, and Archiving in Art*, Munich and New York, 1998, p. 47.
133 Vilém Flusser, *Dinge und Undinge: Phänomelologische Skizzen*, Munich, 1993.
134 Peter Osborne, *Travelling Light*, Manchester, 2000.
134 Irit Rogoff (Beatrice von Bismark et al., eds), *Interarchive*, Cologne, 2001, p. 177.
134 Rogoff, *op.cit.*, p. 179.
134 Jane and Louise Wilson, Interview with Lisa Corrin, Serpentine Gallery, London, 1999, p. 9.
134 Paul Virilio, *Lost Dimension, Semiotext(e)*, New York, 1991.
135 Jean-François Lyotard, *The Postmodern Condition: A Report on Knowledge*, Manchester, 1984, p. 81.

the body of the audience

166 Jonathan Crary, *Suspensions of Perception: Attention, Spectacle, and Modern Culture*, Cambridge, Mass., and London, 1999, p. 1.
167 Crary, *op. cit.*, p. 74.
167 Jacques Lacan, *The Four Fundamental Concepts of Psycho-Analysis*, tr. Alan Sheridan, London, 1977, p. 80.
168 M. Christine Boyer, *The City of Collective Memory*, Cambridge, Mass., 1994.
168 Jean Baudrillard, 'The Ecstacy of Communication', *Postmodern Culture*, London, 1985, p. 128.

bibliography

Monographs and Exhibition Catalogues

Absalon, exh. cat., Tel Aviv Museum of Art, 1992
Absalon. Retrospective, exh. cat., CAPC Bordeaux, 1998
Ackermann, Franz and Rikrit Tiravanija, *RE public*, Grazer Kunstverein, Graz, 1998
Aernout Mik, exh. cat., Van AbbeMuseum, Eindhoven, 1999
Aernout Mik, Primal Gestures, Minor Roles, exh. cat., The Stedelijk Van Abbemuseum, Eindhoven, Rotterdam, 2000
Ahtila, Eija-Liisa, *Fantasized Persons and Taped Conversations*, exh. cat., Tate Modern, London, 2002
Aitken, Doug, *Diamond Sea*, London, 2000
Doug Aitken, London, 2001
Daren Almond, exh. cat., Kunsthaus Zürich, 2001
Francis Alÿs, exh. cat., Musée Picasso, Antibes, 2001
Alÿs, Francis, *The Last Clown*, exh. cat., Fundació 'La Caixa', Barcelona, 2000
Amorales, Carlos, *Los Amorales*, exh. cat., Migros Museum Zurich, Amsterdam, 2001
Ana Miguel, exh. cat., Contemporary Art Center Venâncio-Ecco, Brasilía, 2001
Andrea Zittel, exh. cat., Deichtorhallen, Hamburg, 1999
Anish Kapoor/Germano Celant, London, 1996
Åsdam, Knut, *Works 1995–2000*, exh. cat., Tate Britain, Copenhagen, 2000
Atelier van Lieshout, A Manual, exh. cat., Kölnischer Kunstverein, Cologne, Museum Boijmans Van Beuningen, Rotterdam, 1997
Atelier van Lieshout, *The Good, The Bad + The Ugly*, Rotterdam, 1998
Per Barclay, exh. cat., Galleria Civica di Arte Contemporanea, Trento, Turin, 2000
Per Barclay, exh. cat., The National Museum of Contemporary Art, Oslo, 1999
Barney, Matthew, *The Cremaster Cycle*, New York, 2002
Tatsurou Bashi alias Tazro Niscino: Obdach, exh. cat., Räume von Junge Kunst, Wolfsburg, 1997
Beecroft, Vanessa, *VB 08-36 Performances*, Ostfildern-Ruit, 2000
Bik, Liesbeth and Jos van der Pol, *Moderna Museet Project*, exh. cat., Moderna Museet Stockholm, 2001
Bill Viola, exh. cat., Whitney Museum of American Art, New York, 1999
Bill Viola, Going Forth By Day: Process/Prozess, Deutsche Guggenheim Berlin, 2002
Bock, John, *Gribbohm*, Ostfildern, 2001
Bodys Isek Kingelez, Ostfildern-Ruit, 2001
Christian Boltanski, exh. cat., Galleria d'arte moderna, Milan, 1997
Boltanski, Christian, *La vie impossible. Ce dont ils se souviennent/Woran sie sich erinnern/What People Remember About Him*, Cologne, 2001
Bonde, Peter and Jason Rhoades, *The Snowball*, Ostfildern-Ruit, 1999
Bonvicini, Monica, *Eternmale*, exh. cat., Kunsthaus Glarus and Centre d'édition contemporaine, Geneva, 2001
—, *Scream & Shake*, exh. cat., Le Magasin, Grenoble, 2001
Brüggemann, Stefan, *Intellectual Disaster*, New Mexico City, 2002
Christoph Büchel, exh. cat., Kunsthalle St Gallen, 1999
Bul, Lee, *Korean Pavilion*, exh. cat., 48th Venice Biennale, 1999.
Bulloch, Angela, *Rule Book*, London, 2001
Bunn, David, *Double Monster*, exh. cat., New York, 2000
Cardiff, Janet, *The Missing Voice (Case Study B)*, London, 2000
Christo, *The Reichstag and Urban Projects*, Munich and New York, 1993
Creed, Martin, *Works*, exh. cat., Southampton City Art Gallery, Southampton, 2000
Dalziel+Scullion, *Home*, exh. cat., Fruitmarket Gallery, Edinburgh, 2002
Dávila, Jose, *Temporality Is a Question of Survival*, exh. cat., Camden Arts Centre, London, 2001
Tacita Dean, exh. cat., Museum für Gegenwartskunst, Basle, 2001
Tacita Dean, exh. cat., Tate Britain, London, 2001
Delvoye, Wim, *New & Improved*, exh. cat., New Museum for Contemporary Art, 2002
—, *Skatalog*, exh. cat., Museumkunstpalast, Düsseldorf, 2001
Dion, Mark, *Archaeology*, London, 1999
Stan Douglas, London, 1998
Douglas, Stan, *Journey into Fear 2001*, exh. cat., Serpentine Gallery London and Cologne, 2002
Dutton & Peacock, *On Vanishing*, exh. cat., Site Gallery, Sheffield, 2001
Olafur Eliasson, London, 2002
Eliasson, Olafur, *The Mediated Motion*,

Cologne, 2001

—, *Your only real thing is time*, exh. cat., Institute of Contemporary Art, Boston, Mass., 2001

Elmgreen, Michael & Ingar Dragset, *Taking Place*, exh. cat., Kunsthalle Zürich and Witte de With, Center for Contemporary Art, Rotterdam, 2001

Emin, Tracey, *Diary*, exh. cat., Cornerhouse, Manchester, 2000

—, *Holiday Inn*, exh. cat., Gesellschaft für Aktuelle Kunst, Bremen, 1998

Fischer, Lili, *Leporello-Arie*, Ostfildern-Ruit, 1997

Sylvie Fleury, exh. cat., Galerie der Stadt Esslingen, Villa Merkel, Ostfildern-Ruit, 1999

François, Michel, *La plante en nous/Die Pflanze in uns*, exh. cat., Kunsthalle Bern, Göttingen, 2000

Friis-Hansen, Dana, Octavia Zaya et al. (contributors), *Cai Guo-Qiang* London, 2002

Gilchrist, Bruce and Jo Joelson, *Syzygy/Polaria*, London Fieldworks, 2002

Gordon, Douglas, *Feature Film*, London, 1999

Rodney Graham, Whitechapel Art Gallery, London, 2002

Graham, Rodney, *Cinema Music Video*, exh. cat., Kunsthalle Vienna, 1999

Rodney Graham, Works from 1976 to 1994, Art Gallery of York University, Toronto, 1994

Gygi, Fabrice, *Le Magasin*, exh. cat., Centre national d'art contemporain, Grenoble, 2000

Håkanson, Henrik, *Syndrome*, exh. cat., IAPSIS, Stockholm, 2000

—, *Tomorrow and Tonight*, exh. cat., Kunsthalle Basel, 1999

Halmans, Frank, *Noodvelichting*, Hermen Molendijk Stichting, Centrum Beeldende Kunst, Amersfort, 1999

Hamilton, Ann, *Mattering*, exh. cat., Musée d'art contemporain de Montréal, 1999

—, *Myein*, exh. cat,. The United States Pavilion, 48th Venice Biennale, 1999

—, *Present-Past, 1984–1997*, exh. cat., Musée d'art contemporain de Lyon, 1998

Christine Hill, exh. cat., Galerie EIGEN+ART Berlin and Kunst-Werken, Berlin, 1995

Hill, Gary, *Projective Installations. Nr. 3*, New York, 1997

Hirschhorn, Thomas, *Jumbo Spoons and Big Cake*, exh. cat., The Art Institute of Chicago, 2000

—, *Material. Public Works -The Bridge 2000*, London, 2001

Hirst, Damien, *I want to spend the rest of my life everywhere, with everyone, one to one, always, forever, now*, London, 1997

—, *Theories, Models, Methods, Approaches, Assumptions, Results and Findings*, Gagosian Gallery, New York, 2000

Höller, Carsten, *Glück/Skop*, exh. cat., Kunstverein Hamburg, 1996

—, *Registro*, exh. cat. Fondazione Prada, Milan, 2000

Höller, Carsten and Rosemarie Trockel, *Ein Haus für Schweine und Menschen*, Cologne, 1997

Hoptman, Laura J., *Yayoi Kusama*, London, 2000

Huyghe, Pierre, *The Third Memory*, Editions du Centre Pompidou, Paris, 2000

Christian Jankowski: Play, exh. cat., De Appel, Amsterdam, 2001

Janssens, Ann Veronica, *Une image différente dans chaque œil*, Liège and Brussells, 1999

Ilya Kabakov, Milan, 2001

Kabakov, Ilya, *Installations 1983-1995*, exh. cat., Le Musée national d'art moderne Centre de création industrielle, Paris, 1995

—, *Installations, Catalogue Raisonné 1983–2000*, Düsseldorf, 2000

—, *The Man Who Never Threw Anything Away*, New York, 1996

Kabakov, Ilya and Emilia, *Palace of Projects*, Düsseldorf, 1998

Katase, Kazuo, *Umsicht*, exh. cat., Wilhelm-Hack-Museum, Ludwigshafen am Rhein, Cologne, 1999

Tadashi Kawamata, exh. cat., Middelheimmuseum Antwerpen, 2000

Kruger, Barbara, *Remote Control*, Cambridge, Mass., London, 1993

Kuball, Mischa, *Private Light/Public Light*, exh. cat., 24. Biennale São Paulo, Ostfildern-Ruit, 1998

—, *Project Rooms*, Cologne, 1997

Landy, Michael, *Break Down*, exh. cat., London, 2001

Lane, Abigail, *Tomorrows World, Yesterday Fever (Mental Guests Incorporated)*, exh. cat., Milton Keynes Gallery, London, 2001

Leal, Miguel, *Projecto Bunker (1996–99)*, exh. cat., Circulo de Artes Plásticas de Coimbra, 2000

Maurizio Cattelan, London, 2000

Mori, Mariko, *Dream Temple*, exh. cat., Fondation Prada, Milan, 1999

—, *Esoteric Cosmos*, exh. cat., Kunstmuseum Wolfsburg, 1999

Muñoz, Juan, *Double Bind*, exh. cat, Tate Modern, London, 2001

Muntean/Rosenblum, *Where else*, Secession, Vienna, 2000

Nelson, Mike, *A Fotgotten Kingdom*, London, 2001

Newling, John, *Weight*, exh. cat. Turnpike Gallery, Leigh, 1998

Nicolai, Olaf, *...fading in, fading out, fading away...*, exh. cat., Westfälischer Kunstverein, Münster, 2001

—, *Show Case*, Nuremberg, 1999

Op de Beeck, Hans, *A Selection of Works 1996–2001*, Amsterdam 2001

Julian Opie, exh. cat., Ikon Gallery, Birmingham, 2001

Otto, Catrin, *Einschnitte*, exh. cat., Goldrausch 11, Berlin, 2000

João Penalva, exh. cat., Frac Languedoc-Roussillon and Camden Arts Centre, 1999

Petry, Michael, *The Trouble with Michael*, London, 2001

Pilis, Alexander, *Architecture Parallax: SnackLunch*, exh. cat., St Norbert Arts and Cultural Center, Winnipeg, 1996

Pippin, Steven, *Addendum*, exh. cat., Portikus, Frankfurt am Main, 1994

Jaume Plensa: Love Songs, exh. cat., Kestner Gesellschaft, Hanover, 1999

Rawanchaikul, Navin, *Comm...: Individual and Collaborative Projects 1993–1999*, Cologne, 1999

Rehberger, Tobias, *(whenever you need me)*, exh. cat., Westfälischer Kunstverein, Münster, 2001

—, *Apples and Pears*, Cologne, 2002

Rist, Pipilotti, *Apricots Along The Street*, exh. cat., Museo Reina Sofia, Madrid, Zurich, 2001

Pipilotti Rist, London, 2001

Rondinone, Ugo, *Guided by Voices*, exh. cat., Kunsthaus Glarus and Ostfildern-Ruit, 1999

—, *Hell, Yes!*, Küsnacht, 2000

Sæthre, Børre, *A Million Dreams – A Million Scars*, exh. cat., Galleri Wang, Oslo, 1999

Gregor Schneider, exh. cat., Musée d'Art Moderne de la Ville de Paris, 1998

Schneider, Gregor, *Totes Haus Ur*, Ostfildern-Ruit, 2001

Roman Signer, exh. cat., Swiss Pavilion, 1999 Venice Biennale, St Gallen, 1999

Smith, Terry, *Site Unseen*, London 1997

Sudell, Louise, *Theatre of Ideas*, exh. cat., Picaron Editions, Amsterdam, 1990

Do-Ho Suh, exh. cat., Whitney Museum of American Art, New York, 2001

Sam Taylor-Wood, exh. cat. Hayward Gallery, London, 2002

Taylor-Wood, Sam, *Third Party*, Ostfildern-Ruit, 2000

Diana Thater, Delphine, Secession, Vienna, 2000

Tiravanija, Rikrit, *Untitled*, exh. cat., Migros Museum für Gegenwartskunst, Zurich, 1998

Tolaas, Sissel, *Transitionen*, Ostfildern-Ruit, 1994

Torres, Francesc, *The Repository of Absent Flesh*, exh. cat., List Visual Arts Center, Cambridge, Mass., 1998

Tuerlinckx, Joëlle, *Autour de Film. Cinema. Audio and Visual Days. Journal de Jours. Expositions. Projections*, exh. cat., Brussels, 2000

Tunick, Spencer, *Self*, DeBeyerd Centrum voor Beeldende Kunst, Breda, 2001

Tyson, Keith, *Supercollider*, exh. cat., South London Gallery, 2002

Weigand, Hans, *Jerry Cotto 2002*, Cologne, 2002

Westphalen, Olav, *E.S.U.S. & other works*, exh. cat., Public Art Fund, New York, 2002

Wexler, Allan, *The Fine Art of Applied Art*, Nuremberg, 1997

Wilson, Jane and Louise, *Ellipsis*, London, 2001

BIBLIOGRAPHY

Reference Books

Installation

Arscott, Caroline (ed.), *On installation*, vol. 24 (no. 2), Oxford, 2002

Bahtsetzis, Sotirios, *Der Anfang der Installationskunst*, Berlin, 2003

Kabakov, Ilya and Boris Groys, *Die Kunst der Installation*, Munich, 1996

Kachur, Lewis, *Displaying the Marvelous. Marcel Duchamp, Salvador Dali and Surrealist Exhibition Installations*, Cambridge, Mass., and London, 2001

Kaye, Nick, *Site-specific Art. Performance, Place and Documentation*, London and New York, 2000

de Oliveira, Nicolas, Nicola Oxley and Michael Petry, *Installation Art*, London and Washington, D.C., 1994

Reiss, Julie H., *From Margin to Center. The Spaces of Installation Art*, Cambridge, Mass., and London, 2000

Suderburg, Erika (ed.), *Space, Site, Intervention. Situating Installation Art*, Minneapolis, Minn., and London, 2000

Display

Andriesse, Paul (ed.), *Art Gallery Exhibiting. The Gallery as a Vehicle of Art*, Eindhoven, 1996

Barker, Ema (ed.), *Contemporary Cultures of Display*, London, 1999

Bovier, Lionel and Christophe Cherix (ed.), *Independent Spaces*, Geneva, 1999

Greenberg, Reesa, Bruce W. Ferguson and Sandy Nairne (ed.), *Thinking about Exhibitions*, London and New York, 1996

Putnam, James, *Art and Artifact. The Museum as Medium*, London and New York, 2001

Staniszewski, Mary Anne, *The Power of Display. A History of Exhibition Installations at the Museum of Modern Art*, Cambridge, Mass., and London, 1998

Archive

Bismarck, Beatrice von, et al., *Interarchive*, Cologne, 2002

Clifford, James, *On Collecting Art and Culture*, Cambridge, Mass., 1995

Elsner, John and Roger Cardinal, *Cultures of Collecting*, London, 1994

Groy, Boris, *Die Logik der Sammlung*, Munich, 1997

Site specificity

Büttner, Claudia, *Art Goes Public. Von der Gruppenausstellung im Freien zum Projekt im nicht-institutionellen Raum*, Munich, 1997

Crimp, Douglas, *On the Museum's Ruins*, Cambridge, Mass., and London, 1993

Kwon, Miwon, *One Place after Another. Site-Specific Art and Locational Identity*, Cambridge, Mass., and London, 2001

Möntmann, Nina, *Kunst als sozialer Raum*, Cologne, 2002

Site and Displacement

Augé, Marc, *Non-places: Introduction to an Anthropology of Supermodernity*, London and New York, 1995

Bell, Michael and Sze Tsung Leong (ed.), *Slow Space*, New York, 1998

Borden, Iain, Jane Rendell et al., *The Unknown City*, Cambridge, Mass., and London, 2000

Burgin, Victor, *In/different Spaces: Place and Memory in Visual Culture*, Berkeley and Los Angeles, Calif., and London, 1996

Clarke, David B. (ed.), *The Cinematic City*, London and New York, 1997

Crang, Mike and Nigel Thrift (eds), *Thinking Space*, London and New York, 2000

Deutsche, Rosalyn, *Art and Spatial Politics*, Cambridge, Mass., and London, 1996

Grosz, Elisabeth A., *Architecture from the Outside: Essays on Virtual and Real Space*, Cambridge, Mass., and London, 2001

Kaplan, Caren, *Questions of Travel: Postmodern Discourses of Displacement*, Durham, N.C., 1996

Lacy, Suzanne, *Mapping the Terrain. New Genre Public Art*, Seattle, Wash., 1995

Lippard, Lucy R., *On the Beaten Track: Tourism, Art and Place*, New York, 2000

Low, Seth M., *On the Plaza: The Politics of Public Space and Culture*, Austin, Tex., 2000

Mathews, Gordon, *Global Culture/Individual Identity*, London and New York, 2000

McKenzie, Evan, *Privatopia*, New Haven, Conn., 1994

Morley, David and Keith Robins, *Spaces of Identity*, London and New York, 1995

Osborne, Peter D., *Traveling light: Photography, Travel and Visual Culture*, Manchester and New York, 2000

Vidler, Anthony, *Warped Space. Art, Architecture, and Anxiety in Modern Culture*, Cambridge, Mass., London, 2000

Weibel, Peter (ed.), *Olafur Eliasson: Surroundings Surrounded. Essays on Space and Science*, Cambridge, Mass., and London, 2000

Art in Context

Bätschmann, Oskar, *The Artist in the Modern World: The Conflict Between Market and Self-Expression*, Cologne, 1997

Jones, Caroline A., *Machine In The Studio: Constructing The Postwar American Artist*, Chicago, Ill., 1996

Weibel, Peter (ed.), *Kontext Kunst*, Cologne, 1994

Wu, Chin-Tao, *Privatising Culture. Corporate Art Intervention Since the 1980s*, London, 2002

Perception and Representation

Crary, Jonathan, *Suspensions of Perception: Attention, Spectacle, and Modern Culture*, Cambridge, Mass., and London, 1999

Foster, Hal, The Return of the Real: *The Avant-garde at the End of the Century*, Cambridge, Mass., and London, 1996

Krauss, Rosalind, *A Voyage on the North Sea: Art in the Age of Post-Medium Condition*, London, 1999, and New York, 2000

Manovich, Lev, T*he Language of New Media*, Cambridge, Mass., and London, 2001

McEvilley, Thomas, *Sculpture in the Age of Doubt*, New York, 1999

Rieser, Martin and Andrea Zapp, *New Screen Media: Cinema/Art/Narrative*, London, 2002

Body as Site

Jappe, Elisabeth, *Performance, Ritual. Prozess – Handbuch der Aktionskunst in Europa*, Munich and New York, 1993

Jones, Amelia, *Body Art: Performing The Subject*, Minneapolis, Minn., 1998

Sandford, Mariellen R. (ed.), *Happenings and Other Acts*, London and New York, 1995

Schimmel, Paul (ed.), *Out of Actions: Between Performance and the Object, 1949–1979*, London, 1998

Virtual Environment and Simulation

Hayles, N. Katherine, *How We Became Posthuman: Virtual Bodies in Cybernetics and Literature*, Chicago, Ill., 1999

Holtzman, Steven R., *Digital Mosaics: the Aesthetics of Cyberspace*, New York, 1997

Mitchell, William J., *City of Bits: Space, Place, and the Infobahn*, Cambridge, Mass., and London, 1996

Moser, Mary Anne with Douglas MacLeod (ed.), *Immersed in Technology. Art and Virtual Environments*, Cambridge, Mass., and London, 1996

Negroponte, Nicholas, *Being Digital*, London and New York, 1995

Virilio, Paul, *A Landscape of Events*, Cambridge, Mass., and London, 2000

Weibel, Peter and Timothy Druckrey (ed.), *Net Condition: Art and Global Media*, Cambridge, Mass., Karlsruhe and London, 2001

Wilson, Stephen, *Information Arts. Intersections of Art, Science, and Technology*, Cambridge, Mass., and London, 2001

Memory and fictional topographies

Amato, Joseph Anthony, Dust: *A History of the Small and the Invisible*, Berkeley and Los Angelesl, Calif., and London, 2000

Batchelor, David, *Chromophobia*, London, 2000

Bibliomania, exh. cat., The Henry Moore Foundation, London, 1999

Calvino, Italo, *Invisible Cities*, London, 1997 (originally published in 1972 as *Le Città invisibili*)
Coles, Alex (ed.), *The Optic of Walter Benjamin*, London, 1999
Derrida, Jacques, *Archive Fever: A Freudian Impression*, London, 1996
Harbison, Robert, *Eccentric Spaces*, Cambridge, Mass., London, 2000
Manguel, Alberto and Gianni Guadalupi (ed.), *The Dictionary of Imaginary Places*, London, 1999
Olalquiaga, Celeste, *The Artificial Kingdom. A Treasury of the Kitsch Expirience*, London, 1998
Perec, George, *Species of Space and Other Pieces*, London and New York, 1997
Robbe-Grillet, Alain, *Topography of a Phantom City*, London, 1978
Stewart, Susan, *On Longing. Narratives of the Miniature, the Gigantic, the Souvenir, the Collection*, Durham, N.C., and London, 1993

Mass Culture

Buck-Morss, Susan, *Dreamworld and Catastrophe. The Passing of Mass Utopia in East and West*, Cambridge, Mass., and London, 2000
Chaney, Davis, *Lifestyles*, London and New York, 1996
Frisa, Maria Luisa, Mario Lupano and Stefano Tonchi, *Total Living*, Milan, 2002
Lehmann, Ulrich, *Tigersprung. Fashion in Modernity*, Cambridge, Mass., and London, 2000
Miller, Daniel, *A Theory of Shopping*, Ithaca, New York, 1998
Tester, Keith (ed.), *The Flâneur*, London and New York, 1994

Statements

Detterer, Gabriele (ed.), *Art Recollection. Artists, Interviews and Statements in the Nineties*, Ravenna, 1997
Finkelpearl, Tom (ed.), *Dialogues on Public Art*, Cambridge, Mass., and London, 2000
Hiller, Susan and Sarah Martin (ed.), *The Producers: Contemporary Curators in Conversation*, Gateshead 2000 and Newcastle upon Tyne, 2001
Ramos, María Elena (ed.), *Intervenciones en el espacio. Diálogos en el MBA*, Caracas, 1998
Sâns, Jérome and Marc Sanchez (ed.), *TokyoBook1, 'What do you expect from an art institution in the 21th century?'*, Paris, 2001
Wade, Gavin (ed.), *Curating in 21st Century*, Walsall, 2000

list of illustrations

p. 1 Oswaldo Macia
Columbian artist, born 1960; based in London.
Memory Skip, 1995
Metal skip, pine essence, CD-disc. Installation view: the Museum of Installation, London. Photograph: Edward Woodman. Courtesy: the Museum of Installation, London.

p. 2 + 3 Andrea Zittel
Born 1965 in USA.
RAUGH Furniture: Lucinda, 1998
Foam rubber, 153.6 x 358 x 259 cm (5 ft x 11 ft 9 in. x 8 ft 6 in.). Installation view: Andrea Rosen Gallery, 1998. Photograph: Orcutt & Van Der Putten. Courtesy: Andrea Rosen Gallery, New York.

foreword

p. 10 Tomoko Takahashi
Born 1966 in Japan.
Line Out, 1999
Installation view at 'New Neurotic Realism': the Saatchi Gallery, London, 1999. Courtesy: Hales Gallery, London.

introduction

p. 12 + 13 Michael Landy
Born 1963 in UK (London).
Break Down, 2001
C&A store, Marble Arch, London. Photograph: Dillon Bryden. Courtesy: Karsten Schubert and Thomas Dane, London.

p. 14 Ilya Kabakov
Born 1933 in Russia (Dujepropetrovsk); lives and works in New York.
The Palace of Projects, 1998
Camden Round House, London. Courtesy: Artangel, London.

p. 15 Francis Alÿs
Born 1959 in Belgium (Antwerp); lives and works in Mexico City and New York.
When Faith Moves Mountains, 2002
Performance view: Lima, Peru, April 11th, 2002. Courtesy: the artist and Lisson Gallery, London.

p. 16 Renée Green
Born 1959 in USA (Cleveland, Ohio); lives and works in New York.
Between and Including, 1999
Video. Courtesy: Georg Kargl, Vienna.

p. 17 (left) Meschac Gaba
Born 1961 in Benin (Cotonou); lives in Amsterdam, The Netherlands.
Museum Shop, 2001
3 cardboard boxes for transport.
Courtesy: carlier/gebauer.

p. 17 (right) Bik Fillingham Van der Pol
Liesbeth Bik, Peter Fillingham, Jos van der Pol.
The Bookshop Piece, 1996
Diverse media (books, construction materials, etc.), 385 x 500 x 250 cm (12 ft 7 in. x 16 ft 4 in. x 8 ft 2 in.). Project for Museum Boijmans van Beuningen, Rotterdam. Photograph: Jos van der Pol. Courtesy: the artists.

p. 18 Barbara Kruger
Born 1945 in USA.
Power, Pleasure, Desire, Disgust, 1997
Video and slide projection; dimensions variable. Courtesy: the artist and South London Gallery, London.

p. 19 + 20 (above) Juan Muñoz
Born 1953 in Spain, (Madrid); died 2001.
Double Bind, 2001
Mixed media; exhibiting site: Tate Modern, London. Photograph: Attilio Maranzano. Courtesy: Estate of Juan Muñoz and Marian Goodman Gallery, New York.

p. 20 (below) Blast Theory
Group founded 1991; based in London.
Kidnap, 1998
Performance event. London location and live internet viewing with chat rooms. Camera controllable via the ICA, London, and The Green House, Manchester. Photograph: Gregorio Pagliaro. Courtesy: the artists.

p. 21 Stefan Brüggemann
Born 1975 in Mexico.
Opening, 1998
Installation view: the Museum of Installation, 1998. Photograph: Edward Woodman. Courtesy: the artist and the Museum of Installation, London.

p. 22 Ann Hamilton
Born 1956 in USA (Lima Ohio); lives in Columbus, Ohio, USA.
Salic, 1995
Passenger railroad car, exterior dimensions: 2.95 x 3.2 x 25.9 m (9 ft 8 in. x 10 ft 6 in. x 85 ft); interior dimensions: 2.4 x 14.6 m (7 ft 10 in. x 48 ft). Materials: salt licks; 4 videos (black and white, sound, 50 min. each, continuous play); 4 video laser discs; 4 laser disc players; 22 video projectors. Courtesy: Sean Kelly Gallery, New York.

p. 23 Wendy Bornholdt
New Zealand artist.
Subspace SE8 3NU (Relay), 2001
Installation view of the group show 'Here and Now' at the Museum of Installation, London. Photograph: David Grandorge. Courtesy: the artist and the Museum of Installation, London.

p. 24 + 25 Stan Douglas
Born 1960 in Canada.
'Contemporary' set for *Der Sandmann* at DOKFILM Studios, Potsdam, Babelsberg-12/94. Photograph: the artist. Courtesy: the artist and David Zwirner, New York.

p. 26 Jonathan Hernández
Born 1972 in Mexico.
Everything is OK, 2001
Mirror, acrylic, wood and red carpet. 200 x 122 x 27 cm (6 ft 6 in. x 4 ft x 10½ in.). Courtesy: Kurimanzutto, Mexico City.

p. 27 Matthew Barney
Born 1967 in USA (San Francisco); lives and works in New York.
Cremaster 2: The Drone's Exposition, 1999
Mixed media sculptural installation including 35 mm film transferred from HDTV, 12 C-prints and 5 drawings in acrylic frames. MB139. Courtesy: Barbara Gladstone Gallery, New York.

p. 28 Alexandra Ranner
Born 1967 in Germany
Basement, 2001
Various materials. 210 x 330 x 130 cm (6 ft 8 in. x 10 ft 10 in. x 4 ft 3 in.). Photograph: Gert Jan van Rooij. Courtesy: Galerie Fons Welters, Amsterdam/Six Friedrich Lisa Ungar, Munich.

p. 29 Carl Von Weiler
Born 1964 in The Netherlands; lives and works in London.
Matrix, 1998
Installation detail at the Museum of Installation, London. Monitors, VHS players. Photograph: Edward Woodman. Courtesy: the artist and the Museum of Installation, London.

p. 30 (above) Bruce Gilbert
Born 1946.
Cross over, 1998
Installation view of the exhibition: 'MOI LAB': the Museum of Installation, London. Photograph: Edward Woodman. Courtesy: the artist and the Museum of Installation, London.

p. 30 (below) Sarah Sze
Born 1969 in USA (Boston, Massachusetts); lives and works in New York.
Everything That Rises Must Converge, 1999
Mixed technic. Photograph: Frank Oudeman. Collection: Fondation Cartier pour l'art contemporain, Paris.

p. 31 Olav Westphalen
Born 1963 in Germany (Hamburg); lives and works in New York.
E.S.U.S., Extremely Site-Unspecific Sculpture, 2000
Mixed media, c. 350 x 200 x 200 cm (11 ft 6 in. x 6 ft 6 in. x 6 ft 6 in.). Courtesy: the artist and Maccarone Inc., the Public Art Fund, New York.

p. 33 Spencer Tunick
Born 1967 in USA (Middletown, New York); lives and works in New York.
Maine, 1997
Gelatin silver mounted on aluminium, 125 x 151.7 cm (4 ft 1 in. x 5 ft 2 in.). Courtesy: the artist and Hales Gallery, London.

p. 34 Keith Wilson
Born 1967.
Puddle, 1999
Altered paving and rain water.

p. 35 (above) Rodney Graham
Born 1949 in Canada (Vancouver).
The King's Part, 1999
Anechoic chamber, painted metal staircase, sound equipment. c. 558 cm h x 1067 x 406 cm (c. 18 ft 4 in. h x 35 ft x 13 ft 4 in.). Courtesy: Donald Young Gallery, Chicago.

p. 35 (below) Janet Cardiff
Born 1957 in Canada (Brussels, Ontario); lives and works in Alberta, Canada.
The Missing Voice (Case Study B), 1999
Audio walk (with headphones). Commissioned by Artangel, London. Photograph: Stephen White. Courtesy: the artist and Luhring Augustine Gallery, New York.

p. 36 Carsten Höller, Rosemarie Trockel
Carsten Höller born 1961.
Rosemarie Trockel born 1952.
Ein Haus für Schweine und Menschen, 1997
Installation view Documenta X, Kassel, 1997. Courtesy: Schipper & Krome, Berlin.

p. 37 (above) Maurice Van Tellingen
Born 1957 in The Netherlands (Hilversum); lives and works in Amsterdam.
Shadowman, 1999
Mixed media and LCD projector, 12 x 18 x 10 cm (4¾ x 7 x 3¹⁵⁄₁₆ in.). Photograph: Gert Jan van Rooy, Amsterdam. Courtesy: the artist.

p. 37 (below) Snøhetta AS
Turner Center, Margate England, 2001
Animation. Courtesy: Snøhetta AS.

p. 38 (above) Hans Op de Beeck
Born 1969 in Belgium.
Exercising the Nowhere (2), 2000
Sculptural installation, painted MDF-sculpture on metal structure, improvised architectural model at breast height. 180 x 190 x 272 cm (5 ft 11 in. x 6 ft 2 in. x 8 ft 11 in.), MDF wood, 2K-spray paint, grey primer, Plexi, metal and installed lighting. Photograph: Hein Hage and Gert Op de Beeck. Courtesy: Collection Vlaamse Gemeenschap - MuHKA.

p. 38 (below) Martin Dörbaum
Born 1971 in Germany (Berlin).
Microviseur 2200/H, 2000
Lambdachrome on Aludibond / Diasec 92.6 x 80 cm (36½ x 31½ in.). Courtesy: the artist and Kapinos – Galerie für zeitgenössische Kunst, Berlin.

p. 39 (above) Sven Påhlsson
Born 1965; lives and works in Oslo and New York.
Sprawlville, 2002
3D computer animation/DVD still. 10 min. Courtesy: the artist and Spencer Brownstone Gallery, New York.

p. 39 (below) Martin Dörbaum
Schwimmen mit Vater, der: 'Banana Yoshimoto', Tsugumi, 2000
Iris Giclée on Aquarelles Arches grain fin 32.7 x 43.5 cm (12⅞ x 17⅛ in.). Courtesy: the artist Kapinos – Galerie für zeitgenössische Kunst, Berlin.

p. 40 Paul Noble
Born 1963; lives and works in London.
Unified Nobson, 2001
DVD for projection. Still courtesy: Maureen Paley/Interim Art, London.

p. 41 Damián Ortega
Born 1967; lives and works in Mexico City.
Cosmic Thing, 2002
Volkswagen Beetle, 25.3 m (83 ft), stainless steel wire, acrylic, dimensions variable. Courtesy: Kurimanzutto, Mexico City.

p. 42 Frank Halmans
Born 1963 in Heerlen; lives and works in Utrecht, The Netherlands.
The Bedrooms in which I still wake up, 1996-2002.
View of studio. Photograph: Jeannette Schols, Utrecht. Courtesy: the artist and Gallerie van der Berge, Goes, The Netherlands.

p. 43 Chris Burden
Born 1946 in USA (Boston, Massachussetts); lives and works in Topauga, California.
Mexican Bridge, 1998-99.
Installation view from *The Bridges*, installation at BALTIC, The Centre for Contemporary Art, Gateshead, England.
Photograph: Neville Balszk. Courtesy: the artist.

p. 44 (above left) Francesc Torres
Born 1948 in Spain (Barcelona); lives and works in New York.
The Repository of Absent Flesh, 1998
Mixed media, 27.43 x 9.14 m (90 x 30 ft). Site: List Visual Arts Center Massachusetts Institute of Technology (MIT), Cambridge, Massachusetts. Photograph: Charles Mayer.

Courtesy: the artist and Elba Benítez Gallery, Madrid (collection of the Bohen Foundation, New York).

p. 44 (above right) Francesc Torres
The Crystal Continent (El continent de cristall), 1993–94
Mixed media, 60 x 20 m (197 x 66 ft) Site: Tinglado 2, Tarragona, Spain. Photo Martín García, Barcelona. Courtesy: the artist and Elba Benítez Gallery, Madrid.

p. 45 Steven Pippin
Born 1960 in UK.
Addendum, 1994.
Photonegative on cardboard, 4.6 x 7.6 m (15 ft x 24 ft 11 in.). Installation view: Portikus Frankfurt am Main, Germany, 1994–95. Courtesy: Klosterfelde, Berlin.

p. 46 staatsbankberlin
Einstein On The Beach, 2002
View of the main hall. Opera in four acts by Philip Glass and Robert Wilson
opera/installation idea, concept and stage director: Berthold Schneider; musical director: Ari Benjamin Meyers; installation concept: Veronika Witte; choreography: Tino Sehgal; costumes: Nina Thorwart; singers and staatsbankberlin orchestra. Courtesy: staatsbankberlin.

p. 47 Monica Bonvicini
1965 Born in Italy (Venice); lives and works in Berlin and Los Angeles.
Plastered, 1998
Drywall panels, styrofoam, adaptable dimensions. Courtesy: Chouakri Brahms Berlin.

escape

p. 53 Biefer/Zgraggen
Marcel Biefer, born 1959; lives and works in Düsseldorf and Zurich.
Beat Zgraggen, born 1958.
God, 1998
Styrofoam, construction foam, electronically controlled illumination. 8.4 m (27 ft 6 in.) diameter. Installation view: Neustadtbahnhof, Bremen, Germany. Courtesy: the artists (Biefer/Zgraggen) and Horst Griese.

p. 54 (above) Per Barclay
Born 1955 in Norway.
Pas de deux, 2001
Room constructed from wooden panels, metal gantry, 2 chainsaws, 5 x 7 x 3.05 m (16 ft 5 in. x 23 ft x 10 ft). Installation view Bergen Kunstforening, Bergen, Norway. Photograph: Fin Serck Hansen, Oslo. Courtesy: Galleri Wang, Oslo.

p. 54 (below) Per Barclay
Untitled, 1999–2000
Installations 1991–2000. Installation view, exhibition at the Museum of Installation, 2000. Photograph: David Grandorge. Courtesy: the Museum of Installation, London, and Galleria Persano, Italy.

p. 55 Lee Bul
Born in 1964 in South Korea (Seoul); lives and works in Seoul.
Gravity Greater Than Velocity ll, 1999
Polycarbonate panels, steel frame, velour, sponge, karaoke equipment, LCD monitor,
250 x 184 x 120 cm (8 ft 2 in. x 6 ft x 3 ft 11 in.).
Photograph: Rhee Jae-yong. Courtesy: PKM Gallery, Inc., Seoul, Korea.

p. 56 + 57 (above) Ann Veronica Janssens
Born 1956 in UK
Blue, Red and Yellow, 2001
Installation at the Neuenationale Galerie, Berlin. Photograph: the artist. Courtesy: the artist.

p. 56 + 57 (below) Bruce Gilchrist and Jo Joelson
Both Born in UK
Polaria, 2002
3 m cube. Installation view: Wapping Hydraulic Power Station, London. Photograph: Lenard Smith, Anthony Oliver, Stephen Morgan. Courtesy: London Fieldworks.

p. 58 Jaume Plensa
Born 1955 in Spain
Love Sounds I–V, 1998
Alabaster, iron, plastic, light and sound
212 x 120 x 228 cm/212 x 120 x 115 cm (7 ft x 4 ft x 7 ft 6 in./7 ft x 4 ft x 3 ft 10 in.). Installation view: the Kestner Gesellschaft, Hannover, Germany, 1999. Photograph: Gunter Lepkowski. Courtesy: the artist and Galeria Toni Tàpies, Barcelona.

p. 59 (left + below) Ernesto Neto
Born 1964 in Brazil; lives and works in Rio de Janeiro.
Walking in Venus blue cave, 2001
Stocking, styrofoam, buttons, incandescent lights, 396.2 x 777.2 x 833 cm (13 ft x 25 ft 6 in. x 27 ft 4 in.). Courtesy: the artist and Tanya Bonakdar Gallery, New York (collection Kent and Vicki Logan, Vail, Co.).

p. 59 (above right) Pipilotti Rist
Born 1962 in Switzerland.
Sip My Ocean (Grossmut Begatte Mich), 1994–96
Video, dimensions variable. Courtesy: the artist and Luhring Augustine Gallery, New York.

p. 60 (right) Siobhan Hapaska
Born in 1963 in Northen Ireland (Belfast); lives and works in London.
Here, 1995
Fibreglass, opalescent paint, acrylic lacquer, lambswool, harness, piped water and oxygen, 100.3 x 400 x 200 cm (3 ft 4 in. x 13 ft 1 in. x 6 ft 6 in.). Courtesy: Tanya Bonakdar Gallery, New York.

p. 60 (left) Absalon
Born 1964 in Israel (Ashold); died in Paris 1993.
Cellule nr. 6, 1992
Wood, cardboard, white paint, 300 x 220 x 220 cm (9 ft 10 in. x 7 ft 2 in. x 7 ft 2 in.). Photograph: Ann Katrin Blomqvist. Collection Magasin 3 Stockholm Konsthall. Courtesy: Magasin 3 Stockholm Konsthall.

p. 61 Børre Sæthre
Born 1967 in Norway.
MY PRIVATE SKY, unit 1/trauma white, 2001
Installation view: Astrup Fearnley Museum of Modern Art, Oslo, 2001. Photograph: the artist. Courtesy: Galleri Wang, Oslo.

p. 61 (right) Gregor Schneider
Born 1969 in Germany.
ur12, total isoliertes Gästezimmer, Rheydt, 1995
Courtesy: the artist, VG Bildkunst, Bonn and Galerie Luis Campaña, Cologne.

p. 62 Mischa Kuball
Born 1959 in Germany.
Believe/Disbelieve, 1999
Installation view of the exhibition 'Project Rooms', the Museum of Installation, London. Photograph: Edward Woodman. Courtesy: the artist and the Museum of Installation, London.

p. 63 Kazuo Katase
Born 1947 in Japan.
Winterreise, 1998
White house: wood, gypsum, floor: white felt, 1 swing, see-saw: white wax, blue filtered light. Installation view Overbeck-Gesellschaft, Lübeck, Germany. Photograph: the artist. Courtesy: the artist.

p. 64 (above) Pierre Huyghe
Born 1962 in France (Paris). Lives and works in Paris.
L'expédition scintillante, a musical, Act 1, Act 2, Act 3, 2002
Exhibition view Kunsthaus Bregenz. Photograph: KuB, Markus Tretter. Courtesy: Marian Goodman Gallery, New York/Paris.

p. 64 (below) Yayoi Kusama
Born 1929 Matsumoto-shi Naganoken, Japan.
Dots Obsession, 2000
Dimensions variable. Photograph: André Morin. Courtesy: Le Consortium, Dijon, France.

p. 65 Jon Lockhart and Tom Cox-Bisham
Jon Thomas: Together in Electric Dreams, 2002
Installation view: the Museum of Installation, London, mixed media. Photograph: David Grandorge. Courtesy: the artists and the Museum of Installation, London.

p. 66 Julian Opie
Born 1958 in UK (London).
Imagine that you are moving (detail), 1997
Lightbox and computer installation. Photograph: Stephen White. Courtesy: the artist and the Lisson Gallery, London.

p. 67 Ugo Rondinone
Born 1963 in Switzerland.
It's late and the wind carries a faint sound as it moves..., 1999–2000
6 video projections, 12 video loops, sound, dimensions variable. Installation view 'GUIDED BY VOICES' exhibition, Kunsthaus Glarus, Switzerland, 1999. Courtesy: Matthew Marks Gallery, New York.

p. 68 Doug Aitken
Born 1968 in USA.
Thaw, 2001
Installation view 'New Ocean' exhibition at the
Serpentine Gallery, London, 2001; 3 Channel, 3
projection video installation,
variable dimensions. Produced by the Fondazione
Sandretto Re Rebaudengo, Turin; in association
with the Serpentine Gallery, London. Courtesy: 303
Gallery, New York; Victoria Miro Gallery, London;
Galerie Hauser Wirth & Presenhuber, Zurich.

p. 69 (left) Ann Lislegaard
Born 1962; lives and works in New York and
Copenhagen.
I-You-Later-There, 2000
Architectural object, halogen light, colororgan,
CD-player, 4 built-in wall speakers. Courtesy: the
artist and Galerie Paul Andriesse.

p. 69 (right) Dalziel+Scullion
Matthew Dalziel born 1957 in UK (Irvine, Scotland).
Louise Scullion born in UK (Helensburgh,
Scotland). Dalziel and Scullion have been working
collaboratively since 1993. They live and work in
Dundee, Scotland.
Rain, 2000
Wood plastic, tin, 5 x 5 x 5 m (16 ft 5 in. x 16 ft 5 in.
x 16 ft 5 in.) structure 6 x 6 m (19 ft 7 in. x 19 ft 7
in. x 19 ft 7 in.) pool, 1.5 x 5 x 5 m (5 x 16 ft 5 in.)
ramp, temporary structure commissioned by Oriel
31 and exhibited in Newtown, Wales. Courtesy: the
artists and Houldsworth, London.

p. 69 (below) Ron Haselden
Lives and works in the UK and in France.
Maid of the Mist, 1994
Installation view: the Museum of Installation,
London. Photograph: Edward Woodman. Courtesy:
the artist and the Museum of Installation, London.

p. 70 + 71 Diller+Scofidio
Elisabeth Diller born 1954 in Poland (Lodz).
Ricardo Scofidio born 1935 in USA (New York).
Blur Building, 2002
Media pavilion for Swiss Expo 02, 2002;100 x 65 x
25 m (328 x 213 x 82 ft). Yverdon-les-Bains,
Switzerland. Photograph: Diller+Scofidio (aerial
photos: Beat Widmer). Courtesy: Diller+Scofidio.

p. 72 + 73 (above) Olafur Eliasson
Born 1967 in Denmark
*Die Dinge die du nicht siehst die du nicht
siehst*, 2001
Mixed media, dimensions variable.
Photograph: Jens Ziehe, Berlin. Courtesy:
neugerriemschneider, Berlin.

p. 73 (below) Louise Sudell
Born 1960 in UK; lives and works in Barcelona.
Ascensor Negro, 1998
Lift, metal cell with interior ceiling light and alarm
system, with added features (adapted panel of
controls, timing device on the automatic doors
opening and shutting), 230 x 85 x 125 cm (7 ft 6 in.
x 2 ft 9 in. x 4 ft). Courtesy: the artist.

p. 74 Andrea Zittel
RAUGH Furniture: Lucinda, 1998

p. 75 (above) Andrea Zittel
A–Z Homestead Unit, 2001
Steel, wood, glass and objects, 3 x 3.9 x 3 m
(10 x 13 x 10 ft). Installation view: Sadie Coles,
HQ, Ltd. Courtesy: Andrea Rosen Gallery, New
York, and Sadie Coles, HQ, Ltd., London.

p. 75 (below) Carl von Weiler
Nest, 1993–96
Wood, earth, blanket, heaters, cooling fan and
light, 2 x 6 x 12 m (6 ft 6 in. x 19 ft 7 in. x 39 ft 4
in.). Situated in the basement of an industrial
building at 10 Martello Street, London E8 (open
to the public for 18 months: Jan. 1995–June 1996).
Photograph: Andrew Holligan.
Courtesy: the artist.

p. 76 Lee Bul
Live Forever, 2001
Installation view: The Fabric Workshop & Museum,
Philadelphia, 2001. Created in collaboration with
the Fabric Workshop and Museum. Fibreglass
capsule with acoustic foam and leather upholstery,
electronic equipment,
254 x 152.4 x 96.5 cm (8 ft 4 in. x 5 ft 3 ft 2 in.).
Edition of 3. Photograph: Will Brown. Courtesy:
PKM Gallery, Inc., Seoul, Korea.

p. 77 (above) Doug Aitken
Blow Debris, 2000
9 channel and video architectural environment.
Installation view: Flight Patterns, MOCA, Los
Angeles. Courtesy: 303 Gallery, New York; Galerie
Hauser Wirth & Presenhuber, Zurich; Victoria Miro
Gallery, London.

p. 77 (below) Doug Aitken
new skin, 2002
4 projections onto elliptical x-screen video
installation. Installation at the MACBA, Barcelona.
Commissioned by the Centre Georges Pompidou,
Musée d'Art Moderne and L'IRCAM, Paris.
Courtesy: 303 Gallery, New York; Galerie Hauser
Wirth & Presenhuber, Zurich; Victoria Miro
Gallery, London.

author and institution

p. 82 (above) Mischa Kuball
Private Light Public Light, 1998
Installation view: 24th Biennial of São Paulo,
Brazil, 1998. Photograph: Nelson Kon, São Paulo
1998, Courtesy: Mischa Kuball Archive, Düsseldorf.

p. 82 (below) Kendell Geers
Born 1968 in South Africa; lives and works
in Brussels.
Poetic Justice, 1999
Video installation, dimensions variable. Installation
view: Carnegie International, Pittsburgh, 1999.
Courtesy: the artist and Stephen Friedman
Gallery, London.

p. 83 (above) Beat Streuli
Born 1957 in Switzerland (Altdorf); lives and works
in Düsseldorf.
Portraits, 2002
Duraclear mounted on glass. Installation view:

Palais the Tokyo, Paris. Photograph: the artist.
Courtesy: the artist.

p. 83 (below) Beat Streuli
Billboard Sydney, 1998
Installation view: Biennial of Sydney, 1999.
Inkjet print on vinyl, 2 parts: 3.5 x 35 m (11 ft 6 in.
x 114 ft 10 in.) each. Photograph: the artist.
Courtesy: the artist.

p. 84 (above) Tobias Rehberger
Born 1966 in Germany.
Brancusi, 1997
Wall painting, 5 seats, 3 lamps, wooden floor, 11
original works by artists. Courtesy:
Neugerriemschneider, Berlin.

p. 84 (below) Françoise Bassand
Born 1963 in Switzerland; lives and works in
Zurich in collaboration with Charles Castillo,
Christian Hutzinger, Vreni Spieser, Philippe
Winninger and Markus Schwander.
3D, 1998
Emulsion paint, plastic sheet, adhesive film,
drawing pins, plastic objects, slides. Exhibiting
site: KLINIK Zurich/Morphing Systems (concept
created by Teresa Chen, Tristan Kobler and
Dorothea Wimmer). Photograph: Simone
Ackermann.
Courtesy: Edition Patrick Frey do Scalo,
Zurich, Berlin, New York.

p. 85 (below) Fabrice Gygi
Born 1965 in Switzerland (Geneva).
Tribunal, 1999
Awning, pvc, wood, metal, straps, c. 600 x 400 x
400 cm (19 ft 8 in. x 13 ft x 13 ft). Installation
view, Galerie für Zeitgenössische Kunst,
Leipzig, Germany. Courtesy: Bob van Orsouw
Gallery, Zürich.

p. 85 (above) Fabrice Gygi
Sans nul titre, 1998
Mixed media, dimensions variable. Courtesy:
Bob van Orsouw Gallery, Zurich.

p. 86 (above) Luchezar Boyadjiev
Born 1957 in Bulgaria (Sofia); lives and works
in Sofia.
Gazebo, 1996
Natural location, 4 repaired wooden cinema
chairs, stone platform; platform and chairs: 300 x
300 x 200 cm (9 ft 10 in. x 9 ft 10 in. x 6 ft 6 in.).
Site-specific installation, hills above the city of
Gars am Kamp, Lower Austria. Photograph: Dieter
Graff. Courtesy: the artist & Art in Landscape '96,
Gars am Kamp, Austria.

p. 86 (below) Bob & Roberta Smith
Pseudonym of Patrick Brill. Born 1963 in London.
Jessica Voorsanger
Joe Amrhein at the LCCA, 2001 (The Leytonstone
Center for Contemporary Art, London). Courtesy:
the artists.

p. 87 Michael Smith and Joshua White
The QuinQuag, Arts and Wellness Centre, Touring
Exhibition, 2002.
Installation detail. Courtesy: the artists and

Hales Gallery, London.

p. 88 (above) Mark Dion
Born 1961 in USA (New Bedford, Massachusetts);
lives and works in Beach Lake, Pennsylvania.
Alexander Wilson Studio, 1999
Wooden structure, mixed media, dimensions
variable. Courtesy: the artist and Tanya Bonakdar
Gallery, New York.

p. 88 (below) Jorge Pardo
Born 1963 in Cuba (Havana); lives and works in
Los Angeles (California).
Pier, 1997
Redwood, metal, cigarette vending machine.
Installation view Skulptur Project Münster 1997.
Courtesy: the artist and Friedrich Petzel Gallery,
New York.

p. 89 Ayşe Erkmen
Born 1949 in Turkey; lives in Berlin and Istanbul.
Sculptures on Air, 1997
1 helicopter, 13 sculptures, museum.
Exhibiting site: Münster/Westfälisches
Landesmuseum. Photograph: the artist. Courtesy:
the artist and Sculpture Projects Münster, 1997.

p. 90 (below) Hans Haacke
Born 1936 in Germany (Cologne); lives and works
in New York.
Der Bevölkerung (To the Population), 1999–2000
Installation site: Reichstag, Berlin
Oblong wooden trough, 6.8 x 20.8 x 1.2 m (22 ft 4
in. x 66 ft 6 in. x 4 ft), 14 white neon letters, 1.2 m
(3 ft 11 in.) high, soil, unencumbered plant growth
Courtesy: the artist. Credit: VG Bild-Kunst.

p. 90 + 91 Christo and Jeanne-Claude
Both born 1935.
Wrapped Reichstag, Berlin, 1971–1995
Photograph: Wolfgang Volz. Courtesy: Christo and
Jeanne-Claude.

p. 92 Anish Kapoor
Born 1954 in India (Bombay); lives and works
in London.
Tarantara, 1999
PVC. Installation view: BALTIC, Newcastle,
England. Photograph: Ravi Deepres. Courtesy:
Barbara Gladstone Gallery, New York.

p. 93 (right) Daniel Pflumm
Born 1968 in Switzerland (Geneva); lives and
works in Berlin.
Ohne Titel, 1998
Lightbox on the façade of the South London
Gallery. Photograph: John Mason. Courtesy:
Galerie Neu, Berlin & South London Gallery,
London.

p. 93 (above) Thomas Hirschhorn
Born 1957 in Switzerland (Berne). Lives and works
in Paris.
World Airport/Flugplatz Welt, 1999
Mixed media, 500 m² (5382 ft²). Exhibition view
at the Venice Biennale. Courtesy: the artist and
Galerie Chantal Crousel.

p. 93 (below) Micah Lexier
Born 1960 in Canada.
*Ampersand: A Project for the Sheppard/Leslie
Subway Station*, Toronto (open in 2002).
17,000 custom-printed ceramic tiles 77.4 cm²
(12 in.²). Commissioned by the Toronto Transit
Commission. Courtesy: the artist and Toronto
Transit Commission.

p. 94 Barbara Bloom
Born 1951 in USA.
Pictures from the Floating World, 1995
Installation view: Leo Castelli Gallery,
New York. Mixed media. Courtesy: Gorney
Bravin+Lee, New York.

p. 95 Tatsurou Bashi (alias Tazro Niscino)
Born 1960 in Japan (Nagoya).
Villa Victoria, 2002
Installation at Derby Square, Liverpool,
Sept.–Nov.2002. Mixed media, dimensions
variable. Courtesy: the artist.

p. 96 (above) Stefan Brüggemann
Capitalism and Schizophrenia, 2003
Puerto Rico. Dimensions variable. Courtesy: the
artist.

p. 96 (below) Micah Lexier
The Hall of Names, 1996
Laser-cut stainless steel, 243.8 m (800 ft) long.
Commissioned for the National Trade Centre,
Toronto. Courtesy: the artist.

p. 97 (above) Elmgreen & Dragset
Michael Elmgreen born 1961 in Denmark,
Ingar Dragset born 1969 in Norway.
Powerless Structures, Fig. 111, 2001
Installation view: Portikus Frankfurt am Main,
Germany, 2001. Courtesy: Klosterfelde, Berlin,
Nicolai Wallner, Copenhagen and Tanya Bonakdar,
New York.

p. 97 (below) Elmgreen & Dragset
Taking Place, 2001–2002
Site specific project: remodelling of the exhibition
space Kunsthalle Zürich. Photograph: Burkhard
Meltzer. Courtesy: Kunsthalle Zürich.

p. 98 Miguel Leal
Born 1967 in Portugal (Oporto); lives and works
in Oporto.
Bunker Project, 1999
CAPC, Coimbra, Portugal, 1999. Mixed media,
dimensions variable. Photograph: José Meneses.
Courtesy: the artist and Galeria Marta Vidal.

p. 99 Joëlle Tuerlinckx
Born 1958 in Belgium
*In Real Time, Space Parts/Night Cabin/
Solar-room*, 2002
Installation view: the South London Gallery,
London. Photograph: Marcus Leith. Courtesy: the
artist and the South London Gallery.

p. 100 Michel François
Born 1956 in Belgium; lives and works
in Brussels.
Bureau Augmenté, 1998

Installation, Albi, Berlin, Paris, Charleroi. Mixed
media. Courtesy: carlier/gebauer.

p. 101 (above + below) Dutton/Peacock
Steve Dutton and Percy Peacock live and work in
the UK.
Apocotropes, 1996-97
Prints on M.D.F. Courtesy: the artists.

p. 101 (below) Dutton/Peacock
Europe, 1999
Mail shot. Courtesy: the artists.

p. 102 John Newling
Born 1952 in UK.
Weight, 1998
Mixed media. Installation view: the Turnpike
Gallery, Leigh, Greater Manchester, UK.
Commissioned for Arttranspennine 98.
Photograph: Paula Latham. Courtesy: the artist
and the Turnpike Gallery, Leigh.

p. 103 Henrik Plenge Jakobsen
Born 1967 in Denmark.
Diary of Plasma, 1995–96
Mixed media, c. 1000 x 400 x 300 cm (328 ft x 13 ft
x 9 ft 10 in.). Installation Louisiana Museum,
Copenhagen, Denmark and FRAC Champagne
Ardennes, France. Photograph: Bent Byberg.
Courtesy: the artist and Galleri Nicolai Wallner,
Copenhagen.

p. 104 (above) Martin Creed
Born 1968 in UK
Work No 270 'The Lights Off', 2001
Mixed media, dimensions variable. Photograph:
Achim Kukulis. Courtesy: Johnen & Schöttle,
Cologne, Germany.

p. 104 (below) Renato Niemis
[;], 1994
Installation view: the Museum of Installation,
London. Photograph: Edward Woodman. Courtesy:
the artist and the Museum of Installation, London.

p. 105 Hew Locke
Born in UK (Edinburgh).
Cardboard Palace, 2002
Cut cardboard and paint, variable size.
Installation view: the Chisenhale Gallery, London.
Photograph: Stephen White
Courtesy: the artist and Chisenhale Gallery,
London.

exchange and interaction

p. 110 Cai Guo-Qiang
Born 1957 in China (Quanzhou City, Fulian
Province).
Cultural Melting Bath, 1997
Hot tub with hydrotherapy jets, Chinese herbal
medicine, banyan tree roots, translucent fabric,
live birds, taihusu rocks, triangular space: 7.3 m h
x 20.4 x 24.6 x 25.3 m (24 ft h x 67 x 81 x 83 ft).
Installation view: the Queens Museum of Art,
New York, USA. Photograph: Hiro Ihara. Courtesy:
the artist.

in The Netherlands.
Compostopia, 2002
Mixed media. Installation view: the Camden Arts Centre, London. Photograph: Ahlburg Keate Photography. Courtesy: Atelier van Lieshout and Camden Arts Centre, London.

p. 125 (above) Wim Delvoye
Born 1965 in Belgium (Werwik); lives and works in Ghent and London.
Cloaca - New and Improved, 2001
Mixed media, 2000 x 10,000 x 75 cm (65 ft 7 in. x 328 ft x 2 ft 6 in.). Installation view: the Migros Museum, Zürich. Photograph: Franziska Bodmer, Zürich. Courtesy: the artist.

p. 125 (below left) Sissel Tolaas
Born 1959 in Norway; lives and works in Berlin.
It must be the weather, Part 1: Dirty 1, 2001
Perfume, video, vinyl text, perfume diffuser.
Photograph: David Grandorge. Courtesy: the Museum of Installation, London.

p. 125 (below right) Atelier van Lieshout
Maxi Capsule Luxus, 2002
Installation view: the Camden Arts Centre, London, UK. Photograph: Ahlburg Keate Photography. Courtesy: Atelier van Lieshout.

p. 126 (above) Lili Fischer
Born 1947.
Meute im Museum, 2001
Installation view: the Museum of Installation, London. Photograph: David Grandorge. Courtesy: the artist and the Museum of Installation, London.

p. 126 (below) Simone Michelin
Born 1956 in Brazil (Bento Goncalves, Rio Grande do sul); lives and works in Rio de Janeiro, Brazil.
Bonjour, Bonsoir, Adieu, Tristesse, 2001
Wood, linoleum, LCD monitor, computer system, c. 4 x 10 m (13 x 33 ft). Installation view: the Espaço Cultural Sérgio Porto. Photograph: Wilton Montenegro. Courtesy: the artist.

p. 127 (above) Maywa Denki
Uke-TEL (NAKI-U1), 1998
1200 x 900 x 900 mm (4 ft x 3 ft x 3 ft), 80 kg AC100V 50/60Hz. Drived-Live, Maywa Denki Japan Tour II, 1998. Photograph: Jun Mitsuhashi. Courtesy: Yoshimoto Kogyo Co., Ltd./Maywa Denki.

p. 127 (below) Jeroen Offerman
Born 1970 in the Netherlands (Eindhoven).
Silent Boatman, 2000
Collaborative piece entitled 'Cover Versions' for the exhibition 'Forensic' with artist Simon Morretti, the Museum of Installation, 2000. Photograph: Edward Woodman. Courtesy: the artists and the Museum of Installation, London.

p. 128 (above left) Jose Dávila
Born 1974 in Mexico.
Open Studio, 2000
Installation view: the Brazier's International Workshop in Oxford. Photograph: the artist. Courtesy: the artist and Camden Arts Centre, London.

p. 128 (above right) Veronika Witte
Born 1962 in Germany; lives and works in Berlin.
Institute for socio-aesthetic research (ISF), 2001–2002
6 stalls with chairs, 1 ballot-box, 1 poster, 3 suppliers for the forms, 2000 6-page questionnaires, neon light. Installation view: the Kunstverein Hürth, Cologne, 2001. Photo by the artist. Courtesy: the artist.

p. 128 (below) Allan Wexler
Born 1949 in USA.
Vinyl Milford House, 1994
Prefab storage shed, wood, glass, enamel, 2.1 m h x 2.9 m d x 4.8 m w (7 ft h x 9 ft 6 in. d x 16 ft w, generic furniture. Commissioned by Katonah Museum of Art New York. Courtesy: Ronald Feldman Fine Arts, New York.

p. 129 (above) Christian Jankowski
Born 1968 in Germany.
Mein erstes Buch: Inszeniertes Schreiben, 1998
Installation view: Portikus, Frankfurt am Main, Germany, 1998. Courtesy: Klosterfelde, Berlin.

p. 129 (below) Renée Green
Born 1959 in USA (Cleveland, Ohio); lives and works in New York.
Between and Including Partially Buried in 3 Parts, 1999
Mixed media, dimensions variable. Courtesy: the artist and Georg Kargl, Vienna.

p. 130 (above) Ana Miguel
Born in 1962 in Brazil (Rio de Janeiro); lives and works in Brasilia.
I love you, 2000
Fabric, crochet, sound and winding mechanisms, 400 x 400 x 330 cm (13 x 13 x 10 ft 10 in.). Installation view: the Ecco Gallery, Brasil. Photograph: Edgar Cesar. Courtesy: the artist.

p. 130 (below) Simon Moretti
Born 1974 in UK; lives and works in London.
A Space for Conversation, 2000
Performance/event at Tate Modern, London. Photograph: Effie Paleologou. Courtesy: the artist and Tate Modern, London.

p. 131 (above) Muntean/Rosenblum
Markus Muntean born 1962 in Austria.
Adi Rosenblum born 1962 in Israel.
Where else, 2000
Mixed media, dimensions variable. Installation view: Secession, Vienna, Austria. Courtesy: Georg Kargl, Vienna.

p. 131 (below) Jiri Kratochvil
Born 1946 in Czechoslovakia; lives and works in London.
Joseph, 1998
Mixed media. Installation view: the Museum of Installation, London. Photograph: James Mardsen. Courtesy: the Museum of Installation, London.

time and narrative

p. 135 Mike Nelson
Born 1967 in UK.
The Coral Reef, 2000
Installation view: Matt's Gallery, London. Courtesy: the artist and Matt's Gallery, London.

p. 136 (above) Jane and Louise Wilson
Born 1967 in UK.
Stasi City, 1997
4 channel video installation, 5 min. loop. Photograph: Theo Coulombe. Courtesy: 303 Gallery, New York.

p. 136 (below) David Bunn
Born 1950 in USA.
I feel better now, I feel the same way, 1996
Discarded card catalogue and 53 specific works: ink on paper with catalogue cards, 514 cardboard storage boxes, numbered and alphabetized, on wood shelves, 426 x 121 x 60 cm (14 x 40 x 2 ft), dimensions variable. Installation view: the Burnett Miller Gallery, Los Angeles, 1996. Courtesy: the artist, Brooke Alexander, New York and Burnett Miller Gallery, Los Angeles.

p. 137 (above) Amanda Wilson
Mirror, 1997
Installation view, the Museum of Installation, London. Photograph: Edward Woodman Courtesy: the artist and the Museum of Installation, London.

p. 137 (below) Christian Boltanski
Born 1944 in France.
Les Abonnés du Téléphone, 2000
Telephone directories, lamps, shelves, chairs and ladders, dimensions variable. Installation view: the South London Gallery, London. Photograph: John Mason. Courtesy: artist and the South London Gallery, London.

p. 138 (above) Teresa Serrano
Born 1936; lives in Mexico City and New York.
Vanishing City, 2001
Programa Art Centre, Mexico.

p. 138 (below) Maurizio Cattelan
Born 1960 in Italy (Padua) lives and works in Milan and New York.
Lift, 2001
Two elevators, stainless steel, electronic components, 60 x 86 x 47 cm (23½ x 33⅞ x 18½ in.). Photograph: Attlio Maranzano. Courtesy: Galerie Emmanuel Perrotin, Paris.

p. 139 (above) David Allen
Thames Piece, 2001
Installation view of the group show 'Here and Now': the Museum of Installation, London. Photograph: David Grandorge. Courtesy: the artist and the Museum of Installation, London.

p. 139 (below) Darren Almond
Born 1971 in UK (Wigan); lives and works in London.
H.M.P. Pentonville, 1997

Projection with sound U-matic and CD
c. 3.6 x 4.5 m (12 x 15 ft). Photograph: Stephen White. Courtesy: Jay Joplin/White Cube, London. © the artist.

p. 140 (above) David Davies
Row 01, 2001
View of the installation at the Museum of Installation, London. Photograph: David Grandorge. Courtesy: the artist and the Museum of Installation, London.

p. 140 (below) Massimo Bartolini
Born 1962 in Italy (Cecina); lives and works in Cecina, Italy.
Zwei Horizonte (particolare), 2002
Furniture, tile floor, fibreglass, light equipment, 415 x 550 x 1,500 cm (13 ft 7 in. x 18 ft x 49 ft 2 in.). Manifesta 4. Frankensteiner Hof. Photo Bernd Bodtlander. Courtesy: Galeria Massimo De Carlo, Milan.

p. 141 (above) Juan Cruz
Born 1970 in Spain (Valencia); lives and works in London.
Driving Back, 1999–2000
Sound, speakers. Installation view: the Camden Arts Centre, London. Courtesy: Matt's Gallery, London and Camden Arts Centre, London.

p. 141 (below) 'Archive',
Group Exhibition, 1995
View of the exhibition 'Archive': Museum of Installation, 1995. Exhibition devised by Museum of Installation in collaboration with architects Simon Miller and Alain Chiaradia. Photograph: Edward Woodman. Courtesy: Simon Miller, Alain Chiaradia and the Museum of Installation, London.

p. 142 Jason Rhoades
Born 1965 in USA.
The Great Sea Battles of Wilhelm, 1994–95
Dimensions and materials variable. Installation view: 'Deep Storage' exhibition at Haus der Kunst, Munich, Germany. Courtesy: David Zwirner, New York.

p. 143 (above) Tracey Emin
Born 1963 in UK (London); lives and works in London.
My Bed, 1998
Mattress, linens, pillows, rope, various memorabilia, 79 x 211 x 234 cm (31 x 83 x 92 in.). Installation view: Tate Britain, London. Photograph: Stephen White. Courtesy: Jay Joplin/White Cube, London. © the artist.

p. 143 (below) Liza Lou
Born 1969 in USA (New York); lives and works in Los Angeles.
Trailer, 1999–2000
Mixed media, 365 x 243 x 609 cm (12 x 8 x 20 ft). Courtesy: the artist and Deitch Projects, New York.

p. 144 (above) Ann Hamilton
Born 1956 in USA.
Mattering, 1997
Room dimension: 5 x 3 x 2 m (16 ft 8 in. x 10 ft 8 in. x 6 ft), typewriter ribbon, spindle, porcelain ink

pot, five peacocks, wood and steel perches 3.2 m h (10 ft); silk 3 x 1.5 m d (9 ft 8 in. x 5 ft d circular cutout), motors, cables, wood utility pole, wood and steel seat, safety belt, figure, recorded voice: audio tape, audio tape player. Installation view of the exhibition 'Ann Hamilton: Present-Past, 1984–1997': the Musée d'art contemporain de Lyon, France. Photograph: Thibault Jeanson. Courtesy: Sean Kelly Gallery, New York.

p. 144 (below) Dermot O'Brien
Lives and works in the UK.
Untitled, 1995
Installation view: the Museum of Installation, London. Photograph: Edward Woodman. Courtesy: the artist and the Museum of Installation, London.

p. 145 (above) Sam Taylor-Wood
Born 1967 in UK (London); lives and works in London.
Third Party, 1999
Seven 16 mm film projections with sound (duration: 10 min.). Courtesy: Jay Joplin/White Cube, London. © the artist.

p. 145 (below right) David Wilkinson
Untitled, 1996
Latex, pigment, video projection, convex mirrors, lighting gel. Courtesy: the artist and empty rooms e.V., Berlin.

p. 145 (below left) David Wilkinson
Untitled, 1999
16mm loop, aluminium, ripstop nylon, sherman tank, slip ring. Installation view of the exhibition 'Day for Night': the Museum of Installation, London. Photograph: Edward Woodman. Courtesy: the artist and the Museum of Installation, London.

p. 146 Damien Hirst
Born 1965 in UK.
Love Lost (Large River Fish), 2000
Aquatic tank and filtration unit, couch, table, stool, surgical instruments, computer ring, cup, watch and fish. 274.3 x 213.4 x 213.4 cm (9 ft x 7 ft x 7ft). Courtesy: Damien Hirst/Science Ltd. and Gagosian Gallery, New York.

p. 147 (above) Phyllida Barlow
Born 1944; lives in London.
Depot, 1995
Installation view: the Museum of Installation, London. Photograph: Edward Woodman. Courtesy: the artist and the Museum of Installation, London.

p. 147 (below left) Knut Åsdam
Born 1968 in Norway (Trondheim).
Psychasthenia (5), 1998
Architectural installation with video programme, 17.5 x 10.5 x 3 m (57 ft 5 in. x 34 ft 5 in. x 9 ft 10 in.). Installation in 3 sections (installation detail: view of entrance to video-booths). Installation view: the Pakkhus, Momentum Biennial of Nordic Art, Norway. Photograph: Stein Jørgensen, Oslo. Courtesy: the artist; Galeria Sonia Rosso, Pordenone/Torino, Italy; Klemens Gasser & Tanja Grunert Inc, New York.

p. 147 (below right) Mona Hatoum
Born 1952 in Lebanon (Beirut).
Homebound, 2000
Installation view: Tate Britain, London. Kitchen utensils, furniture, electric wire, light bulbs, computerised dimmer switch, amplifier, speakers, dimensions variable. Photograph: Edward Woodman. Courtesy: Jay Jopling/White Cube, London. © the artist.

p. 148 (above) Hans Op de Beeck
Born 1969 in Belgium.
Border, 2001
Video installation, variable length and edit (3 versions/languages), projection of 12 m w x 9 m h (39 ft 4 in. w x 29 ft 6 in.), DVD video, video projector, amplifier and speakers. View at the Big Biennial, Torino (Italy). Photograph: Gert Op de Beeck and Hans Op de Beeck. Courtesy: the artist.

p. 148 (below) Alexander Brodsky
Born 1955 in Russia.
Coma, 2000–2001
Mixed media, 290 x 800 x 400 cm (9 ft 6 in. x 26 ft 3 in. x 13 ft). Installation view: the Palazzo della Triennale, Milan, Italy. Photograph: Mario Tedeschi, Milan. Courtesy: Municipality of Milan and Museo del Presente, Milan.

p. 149 (above) Hans Op de Beeck
Location I, 1998
Installation view: the Museum of Installation, London, 2002, 8 m² (86 ft²) model, 200 x 260 x 310 cm (6 ft 5 in. x 8 ft 5 in. x 10 ft), waist height, wood, polystyrene, sand, modelling paste, PVC, plastics, plexiglas, lets, electronics, paint, light box. Photograph: David Grandorge. Courtesy: the artist and the Museum of Installation, London.

p. 149 (below) Marc Quinn
Born 1964 in UK (London).
Garden, 2000
Refrigerating room, stainless steel, acrylic tank, heated glass, refrigeration equipment, mirrors, liquid silicone at -20°C, turf, plants, 320 x 1,270 x 543 cm (10 ft 6 in. x 41 ft 17 ft 10 in.). Photograph: Attilio Maranzano. Courtesy: Jay Joplin/White Cube, London. © the artist.

p. 150 Tadashi Kawamata
Born 1953 in Japan.
Les chaises de traverse, 1998
Installation view: the Hôtel Saint-Livier, Metz & Synagogue of Delme. Commissioned by Fonds régional d'art contemporain de Lorraine and Synagogue de Delme. Photograph: Leo van der Kleij.
Courtesy: Frac Lorraine.

p. 151 Rosemarie McGoldrick
Lives and works in London.
What Katy Did, 1999
Steel, wire, cable, speakers, recorded sound. View of installation for the exhibition 'Day for Night', six projects in Portakabin buildings: the Museum of Installation, London. Photograph: Edward Woodman. Courtesy: the artist and the Museum of Installation, London.

p. 152 (above, above left + left) Loriot/Mélia
François Loriot and Chantal Mélia born 1947
in France.
Le Leurre et L'agent du Leurre, 1994–2000
Ready Made in China, 2000
Le Diable Probablement, 1993–2000
Installation views: the Museum of Installation,
2000. Photograph: David Grandorge.
Courtesy: the artists and the Museum of
Installation, London.

p. 153 Bob & Roberta Smith
Paint it Orange, 1997
Mixed media, videos and painted signs. Installation
view: 'Don't Hate Sculpt' exhibition: Chisenhale
Gallery, London. Courtesy: the artist and
Chisenhale Gallery, London.

p. 154 (below) Sarah Lucas
Born 1962 in UK (London).
Chuffing Away to Oblivion, 1999 (detail)
Newspapers, shellac, wood, door, picture rail,
light and linoleum, 110 x 281 cm (3 ft 7 in. x 9 ft
2 in.). Courtesy: Barbara Gladstone, New York.

p. 154 + 155 João Penalva
Born 1949 in Portugal (Lisbon); lives and works
in London.
From R., 2001
Video projection, furniture, painted cloths,
photographs, books and lights, dimensions
variable. Installation view: the Venice Biennale
2001. Photograph: Stephen White. Courtesy:
the artist.

p. 156 (above) Miguel-Angel Rios
Born 1943.
*Si me buscas...no me encuentras (If you look for me,
you will not find me.)*, 2001.
Courtesy: the artist.

p. 156 (below) Jeremy Wood
Born 1967 in UK; lives and works in London.
*The Map of Hope and Other Improbable
Locations*, 2002
Installation with video animation for exterior
projection, 35 mm mini DV film essay for monitor,
furniture arrangement & additional objects. Site:
empty rooms at the THU, Berlin, Germany.
Photograph: Gisela Dilchert. Courtesy: empty
rooms e.V., Berlin, Theater am Halleschen Ufer,
Berlin and the artist.

p. 157 (above) Joe Banks
Soundproofs, 1998
Installation view: the Museum of Installation,
London. Photograph: Edward Woodman. Courtesy:
the artist and the Museum of Installation, London.

p. 157 (below) Markus Wirthmann
Born 1963 in Germany; lives and works in Berlin.
*The Twentieth Century. Chapter V: The Total
Eclipse*, 2000
Theatre headlight, mirror ball, video camera and
monitor on mobile tripod system, mural
wallpaper, measurements variable. Installation
view: the Goethe-Institute Dakar, Senegal.
Courtesy: the artist.

p. 158 (left) Diana Thater
Born 1962 in USA San Francisco; lives and works
in Los Angeles.
Broken Circle, 1997
Interior view: the Buddenturm. Floor 2 (view B). 6
LCD video projectors, 1 video monitor, 7 laserdisc
players, 1 laserplay-2 synch, dimensions variable.
Courtesy: the artist and David Zwirner, New York.

p. 158 (right) A. K. Dolven
Born 1953 in Norway (Oslo); lives and works in
Lofoten and London.
Stairs, 2002
Video installation, digital video on DVD. Courtesy:
carlier/gebauer.

p. 158 (below) Eija-Liisa Ahtila
Born 1959 in Finland (Hämeenlinna); lives and
works in Helsinki.
Tuuli/The Wind, 2002
14 min. 20 seconds, 3-screen DVD. Installation
with sound, PAL 16:9, Dolby Digital 5.1. Edition:
5 + 1 ap, dimensions variable. View at Klemens
Gasser & Tanja Grunert Inc., New York.
Photograph: Mark Luttrell. © Crystal Eye Ltd.,
Helsinki. Courtesy: Klemens Gasser & Tanja
Grunert Inc., New York.

p. 159 Eija-Liisa Ahtila
Anne, Aki and God, 1998
Video installation, view at Klemens Gasser & Tanja
Grunert Inc., New York. © Crystal Eye Ltd.,
Helsinki. Courtesy: Klemens Gasser & Tanja
Grunert Inc., New York.

p. 160 Michael Petry
Born 1960 in USA (El Paso, Texas); lives and works
in London.
Contagion, 2000
Gardner Arts Centre, Brighton Festival 2000. 144
red crystal hearts, steel wire, rubber discs, red
theatre lights. Photograph: David Grandorge.

p. 161 (below) Catrin Otto
Born 1964 in Germany; lives and works in Berlin.
Full House, 1998
Various materials and cibachrome in aluminium.
Photograph: Jürgen Baumann. Courtesy: the artist
and empty rooms e.V., Berlin.

p. 161 (above) Gabriel Kuri
Born and based in Mexico City.
Momento de importancia, 2001
Conference table, chairs, green felt, microphones,
desk lamps, cold steam machine, blue walls,
ornamental plants, spotlights, water drinking unit,
dimensions variable. Courtesy:
Kurimanzutto, Mexico City.

p. 162 (left) Teresita Fernández
Born 1968 in USA (Miami); lives and works in
New York.
Bamboo Cinema, 2001
Acrylic, steel, 244 x 843 cm d. (8 ft x 27 ft 7 in. d).
Project commissioned by Public Art Fund.
Installation in Madison Square Park, April–Sept.
2002. Courtesy: the artist and Lehmann Maupin
Gallery, New York.

p. 162 (right) Daniel Guzmán
Born 1964; lives and works in Mexico City.
Untitled, 2000
Drawings, table, tablecloth, plant, dimensions
variable. International Studio Program, New York.
Courtesy: Kurimanzutto, Mexico City.

p. 162 (below) Bodys Isek Kingelez
Born 1948 in Kimbembele Ihuga; lives and works
in Kinnshasa, Congo.
Ville Fantome, 1996
Balsa, paper, cardboard, plastic, ink, misc.
120 x 170 x 240 cm (4 ft x 5 ft 6 in. x 8 ft).
Photograph: I. Kalkkinen & D. Dennehy. Courtesy:
the C.A.A.C, The Pigozzi Collection, Geneva.

p. 163 Karsten Bott
Born 1960 in Germany (Frankfurt am Main).
Von Jedem Eins (One of Each), 2001
Frankfurt. Courtesy: the artist

p. 164 (above) + 165 Bill Viola
Born 1951 in USA (New York); lives and works
in Long Beach.
Going Forth By Day, 2002
The Deluge, panel 3
The Voyage, panel 4
The First Light, panel 5
Video/sound installation, production stills.
Exhibiting site: Deutsche Guggenheim Berlin.
Photograph: Kira Perov. Courtesy: the artist;
Deutsche Bank and Solomon R. Guggenheim
Museum of Art.

p. 164 (below) Do-Ho Suh
Born 1962 in Korea (Seoul).
*Seoul Home/L.A. Home/New York Home/Baltimore
Home/London Home*, 1999
Silk and metal armateurs, 378 x 609 x 609 cm
(12 ft 5 in. x 20 ft x 20 ft). Courtesy: MOCA,
Los Angeles.

the body of the audience

p. 169 Carlos Amorales
Born 1970 in Mexico; lives in Mexico City.
Funny 13, 2001
Wall paint, tape, sound system, devil suit.
Photograph: Philippe Boel. Courtesy: Galerie
Micheline Szwajcer, Antwerp.

p. 170 Christoph Draeger
Born 1965 in Switzerland (Zurich); lives and works
in New York.
Apocalypso Place, 2000
Dimensions variable. View at the Kunsthaus
Zürich, Biennale Torino, Italy
Photograph: Jules Spinatsche. Courtesy: the artist
and Galerie Anne de Villepoix, Paris.

p. 171 Aernout Mik
Born 1962 in The Netherlands.
Piñata, 1999
Video installation, digital video on DVD
edition of 2 + 1 a.p. Installation view: ARCO,
Madrid, 2000. Courtesy: carlier/gebauer.

p. 191 (below) Gary Hill
Born 1951 in USA.
Viewer, 1996
Five-channel video installation (5 projectors,
1 five-channel synchronizer, 5 laserdisc players
and 5 laserdiscs edition of 2 and 1 artist's proof).
Courtesy: Gary Hill Studio and Donald Young
Gallery, Chicago.

p. 192 Tacita Dean
Born 1965; lives and works in London.
Fernsehturm, 2001
16 mm colour anamorphic film, optical sound,
44 min. Courtesy: the artist, Frith Street Gallery,
London and Marian Goodman Gallery, New York.

list of contributors

Research Co-ordination: Sotirios Bahtsetzis
Picture Research: Sarah Loriot
Administrative Assistant: Clare Fitzpatrick
IT Support: Kenichi Nakayama
Liaison: Rie Watanabe
Consultants: Sotirios Bahtsetzis, Jeremy Wood

With thanks to all contributing artists and
galleries, and to Robert Preece and Russel
Keziere for their support and advice.

index